BATTLE GROUND

THE GREATEST TANK DUELS IN HISTORY

GROUND

OSPREY
PUBLISHING

BATTLE
THE GREATEST TANK DUELS IN HISTORY
GROUND

EDITOR
STEVEN J. ZALOGA

" ... it is not, of course, enough that the Tank offers protection to those who fight in it. A trench or a hole in the ground will do the same. But the Tank is essentially a mobile weapon of *offense*. It is the weapon for the nation that does not fight willingly, but when it fights, fights to win, and to win quickly with as little bloodshed as possible. "

Major Clough Williams-Evans, *The Tank Corps*, 1919

First published in Great Britain in 2011 by Osprey Publishing,
Midland House, West Way, Botley, Oxford, OX2 0PH, UK
44-02 23rd Street, Suite 219, Long Island City, NY 11101, USA
E-mail: info@ospreypublishing.com

A CIP catalog record for this book is available from the
British Library

ISBN: 978 1 84908 551 9

Page layout by: Ken Vail Graphic Design, UK
Index by Alan Thatcher
Typeset in Garamond and Conduit ITC
Maps by bounford.com
Tactical diagrams by Peter Bull Art Studio
Originated by Blenheim Colour
Printed in China through Worldprint Ltd

11 12 13 14 15 10 9 8 7 6 5 4 3 2 1

Osprey Publishing is supporting the Woodland Trust, the UK's
leading woodland conservation charity, by funding the dedication
of trees.

www.ospreypublishing.com

Imperial War Museum Collections

Many of the photos in this book come from the Imperial
War Museum's huge collections which cover all aspects of
conflict involving Britain and the Commonwealth since
the start of the twentieth century. These rich resources are
available online to search, browse and buy at
www.iwmcollections.org.uk. In addition to Collections
Online, you can visit the Visitor Rooms where you can
explore over 8 million photographs, thousands of hours of
moving images, the largest sound archive of its kind in the
world, thousands of diaries and letters written by people
in wartime, and a huge reference library. To make an
appointment, call (020) 7416 5320, or e-mail
mail@iwm.org.uk.
Imperial War Museum www.iwm.org.uk

Material in this book has been previously published as:
Panther vs T-34: Ukraine 1943
Sherman Firefly vs Tiger: Normandy 1944
T-34-85 vs M26 Pershing: Korea 1950
Centurion vs T-55: Yom Kippur War 1973
M1 Abrams vs T-72 Ural: Operation Desert Storm *1991*

Image on p12 is courtesy Nik Cornish; p13, Robert
Forczyk; p86, Bovington Tank Museum; p87, IWM;
p154 & p155, NARA; p220, IGPO; p221, UN; p290,
Capt Mark Gerges; p291, US DoD

Front cover image © Osprey Publishing
Back cover images © Osprey Publishing

CONTENTS

INTRODUCTION

Tanks were the signature weapon of land warfare in the 20th century. Although seldom the dominant land weapon in terms of the numbers employed, the casualties inflicted, or the terrain captured and held, it was their success or failure on the battleground that was often the decisive influence in many major land campaigns.

Tanks were developed during World War I as a riposte to the novel army technologies and tactics that led to the bloody stalemate of trench warfare. There were three new threats that had to be overcome: barbed wire, trenches, and the lethal increase in defensive firepower. These three adversaries were a synergistic combination that shifted the technological and tactical balance back to the defense and led to tactical stalemate. Barbed wire deprived the attacking side of mobility and left the attacking infantry vulnerable to enemy machine guns. Trenches provided the defender with the means to protect himself against attacking firepower, and the enhanced defensive firepower of 1914–18 made the advancing infantryman vulnerable at greater ranges than ever before. As they advanced towards enemy lines, the infantry had to endure artillery fire at longer ranges than was previously the case, and then to face the murderous scythe of machine guns and long-range rifle fire.

Before the advent of the tank, a variety of armored vehicles were tested but failed. Armored cars and armored trains provided protection and firepower, but their mobility was severely limited. Tanks were a further evolution of these concepts, but with tracked suspension for better mobility in a wider range of ground conditions. By the end of World War I, both the British and French armies were fielding large tank forces, with several hundred tanks deployed in some of the final battles in fall 1918. Even though the early tanks held the promise of returning mobility to modern battlefield tactics, there were enormous technical and tactical issues that needed to be addressed. Early tanks were mechanically unreliable and often broke down after a day or two of combat use. From the tactical perspective, the interaction of the tanks with the other combat arms, especially the infantry, remained a difficult conundrum well into World War II. The tank's reliability problems were gradually

A British Army Mark IV male tank, improbably named "Hyacinth," ditched in a German trench one mile west of Ribecourt, Cambrai, November 20, 1917. With a top speed of 4mph (less in heavily churned terrain) and a maximum of 12mm of armor, the protection, mobility and firepower the tank offered was nevertheless revolutionary. (Imperial War Museum, Q 6432)

solved as tank design matured, and the tactical dilemmas were addressed both by new organizations and doctrine as well as the advent of new technologies such as armored infantry vehicles and tank–infantry radios. The technology and tactics of the tank reached maturity during World War II.

Tank-versus-tank combat was a rarity until the 1940 battle of France. Most early tanks were not designed to fight enemy tanks, and their principal mission was to support the infantry in its timeless battlefield tasks. As tanks became more and more numerous by 1940, the probability of armored clashes greatly increased. Nevertheless, the armored clashes of the 1940 France campaign were fought between tanks that had

not been optimized for tank-versus-tank action. In response to the lessons of the Spanish Civil War of 1936–38, the Polish campaign of 1939, and the battle of France in 1940, armies began to more seriously address the need to factor in tank-versus-tank fighting as a significant requirement for their new designs.

The Soviet T-34 tank, based heavily on the lessons of tank combat in the Spanish Civil War, became the benchmark tank design of World War II. It represented the essence of the "Holy Trinity" of tank design – firepower, mobility and armored protection – in a simple and robust design that was well suited both to infantry cooperation and tank-versus-tank fighting. The Germans responded to the T-34 in a lopsided fashion. Their Tiger and Panther tanks were exceptionally well-suited to tank-versus-tank combat, but neither the Tiger nor the Panther were ideal for other aspects of tank warfare such as infantry support, and the proper balance of capabilities remained a central dilemma in tank design in the final years of the war.

The chapter here on the Korean War uses this regional conflict to compare Soviet and American design practices during World War II as a stepping stone to the development of tanks in the Cold War. The Korean War provides a useful perspective on some of the lessons of tank warfare in World War II – as well as highlighting the proliferation of tanks away from their origins in European warfare, as a critical weapon on the global battlefield.

The prevalence of tank-versus-tank combat has always been heavily dependent on the texture of the battlefield, whether it is open desert, built-up urban areas, or temperate farmland or forest. Tank-versus-tank combat has been especially dominant in desert warfare, as is examined in some detail in the final two sections of the book. The Yom Kippur War clashes between the Centurion and T-55 provide a perspective on the first postwar generation of main battle tanks, as well as the influence that the Arab–Israeli wars had on tank development in the broader Cold War context. Indeed, it can certainly be argued that the wars of 1967 and 1973 were instrumental in the design of the American M1A1 Abrams and Soviet T-72 tank, which are profiled in the final chapter on the tank battles of *Desert Storm*.

Steven J. Zaloga, 2011

T-34

UKRAINE 1943

The German Wehrmacht invaded the Soviet Union in June 1941, confident that its superior doctrine, training, equipment, and leadership would carry it to a swift victory over the large but clumsy Red Army. In particular, the German panzer divisions, composed primarily of Panzer III and Panzer IV medium tanks, had proved to be powerful spearhead units in the Polish and French campaigns, and it was assumed that they could deal with any Soviet tanks. However, German intelligence had failed to detect that the Red Army was reequipping with a whole new generation of weapons, including the T-34 and KV-1 tanks. Within the first weeks of the invasion, it quickly became apparent that the new Soviet tank models had superior firepower, mobility, and armor protection to that of the Panzer III and Panzer IV tanks. German panzer officers were shocked that an army that they had regarded as backward was equipped with tanks that could destroy any German tank, and they demanded a quick technological solution to match the T-34. Yet in many respects, the T-34 had not reached its full combat capability. Inadequate training and doctrine had marred the T-34's combat debut in 1941, and the Red

S Panther

Army spent most of 1941–42 trying to figure out how to best use their technical edge. It was not until the Stalingrad counteroffensive in November 1942 that the Red Army could use the T-34 to its full potential.

By mid-1943, the Red Army had perfected the T-34's early technical defects and had a cadre of trained tankers who knew how to use it properly in combat. However, the German technical solutions to the T-34 – first the heavy Tiger tank and then the medium Panther tank – would not be available in significant numbers in the summer of 1943. As the war in the East approached a decisive climax in mid-1943, both sides sought to achieve dominance in the realm of armored combat. The Soviet approach was based partly on numerical superiority but also on fielding a reliable, well-rounded tank. The German approach was to build smaller numbers of high-quality tanks that excelled in one or two areas, such as armored protection and gunnery. The stage for this decisive clash between two competing philosophies of armored warfare was set primarily in the Ukraine, which offered the best terrain for operational maneuver and which contained key economic resources that Germany needed for survival. If Germany could maintain its control over the Ukraine, there was a chance that the Red Army could be fought to a standstill. For the Soviets,

> **" We had nothing comparable. "**
>
> Major-General F. W. Mellenthin,
> Chief of Staff of XLVIII Panzer
> Corps, referring to the T-34 tank

victory in the Ukraine would establish the necessary preconditions for a successful drive westward into the Axis heartland. Ultimately, the battle for the Ukraine would determine the remaining course of World War II.

The actual combat effectiveness of each combatant's armor units was the sum of the quality of their tanks and crew training as well as tactical doctrine, battalion-level leadership, and logistic support. By 1943, the German advantages began slipping, in part due to heavy German losses but also due to the Soviet ability to learn from defeat. With fewer available tanks than the Red Army and a diminishing cadre of veteran tankers, the Wehrmacht sought to gain superiority in tank warfare through technological advantage, such as the new Panther tank. The Panther was designed specifically to outclass the T-34 in firepower, mobility, and armored protection, and the Third Reich put enormous financial, labor, and industrial resources into developing and deploying the Panther for the decisive clash in the Ukraine. Hitler in particular had an almost religious faith that new weapons such as the Panther would turn back the tide in Germany's favor.

While the Germans focused on the technical potential of their new tank designs, the Red Army doggedly developed their T-34 into a no-nonsense weapon with great operational potential. Possession of the reliable T-34 in large numbers would enable the Red Army to conduct multi-echeloned attacks on a vast scale, using the newly created tank armies to rip open the increasingly flimsy German frontlines time and again. As for individual tank engagements, Soviet commanders realized in 1943 that the new German tanks would inflict heavy losses on a local, tactical level, and they accepted these losses as the price of victory until better Soviet tanks could arrive in 1944.

Much of the historical writing about the role of the Panther and T-34 tanks has been dominated by simplistic generalizations rather than sober analysis of their actual combat performance. For decades, the Panther has often been praised as "the best tank of World War II," while the T-34, by 1943, has been criticized as inferior and capable of winning only through vast numbers. In particular, some German sources have depicted German weapons technology as superior, overcome solely by the avalanche of inferior Soviet weapons. However, the quality versus quantity argument tends to overlook the fact that any technical edge in warfare tends to be short-lived and that the cost, in terms of pursuing a potential combat advantage, often means surrendering the production front to the enemy. In 1943, the Third Reich bet its future on the Panther while the Red Army played it safe and single-mindedly focused on fielding as many T-34s as possible. As always, the validation was on the battlefield, where the Panther met the T-34 in their duel for supremacy.

THE TANKS

The Panther

In 1938, the German Heereswaffenamt (Army Ordnance Department)[1] began looking at follow-up vehicles to eventually replace the Panzer III and Panzer IV series tanks, since these designs were viewed as only interim medium tanks. Daimler-Benz, Krupp, and Maschinenfabrik Augsburg-Nürnberg (MAN) were involved in designing a replacement tank, which was originally conceived as a 20-ton machine. Given the quick success of the Blitzkrieg in the Polish and French campaigns, development proceeded at a leisurely pace and had not even reached the prototype stage before the beginning of Operation *Barbarossa*, the invasion of Russia. After the appearance of the heavily armored French Char B and the British Matilda tanks in 1940, the Heereswaffenamt decided that the Panzerwaffe needed both a new medium and a heavy, or "breakthrough" tank. The new heavy tank, which eventually became the PzKpfw VI Tiger, was given greater priority than the languishing medium tank designs, and in May 1941 Hitler personally decided that the new heavy tank would mount the 88mm KwK 36 gun.

Once the Wehrmacht invaded the Soviet Union and began to encounter T-34 and KV-1 tanks, German panzer leaders realized that their current tanks were outgunned and underarmored. While the T-34 caused concern, the situation finally reached crisis proportions when General Heinz Guderian's 2nd Panzer Army spearhead was ambushed near Mtensk on October 6, 1941, by a brigade of T-34s. In a brief action, T-34s under Colonel Mikhail Katukov destroyed ten Panzer III and Panzer IV tanks for the loss of only about five of their own. Guderian, creator of the German panzer force, was shocked. With their short 50mm and 75mm guns, the German panzers could only penetrate the thick armor of the T-34 from point-blank ranges of 100m or less, but the T-34 could destroy the poorly armored Panzer III and Panzer IV from up to 1,000m. The T-34's mobility over muddy terrain and poor roads astounded the

---

[1] In peacetime, the Heereswaffenamt (HWA) fell under the German Army High Command (OKH), but in wartime it worked for the Replacement Army

German tankers. Furthermore, the use of sloped armor on the T-34 and KV-1 tanks indicated that German tank design had fallen woefully behind. In order to restore the Panzerwaffe's technical superiority on the battlefield – a necessary prerequisite for the Third Reich's victory – German industry needed to quickly develop new tanks that were not merely evolutionary improvements over their predecessors but revolutionary designs that could ensure battlefield superiority for years to come.

Inside the Heereswaffenamt was Waffenprufamter 6 (Wa Pruef 6), headed by Oberst Sebastian Fichtner from 1937 to 1942. The senior engineer in Wa Pruef 6 was Heinrich Ernst Kniepkamp, who had worked as a designer at MAN for three years before becoming a government employee in 1926.[2] By 1936, Kniepkamp had been made responsible for all new tank development projects. Unlike his Russian counterpart, engineer Mikhail I. Koshkin, Kniepkamp had no grand vision of what a medium tank should look like. He had only many small ideas that he wanted to incorporate into a new tank. Kniepkamp was particularly fond of incorporating torsion bar suspension into new tank designs, but he had been frustrated in his dealings with Daimler-Benz and Krupp on the Panzer III and Panzer IV development projects.

After the battle of Mtsensk, a special German armor investigation committee comprised of Oberst Fichtner, Kniepkamp, and officials from Daimler-Benz, Henschel, Krupp, and MAN visited Guderian's 2nd Panzer Army on November 18, 1941. The commission listened to Guderian's concerns about the T-34 and inspected several captured Soviet tanks. One week later, based upon orders from Reichsminister for Armaments Production Fritz Todt, Wa Pruef 6 established the requirement for a new 30-ton tank with 60mm sloped frontal armor to be known as the VK 30.02. Fichtner argued that MAN's VK 24.01 project was nearly completed and that designing a whole new tank would waste vital time. However, Todt overruled him. Guderian specifically demanded that the new tank have "heavier armament," "higher tactical mobility," and "improved armor protection." Therefore, both Daimler-Benz and MAN began working on their own versions of the new VK 30.02. Krupp dropped out of the medium tank design work, preferring instead to focus on the new heavy tank. The Heereswaffenamt had awarded contracts to Rheinmetall-Borsig on July 18, 1941, to design a new 75mm gun, and it was decided that this weapon would probably equip the VK 30.02. On December 9, 1941, Wa Pruef 6 set the weight for the VK 3002 at 32.5 tons but raised it to 36 tons on January 22, 1942.

Daimler-Benz, which designed the Panzer III tank, adopted a conservative approach for the development of the VK 30.02, envisioning a tank similar in appearance to the T-34 and powered by a 650hp diesel engine equipped with leaf-spring suspension and rear wheel drive. The Daimler-Benz design tried to incorporate everything Germany

[2] Kniepkamp also patented the design for the Kettenrad semitracked motorcycle in June 1939

The agility of the T-34 constantly astonished the Germans. Soviet tankers often drove their vehicles at maximum speed to cross the German "kill zone" as rapidly as possible. (From the fonds of the RGAKFD at Krasnogorsk via Nik Cornish)

had learned about the Soviet tank. Additionally, MAN had far less experience than Daimler-Benz in tank design, having only produced the small Pz I and Pz II light tanks. The MAN design team, led by Paul Max Wiebicke, rejected equipping its version of the VK 30.02 with a diesel engine since developing a new engine would require too much time. Instead, Wiebicke decided to use the new Maybach HL 210 gasoline engine, which had just entered production in February 1942. Overall, the MAN design did not resemble the T-34 since its turret was further back, and it featured front wheel drive and torsion bar suspension, which guaranteed immediate approval by Kniepkamp.

Hitler was impressed by the Daimler-Benz design, which made Kniepkamp almost apoplectic because above all else he wanted the new tank to have torsion bar suspension. Apparently, Kniepkamp was oblivious to the fact that the Daimler-Benz design had rear wheel drive like the T-34 and that Guderian had not asked for torsion bar suspension. Despite Kniepkamp's objections, Hitler decided on March 6 to select the Daimler-Benz design for series production. In particular, Hitler regarded the diesel engine as imperative for the new tank, and only Daimler-Benz was committed to using it. Fretting over the Führer's decision, Kniepkamp and Oberst Fichtner at Wa Pruef 6 began a "whisper campaign," claiming that the Daimler-Benz design looked "too Russian" and that the MAN design was a more "German-looking" tank. Apparently, Kniepkamp and other officials in Wa Pruef 6 leaked Daimler-Benz proprietary information about their design to the MAN design team, which allowed MAN to make refinements to its technical proposal.

The Panther through 360 degrees

SPECIFICATIONS:
Panther Ausf. A

General
Production run: Ausf. D: January–September 1943
        Ausf. A: August 1943–July 1944
Vehicles produced: Ausf. D: 842
        Ausf. A: 2,200
Combat weight: 44.8 tons (metric)
Crew: Five (tank commander, gunner, loader, driver,
   radio operator)

Dimensions
Overall length: 8.86m
Hull length: 7.10m
Width: 3.42m (with side skirts)
Height: 2.95m

Armor
Hull front: 80mm (at 55 degrees)
Hull sides: 40mm (at 50 degrees)
Hull rear: 40mm (at 30 degrees)
Hull roof: 16mm (at 90 degrees)
Turret front: 100mm (at 12 degrees)
Turret sides: 45mm (at 25 degrees)
Turret rear: 45mm (at 25 degrees)
Turret roof: 16mm (at 90 degrees)

Armament
Main gun: 1 x 75mm KwK 42/L70
Secondary: 2 x 7.92mm MG 34
Main gun rate of fire: 3–5rpm

Ammunition stowage
Main: 79 rounds (typically 40 rounds Pzgr 39/42 APC
   and 39 rounds Sprgr 42 HE)
Secondary: 4,200 rounds

Artwork by Jim Laurier, © Osprey Publishing

A Panther Ausf. D from the battle of Kursk in July 1943. The number 521 indicates the first tank in the 2nd Platoon of the 52nd Panzer Battalion. Panthers used a wide variety of camouflage schemes during the period July–August 1943 and the stylized panther heads disappeared from turrets after Kursk.

Communications
Fu-5 transmitter/receiver; intercom

Motive power
Engine: Maybach HL 230 P 30 12-cylinder gasoline engine
Power: 600hp at 2,500rpm
Fuel capacity: 720 liters
Power-to-weight ratio: 15.5hp/ton

Performance
Ground pressure: 0.73kg/cm²
Maximum road speed: 55km/h
Maximum cross-country speed: 30km/h
Operational range (road): 250km
Operational range (cross-country): 100km
Fuel consumption (road): 2.8 liters/km
Fuel consumption (cross-country): 7.3 liters/km
Cost: RM 129,000 ($51, 600)

After Todt's death in February 1942, Albert Speer became head of the Reich's Armaments Ministry and his principal deputy was Karl-Otto Saur, an ambitious and sycophantic Nazi engineer. Saur's main goal was to gain favor with Hitler by "achieving the impossible," and he saw the new medium tank program as a means to that end. While Speer also preferred the Daimler-Benz design, Saur realized that it would take time to develop a diesel tank engine, and that did not fit his personal agenda. Saur was able to convince Speer that the new tank had to enter production by December 1942, although this goal was not based on strategic considerations. Yet Saur's December deadline caused immediate problems for Daimler-Benz. Neither their new diesel engine nor their turret would be ready to begin production in December, allowing Saur and Kniepkamp to recommend another look at the MAN technical proposal. On May 11, a special design committee recommended the MAN design primarily due to its ability to enter production sooner than the Daimler-Benz design. Hitler was not convinced and still thought the Daimler-Benz design superior, but he was eventually persuaded by Saur that getting the MAN design into production as soon as possible was more important than any technical factors. On May 15, Hitler ordered the MAN design to begin series production as soon as possible, but he stipulated that the frontal armor had to be increased to 80mm. While Hitler's concerns about the armor were valid, his arbitrary decision to increase the armor thickness raised the weight of the tank to 45 tons. Speer ordered all work on the Daimler-Benz VK 30.02 terminated. On July 2, Hitler ordered that an air-cooled diesel tank engine be given top developmental priority, but Wa Pruef 6 and Speer ignored him. This decision was a disaster for the Panther tank development program since it meant that getting the best tank possible to German tankers was set aside in favor of merely fielding a new tank design as rapidly as possible.

Although the Daimler-Benz VK 30.02 may not have "looked German," its rear wheel drive and diesel engine would have provided the German Panzerwaffe with a more mechanically reliable tank. Furthermore, Kniepkamp's obsession with torsion bar suspension and his blatant bias toward his former employer seriously compromised the technical competition. Instead of focusing on a noncritical aspect of the design, Kniepkamp should have been more concerned that the design weight had grown by 50 percent in less than three months. Once awarded the contract, it was clear that MAN lacked the ability to construct large numbers of Panther tanks on its own and would need to dole out much of the manufacturing to subcontractors. The initial contract called for the construction of 850 Panther Ausf. D model tanks, with production occurring at MAN (Nürnberg), Daimler-Benz (Berlin), Maschinenfabrik Niedersachsen Hannover (MNH, Hannover), and Henschel (Kassel). Hitler specified that at least 250 Panthers should be available for combat by May 12, 1943. However,

A Panther Ausf. D of the 15th Replacement Tank Battalion conducting crew familiarization training at Sagan in Silesia during the late summer of 1943. Note that the driver appears to be a civilian technician. (The Tank Museum)

Saur ordered that no resources would be diverted from existing Panzer III or Panzer IV production to assist in Panther production.

It soon became evident that MAN had promised far more than it could deliver, and it had to ask for design assistance from Henschel and MNH to complete the prototype. However, several inherent technical flaws in the basic Panther design would undermine the vehicle's combat debut. First, the decision to increase the vehicle's gross weight to 45 tons was made after the design work had been completed on the transmission and running gear. This 50 percent increase induced great strain on an untested engine and final drive. Despite efforts to improve the final drive, MAN's front-wheel-drive design was too weak for a 45-ton vehicle, and the Panther continued to shear off the teeth of drive sprockets throughout 1943. Second, MAN had decided to offer extra features in order to clinch the contract award: its Panther would be amphibious. The MAN Panther Ausf. D Panthers were built with a special rubber lining in the engine compartment that would keep out water. Unfortunately, the rubber seal also kept in a great deal of heat and contributed greatly to engine fires during Operation *Zitadelle* in July 1943. Thus, a requirement that the German tankers had not even asked for was allowed to corrupt the tank that was so desperately needed at the front. Finally, there was a general shortage of automotive components in Germany in late 1942, and MAN was forced to turn to French subcontractors and second-rate sources for many parts in order to meet the December 1942 deadline.

MAN demonstrated its first prototype V2 Panther to Reichsminister Albert Speer on November 2, and he test-drove the vehicle. However, MAN failed to meet its December deadline and did not assemble its first preproduction Panther until January 11, 1943. Three preproduction Panther Ausf. D tanks were delivered for testing at Grafenwöhr between January 24 and 26. A live-fire and maneuver demonstration by the newly formed 51st Panzer Battalion with 13 Panther tanks was put on for Speer at Grafenwöhr on February 22. Although Speer was impressed by the new tank, it was an indication of the rushed nature of the Panther that six of 13 vehicles broke down during the demonstration, including one tank that caught fire. Since the initial batch of Panthers had major problems with their final drives, fuel systems, and engines, as well as a host of other corrections needed on the turret, it was decided in late March to begin rebuilding the early Panthers at DEMAG's Falkensee plant. In addition, *Schuerzen* (armored side skirts), designed to provide additional ballistic protection for the Panther's vulnerable sides from Soviet antitank rifles, were introduced in April. Further technical problems with the automotive systems required additional rebuilding of the first 250 production Panthers (known as Panther Ausf. D1) at Grafenwöhr in June. Indeed, German designers kept tinkering with the Panther through late June, right up to the moment the tanks were loaded on trains for movement to the front. On June 16, Guderian, serving as Inspector for Panzer Troops, refused to certify the Panther as combat ready, but his technical evaluation was rejected by Speer's assistant, Saur. Saur had personally promised Hitler that the Panther would be ready for Operation *Zitadelle*.[3]

The Panther's development was marked by a constant tendency to tinker with the basic design of the vehicle, which severely hindered the production and deployment of the Panther to combat units in 1943. Just as the first handful of Ausf. D models began to roll off the production lines in January 1943, the Armaments Ministry decided that an improved Panther with heavier armor protection, dubbed the "Panther II," should supersede the Ausf. D models beginning in September 1943. Like the T-34M project, the Panther II was an attempt to get an even better tank before the original design had even achieved operational status. However, the early technical problems with the Ausf. D Panthers diverted considerable resources from MAN and Daimler-Benz into rebuilding the original models, and it made the early introduction of an upgraded Panther impossible. With the Panther Ausf. D delivery

---

[3] Saur later used the July 20 plot (the attempt to assassinate Hitler on July 20, 1944) to accuse Colonel Fichtner and General Schneider of the Heereswaffenamt of not properly supporting Hitler's tank programs. Although Speer saved their lives, both officers were cashiered

schedule slipping behind by May, the decision was made to defer the Panther II project but to incorporate improvements into new models of the Panther. A total of 842 Panther Ausf. D tanks were built before production shifted to the improved Ausf. A model in September 1943. The Ausf. A incorporated many of the ad hoc corrections that had been directed for the Ausf. D and standardized them into the new model. About 908 Panther Ausf. A tanks were built in 1943, and the model remained in production until July 1944.

If ever there was an example that "haste makes waste" in warfare, it lies in the Panther development program. Instead of taking the time to ensure that a truly superior tank was fielded, bureaucrats at the Wa Pruef 6 and the Reich's Armaments Ministry succumbed to the temptation to rush it into production without proper testing. Unlike the T-34, the Panther Ausf. D never underwent serious mobility or field trials, probably because it would have failed embarrassingly. Guderian knew that the Panther was a loser, but he was silenced by Saur. Furthermore, the decision to add the Panther program on top of the existing tank and assault gun programs led to a harmful competition for resources. The Panther design did have several innovative features as well as the superb KwK 42 L/70 75mm gun and thick, sloped armor, but the vehicle as a whole fell short of Guderian's initial requirements. Given the Reich's increasing shortfalls in fuel production, the abandonment of a fuel-efficient diesel tank engine made no long-term sense. The need for the Panther tank developed because of battlefield realities discovered in 1941, but German developers erred grievously by building a tank that essentially ignored these realities.

> **"** We will pay a big price if our vehicles are not battle worthy enough. **"**
>
> General Dmitri G. Pavlov speaking to Josef Stalin, March 18, 1940

The T-34

In 1936, the Red Army had the largest fleet of tanks in the world, but its armor leaders had limited experience with using them in actual combat. Soviet tank designers had borrowed liberally from British and American tank designs of the early 1930s in order to produce the first generation of Soviet tanks. The bulk of Soviet tanks in 1936 were light T-26 and BT-5/7 series, weighing 10–13 tons, armed with a 45mm gun, and having no more than 22mm of armor. The Soviets also had about 270 T-28 medium tanks and 60 T-35 heavy tanks. All Soviet tanks at this time employed gasoline engines and were designed primarily as infantry support weapons.

The first major combat experience for Soviet armor occurred with the Russian intervention in the Spanish Civil War in October 1936. The Soviets sent 281 T-26B and 50 BT-5 light tanks to Spain to support the Republican forces. In general, the T-26B performed well in Spain, but the destruction of several tanks at the battle of

Building a T-34 in the Urals. A T-34 in 1943 cost 135,000 rubles ($25,470) and required about 3,000 man-hours to complete. A Panther cost about 129,000 Reichsmarks ($51,600) and 55,000 man-hours to complete. (The Tank Museum)

Jarama in February 1937 by German 37mm antitank guns caused the Soviet tankers to reconsider the thin armor on their tanks. General Dmitri G. Pavlov, the commander of the first Soviet armor sent to Spain and later head of the Soviet Armored Forces Directorate (GABTU), was particularly concerned about the flammability of the gasoline-fueled T-26. Based upon early reports from Spain, the GABTU recommended developing a "shell-proof" tank that could withstand 37mm antitank fire. In 1937, the Soviet Union had two main tank production centers: the Leningrad complex (Bolshevik, Kirov, and Voroshilov factories) and the Kharkov Locomotive Factory (KhPZ). GABTU initially recommended that the Leningrad factories design an improved variant of their T-26 light tank while KhPZ was ordered to design an improved BT-7. The result of this recommendation was the T-26S tank with a new conical turret and the BT-7M with an experimental V-2 diesel engine.

KhPZ had developed the BT-series "fast tanks" and the T-35 heavy tank. The chief engineer was Mikhail Koshkin, who took over in December 1936 after his predecessor had been arrested in the Stalinist purges. Koshkin had been a candy maker outside Moscow before the Russian Revolution, but he managed to get a technical education afterward and proved to be a brilliant engineer. Despite his technical prowess and vision, Koshkin was not above using his Communist Party connections to rise rapidly in the "Oboronka" (Russian slang for "military industrial complex"). Once at KhPZ, Koshkin was given the assignment of developing the improved BT-7M design as well as another variant known as the BT-SV that incorporated sloped armor. While Koshkin quickly completed these designs, he felt that such incremental improvements were too conservative to offer any real technological advantage. Instead, Koshkin saw the wheeled-tracked configuration utilized by the BT-series as a technical dead-end and preferred to develop a new tracked-only tank that would utilize the new diesel engine as well as sloped armor and a larger gun. KhPZ had been experimenting with diesel engines since 1933 and was on the verge of developing the first practical diesel engine for a tank. Koshkin's deputy, Alexsander Morozov, was responsible for developing the V-2 diesel engine from an earlier prototype. The V-2 was a huge breakthrough in tank engine development, allowing Koshkin to emphasize mobility and fire safety in the new design. In addition to using aluminum to reduce weight, the new V-2 offered better range, reliability, and 30 percent more power than any other contemporary tank engine.

By the fall of 1937, planners at GABTU began to realize that merely building improved variants of the T-26 and the BT-7 would not solve Soviet armor deficiencies. Even the improved versions were still thinly armored and undergunned vehicles that would soon be obsolete. GABTU recognized that Soviet armored forces needed completely new tank designs that would provide the firepower, protection, and mobility to triumph on a modern battlefield. Consequently, in November 1937 GABTU ordered KhPZ to begin design work on a new medium tank while the Voroshilov and Kirov factories in Leningrad were ordered to begin designing a new heavy tank. The new medium tank, designated the A-20, still reflected very conservative thinking, the requirement being for a 20-ton tank with a 45mm gun, 20mm of armor, and a wheeled-tracked system – not really much of an improvement over the BT-7.

Six months later, the Soviet Defense Council of the Soviet People's Commissars (SNAKE) decided that the initial A-20 requirement was still vulnerable to the German 37mm Pak 36 and ordered KhPZ to develop a variant known as the A-30, which increased armor to 30mm and increased the gun to 76.2mm. However, Koshkin and Morozov disliked the wheeled-tracked system used on the A-20, and on their own initiative they designed a further tracked-only variant known as the A-32 or T-32. General Pavlov, now head of GABTU, favored maintaining a capability to remove the tank's tracks and run it on its road wheels because this method offered superior operational mobility – a not-insignificant factor in a large country with a poor internal transportation system. Thus, by the summer of 1938, KhPZ had three new medium tank prototypes in various stages of development: the A-20, A-30, and A-32.

At a conference on new tank designs in Moscow in August 1938, Josef Stalin took a personal interest in the medium tank prototypes. Like Hitler, Stalin got directly involved in major weapons projects. Although SNAKE favored the wheeled version of the A-30, Koshkin convinced Stalin that the tracked A-32 would have superior armored protection and that wheeled tanks had poor off-road mobility.

The T-34 through 360 degrees

SPECIFICATIONS:
T-34

General
Production run:
   T-34: September 1940–March 1944
   Model 1943: October 1943–March 1944
Vehicles produced:
   All T-34: 34,902
   Model 1943: 10,760
Combat weight: 30.9 tons (metric)
Crew: four (tank commander, loader, driver mechanic,
   radio operator)

Dimensions
Overall length: 6.75m
Hull length: 6.09m
Width (with battle tracks): 3m
Height: 2.6m

Armor
Hull front: 47mm (at 30 degrees)
Hull sides: 60mm (at 50 degrees)
Hull rear: 47mm (at 45 degrees)
Hull roof: 20mm (at 0 degrees)
Turret front: 70mm (at 60 degrees)
Turret sides: 52mm (at 70 degrees)
Turret rear: 52mm (at 70 degrees)
Turret roof: 20mm (at 0 degrees)

Armament
Main gun: 1 x 76.2mm F-34 gun
Secondary: 2 x 7.62mm DT
Main gun rate of fire: 4–8rpm

Ammunition stowage
Main: 100 rounds (typically 75 OF-350 HE-Frag and 25
   BR-350A APHE)
Secondary: 3,600 rounds

Artwork by Jim Laurier, © Osprey Publishing

A Soviet T-34 Model 1943 from the summer of that year. Most T-34s arrived from the factory without any exterior markings and turret numbers were rarely used in typical units at this phase of the war. However, Guards tank units were often encouraged to display numbers, slogans and Soviet symbology on their turrets for propaganda purposes.

Communications

9R AM receiver/transmitter on 80 percent of tanks; intercom

Motive power

Engine: V-2 34 12-cylinder diesel engine
Power: 500hp at 1,800rpm
Fuel capacity: 610 liters
Power-to-weight ratio: 16.1hp/ton

Performance

Ground pressure: 0.83kg/cm^2
Maximum road speed: 55km/h
Maximum cross-country speed: 40km/h
Operational range (road): 432km
Operational range (cross-country): 57km
Fuel consumption (road): 1.41 liters/km
Fuel consumption (cross-country): 1.65 liters/km
Cost: 135,000 rubles

Furthermore, when Koshkin pointed out to Stalin that the L-11 76.2mm gun would not fit in the A-30's small turret, Stalin ordered that project halted. However, the A-32 was opposed by Defense Commissar Marshal Klimenti Voroshilov, whose son-in-law, Zhosif Kotin, was developing the KV-series heavy tank in Leningrad. Voroshilov and Kotin did not want KhPZ to develop a tank that was a direct competitor to the KV-series. By late 1938, KhPZ was pressing ahead with developing a wheeled-tracked A-20 to satisfy GABTU's initial requirement, but Koshkin was still developing the tracked-only A-32.

In July 1939, both prototypes of the A-20 and A-32 were completed by KhPZ and sent to Kubinka for evaluation. General Pavlov still preferred the A-20 because the smaller, less-complicated tank would be inexpensive to mass-produce. However, there was no hiding from Stalin the fact that the A-20 performed poorly in its off-road mobility tests when used in its wheeled mode and that the A-32 clearly had superior firepower and armored protection. Stalin was unconcerned about cost issues, but he wanted a medium tank that could be built in large numbers. When Pavlov and Voroshilov suggested that the A-32 was too complex for KhPZ to manufacture in quantity, Stalin agreed to defer on an immediate decision. Stalin did not want another T-28 or T-35 that could only be built in token numbers. For the next several months, the final decision was left floating in bureaucratic limbo, pending more testing with the prototypes. At the same time, the Kirovsky heavy tank project was finally making progress, and the KV-1 design was approved for production in August 1939. GABTU agreed that both the new medium tank and the KV-1 would utilize the new V-2 engine, sloped armor, and either the L-11 or F-34 76mm tank gun.

The realities of actual warfare also had a profound influence upon the development of the T-34 tank. On November 30, 1939, the Soviet Union attacked Finland, but in the first week the Soviets lost 80 tanks to a handful of Finnish

MEDIUM TANK PROTOTYPES 1938				
BT-7M	A-20	A-32	T-34	Model 1940
Weight (metric tons)	14.6 (16.1 US tons)	18 (19.8 US tons)	19 (21 US tons)	26.3 (29 US tons)
Main gun	45mm	45mm	76.2mm	76.2mm
Maximum armor	22mm	25mm	30mm	45mm
Engine	V-2 diesel	V-2 diesel	V-2 diesel	V-2 diesel
Drive configuration	Wheel-track	Wheel-track	Tracked	Tracked

antitank guns. Furthermore, the Soviet 45mm tank gun proved completely ineffective at neutralizing Finnish bunkers. As Soviet tank losses mounted in Finland, it became apparent to GABTU that the new medium tank needed better protection and firepower. On December 9, SNAKE selected the A-32 as the new medium tank and canceled the A-20. The Defense Council ordered KhPZ to immediately build 220 A-32 tanks. Although this seemed like a victory for Koshkin, Voroshilov had not agreed to authorize production of Koshkin's latest version of the new tank, known as the T-34. This variant was 38 percent heavier than the A-32 and had a maximum of 45mm of sloped armor, which Koshkin felt would ensure the tank's invulnerability to 37mm fire. Instead, Voroshilov demanded that the T-34 should undergo further "testing" before he would authorize production. Apparently, Voroshilov hindered the T-34's development in order to boost the prestige that he would gain when his son-in-law's KV-1 tank entered service in spring 1940.

Koshkin was undaunted by Voroshilov's meddling and was unwilling to see his revolutionary design pushed aside. Instead of simply sulking in Kharkov, Koshkin ventured upon a dramatic demonstration by driving the first two unarmed T-34 prototypes to Moscow. Between March 5 and 17, Koshkin and two crews drove the T-34s roughly 700km from Kharkov to Moscow, where the tanks were presented to Stalin. On this grueling road test, Koshkin contracted the pneumonia that would kill him six months later. Voroshilov, who was present at the demonstration, was visibly upset by this stunt, but he could not deny the T-34's qualities. After showing the T-34 to Stalin, both prototypes were driven to the Kubinka test area where the tanks' sloped armor successfully withstood fire from 45mm antitank guns. The T-34s also conducted mobility trials at Kubinka with a Panzer III purchased

The large driver's hatch on the T-34 made ammunition loading easier and offered better chances for escape in the event of the tank being hit. (Courtesy of the Central Museum of the Armed Forces Moscow via Nik Cornish)

from Germany. In order to further demonstrate the new tank's mechanical reliability, both prototypes were then driven back to KhPZ via Smolensk and Kiev, completing a 2,900km (1,802-mile) road test. In late March, one prototype was sent by rail to the Finnish front, where it demonstrated that its L-11 76.2mm gun could demolish captured Finnish bunkers. On March 31, 1940, the Defense Ministry approved full-scale production of the T-34 at KhPZ and the Stalingrad Tractor Works (STZ).

This type of road test was far beyond the abilities of any other contemporary tank and proved the inherent robustness of the T-34's diesel engine. However, the road test revealed a tendency for the engine to overheat and it also showed that the steering controls were rather primitive. The transmission designed by Morozov – similar to the one used on the BT-series light tanks – proved problematic for much of the T-34's early career. GABTU was also concerned that the two-man turret on the T-34 was too small and cramped compared to the three-man turret on the Panzer III. Thus, General Pavlov ordered the KhPZ to address these improvements to the basic T-34 design before proceeding with mass production. KhPZ recommended two potential variants: the A-41 with a three-man turret and the A-43, also known as the T-34M.

As KhPZ began to prepare for series production of the T-34 in late 1940, it had to integrate key components such as the L-11 76.2mm gun from the Kirovski Works and V-2 diesel engines from Factory #75 in Kharkov. Although SNAKE increased the order for T-34s to 600 after the fall of France, KhPZ's pace of development slowed during the summer of 1940 because it had to work on improving the basic design as well as planning for short-term improvements.

By September 15, seven months after the first prototypes appeared, three production Model 1940 T-34 tanks were completed. However, the T-34's development was plagued during the winter of 1940–41 by bureaucratic interference and material shortages. Therefore, KhPZ was only able to complete 115 of the planned 600 tanks for 1940. Marshal Grigory Kulik, Commander of the Artillery Directorate, curtailed deliveries of the L-11 gun while Vorishilov and Pavlov argued that T-34 production should be suspended until the T-34M variant was ready. With plans for a new turret, torsion bar suspension, and a new V-5 diesel engine, the T-34M was indeed superior to the basic T-34. Several prototypes of the T-34M were nearing completion in June 1941, but this advanced design would not be ready for full-scale production until 1942. In warfare, the "best" is often the enemy of the "good," and the T-34M wasted a great deal of design and production energy on a tank that would not be ready for some time. Given the tendency for Soviet committees to suggest new variants and to push "pet theories," it is almost a miracle that any T-34 tanks were available in 1941.

The initial T-34 Model 1940 weighed in at 26.3 tons and was armed with the L-11 76.2mm gun. Koshkin viewed the L-11 as an interim weapon until the new F-34 76.2mm gun became available, and this gun, as well as a cast turret with thicker armor, was earmarked for the Model 1941. However, Koshkin died in September 1940, leaving the Model 1941 without a firm advocate. (Morozov succeeded him at KhPZ.) When the improved T-34 Model 1941 with the F-34 gun and turret began production in February 1941, GABTU and SNAKE allowed the outmoded Model 1940 to remain in production as well. On May 5, SNAKE increased the order for T-34 tanks to 2,800 and authorized production of the upgraded T-34M.

By the time of the German invasion of the Soviet Union on June 22, the KhPZ and the Stalingrad Tank Factory had built about 1,226 T-34 tanks for the Red Army, which was roughly an equal mix of Model 1940 and Model 1941. However, at the start of Operation *Barbarossa*, only 5 percent of the Red Army's tanks were T-34s and 2 percent were KV heavy tanks, meaning that the bulk of Soviet armored forces were still composed of obsolescent light tanks. Approximately 982 T-34 and 466 KV-1 tanks were deployed in the Western military districts at the start of the invasion. Yet despite all its technical promise, the initial combat debut of the T-34 in 1941 was a disaster due to inadequate training and skimpy logistics. The T-34's baptism of fire occurred in Lithuania near Rassinye, when about 50 T-34s from the 3rd Tank Regiment/2nd Tank Division mounted a clumsy counterattack against the spearheads of the 1st and 6th Panzer Divisions between June 24 and 25. Although the T-34s caused a brief panic when 37mm antitank guns failed to penetrate their armor, the Soviet attack was stopped by a few 88mm Flak guns.

A T-34 crew "punches the gun tube" in order to clean the F-34 barrel of carbon residue after firing a significant number of rounds. (The Tank Museum)

General Pavlov had left GABTU to command the Western Front just before the start of the war. Pavlov's command included the 6th Mechanized Corps, one of the Red Army's strongest armored formations with 238 T-34 tanks. Unfortunately for Pavlov, the 6th Mechanized Corps had no armor-piercing (AP) rounds for the T-34s and only one load of fuel per tank. Due to security concerns, few T-34 crewmen had actually been trained. The best-designed tank in the world is merely scrap iron if it does not have ammunition, fuel, or a trained crew, and that was the condition of virtually all the T-34 units in the summer of 1941. The 6th Mechanized Corps and all its vital T-34s were annihilated in the first two weeks of the war without accomplishing anything of consequence. By early July, about half the available T-34 and KV-1 tanks had been lost as the Soviet border armies were destroyed, and most of the remaining prewar T-34s were lost in the Kiev Pocket. When Pavlov's command was wiped out in the Minsk Pocket, he was recalled to Moscow and executed.

Once the extent of Soviet armor losses in the opening battles became apparent, the Soviet National Defense Committee (GKO) decided that quantity, not quality, was the key to victory. Production of the T-34M was canceled. The Model 1941 T-34 became the standard model, and another 1,886 were built in the last half of 1941. However, a total of 2,300 were lost. Once the KhPZ was relocated at Nizhni Tagil in the Urals, Morozov began work on designing the T-34 Model 1942. The main emphasis on the Model 1942 was to simplify the design in order to increase production. This result was admirably achieved, although some of the T-34s were built with inferior or incomplete components. The only significant change in the Model 1942 was an increase in the maximum frontal armor to 65mm, thereby adding two tons to the vehicle's weight. Problems with the KV-1 heavy tank also forced the Red Army to place greater reliance on the T-34 because it was essentially the only effective Soviet design in production. A total of 12,553 T-34s were built in 1942 but 6,500 were lost – a disappointing 51 percent loss rate.

In mid-1942, Morozov began designing the T-34 Model 1943, which would use the newly developed hexagonal turret with two hatches instead of the one large hatch on earlier models. The new turret also had slightly thicker armor of 70mm, but the poor visibility problem was not corrected until mid-1943 when a cupola was introduced. The T-34 Model 1943 would comprise the bulk of T-34s available for the campaigns in the Ukraine in 1943. The Model 1943 was a good tank, but it indicated that Soviet tank design had stagnated in the 18 months since the war began: the T-34 was still armed with a 76.2mm gun and armor that was no longer immune to the improved German antitank guns. The Red Army would have to fight for the remainder of 1943 with the T-34, no longer enjoying a major technical advantage over German tanks. However, the model was at least finally available in quantity.

TECHNICAL ASSESSMENT

Armor protection

Both the Soviets and the Germans sought to develop a medium tank that could withstand a hit from contemporary antitank guns. However, it was easier to increase the size of antitank weapons than it was to increase armor on tanks, which meant that by 1943 it was accepted that only heavy tanks could carry enough armor to defeat weapons in the 75–85mm range. The introduction of sloped armor on the T-34 succeeded in increasing armored protection while keeping the vehicle's gross weight within reason. Wa Pruf 6 was quick to realize that all new German tank designs should incorporate at least some sloped armor.

The armor on the T-34 was initially designed to withstand hits from antitank guns in the 37–50mm range, but when the Germans introduced the long 75mm KwK 40 L43 gun on their Panzer IV Ausf. F2 in May 1942, the comfortable margin of safety on the Soviet tank disappeared. Suddenly, German tanks armed with the new long-barreled guns could destroy T-34s at 1,000m instead of being limited to only point-blank attacks. Furthermore, from 1940 to 1943 the T-34's armor was only increased from a maximum of 45mm to 70mm, but at least 90mm of frontal armor was needed to provide some degree of protection against the KwK 40. Additionally, the quality of Soviet armor plate was often poor, and the nickel content used to harden steel plate – typically 1 to 1.5 percent – was less than on German tanks. The weaker Soviet armor plate tended to spall (or break off in chips on the inner surface) more easily when hit, and metal splinters caused the majority of Soviet tanker casualties. By the time of *Zitadelle*, the T-34 had lost its edge in armored protection and was now vulnerable to destruction at long range from a wide variety of German weapons, including the new Panthers and Tigers.

Although the Panther's sloped armor is often described as revolutionary for German tank design, this characterization is misleading. The frontal armor protection on the Panther Ausf. D was thicker than the Panzer IV Ausf. H, having 100mm at

> **"** The engine of the panzer is its weapon just as much as the cannon. **"**
>
> Generaloberst Heinz Guderian

12 degrees on the turret front (instead of 50mm) and a sloped glacis plate (the heavily armored front of a tank's hull) that was 80mm thick at 55 degrees (versus 80mm at 78 degrees). While the 100mm-thick gun mantlet was generally impervious to most AP rounds in 1943, Soviet AP rounds fired from close range during *Zitadelle* cracked the mantlet on at least three Panthers from the 52nd Panzer Battalion. Moreover, the side and rear armor on the Panther was only marginally thicker than the Panzer IV Ausf. H. The Panther had 40mm of hull side armor (versus 30mm), the Panther's turret side armor was 45mm at 25 degrees (instead of 50mm at 79 degrees), and rear armor was 40–45mm (instead of 20–30mm). In fact, the Panther was quite vulnerable to flanking fire, which often ignited the fuel tanks.

Ostensibly, the Panther's armor was designed to meet Guderian's specification for a tank that could withstand the T-34's 76.2mm gun. Based upon examination of captured T-34s, the Germans were aware that the F-34 gun was capable of penetrating up to 63mm of sloped armor at 1,000m. Thus, Wa Pruf 6 should have realized that the Panther's 40–45mm of side armor was insufficient to withstand flanking shots from T-34s at normal combat ranges. While the Panther's frontal armor was as good as the Tiger's, its side armor offered only a modest improvement over the Panzer IV. Hitler realized that the Panther wasn't well armored enough, and he kept demanding that Wa Pruf 6 increase the level of armored protection.

T-34 turret interior. The eyepiece for the PT-4? rotating periscope is toward upper left of this photo. The padded eyepiece for the TMFD sight is just to the left of the main gun breech, and next to the turret elevation handle. (Author's collection)

In response, Wa Pruf 6 developed the *Schuerzen* armored side skirts for the Panther and began work on a more heavily armored variant, the Panther II. While the Panther II offered 60mm of side armor, the increased armor raised the Panther's weight to over 50 tons. After several months of technical discussion between Wa Pruf 6 and MAN, the Panther II design was shelved in May 1943, and the decision was made to incorporate some of its features into future versions of the Panther. As for the side skirt armor, this ad hoc measure proved to be of limited value since most of these broke off under combat conditions. Thus, the Panther Ausf. D and Ausf. A models that fought in the Ukraine in 1943 were too lightly armored and did not meet Guderian's 1941 specifications. Overall, the Panther Ausf. D clearly had better frontal armored protection than the T-34 Model 1943, but the level of protection still fell far short of what was needed.

Firepower

An AP round can achieve various levels of penetration on the battlefield, depending upon the range and the striking angle. A round can achieve target destruction by physically penetrating the armor, but it may also inflict serious damage by causing the armor to spall inside. In general, fewer than 50 percent of actual hits in 1943 either knocked out or destroyed a tank, and only about 25 percent of tanks that were immobilized were permanently lost.

The T-34 Model 1943 typically carried 75 OF-350 HE-Frag and 25 BR-350A APHE rounds (including four tungsten-cored BR-350P rounds after October 1943). The Panther usually carried 40 rounds of Pzgr 39/42 APC and 39 rounds of Sprgr 42 HE (high explosive) ammunition. Soviet gunners tended to fire a lot of ammunition – often half their basic load in a single engagement – while German gunners had to be more conservative because their ammunition resupply was not always reliable.

Like its sloped armor, the T-34's F-34 gun was designed for the battlefield of 1941, not 1943. The standard BR-350A 76.2mm AP round used on the T-34 fired a steel projectile with a muzzle velocity of 662m/s (1,480mph). This round could penetrate the Panther's side armor out to about 1,000m, but it could only penetrate the glacis armor at about 300m and could not penetrate the turret frontal armor. The BR-350P APDS round introduced in October 1943 could damage the Panther's frontal armor at ranges under 100m but could not achieve reliable target destruction. The T-34's firepower was also handicapped by the lack of a dedicated gunner, forcing the tank commander to first acquire the target with the PTK periscope and then switch to the TMFD gunner's sight. The TMFD was inferior to the Panther's TFZ12 sight,

Inside the Panther

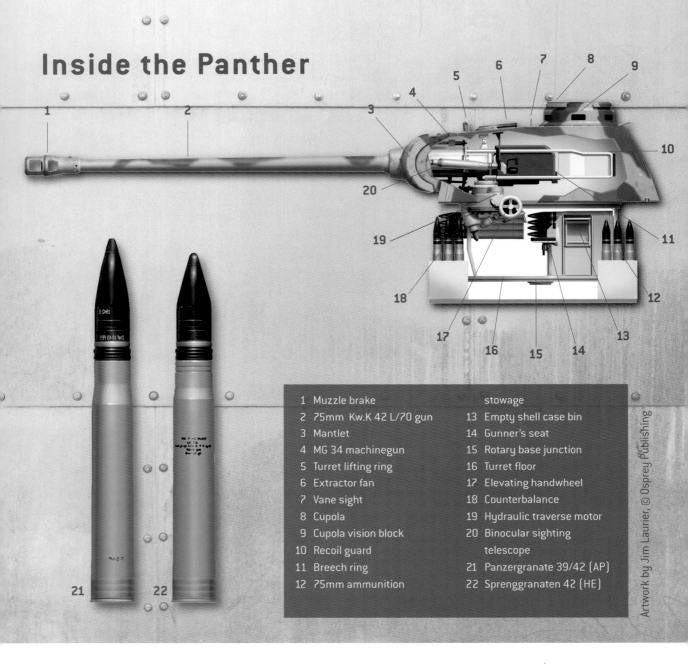

1 Muzzle brake
2 75mm Kw.K 42 L/70 gun
3 Mantlet
4 MG 34 machinegun
5 Turret lifting ring
6 Extractor fan
7 Vane sight
8 Cupola
9 Cupola vision block
10 Recoil guard
11 Breech ring
12 75mm ammunition
stowage
13 Empty shell case bin
14 Gunner's seat
15 Rotary base junction
16 Turret floor
17 Elevating handwheel
18 Counterbalance
19 Hydraulic traverse motor
20 Binocular sighting
telescope
21 Panzergranate 39/42 (AP)
22 Sprenggranaten 42 (HE)

Artwork by Jim Laurier, © Osprey Publishing

having a narrower field of view and less magnification. However, the T-34 did have one advantage over the Panther in terms of firepower, and that was its turret traverse speed. The T-34 had a turret traverse speed of 30 degrees per second, or 12 seconds for a full rotation, which was five times faster than the Panther Ausf. D and 50 percent faster than the Panther Ausf. A. Faster turret rotation allowed T-34 gunners to redirect fire more quickly, particularly at close range.

The 75mm KwK 40 L43 gun on the Panzer IV F2 fired an AP round with a muzzle velocity of 740m/s (1,655mph) that could penetrate up to 87mm of armor at 1,000m, easily guaranteeing destruction of the T-34. The 75mm KwK 42 L70 developed for the Panther was an even more powerful gun that fired a standard AP round that could penetrate 111mm of armor at 1,000m, far more armor than carried on any existing Soviet tank. Furthermore, the tungsten-cored Panzergranate 40/42 round had an even better performance, with a 1,120m/s muzzle velocity and the ability to penetrate 150mm of armor at 1,000m. With the excellent TFZ12 sight, Panther gunners could theoretically engage targets out to 3,000m, although commanders usually forbade firing at very long ranges in order not to waste rounds. Thus, the Panther's main gun was well designed for long-range killing, and it clearly was superior to the F-34 gun, but it offered few significant advantages over the KwK 40. In firepower, the Panther met Guderian's requirement, and it did outclass the T-34, but it should also be remembered that the trade-offs for gaining this superior gun were significant. The larger KwK 42 meant a bigger turret and, therefore, a wider hull, resulting in greater weight and less mobility.

Mobility

The T-34 was built around its V-2 diesel engine, and the automotive design was so sound that its successor, the T-34-85, was able to keep the same chassis. While the T-34's armor protection and firepower advantages had largely disappeared by 1943, its superior mobility was clearly demonstrated when 5th Guards Tank Army was able to move its T-34s 300km on their own tracks to the front between July 7–9 and still had about 90 percent of its tanks operational. No Panther unit could ever have moved this distance without losing most of its tanks to mechanical breakdowns.

Although Guderian asked for a tank with superior mobility, Wa Pruf 6 and MAN had different conceptions about what this meant. The design team's fixation on torsion bar suspension and quick dismissal of equipping the Panther with a diesel engine led to the development of a tank that essentially ignored the T-34's mobility advantages. While the T-34 was a 30-ton tank equipped with rear wheel drive and a diesel engine, the Panther was a 45-ton tank equipped with front wheel drive and a gasoline engine. Amazingly, Wa Pruf 6 even overlooked the simple efficiency of the T-34's Christie suspension and instead opted for complex interleaved road wheel running gear, which would quickly clog up with mud in the soft fields of the Ukraine. Furthermore, replacing an inner road wheel on the Panther was more difficult because it required removing the adjacent road wheels as well. Obviously, the engineers who designed the Panther put little thought into how the vehicle would be operated or maintained under field conditions.

Some of the T-34's advantages in mobility declined as new models added weight but without any increase in engine output. The introduction of the new hexagonal turret in 1942 added about two tons to the T-34's overall weight. In terms of statistical comparison, the Panther Ausf. D did appear to have equal or better mobility to the T-34, having lower ground pressure and better road speed. However, in reality, the Panther could only move faster than the T-34 once it reached seventh gear, which was unlikely to occur under combat conditions. In tactical driving using third gear, the Panther was considerably slower than the T-34, being able to achieve only 13km/h (8mph) versus 29km/h (18mph). Certainly, one of the biggest problems with the Panther Ausf. D and A models was the fuel-guzzling character of its Maybach HL 230 engine, which required almost double the amount of fuel to go 1km as a Panzer IV and nearly four times as much as a T-34. As the Wehrmacht began to run seriously short of fuel in late 1943, the Panther's poor fuel efficiency would further degrade its operational and tactical mobility.

Panther 824 from the 52nd Panzer Battalion, which was captured by the Soviets. Note the multiple 45mm antitank hits on the gun mantlet, which damaged the TFZ sights. (Courtesy of the Central Museum of the Armed Forces Moscow via Nik Cornish)

The rugged and simplistic construction of the T-34 paid off with an operational reliability rate of around 70–90 percent in most Soviet armor units in 1943. In contrast, no German panzer unit equipped with Panther Ausf. D or A model tanks was able to sustain an operational readiness rate above 35 percent for any sustained period in 1943. Far more Panthers were lost to mechanical failure in 1943 than to enemy action, while the opposite was true for T-34s. Although the Panther's AK 7-200 transmission was nominally superior to the clumsy transmission on the T-34, about 5 percent broke down within 100km and over 90 percent within 1,500km in combat. The final drive on the Panther Ausf. D was so weak that the tank could not even turn while it was backing up, which occurred frequently in the retreat to the Dnepr River. The two fuel pumps were probably the biggest mobility weakness in the Panther Ausf. D because they were prone to leaks and caused serious engine fires. At least three Panthers were destroyed by fuel pump-caused fires during *Zitadelle*, and a high proportion of mechanical breakdowns was caused by this troublesome component. Nor did this problem go away after Kursk: the initial batch of Panther Ausf. A tanks that were handed over to the SS-Leibstandarte in Italy in September 1943 were so problematic that every one was rejected for service.

The Panther's poor mobility forced the Wehrmacht to move units around by rail and get them as close to the front as possible before unloading. Throughout 1943, the Panther was essentially tied to conducting all major movements by rail, as was the equally short-legged Tiger, and units could not even move 100km without significant losses. Thus, the Panther did not meet Guderian's requirement for a tank with superior mobility, and it was the T-34's continued advantage in mobility and reliability that contributed greatly to the Soviet victory in the Ukraine in 1943.

Communications

The standard Panther Ausf. D was equipped with an intercom system that allowed all five crew members to communicate in combat. A Fu 5 transmitter and a UHF receiver were also standard equipment. Normally, a platoon leader would operate with his platoon frequency on the Fu 5 and monitor his company frequency on the UHF receiver. The command versions of the Panther would typically carry a long-range Fu 7 or Fu 8 transmitter to communicate with higher headquarters, a Fu 5 to talk with subordinate commanders, and an additional receiver to monitor other radio nets. Soviet tankers were quick to notice the extra antennas on command Panthers, and these were usually marked as high-priority targets. While about 80 percent of T-34s were equipped with the 9R AM radio by late 1943, the radio did not function well on the move, and company and battalion commanders were

Inside the T-34

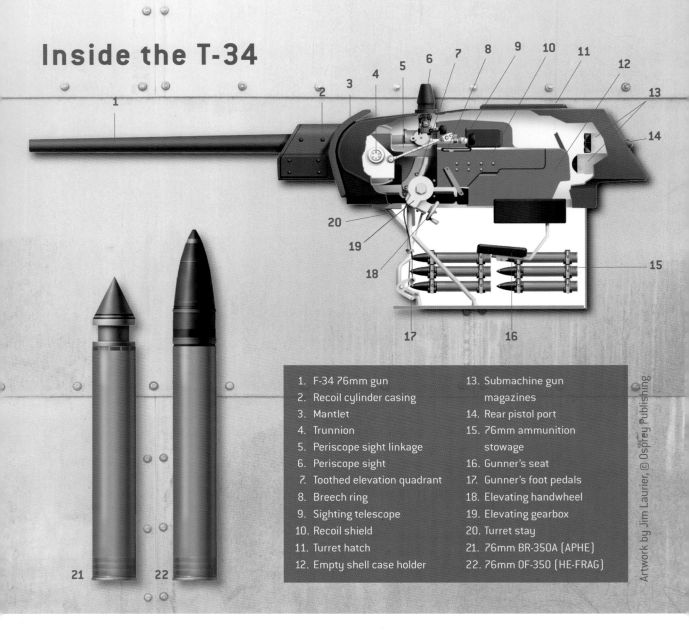

1. F-34 76mm gun
2. Recoil cylinder casing
3. Mantlet
4. Trunnion
5. Periscope sight linkage
6. Periscope sight
7. Toothed elevation quadrant
8. Breech ring
9. Sighting telescope
10. Recoil shield
11. Turret hatch
12. Empty shell case holder
13. Submachine gun magazines
14. Rear pistol port
15. 76mm ammunition stowage
16. Gunner's seat
17. Gunner's foot pedals
18. Elevating handwheel
19. Elevating gearbox
20. Turret stay
21. 76mm BR-350A (APHE)
22. 76mm OF-350 (HE-FRAG)

Artwork by Jim Laurier, © Osprey Publishing

limited to the same short-range system. The T-34's intercom system was also limited to only the commander and the driver, leaving the other two crew members virtually isolated. The T-34's intercom was so unreliable that most tank commanders preferred to tap with their boots on their drivers' left or right shoulder to indicate direction. Simple sign language was used to communicate with the loader. Overall, the Panther enjoyed a communications advantage over the T-34 at both the crew and unit levels, which contributed to some German tactical successes. However, the hasty manner in which Panthers were often thrown into combat in the Ukraine in 1943 – often straight off the rail cars they arrived on – led to units getting no chance to establish functioning radio nets.

Overall assessment

Over the years, the PzKpfw V Panther has been commonly described as "the best tank of World War II" but such simplistic assessments have been made with little regard for the Panther's actual capabilities or performance. In many respects, the Panther was merely an enlarged MAN VK 24.01 with sloped armor and a bigger gun tacked on that was rushed into production and combat. MAN's engineers designed the chassis and running gear for a 24-ton tank but ended up carrying a 45-ton load, which severely strained the engine and transmission. While the "teething problems" of the Panther at Kursk are well known, less appreciated is the fact that these problems dogged the tank for the rest of 1943 and, indeed, its entire career. A report by Generaloberst Guderian's Panzer Commission in January 1945 reported that the final drives on 370 Panthers on the Eastern Front had failed and that the troops were losing confidence in "defective weapons." The Panther did enjoy a huge advantage in firepower over any other existing medium tank, but in terms of mobility, armored protection, and overall reliability, the Panther failed to either best the T-34 or to meet Guderian's initial requirements. In contrast, the T-34 was a mature design by 1943, with an optimum blend of armored protection and firepower. It was the T-34's superior mobility and reliability, combined with the ease of production that guaranteed a steady flow of replacement tanks, that allowed the Red Army to seize and maintain the operational initiative in the Ukraine.

THE MEN

The Panther tank company

Organization

A standard Heer (army) Panther tank platoon in 1943 consisted of five tanks and 25 soldiers, led by a platoon leader (either a Leutnant or Oberfeldwebel). The Panther companies in Panzer Battalions 51 and 52 that fought in *Zitadelle* each had 22 tanks and 172 soldiers, led by an Oberleutnant. There were two different Panther company organizations: one with four platoons and one with three platoons. A Panther tank battalion in 1943 was assigned between 71 and 96 tanks and up to 1,160 soldiers, led by a Hauptman or Major. A Panther tank battalion also included eight Panther tanks that belonged to the Headquarters Company, an armored pioneer platoon supported with halftracks, and towed antiaircraft guns. Compared to the Soviets, the Germans lavishly equipped their tank battalion with support assets: each tank company was supported by a J-Gruppe with six vehicles loaded with spare parts and capable of pulling an engine out. The key asset in each Panther battalion was the recovery section, which might have a couple of Bergepanthers or up to nine Zgkw 18-ton semitracks. These were the primary means of recovering damaged or inoperative Panthers. The Panther battalions also had a large supply platoon, with 47 heavy trucks capable of hauling ammunition or fuel. Although it was intended for Panther units to operate attached to existing Panzer divisions, during the chaotic summer of 1943 most Panther units operated semi-independently, and it was not unusual for companies to be temporarily attached to other commands.

The German Panzer soldier, 1943

Unlike their Soviet counterparts, German Panzer soldiers usually volunteered for the armor branch. Furthermore, most of the German Panzer soldiers were considerably older and more experienced than the Russian crews. Typical Panther tank platoon leaders were 26 to 30 years old, and company commanders were 27 to

31 years old. At least half the platoon leaders and noncommissioned officers (NCOs) had been in the Wehrmacht since 1938 or 1939 and had some combat experience, although often in the infantry or other branches. Typical Panther Unteroffiziers were 22 years old and already had three years of military experience under their belts. However, the German NCO corps by 1943 could no longer be so selective, and not all men promoted were of a high caliber. The heart of each Panther company was the "Spiefl" ("mother of the company") – a Hauptfeldwebel (first sergeant). While the average soldier in a Panther unit had an edge in experience over his Soviet counterpart, it is also important to note the negative impact of wounds and combat fatigue upon the surviving cadre of veterans after two continuous years of war in Russia.

Training schools

The Third Reich went to great effort to train its Panzertruppen as combat-ready "hunters," but as the war progressed, the training programs were shortened and resources such as fuel became increasingly scarce. The formation of the first Panther units coincided with the appointment of Generaloberst Guderian as Inspector of Panzer Troops in February 1943. Guderian took charge of an already good training system and streamlined it to produce tankers who were prepared for actual combat conditions. Unfortunately, the technical problems with the early Panther Ausf. D models severely distracted the troops of the 51st and 52nd Panzer Battalions, and units formed later received much better training.

Enlisted soldiers completed 16 weeks of basic infantry training before going to basic tank training at Panzerschule 1 in Wünsdorf for four more months. The Panzer school provided extremely thorough driver and basic maintenance training to enlisted soldiers as well as cross-training on other crew functions. After completing the Panzer school, promising soldiers could be sent to either NCO or officer candidate training, which might require another six to nine months. Once all individual training was complete, new officers, NCOs, and enlisted troops were then assigned to a Panzer Ersatz Abteilung, a replacement tank battalion for each panzer division. Temporary crews and subunits were formed in the replacement battalions in order to conduct crew, platoon,

A typical example of recruiting posters for the Panzerwaffe. With exhortations such as "Panzer – Your Weapon!," "Volunteers Forward!" and "Come Join Us" they are an accurate reflection of the German military recruiting drive prior to and during the war. The Panzerwaffe was one of the most popular branches of service as well as one of the most difficult ones of which to become a member. (Bundesarchiv Plak 003-025-018)

and company training. While at the replacement battalion, selected crews or individuals would be sent to specialist schools such as the superb gunner's course at the Army Gunnery School at Putlos.

Guderian ordered that the primary focus on unit training should be the live-fire "battle run," and he instituted an abbreviated tank training program in May 1943 that put primary emphasis on gunnery. During the battle run, crews had to engage a series of moving and pop-up stationary targets, with both AP and HE rounds, at ranges from 800 to 2,000m. Against stationary tanks, a Panther crew was expected to obtain at least one hit out of four rounds fired against a frontal tank target at 1,200 to 2,000m. Another sequence was to engage a target moving at 20km/h on a sled at a range of 800 to 1,200m. The target had to be hit with one of three rounds and within

Major Karl von Sivers

Major Karl von Sivers (1912–1944), commander of the 52nd Panzer Battalion, was commissioned as a cavalry officer in 1934, and served in the 1st Cavalry Division in 1939–41. Von Sivers was a traditional horse cavalryman but he came from an educated background, speaking four languages including Russian. In December 1941, von Sivers' regiment began converting into the 2nd Battalion, 24th Panzer Regiment and he served in that unit during the advance to Stalingrad in 1942, but he managed to avoid the fate of most of his unit. On March 15, 1943, von Sivers took command of the 1st Battalion, Panzer Regiment 15, which was forming the 52nd Panzer Battalion. Although von Sivers helped to form the new battalion at Grafenwöhr, he was not able to deploy with the unit for Operation *Zitadelle* due to illness. He rejoined the 52nd Panzer Battalion near Tomarovka on July 22, 1943 and conducted a skillful withdrawal down the Vorskla River valley in the face of the Soviet onslaught in August 1943. Von Sivers remained in command of the battalion after it was redesignated as the 1st Battalion, Panzer Regiment 15 on August 24 until he was killed in action in March 1944. Von Sivers was typical of the mid-war German panzer leader, who was not a "tank ace" himself, but whose experienced leadership enabled the Panther units to hold together under extreme conditions.

Courtesy of Jason Mark

Oberfeldwebel Gerhard Brehme

Oberfeldwebel Gerhard Brehme (1912–1943), a platoon leader in 1st Company, Panzer Battalion 52, was typical of the German mid-war tank sergeant. He had served in the 1st Battalion, Panzer Regiment 15 since Operation *Barbarossa* began. On January 9, 1943, Brehme was a platoon leader in Group Wöhler, the effort to relieve the trapped German garrison at Velikiye Luki. Although the effort failed, Brehme was credited with destroying eight Soviet tanks during the operation. Brehme then was sent back to Grafenwöhr where he trained on the new Panther tank with the 52nd Panzer Battalion. However during Operation *Zitadelle*, Brehme was one of the first casualties. His Panther – probably Number 521 – was hit in the thin hull side armor by two 76mm armor-piercing rounds near Dubrova on July 6, 1943. Brehme was badly burned and he died in the military hospital in Kharkov on July 17, 1943. After *Zitadelle*, Brehme's Panther ended up on display in Gorky Park in Moscow. Brehme was an experienced tanker who was credited with destroying 51 enemy tanks during his career and it was this type of steadfast NCO who held the Wehrmacht together during the tough summer and fall of 1943.

30 seconds. German target silhouettes in 1943 were 4m long and 2m high, which was smaller than an actual T-34. Guderian also mandated that that at least 30 percent of training should be conducted at night or under low-light conditions.

Once the order came from the OKH to begin forming the first Panther battalions, the decision was made on March 1, 1943, to establish a Panther training course at Erlangen, near Grafenwöhr, where much of the Panther testing occurred. The Panther course included both an individual phase for training soldiers on the new features of the tank as well as a collective phase for training platoons and companies. Generally, the Panther course was intended to last about two months, but because some battalions such as I/Panzer Regiment 1 did not go through it all at once, the process could be stretched out. By May, when the school was fully functional, it could produce one trained battalion per month, plus individual replacements. Panzer Battalion 51, based upon the II/Panzer Regiment 33 from 9th Panzer Division, began forming at Grafenwöhr on January 13, 1943, and Panzer Battalion 52 was formed from the 11th Panzer Division's I/Panzer Regiment 15 on

February 6. Between January and June 1943, these battalions spent much of their time working with MAN engineers to identify and correct the numerous defects in the first batch of Panther Ausf. D tanks rather than engaging in collective training. A few Panther crews were sent to the Putlos gunnery school, but collective training above the platoon level never occurred at Erlangen. In April 1943, both battalions had to turn all their Panthers in for modifications, and since the troops now lacked tanks, a ridiculous decision was made to ship the troops to Mailly le Camp in France for "training." Unlike Soviet training camps in the Urals, the German Panzer crews were at risk of enemy air attack while in the rear areas. On April 17, four Panther crewmen from 2 Company of the 51st Panzer Battalion (2./Pz. Abt.51), including an experienced company commander and a platoon leader, were killed by an RAF bombing raid on Mannheim when en route to France. The battalions were finally reassembled at Grafenwöhr in June, just in time to be reissued their tanks and to begin rail loading for the Eastern Front.

Crew and unit formation

Once the 51st and 52nd Panzer Battalions began forming at Grafenwöhr, the newly raised companies began assembling tank crews. Experienced tank commanders did have some choice regarding who was placed on their tank, although the company commander and platoon leaders usually received the better gunners and drivers.

A Panther company massing for an attack. In order to avoid Soviet air and artillery attacks, the Panthers had to be dispersed and well camouflaged until the moment for action arrived. (Author's collection)

Once formed, a crew would tend to stay together until casualties occurred. By the time that 1./Pz. Abt.51 arrived by rail near Borisovka on July 1, it had grown to four officers and 190 enlisted men. Of the 194 troops in the company, 49 percent were veterans from Panzer Regiment 33, 43 percent were replacements, and 8 percent were from other units. The commander of the company was Oberleutnant Rudolf Köhler, an old hand who had served first as a tank platoon leader in Poland, Holland, France, and Greece, then as a company commander in southern Russia from 1941 to 1942. While the company had a solid core of experienced veterans, slightly more than half the troops had not previously seen combat.

Although the OKH had specified in June 1943 that all panzer divisions on the Eastern Front would receive one Panther battalion in the next six months, the decision was made to group the 51st and 52nd Panzer Battalions under the provisional 39th Panzer Regiment, led by Major Meinrad von Lauchert. Interestingly, von Lauchert had been in the 4th Panzer Division's Panzer Regiment 35 during the fighting around Mtsensk against Katukov's T-34s in October 1941. Now he stood to lead Germany's answer to the T-34 into its first battle.

Crew roles and functions

The five-man crew of a Panther consisted of the Panzerführer (tank commander; usually a Leutnant, Feldwebel, or Unteroffizier), the Richtschutze (gun layer, or gunner; usually an Unteroffizier or Obergefreiter), the Ladeschutze (loader; typically an Obergefreiter or Gefreiter), the Funker (radio operator; a Gefreiter or Schütze), and the Fahrer (driver; an Obergefreiter or Gefreiter). By having a dedicated gunner, the Panther commander could concentrate on not only fighting his own tank but leading his section, platoon, or company. Unlike Soviet T-34 drivers, the Panther driver was trained to make independent decisions and to use terrain for concealment as much as possible. The Panther crew was trained to think and fight as a team with every member participating in combat. For example, the radio operator would spot for the gunner and pass him any corrections over the intercom. Since all five crew members were hooked into the tank's intercom system, the situational awareness and coordination between them was easier.

The T-34 tank company

Organization

The T-34 tank platoon consisted of three tanks and 12 soldiers, usually led by a Leytenant Platoon Leader. It was therefore much smaller than a Panther company. In theory, each tank was supposed to be commanded by an officer, but in practice, two

Leytenant Pavlovich Vasily Bryukhov

Leytenant Pavlovich Vasiliy Bryukhov (born 1924), T-34 platoon leader in 99th Tank Brigade, July 1943. Bryukhov was born in the Urals and had just completed high school at the start of the German invasion. Initially, Bryukhov served in a ski battalion in the defense of Kalinin in November 1941, where he was wounded. After recovering, Bryukhov was sent to Kurgan in September 1942 to receive initial tanker training and he was commissioned a junior lieutenant in April 1943. He joined up with his first crew at Chelyabinsk in May 1943. Bryukhov arrived at the 2nd Tank Corps just prior to the battle of Kursk and he fought as a T-34 platoon leader in the Ukraine for the rest of 1943. Bryukhov would eventually destroy a Panther tank at pointblank range in early 1944 and rose to battalion commander by the end of 1944 (at the age of 20).

During 1943–45 Bryukhov was involved in numerous tank battles and had nine T-34s destroyed under him. Bryukhov was eventually made a Hero of the Soviet Union and he claimed to have destroyed 28 German tanks.

Author's collection

out of three tanks were commanded by a Serzhant (Sergeant). The tank company had three platoons totaling ten T-34 tanks and 42 soldiers, including the company commander, who in 1943 was typically a Starshiy Leytenant (Senior Lieutenant). A Soviet tank battalion in 1943 was authorized 31 T-34 tanks and about 180 soldiers and was led by a Kapetan or Major. The tank battalion also included a small 11-man tank and weapons repair section, a transportation section with a truck for fuel, and several supply trucks for ammunition, and a four-man medical section. Some units had a "Zhuchka," a turretless T-34 equipped as a recovery vehicle, but many just had a GAZ-AA repair truck or captured German vehicles. Normally, the smallest Soviet armored unit given independent missions was a tank brigade, with two to three tank battalions.

The Soviet tank soldier, 1943

Soviet tank platoon leaders were usually 19 to 21 years old, while company commanders were 22 to 27 years old. Many junior officers had been members of the Communist Komsomol organization as teenagers and typically were high school graduates. Sergeants were usually 18 years old and might have been in the Red Army for six months, although there were a handful of surviving enlisted men from the 1942 fighting who were often made the company Starshina (Master Sergeant). Each tank platoon usually had a Starshiy Serzhant (Senior Sergeant) who acted as a platoon sergeant, or even as the platoon leader in case the Leytenant was a casualty. Petr Kirichenko, who served in the 159th Tank Brigade, was made a senior sergeant after only one month of training.[4]

[4] See Artem, Drabkin and Oleg Sheremet, *T-34 in Action*, Pen & Sword, Barnsley, UK, 2006, pp. 110–111

Soviet female tankers

Approximately one million women served in the Red Army in 1941–45, but fewer than 10 percent served in combat roles. A few female volunteers served as tank drivers early in 1942, but it was not until women were sent to serve as cadres in tank training regiments in January 1943 that their presence became more widespread. By the summer of 1943 the pool of Soviet manpower was beginning to run dry and a number of women who had served in the training units were sent as individual replacements, usually to Guards tank brigades. While the total number of female T-34 tank crew members is unknown, it was not large, although Communist propaganda tended to focus on these individuals. A few women who survived their initial combat rose to become tank commanders, but most served innocuously as drivers, who tended to have a low survival rate in combat. In one action near Fastov on November 8, 1943, SS Leibstandarte engaged two T-34s from the 3rd Guards Tank Army and discovered afterwards that both tanks had female crew members. Mariya Oktyabrskaya was the first female tank driver to become a Heroine of the Soviet Union, the most prestigious award for bravery.

A widow of a soldier killed defending the Motherland, she sold all her possessions to raise the money to donate a tank to the military. Her only stipulation was that she would be its driver. She was posted to the 26th Guards Tank Brigade in September 1943 and saw repeated action throughout the Eastern Front, in particular serving courageously in the fighting around the Vitebsk region in November 1943. Sr/Sgt Mariya Oktyabrskaya was eventually mortally wounded in combat in March 1944.

Most young Soviet soldiers had been raised under conditions of poverty, limited education, and with poor diets compared to their German counterparts. According to platoon leader Evgeni Bessonov, "Most of the 18-year-old Soviet soldiers in 1943 were not physically strong, mostly small and frail youngsters."[5] Virtually to a man, the primary complaint for Soviet soldiers was the lack of food, a condition that was endemic in both the rear areas and at the front. Soviet battlefield logistics were so primitive that as tank units advanced through the Ukraine, soldiers relied on "grandmother's rations" – food from local civilians. However, alcohol was plentiful, and Soviet commanders were often very lenient about allowing troops to drink before battle in order to allay fears about heavy losses. Soviet tankers were under orders not to abandon their T-34s unless they were either burning or the main gun was disabled. To do otherwise was to risk being sent to a *shtrafbat* (punishment battalion). Thus, fear of harsh punishment by the People's Commissariat for Internal Affairs (NKVD) caused Soviet tankers to stick with their tanks to the end.

Training schools

The three main T-34 production centers in Nizhniy Tagil, Sverdlovsk, and Chelyabinsk all had colocated tank training regiments (TZAP). There were also tank schools at Kurgan, Ufa, Ulyanovsk, and Saratov that taught basic skills such as driving and familiarization with the V-2 diesel engine to both officer cadets and enlisted troops. By 1943, Soviet enlisted soldiers usually spent four to eight weeks receiving basic training in a tank training battalion. There were separate battalions for drivers, loaders, and radiomen. Unlike at the German tank schools, Soviet tank drivers were generally not taught how to make use of battlefield terrain, nor were they taught to make independent decisions. Soviet schools considered a T-34 driver trained if he could start the vehicle and drive it in a column of other tanks or in a simple wedge, all conducted under noncombat conditions. Soldiers selected as loaders spent endless hours practicing loading dummy rounds into a breech and loading machine gun drums. Radio operators were given only the basics: how to turn on the receiver/transmitter (R/T) and how to change frequencies. Cross-training of crew members was rare, and usually only the designated driver was capable of driving the tank.

After initial basic training was judged completed, the more promising trainees were sent to either NCO or officer candidate training. Some candidates may also have been sent to other technical schools in order to be trained as tank mechanics. Even in 1943, much of the tank training was conducted on worn-out BT-7 or T-26

---

[5] See Bessonov, Evgeni, *Tank Rider: Into the Reich with the Red Army*, Casemate, Philadelphia, 2003, p. 44

tanks, with only a few T-34s available for training. Soviet training units in rear areas often wasted their trainees' limited time with pointless drills, the memorizing of field manuals, and endless political lectures. Training under simulated combat conditions was negligible. Leytenant Bessonov, of the 49th Mechanized Brigade in 1943, said that, "The level of training was poor, as the teachers did not understand the subject themselves" and some martinets still managed to include "ceremonial march step" in the officer training syllabus in 1942.[6] Leytenant Pavlov V. Bryukhov, who trained at the Kurgan Tank Training School from January to April 1943, said that "training at the base was very weak" and the tank gunnery ranges lacked the kind of pop-up or moving targets that he observed on tank ranges in Germany after the war. Bryukhov said that most training consisted of driving on old BT tanks with new leytenants conducting only a single exercise dubbed "tank platoon in the offensive."[7] An even more telling indictment of Soviet tank training is that many platoon leaders could not even read a map, which became a frequent problem during the advance to the Dnepr River.

Once a soldier finished his basic training, he was usually sent to one of the tank training regiments located near a T-34 production center to receive his tank. The training regiments could typically process about 2,000 soldiers at a time. In theory, the soldier would spend only about one month at the tank training regiment, but in some cases, soldiers might stay there for a year or longer. The tank factories were perennially short of labor, and tankers awaiting their tanks were often put to work on the assembly lines. When Leytenant Bryukhov completed training at Kurgan, he was sent to the 6th Tank Training Regiment at Chelyabinsk, but instead of receiving a T-34 tank, Bryukhov was put to work on a machine lathe in the Chelyabinsk tank plant for two weeks. The training regiments usually conducted simple platoon and company-level training such as practicing moving in a wedge or line, but there was little tactical training.

Actual crew training in Soviet tank units was incredibly brief. After the new T-34 was received at the factory, a group of about ten tanks would be assembled into a "march company" under the Senior Leytenant who then conducted a road march to a local gunnery range. According to several Soviet T-34 platoon leaders, familiarization firing in 1943 typically consisted of firing only three 76.2mm rounds and one drum of machine gun ammunition at static targets. Even if a newly formed crew performed miserably at this seemingly simple task, the tank was judged combat-ready and ordered to move to a nearby railhead for shipment to the front. Some crew members were still not comfortable around tanks: Junior Leytenant

[6] See Bessonov, p. 28
[7] See Drabkin, pp. 128–129

Sergei Burtsev noted that his loader was so frightened by the recoil from the first round fired on the range that he jumped out of the T-34 and ran off. Once the march company arrived at a railhead near the combat zone, it often had to move considerable distances by track to link up with the battalion it had been assigned to. As the Germans retreated to the Dnepr River, it became vital for the Soviets to sustain their forward tank units by regular infusions of new tanks and crews. Even when a company arrived at the front and was integrated into a tank battalion there was usually little time for training. Just prior to Kursk, many Soviet tankers were sent to assist getting the local harvest in – so dire was the Red Army's food shortage – rather than conducting gunnery or maneuver training.

Despite the shortcomings in Soviet tactical training taught at the schools, frontline units were gradually learning how to counter German tanks. Unlike the battles in 1941–42, in which one inexperienced Soviet tank unit after another was annihilated, more Soviet tankers survived the winter battles of 1942–43 and provided a cadre of experienced tank crews who would make a big difference at Kursk and later engagements. In particular, the creation of Guards units pooled veteran tankers and experienced commanders, helping to bridge the gap between the Wehrmacht's qualitative approach to tank warfare and the Red Army's quantitative approach.

Crew formation and march companies

Once an officer, NCO, or enlisted soldier arrived at the tank training regiment, the process of starting to form companies, platoons, and individual tank crews began. In addition to replacements, the training regiment was also a repository for wounded soldiers returning to duty, soldiers reassigned from other branches, and survivors of tank units that had been shattered in combat. Leytenant Burtsev recalled that none of his four-man crew had any combat experience when they formed up at the Nizhniy Tagil Tank Plant and that the Red Army was beginning to scrape the bottom of the manpower barrel after Kursk. Burstev's driver was a malcontent with a long criminal record, his radio operator/gunner was a former restaurant waiter, and his loader was "a mental defective." Once at the front, the Soviets made little effort to keep crews together: Leytenant Bryukhov had ten different crews from 1943 to 1945.

Crew roles and functions

The four-man crew of the T-34 consisted of the Komandir tanka (KT; tank commander), the Zatyajaletel (loader), the Mekhanik-voditel (MV; driver-mechanic), and the Radist pulemetchik (RP; radio operator/machine gunner). As with the French Char B and Somua 35 tanks, the commander in the T-34 tank was expected

to both direct his own tank – plus others if he was a platoon leader or company commander – and to aim and fire the main gun. This lack of a dedicated gunner in the T-34 seriously slowed down the process of target acquisition and overburdened small-unit leaders with too many tasks to perform. Soviet T-34 drivers were also ostensibly mechanics and responsible for the vehicle's maintenance needs, but in practice, the drivers mostly remained in their "holes" and drove the vehicle where they were told. The loader on the T-34 was also supposed to function as an observer and to fire the coaxial machine gun, but most loaders tended to view themselves as "passengers" and assumed a rather passive role unless kept under tight rein by the tank commander. The RP on the T-34 was fairly useless since at least one-third of tanks still lacked radios in the summer of 1943 and the hull machine gun was difficult to use. His main function was to help the driver shift gears while moving and to help with vehicle maintenance.

A Soviet T-34 tank company commander briefs his commanders on their mission prior to a deliberate attack in 1943. Note the "two up, one back" platoon battle drill, with the commander's tank located right in the center of the formation. This was a common Soviet formation, with two tank platoons deployed on line in front, followed by a third platoon that could respond to enemy actions. (The Tank Museum)

BATTLEGROUND: UKRAINE 1943

After the surrender of the German 6th Army at Stalingrad on February 2, 1943, it became obvious to the OKH, if not Hitler, that the war in the East was turning against Germany. Yet despite the catastrophic situation facing the Ostheer (German Army in the East) in southern Russia in early 1943, the Germans still had some hope of regaining the initiative. A bold counterattack by German commander Erich von Manstein from February 18 to March 20 virtually destroyed the overextended Soviet 3rd Tank Army, retaking Kharkov and pushing back the Red Army from the approaches to the Dnepr River. With the spring thaw in late March 1943, an operational pause ensued for several months, giving both sides time to rebuild their depleted armor units and to make plans for future offensives.

Operation *Zitadelle*

Hitler realized that with his limited resources, a major summer offensive was no longer possible. He did hope, however, that bold, local offensives could inflict punishing losses and prevent the Red Army from seizing the initiative. Generaloberst Kurt Zeitzler, OKH chief of staff, issued a plan named *Zitadelle* on April 15, that envisioned encircling and destroying Soviet forces in the Kursk salient. Zeitzler hoped to repeat von Manstein's successful March 1943 counterattack but with better equipment and on a bigger scale. Realizing that the Soviets now held a significant numerical advantage, Zeitzler's plan was based on regaining the battlefield initiative through qualitative superiority provided by the new Panthers, Tiger heavy tanks, and Ferdinand tank destroyers. The attack was originally planned to begin on May 3, but Karl-Otto Saur, Speer's deputy, succeeded in convincing Zeitzler and Hitler that the offensive should wait until June when significant numbers of Panthers and Tigers would arrive at the front. Serious technical problems with the Panther resulted in the postponement of the operation several times. Finally, realizing that either Soviet or Allied offensives were imminent, Hitler set July 5 as the start date for *Zitadelle*.

Operationally, Zeitzler opted for the proven method of a pincer attack by Army Group Center's 9th Army and Army Group South's 4th Panzer Army to cut off the six Soviet armies within the Kursk salient. *Zitadelle* was unusual in that it committed the bulk of Germany's armor to several narrow attack sectors, leaving few tanks on the rest of the Eastern Front. On July 1, Army Group South had a total of 23 panzer battalions and nine assault gun or panzerjaeger battalions with a total of about 1,850 tanks and assault guns, or about 60 percent of all German armor on the Eastern Front.

Operation *Zitadelle* was a seriously flawed plan that ignored Soviet improvements in defensive capabilities and simply assumed that the reinforced panzer divisions could defeat anything in their path. Zeitzler and Hitler allowed their optimism about the Panther and Tiger tanks to shape their belief that Soviet quantitative superiority was irrelevant and a decisive victory could be achieved.

Despite Saur's promises to Hitler, the Panthers of the 39th Panzer Regiment barely arrived in time for the Kursk offensive. The battalions arrived by rail between July 1 and 4, and the trail elements did not reach their assembly areas until the day before the attack began. There was little or no time to brief the battalion commanders, and the junior leaders were virtually in the dark about the mission or objectives. The battle plan was amazingly simplistic and virtually ignored the terrain and the enemy defenses. As part of the 48th Panzer Corps' attack toward Oboyan, the 39th Panzer Regiment would attack with Panzer Regiment *Grossdeutschland* and smash through the Soviet lines in a great armored fist with over 300 tanks deployed on a very narrow attack sector.

Operation *Rumantsyev*

Soviet intelligence had provided warnings of the impending German offensive against the Kursk salient and for once, the Stavka (the General Headquarters of the Soviet Union) was able to convince Stalin that it was better to defeat the German attack and then switch to the counteroffensive. The three months of relative quiet from April to June 1943 allowed the Red Army to replenish and rebuild its depleted tank units and create significant reserve forces. The Voronezh Front,[9] under General Nikolai Vatutin, was tasked with stopping the 4th Panzer Army's offensive and depleting its armored spearheads in a series of grinding battles. Vatutin's main armored force was Lieutenant General Katukov's 1st Tank Army, which had about 500 T-34s. Katukov intended to use many of his T-34s and antitank guns from

---

[9] The term "Front" denotes an army group-size formation, rather than a geographical area

dug-in, mutually supporting positions to fix and wear down the German panzer wedges while keeping some T-34 battalions to conduct flanking attacks as the Germans advanced into the Soviet defensive belts. Once the German offensive was halted, the Soviets would commit their reserves from Colonel-General Ivan Konev's Steppe Front, which included the 5th Guards Tank Army under Lieutenant-General Pavel Rotmistrov. Together, the Soviet Voronezh and Steppe Fronts that opposed the 4th Panzer Army and Army Detachment Kempf, a panzer unit, possessed a total of 123 tank battalions with about 3,350 tanks, including about 2,300 T-34s. For the

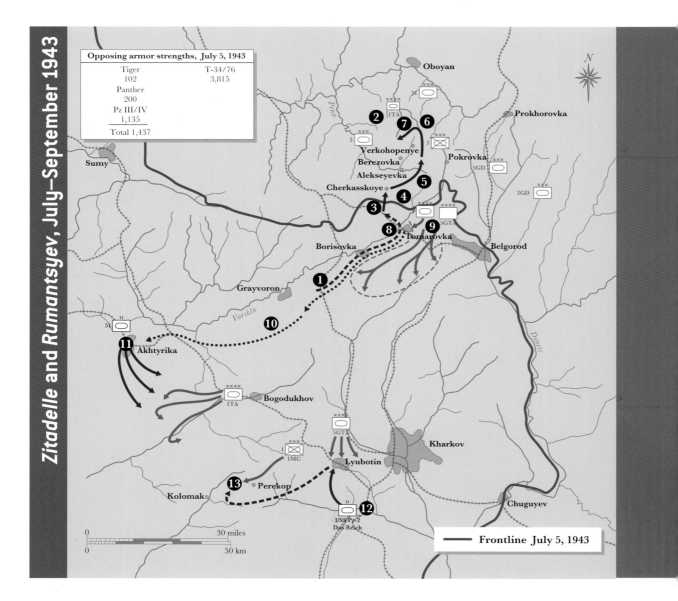

Zitadelle and Rumantsyev, July–September 1943

Opposing armor strengths, July 5, 1943	
Tiger	T-34/76
102	3,815
Panther	
200	
Pz III/IV	
1,135	
Total 1,437	

Frontline July 5, 1943

first time in the war, the Soviets would be able to mass a large force of their best armor and about 50 percent of their available tanks.

Before the battle of Kursk began, Marshal Georgi Zhukov envisioned that the Voronezh Front would launch the main counteroffensive toward Kharkov as soon as the German offensive had culminated, but Soviet tank losses were more serious than expected during the defensive phase and it required two weeks to repair battle-damaged vehicles. On July 24, the Stavka ordered Vatutin and Konev to begin detailed planning for Operation *Rumantsyev*, which was to begin in ten days.

1. July 1–3 : 51st and 52nd Panzer Battalions arrive by rail near Borisovka. Around 20 Panthers break down during a 35km road march to assembly area northwest of Tomarovka.
2. Soviet 1st TA has 3rd MC (Mechanized Corps), 6th TC (Tank Corps), and 31st TC with 500 T-34 tanks in first echelon of Soviet defense. 230 T-34 tanks in reserve.
3. 0815hrs July 5: 39th Panzer begins attack north toward Cherkasskoye with about 166 Panthers. Soviet counterattack is repulsed but the Panthers are stalled crossing a ravine.
4. 1040hrs July 6: 39th Panzer reassembles around Cherkasskoye and continues attacking. Only about 50 Panthers are still operational. The attack is slowed by an antitank ditch.
5. 0840hrs July 7: 39th Panzer continues attack and runs into prepared defenses of 3rd MC on Pena River. The Panthers are stopped by a mine and wire obstacles at a ravine and come under deadly crossfire from about 60 dug-in T-34s from the 1st and 3rd Mechanized Bdes. The Panthers "freeze" in the Soviet kill sack and 27 are knocked out, including some by flank shots from T-34s. However, the Panthers' superior gunnery is able to take a toll of the T-34s as well, and the Soviets pull back around 1500hrs. The Panthers continue the attack against the 112th Tank Bde. During the day, the Panthers destroyed about 30 T-34s. This is the first major Panther vs T-34 engagement of the war.
6. July 12: 39th Panzer continues attacking toward Verkhopen'ye with only 10–15 Panthers operational. Panthers engage counterattacking T-34s from 1st Guard Tank Bde and 200th Tank Bde with some success.
7. 0500hrs July 14: 39th Panzer launches one last attack to contain Soviet 10th TC counteroffensive west of Verkhopen'ye, but six Panthers are destroyed and ten more break down. A total of 56 Panthers have been lost since the start of *Zitadelle*, but the Germans claim that the Panthers destroyed over 200 Soviet T-34s.
8. July 17–19: 39th Panzer is disbanded at Tomarovka. 51st Panzer hands over all its remaining Panthers to 52nd Battalion. 51st receives 96 new Panthers while in the rear. 52nd Panzer is attached to 19th Panzer Division. On August 6 51st Panzer Battalion returns to 4th Panzer Army.
9. 0500hrs August 3: Soviets launch Operation *Rumantsyev* counteroffensive; 1st TA (Tank Army) and 5th Guards TA attack with about 800 T-34s on a narrow 12km front between Tomarovka and Belgorod. Within two days, the Soviet armor has ripped a huge hole in the German defenses. The 52nd Panzer defends Tomarovka with 27 Panthers and destroys seven T-34s from 6th TC.
10. August 6–8: 52nd Panzer retreats down Vorskla River valley, fighting running battles with 1st TA, destroying about 40 T-34s but is reduced to 11 Panthers.
11. August 9–26: 51st Panzer fights a series of battles around Achtyrka against the Soviet 1st TA and helps in isolating the 4th Guards TC. In two weeks of heavy fighting, the battalion loses 36 Panthers and 24 KIA, but the 1st TA is severely damaged.
12. August 22: SS *Das Reich*'s Panther battalion arrives as Kharkov is falling and counterattacks 5th Guards TA at Lyubotin, destroying 53 tanks. The next day, seven more T-34s from 29th TC are destroyed by Panthers near Lyubotin.
13. September 12–13: SS *Das Reich* Panthers destroy 35 T-34s from 219th Tank Bde (1 MC) in Kolomak area with no losses.

Colonel V. Sytnik, commander of the 24th Tank Brigade, briefs his three battalion commanders on their next mission objective in July 1943. Soviet tank officers were expected to "fight to the last tank" and leaders were expected to switch to other tanks if their own was disabled. Colonel Sytnik was killed in action on July 17, 1943. (From the fonds of the RGAKFD at Krasnogorsk via Nik Cornish)

Vatutin's Voronezh Front would attack with the 1st Tank Army and 5th Guards Tank Army to envelop Kharkov from the west while other armies assaulted from north and east. The operation's intent was to seize Kharkov and breach the 4th Panzer Army lines in about two weeks. Once Kharkov was recovered, Zhukov and Stalin anticipated offensives by the southern and southwest fronts to clear the Donbas in late August and reaching the Dnepr River at Zaporozh'ye in September. Meanwhile, the Voronezh and Steppe Fronts would drive west toward the Dnepr River at Kremenchug. The chances of Operation *Rumantsyev* succeeding were enhanced by the Soviet ability to maintain large armored forces on other fronts and to mount successful diversionary attacks. While the Germans had to strip virtually the entire Eastern Front of armor in order to mount *Zitadelle*, the Soviet Southwest and Southern Fronts still had over 1,600 tanks available.

THE ACTION

Kursk, July 5–14

The Panthers of the 39th Panzer Regiment reached the *Grossdeutschland* Division's assembly area north of Moshchenoye late on July 4. Ominously, two Panthers were destroyed by engine fires on the short road march from the railhead, and 18 others broke down. *Grossdeutschland* began its own attack at 0400hrs on July 5, but the late-arriving Panthers were not in the first echelon, giving commander Major von Lauchert a few more hours to finish fueling and attempting to establish functioning radio nets.

At 0815hrs, von Lauchert began moving his two battalions with about 184 Panthers northward out of the assembly area and over the rail line northwest of Tomarovka. At least four Panthers caught fire from fuel leaks shortly after leaving the assembly area. On each remaining Panther, loaders slammed a Panzergranate 39/42 AP round into the breech for "battle carry" while gunners zeroed their sights to 1,000m. The regiment moved with Hauptman Heinrich Meyer's 51st Battalion in the lead, followed by the 52nd Panzer Battalion under the command of Major Gerhard Tebbe with its four companies in double row formation. The entire Panther regiment covered an area about 500m wide and almost 3km long. Smoke from burning corn set afire by artillery hung over the battlefield, limiting visibility. *Grossdeutschland*'s advance guard was supposed to breach the first Soviet obstacle belt, and then the Panthers would exploit through the gap. However, this plan quickly fell apart. When the lead Panthers reached the 80m-wide Berezovyi Ravine, they found barbed wire obstacles, as well as mines, strewn over marshy area that was made virtually impassable by heavy rains the previous night.

Like most untried armor units, the 39th Panzer Regiment came to a virtual halt upon encountering the unexpected obstacle and began to bunch up. *Grossdeutschland*'s pioneers had already assessed the initial crossing site as unsuitable for tanks and were looking for alternate crossing sites when the Panthers arrived. After a few minutes of confusion, either von Lauchert or Meyer decided to cross the ravine. Several Panthers

A Panther Ausf. A command tank on the outskirts of a burning village. The Panther's thinner side armor was vulnerable if ambushed by Soviet antitank guns or T-34s lurking in such villages. (Author's collection)

from both the 1st and 2nd Companies attempted to cross through the narrow, cleared lane, but all of them quickly bogged down in the thick mud at the bottom of the ravine, and their weak final drives could not get them up the opposite slope. Seeing this pile-up, Oberleutnant Helmut Langhammer tried to maneuver his trailing 4th Company westward to cross at a different spot. However, he quickly ran into an uncleared minefield and was wounded when his tank was disabled. The Soviet TM-41 antitank mine, with 4kg of Amatol, could break the track on a Panther and damage the road wheel arms. In short order, about 25 Panthers from the 51st Panzer Battalion and Regimental Stab were immobilized in the ravine due to the combination of mud, mines, and breakdowns. Furthermore, the weak final drive on the Panther Ausf. D could not easily reverse on muddy slopes, and the tanks began shearing teeth from their drive sprockets and overheating in a futile attempt to escape. Soviet artillery began pounding the huge, immobilized mass of German armor in their "kill zone." Although the Panther's armor was generally impervious to this barrage, Langhammer's Panther 401 was destroyed by a lucky ricochet into its belly armor; many other tanks suffered moderate damage and at least six crewmen were killed.

The advance guard from the *Grossdeutschland* Division found a better crossing site 1.5km to the west, and by early afternoon their pioneers established two narrow breaches. Von Lauchert shifted his regiment to the new site, and by 0400hrs, about 30 Panthers, 15 Panzer IVs, and four infantry battalions were across. The main Soviet defense in this area was centered upon the town of Cherkasskoye, held by the 196th Guards Rifle Regiment and two antitank regiments. As dusk approached, the *Grossdeutschland*'s infantry and assault guns broke into the town. Von Lauchert's Panthers assisted mopping up the village and thwarting a Soviet counterattack.

Panther: through the gunsights

Commander: "Panzergranate! Laden und sichern!"
 "Load armor-piercing!"
Loader: "Panzergranate geladen!" *"Armor-piercing loaded!"*

Commander: "3 Uhr! Panzergranate – 800 – Panzer!"
 "3 o' clock! Armor-piercing – 800m – tank!"
Gunner: "Achtung!" *"On the way!"*

A Panther platoon is crossing the line of departure in *keil* or "arrow" formation. Doctrine is to "battle carry" armor-piercing Pzgr 39/42 rounds, with battle sight set at 1,000m. The Panther advances with cupola hatch open, commander scanning forward with binoculars. The platoon commander has assigned each tank a specific area and the gunner periodically traverses the turret about 30 degrees left to right to scan his zone with his TFZ12 sight.

The commander spots a stationary T-34 tank in defilade about 800m to his right flank. The telltale grimy exhaust gives away the T-34's position. Even before he speaks, he taps the gunner's right shoulder with his boot in order to alert him.

The driver brings the vehicle to a smooth halt to stabilize the firing platform. The gunner uses his foot pedal to traverse so that the center triangle of the left reticule is on the T-34's turret ring and uses 5x magnification. He fires the main gun with his center foot pedal. The brief flash and smoke rising from the T-34 turret shows that the target has been destroyed.

The Panthers had accomplished very little on their first day of combat yet had suffered heavy losses from tactical ineptitude and mechanical unreliability. By the morning of July 6, von Lauchert had only 50 to 80 Panthers operational in Yarki, although recovery was continuing in the Berezovyi Ravine. The commander of the

48th Panzer Corps decided to reorient the German attack toward the northeast, in part to avoid the thick Soviet defenses along the Pena River and also to avoid a repetition of the Berezovyi disaster. *Grossdeutschland*'s Panzer regiment kicked off the attack at 1040hrs, with its tanks on the right side of the road toward Dubrova and the Panthers supposedly on the left side. However, von Lauchert was too busy trying to reorganize his disrupted regiment and failed to move out on schedule, while 10th Tank Brigade commander, Oberst Decker, failed to coordinate with the *Grossdeutschland*'s panzers. Consequently, the Panther regiment blundered forward with little idea where friend or foe was located.

Meanwhile, in the low ground near Alekseyevka on the south side of the Pena River, there were three companies of dug-in T-34 tanks from the 14th Tank Regiment (3rd Mechanized Corps) deployed to reinforce the second defensive belt. The T-34s were well camouflaged and their hulls dug-in, presenting very small targets. Despite the lack of formal tactical training, veteran Soviet tankers had learned from bitter experience how to use terrain to counteract superior German gunnery. The T-34s covered an antitank ditch and minefield to their south, backed up by three battalions of motorized infantry and antitank guns. To the southeast, the 16th Tank Regiment and the rest of the 3rd Mechanized Brigade covered the other side of the antitank ditch and minefield. The Soviet defense formed an L-shaped ambush as the Germans approached across flat, grassy terrain and cornfields. *Grossdeutschland*'s advance guard came under direct, heavy fire, and the regimental commander, Oberst Graf von Strachwitz, was incensed about the lack of support from the Panthers.

Von Lauchert's Panthers were lost, inching forward through unfamiliar terrain, still uncertain where their objective lay. The regiment was deployed mostly in double columns with only the lead company in a wedge. Without infantry support, the Panthers never spotted the obstacle or enemy infantry and tanks until they bumped into the first mines 2km east of Cherkasskoye. Several tanks were immediately immobilized. Major Gerhard Tebbe's battalion was in the lead, and he froze in the kill zone. Soviet artillery began to pound the stalled cluster of Germans. In the first Panther versus T-34 duels of the war, the T-34s from the 14th Tank Regiment began to engage the clustered Panther column with flank shots from about 1,000–1,200m. Although Soviet gunnery was not particularly good, the Panthers were not moving much and were presenting their thin side armor to the enemy. Oberfeldwebel Gerhard Brehme, a platoon leader in the 5th Company of the 52nd Panzer Battalion, apparently became one of the first Panthers to fall victim to a T-34 when his tank was hit with a 76mm AP round that punched into his left side armor and ignited one of the fuel cells. Brehme managed to bail out of his burning Panther but was so badly burned that he died 12 days later. Major Tebbe lost control, and the

A T-34 tank company in the attack. Unlike the Germans, the Soviets usually did not use "overwatch" tactics, using one element to cover the movement of another. (Courtesy of the Central Museum of the Armed Forces Moscow via Nik Cornish)

veteran 8th Company commander, Oberleutnant Erdmann Gabriel, took charge, attempting to maneuver out of the zone.

Gabriel ordered his Panthers to engage the well-hidden T-34s, and some of the veteran German gunners hit a few of their elusive foes. The long hours invested in gunnery training on the ranges at Putlos and Grafenwöhr now proved its worth. Soviet tank commanders were surprised by the effectiveness of the new 75mm guns, and some T-34 platoons began to reposition to avoid the heaviest fire. Several T-34s were destroyed while pulling out of their hull-down positions – betrayed by their telltale grimy exhaust – thus becoming the first victims of the Panther's KwK 42 gun. Shortly, Soviet direct fire slackened, and von Lauchert was able to extract the surviving Panthers from this ambush and head southeast in the tracks of *Grossdeutschland*. Von Lauchert's Panthers caught up with *Grossdeutschland*'s tanks shortly after the main antitank ditch was breached, and an angry von Strachwitz ordered the Panther unit to take the lead. Upon crossing the ditch, the Panthers moved off in the general direction of Dubrova, but some tanks became disoriented in the dust and smoke that surrounded the breach site. Eventually, the remnants of von Lauchert's battered regiment and Kampfgruppe von Strachwitz reached a hill on the outskirts of Dubrova and settled into a defensive laager for the night. July 6 had been another bad day for the 39th Panzer Regiment with 19 Panthers knocked out or destroyed compared to the destruction of no more than ten or 12 T-34s. Major Tebbe was quietly replaced by Hauptman Georg Baumunk, a combat-experienced officer from the disbanded 22nd Panzer Division. With the brigade's command and control totally disrupted after less than 48 hours of combat, Oberst Decker decided to leave this mess, and the remaining Panthers were put under von Strachwitz's command.

T-34: through the gunsights

Artwork by Jim Laurier, © Osprey Publishing

The view through the PT-47 sight. Unlike the Panther, the T-34 did not have a gunner so there was no one to give commands to, the commander firing the gun himself.

The view through the TMFD-7 sight as an AP round richochets off the Panther. Other than telling the driver to stop or the loader to load a shell there was little crew interaction.

A T-34 platoon is on line in a defilade position in a dried-out stream gully, awaiting a German armor attack. The tanks all have BF-350A armor-piercing high explosive rounds loaded. The sergeant is scanning to his left with the rotating PT panoramic sight when the first rounds from a Panther land 80m to his right rear. He immediately scans to the right and spots a Panther 800m away and switches to the TMFD sight. The loader releases the main gun's safety and cradles an AP round in his arms.

The commander lays the crosshairs on the Panther and fires with his foot pedal. The round impacts in front of the Panther and throws up a splash of dirt. The loader instantly loads another AP round. The commander uses his hand elevation wheel to add 5 degrees and fires again. He sees a brief spark as his second round strikes the Panther's front slope and ricochets off.

Having seen the ineffectiveness of his APDS rounds against the Panther's front slope, the commander decides to fall back to the next ravine and try to work around for a flank shot. As the T-34 traverses down into the streambed, the driver reports that both adjacent tanks from their platoon are burning.

July 7 was a hot, hazy day. By dawn, Major von Lauchert had only 50 operational Panthers remaining under his command. At 0845hrs, von Strachwitz ordered the attack into the Soviet second defensive belt to continue, with the objective being to seize Dubrova and then move north to envelop the Soviet defenses at Syrtsev. Kampfgruppe von Strachwitz attacked with about 50 Panthers and 30 Panzer III/IV. Most of the Soviet defenders had pulled out of Dubrova during the night, but the 3rd Mechanized Corps had established excellent defensive positions around Syrtsev, with about 20 dug-in T-34s from the 16th Tank Regiment and a few 85mm antitank guns from the 756th Antitank Battalion. The Soviet defenders saw the approaching German armor but did not open up with their antitank weapons until the Panzers ran into a minefield in a ravine just east of Syrtsev. Once again, the Panthers presented their vulnerable side armor to the Soviet gunners, and in minutes, about 15 Panthers were hit and set afire by 76mm and 85mm AP shells.

The Soviet gunners held a higher position than the Panthers who were stuck in the ravine, allowing them to hit the thinner armor on the turret roof. Soviet T-34 commanders fired as rapidly as possible, and their loaders, who were not issued asbestos gloves as were the German tankers, scorched their hands as they labored to throw red-hot spent shell casings out of the turret. Leytenant Vasiliy Bryukhov, a T-34 platoon leader in the nearby 2nd Tank Corps, described engaging German tanks during *Zitadelle*:

> I'd get a target in the gun sight – a short stop, one shot, another one. I'd traverse the gun from left to right and shout: "Armor-piercing! Fragmentation!" The engine would be roaring so one couldn't hear the explosions outside, and when I opened fire myself I didn't hear anything that was happening outside the tank. Only when the tank was hit by an armor-piercing round … would I realize that there were also some guys firing at me."[9]

The situation was no easier for German tank crews. Oberleutnant Gabriel, in Panther 801, tried to assault through the ambush but did not get very far. Gabriel later wrote:

> I was severely hit by an anti-tank round that penetrated the munitions chamber at the left side causing the latter to explode immediately … I tore off the smoldering headset and microphone with my severely burnt hands, which already had the fingernails popped off. By then the gunner was pushing out from below, but I had to push his head so as to get out of the turret myself. This all happened very fast … After me, the gunner was still able to rescue himself. He had suffered burns, mainly on his face.

[9] See Drabkin, p. 130

Despite heavy casualties, von Lauchert, Baumunk, and Meyer were able to get some of their Panthers to lay down suppressive fire against the dug-in T-34s and antitank guns while a few tanks and infantrymen struggled to get through the obstacle. The veteran NCO tank gunners in the Panthers put the KwK 42 to good use by engaging T-34s over 1,000m away. Although the T-34s were virtually immune to fire in their hull-down positions, the Panther gunners merely waited until they rose up to fire and then rapidly pumped several rounds into their turrets. Gradually, the Panther gunners gained the upper hand, and the Kampfgruppe was finally able to cross the ravine and push north of Syrtsev. After overrunning some of the dug-in T-34s and infantry positions, about 20 Panthers were able to reach the vicinity of Gremuchy by dusk. It had been a disastrous day for the Panther regiment with 27 Panthers knocked out or destroyed. Von Strachwitz claimed that his Kampfgruppe destroyed 62 enemy tanks – about 35 to 40 by the Panthers – and the Soviet 3rd Mechanized Brigade had lost almost all its T-34s. Although the Panther had demonstrated its superior gunnery over the T-34, the heavy losses seriously affected morale in the regiment. Walter Rahn from the 52nd Panzer Battalion noted, "We felt the day was a defeat and long thereafter referred to the "Panther cemetery at Dubrova."

Over the next four days, the remnants of the Panther regiment attempted to exploit the small gap created in the Soviet second defensive belt, engaging in much heavy fighting around the village of Verkhopen'ye. Kampfgruppe von Strachwitz had about ten to 20 Panthers, a handful of Tigers, and about 25 Panzer III/IV at this time, opposing the fresh 112th and 200th Tank Brigades from the 6th Tank Corps. Katukov, the 1st Tank Army commander, committed the 6th Tank Corps to stem the German breach in his lines, and the Panther and T-34 met in a series of small-scale engagements. Some 13 Panthers were knocked out or destroyed in these four days, and many more broke down from increasingly serious mechanical defects. Both Soviet tank brigades were badly hurt in these battles, suffering about 60 percent losses, and the Germans were left in possession of a small salient around Verkhopen'ye. By July 12, the 39th Panzer Regiment was combat-ineffective from losses and virtually out of ammunition, and it was pulled out of the line for resupply and reconstitution. A total of 31 Panthers had been destroyed in the first week in combat and 148 were under repair, leaving only 25 operational. The very high number of mechanical breakdowns indicated that Guderian had been correct: the Panther was not ready for combat.

The Panther regiment fought its last action on July 14 when 36 Panthers participated in a counterattack to repulse an attack by the 1st Tank Army's 86th Tank Brigade near Verkhopen'ye. For the first time, the Panther fought on the defensive, and it was now the T-34s who were moving across open terrain. The Panthers and a company of Panzer IVs destroyed 28 T-34s at a cost of six Panthers and three Panzer IVs. The next day,

Operation *Zitadelle* was canceled and von Lauchert began assembling his remaining Panthers to withdraw to Tomarovka. The German armor had not broken through to Kursk, and the Panthers had not proven decisive, or even mechanically reliable.

Von Lauchert and Decker claimed that the Panthers destroyed 263 enemy tanks during the period July 5 to 14. They also made absurd claims that Panthers routinely destroyed T-34s at 1,500–2,000m and even destroyed a T-34 at 3,000m. These claims are suspect and were probably made to overshadow the poor performance of the regiment during *Zitadelle*. Most of the Panther versus T-34 engagements in the first week of *Zitadelle* were against camouflaged, dug-in Soviet tanks, which made long-range engagements unlikely. In fact, most Panther versus T-34 engagements in this period were in the range of 800–1,200m, and Soviet records indicate that only a handful of T-34s were destroyed at ranges above 1,500m. Furthermore, the large numbers of Panthers knocked out indicates that Soviet T-34s were engaging them from 1,200m or less, the maximum at which flank shots were likely to be effective. Given the fact that the regiment was ambushed three times in the first three days and had only a company or two operational for the rest of *Zitadelle*, the claim that the Panthers destroyed more than half the enemy tanks destroyed by the 48th Panzer Corps is absurd. The total number of enemy tanks knocked out or destroyed by the Panthers was probably about 120, of which fewer than 100 were T-34s. On July 20, the 39th Panzer Regiment reported that it had 41 operational Panthers, 85 under repair, and 58 total losses, of which 49 were blown up by the Germans themselves. Although Hitler had ordered that no Panthers were to fall into Soviet hands, seven knocked-out Panthers were captured on July 19. The first round of the duel between

Given the superb mobility of the T-34, Soviet armor units were able to advance rapidly to the Dnepr, upsetting German plans to defend behind the river. Throughout 1943, the Soviet ability to shift tank corps 200km or more in a couple of days and then attack shocked the Germans. (From the fonds of the RGAKFD at Krasnogorsk via Nik Cornish)

Panthers and T-34s had clearly gone to the Soviet tankers, who, while bloodied, had prevented a German breakthrough, and were still capable of offensive operations.

Akhtyrka and Kharkov, August 3–26

Between July 17 and 19, the 39th Panzer Regiment moved back to Tomarovka and was disbanded. The 51st Panzer Battalion handed over its remaining Panthers to the 52nd Battalion, and its personnel proceeded by rail to Bryansk, where they received 96 factory-fresh Panthers. The 52nd Panzer Battalion, with Major von Sivers back in command, was attached to the 19th Panzer Division and concentrated on repairing its damaged Panthers. In one of the great tactical surprises of the war, the Voronezh Front launched Operation *Rumantsyev*, the counteroffensive against the Belgorod salient, at 0500hrs on August 3. Vatutin concentrated the 1st Tank Army (1TA) and 5th Guards Tank Army (5GTA) with about 800 T-34s on a narrow 12km front between Tomarovka and Belgorod. By the end of the first day, the 5GTA had penetrated 26km into the German defenses. The Soviet offensive caught von Sivers with only 27 operational Panthers and 109 under repair. Since most of his tanks were immobile, von Sivers was ordered to organize a defensive hedgehog around Tomarovka and prepare for local counterattacks. By August 4, the Soviet 6th Tank Corps had already pushed south of Tomarovka and was threatening to cut off the 52nd Panzer Battalion and the 19th Panzer Division. Von Sivers's Panthers destroyed seven T-34s from the 200th Tank Brigade outside Tomarovka, but on August 5, he decided to retreat down the Vorskla River valley toward the repair depot in Borisovka.

After blowing up 72 immobilized Panthers, von Sivers's Kampfgruppe began retreating southwest with an assortment of about 2,000 German troops. Although this "floating pocket" was virtually surrounded by the Soviet 1TA, the Panther's long-range gunnery was able to keep Soviet armor at a distance. Late on August 6, the Soviet 31st Tank Corps tried to cut off the column south of Borisovka, but the Panthers destroyed 17 T-34s at no cost to themselves. By August 8, von Sivers's group had reached Grayvoron, where the Soviet 5th Guards Tank Corps had already encircled the town. On the afternoon of August 8, a company-size probe from the 13th Guards Tank Brigade found von Sivers's Kampfgruppe. Walter Rahn wrote, "Early in the afternoon, armor-piercing shells hit our position. A few minutes later, 12 enemy tanks with mounted infantry attacked our all-round defensive positions. After eight T-34s had been put out of action, the remaining Russian tanks withdrew."[10] However, von Sivers's Panthers were virtually out of fuel and were only kept moving thanks to Luftwaffe aerial resupply. On August 9, von Sivers's Kampfgruppe linked up with the *Grossdeutschland* Division near Akhtyrka, which had broken out from Soviet encirclement, destroying 40 T-34s in the process for no combat loss to themselves. However, 16 out of 27 Panthers broke down on the 100km march and only nine were operational once they reached Akhtyrka.

The 51st Panzer Battalion returned to the 4th Panzer Army in early August and was attached to *Grossdeutschland* at Akhtyrka, but it was committed into combat piecemeal as it arrived by rail. On the morning of August 9, a Kampfgruppe of seven Panthers from the 4./Pz. 51 and four Tigers under the command of Hauptman Kikibusch attacked to clear away elements of the Soviet 10th Tank Corps from the rail station at Trostyanets north of Akhtyrka. While moving out of the assembly area, a Panther's engine caught fire and the tank burned out. Unteroffizier Peter Schamberger, the gunner on Panther 442, described the movement:

> Our tubes point forward and to the flanks, we advance nervously, watching the trail… Two hundred meters after leaving the woods, we make a short halt. Suddenly, anti-tank weapons start shooting at us from a higher elevation. We react immediately and radio our position to the tanks remaining on the edge of the woods. Before we can receive new orders, our Panther receives some hits and we take shelter in…Very quickly, we leave in a group toward the village of Trostyanets, 7 kilometers away… Suddenly, a large number of tanks emerge in front of us. "Halte!": we hear on the radio. "Fire on the left!" The action is short and violent. Some T-34s begin to burn. We are favored compared to the T-34 because our Panther has thicker armor and our 75mm guns are surprisingly precise.[11]

By the time the small German Kampfgruppe reached the outskirts of Trostyanets it was surrounded by Soviet tanks and antitank guns and had to fight its way back to friendly lines. However, only a single Panther made it. Two Tigers and six Panthers were lost against a Soviet loss of three to five T-34s. This company-size action is illustrative of how the lack of reconnaissance, infantry support, and artillery seriously undermined the performance of Panthers and Tigers, which had to fight T-34s that were operating as part of a combined arms team. While the T-34 may have had

Overleaf: Combat in the East

Haupsturmführer Friedrich Holzer's SS Panther company ambushes the lead battalion of the Soviet 219th Tank Brigade around Kraschanitschen, northeast of Kolomak, September 12, 1943. This scene depicts the opening moments, with a company-size force of Panther tanks engaging an attacking Soviet tank brigade, arrayed in two battalion wedges. Holzer was awarded the Knight's Cross for this action. (Artwork by Howard Gerrard, © Osprey Publishing)

---

[10] See Rahn, Walter, "Fighting Withdrawal of Kampfgruppe Von Sivers…" an unpublished paper by the former orderly of 52nd Panzer Battalion

[11] See Schamberger, Peter, "Le Bataillon de Panther de la 9.Pz.Div. en Russie ou l'historique de la Pz.Abt. 51 (2e partie) by Didier Lodieu, *39/45 Magazine*, No. 187, February 2002, pp. 16–19

inferior armor and firepower to the Panther and Tiger, the presence of infantry, antitank guns, and plentiful artillery more than made up the difference. Thus, the idea of "pure" tank duels just did not fit the reality of the Eastern Front in mid-1943.

Grossdeutschland and the 51st Panzer Battalion arrived in Akhtyrka just ahead of Major General Pavel Poluboyarov's 4th Guards Tank Corps (4GTC), which made rapid progress down the east side of the Vorskla River valley. Poluboyarov tried to attack directly into the city with his 12th and 14th Guards Tank Brigades on August 10 and 11 but was repulsed. The 51st Panzer Battalion claimed 16 T-34s destroyed in these actions but lost 11 Panthers. Barred from direct entry into Akhtyrka, Poluboyarov attempted to envelop Akhtyrka from the south with his 13th Guards Tank Brigade (13GTB) while maintaining pressure from the east. Scraping together about 15 Panthers and ten Tigers, *Grossdeutschland* Division succeeded in stopping the 13GTB. By holding Akhtyrka, *Grossdeutschland* threatened the flank of Katukov's 1st Tank Army around Kotelva. The Germans decided to try and cut off the Soviet spearhead. On August 18, *Grossdeutschland* mounted a major counterattack into the 1st Tank Army's right flank in the hope of linking up with the SS-Totenkopf division's counterattack from the east. The attack was a complete success and was able to isolate both the 4th and 5th Guards Tank Corps around Kotelva. However, the attack was costly for the 51st Panzer Battalion. Hauptman Meyer was killed in action on August 19, and the battalion lost another 15 Panthers over the next week. Although the German counterattack succeeded in isolating Katukov's spearhead, the 4th Panzer Army could not hold its positions and was forced to yield Akhtyrka on August 24. The 51st Panzer Battalion claimed to have destroyed about 100 enemy tanks in August, but it was reduced to only 15 operational Panthers and had lost 53.

While *Grossdeutschland* was trying to keep Katukov's 1st Tank Army out of Akhtyrka, the 3rd Panzer Corps was fighting desperately to keep Rotmistrov's 5th Guards Tank Army out of Kharkov. The SS *Das Reich* and *Wiking* Divisions returned from the Mius front, but they could only delay the inevitable as overwhelming Soviet force gradually wore down the defense. In the final act of the battle of Kharkov, the *Das Reich*'s Panther battalion, the I/SS Panzer 2, arrived just as the city was about to fall. SS-Haupsturmführer Hans Weiss arrived with two companies of Panthers and was immediately ordered to counterattack a Soviet breakthrough near Korotich and Lyubotin, southwest of Kharkov. The Soviet 24th Guards Tank Brigade under Lieutenant-Colonel V. P. Karpov had 110 T-34s but lost 53 in a three-hour battle with the Panthers. Junior Leytenant Yuri M. Polyanovski, a platoon leader in the 24th Guards Tank Brigade, described what happened when his platoon tried to cross a railway embankment near Korotich:

As soon as our tank tried to drive through the crossing – bang, it was finished. My tank became just another victim… Smoke filled the crew compartment, the tank halted and we had to bail out…[12]

Leytenant Vasiliy Bryukhov, also a platoon leader in the 5GTA, described his platoon's attack:

We were about 200 meters from the enemy when the Germans hit my tank head-on with an armor-piercing round. The tank stopped but didn't catch fire … the round had penetrated our front armor by the radio operator's seat, killing him with splinters … I was shell shocked and fell on top of the ammo storage. At that moment another round penetrated the turret and killed the loader.[13]

Both Polyanovski and Bryukhov survived the battle but losses were heavy. In Polyanovski's battalion, only a single platoon of T-34s was left, and Bryukhov lost

A Soviet propaganda photo of a T-34 unit liberating a Ukrainian village. The reality of liberation was that advance guard Soviet tank units were often forced to beg or steal food from the locals – "known as grandmother's rations" – since their own supply lines were far in the rear. (Courtesy of the Central Museum of the Armed Forces Moscow via Nik Cornish)

---

[12] See Drabkin, p. 66
[13] See Drabkin, p. 134

all three of his T-34s and ten of 12 crewmen in a matter of minutes. The more experienced Soviet tankers learned to take the springs out of their turret hatches, allowing them to escape more rapidly in the event of a hit. The Waffen SS Panthers had the tactical edge in this action because they were occupying hull-down positions and were supported by assault guns and 88mm Flak guns. However, this tactical success did not prevent the fall of Kharkov. Operation *Rumantsyev* had cost the Soviet 1TA and 5GTA over 1,700 T-34 tanks but had decisively seized the initiative from von Manstein.

Retreat to the Dnepr, September 8–29

After the fall of Akhtyrka and Kharkov, the Soviets began their advance to the Dnepr River against fierce resistance from Army Group South. Soviet probing attacks often ran into German ambushes. Junior Leytenant Polyanovski was given a new tank and crew for the pursuit phase:

> At dawn on 2 September, our three tanks were sent out to conduct a reconnaissance in force – that's the military term for it, but in reality to get killed. The Germans opened fire and we fired back … I had to look into the periscope and bend toward the gun sight, and it was when I was looking through the sight that we got hit. The round pierced the turret above my head. It didn't hit me, but slivers of armor struck my head, tore my helmet and damaged my skull. I fell on the tarpaulin covering the ammo. After that a fire started, since the next thing to get hit was the engine compartment. Much later I found out that the loader's head was smashed…[13]

Polyanovski survived the destruction of his second T-34. However, the German panzer units were so depleted after seven weeks of continuous combat that von Manstein realized that he lacked the resources to stop the Soviet juggernaut. On September 8, von Manstein asked permission to withdraw his forces behind the Dnepr River, but Hitler refused. Although *Das Reich*'s Panther battalion scored an impressive small rearguard victory near Kolomak against the Soviet 1st Mechanized Corps on September 12 and 13, Army Group Center was no longer capable of maintaining a continuous front. Hitler finally authorized a withdrawal on September 15, but it was nearly too late. On September 18, Stavka gave Vatutin the 3rd Guards Tank Army (3GTA) under Colonel-General Pavel Rybalko. Two days later, this mass of armor began a rapid advance toward the Dnepr. After marching over 160km in two days, Rybalko's 56th Guards Tank Brigade established a bridgehead over the

[13] See Drabkin, p. 68

Tank ambush

On September 12, 1943, the 219th Tank Brigade with about 60 T-34 tanks and part of the 19th Mechanized Brigade with about 25 tanks began to penetrate the German lines around Kraschanitschen.

The T-34s advanced in v-shaped wedges easily overcoming the antitank trenches (**1**). The first wave of T-34 tanks destroyed the forward German positions and the infantry were forced to retreat (**2**). However, the Soviets did not notice that a small group of Panther tanks from I/SS Panzer Regiment 2, commanded by Haupsturmführer Friedrich Holzer, were approaching from the west and had just moved into hull-down ambush positions. Holzer split his outnumbered Kampfgruppe into two teams, one to hit the Soviets from the flanks (**3**) and one from the front (**4**). In around 40 minutes, the Panthers destroyed 28 T-34s in the "kill zone" without any losses (**5**).

Artwork by Peter Bull © Osprey Publishing

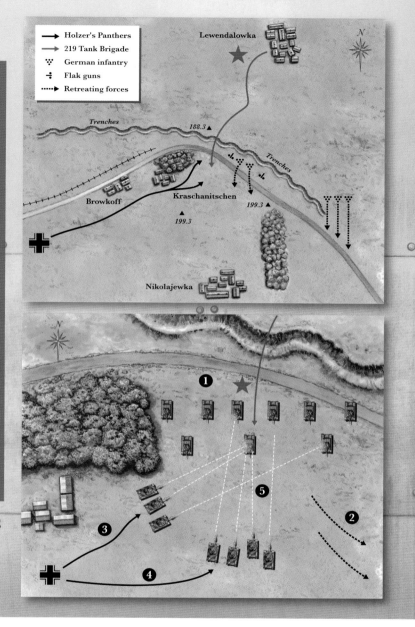

Dnepr at Bukrin on September 22. The operational mobility of the T-34 prevented von Manstein from establishing an effective defense behind the Dnepr.

The retreat to the Dnepr was a disaster for the three Panther battalions in *Grossdeutschland*, *Das Reich*, and the 11th Panzer Division (52nd Panzer Battalion was now redesignated as I/Panzer 15). Eighty Panthers were lost in September, mostly immobilized vehicles blown up to prevent capture. *Grossdeutschland*, with 18 Panthers and a few Tigers left, tried to establish a defensive position around Kremenchug but failed to prevent the 5GTA from gaining a crossing there on September 29.

Melitopol, October 2–24

After Army Group South began retreating to the Dnepr, Hitler briefly hoped that Army Group A's 6th Army might prevent the Soviet South and Southwest Fronts from reaching the lower Dnepr. Two of the new Panther battalions were directed toward this sector in the hope of preventing a Soviet breakthrough. A single company of Major Fritz Fechner's II/Panzer Regiment 23 arrived at Stalino on September 4, but quickly got itself surrounded and had to be rescued. The rest of the battalion was assigned to the 23rd Panzer Division but by then the 6th Army was in full retreat toward the Dnepr. Fechner was able to mount a counterattack against the 23rd Tank Corps near Pavlograd and inflict some losses, but by the end of the month his battalion was combat-ineffective. Fechner's battalion had to blow up most of its disabled Panthers in the retreat to the Dnepr and only had three to six operational tanks for the rest of the year.

The German 6th Army established the Wotan Line around Melitopol, and on October 8, the I/Panzer Regiment 2 of the 13th Panzer Division arrived to provide a mobile reserve. However, before the battalion was fully assembled, the Soviet 20th Tank Corps and 4th Guards Mechanized Corps (4GMC) with over 200 T-34s launched a major attack against the Wotan Line. On October 10, part of I/Panzer 2 fought in the "tank battle of Oktoberfeld" in which the Soviet attack was repulsed with 30 percent losses. Melitopol finally fell on October 23, but Oberleutnant Graf Ledebur, commander of the 2nd Company, led a counterattack against the 4GMC at Kalinovka on October 24 that destroyed 35 T-34s. In the first two weeks in combat, the I/Panzer Regiment 2 had destroyed over 80 enemy tanks, but the constant road marches had incapacitated more than half the battalion due to mechanical breakdowns, and once the battalion had to retreat, most of the immobilized Panthers were blown up. Even the new Panther Ausf. A lacked the mechanical reliability to compete with the fast-moving T-34s in protracted mobile warfare.

After fighting off the Soviet advance guard for several more days, the last Panthers crossed the Dnepr at Kherson, and the Germans blew up the bridges. Neither the II/Panzer 23 nor the I/Panzer Regiment I had seriously delayed or even hurt the Soviet advance to the Dnepr, and within a month of deployment, these battalions were reduced to ineffective remnants.

Fastov, Brusilov, and Radomyshl, November 15–December 31

Despite desperate German counterattacks during October, Army Group South was unable to crush any of the Soviet bridgeheads over the Dnepr or to prevent the capture of Kiev by the 1st Tank Army on November 6. However, the Soviet armor spearheads were overextended after fanning out from Kiev, and von Manstein saw a chance to repeat his successful "backhand blow" formula. Von Manstein persuaded Hitler to give him all available armor reinforcements, and by November 9, he was able to mass six Panzer divisions in General Herman Balck's 48 Panzer Corps near Berdichev. Two new Panther units arrived for the counterattack: the I/Panzer Regiment 2 under Major Ernst Phillip and the SS-*Leibstandarte*'s I/SS Panzer Regiment 1 under Sturmbannführer Herbert Kuhlmann. Combined, the Germans were able to mass 585 tanks for the counterattack, including about 70 Panthers and 30 Tigers. Von Manstein intended to attack into the left flank of Rybalko's 3rd Guards Tank Army (3GTA) near Fastov, encircle the Soviet armies on the west bank of the Dnepr, and recapture Kiev.

The German counteroffensive began in heavy rain on November 15. During the nine days of the counterattack, Kuhlmann's I/SS Panzer Regiment 1 destroyed about 40 enemy tanks but lost seven Panthers destroyed and 54 broken down or damaged. Phillip's I/Panzer Regiment 2 also destroyed about 40 tanks but lost six Panthers destroyed and about 30 out of action. The 7th Guards Tank Corps and part of the 9th Mechanized Corps suffered about 30 percent losses in the German counterattack, but the *Leibstandarte* had failed to capture Brusilov and the 3GTA was not encircled. The superiority of the KwK 42 gun on the Panther mattered little in this battle since most actions had been fought at ranges of 600–800m among wooded areas and small villages. The Panther units also found it increasingly difficult to come to grips with the T-34s without running through a gauntlet of 76mm and 85mm antitank guns, hidden in the woods and villages. By this time, Soviet tank battalions had developed a tactic to fight Panthers and Tigers that, while costly, usually worked. Upon running into Panthers, a T-34 battalion would deploy two companies on line to fix the enemy while using the third company to flank the Germans. Having greater numbers and more mobile tanks allowed Soviet commanders to seize and retain the initiative in spite of better German gunnery.

Von Manstein's counterattack at Fastov pushed the 3GTA onto the tactical defensive, and the Germans wanted to renew the push before the Soviets could recover. On December 6, the 48th Panzer Corps attacked toward Radomyshl and succeeded

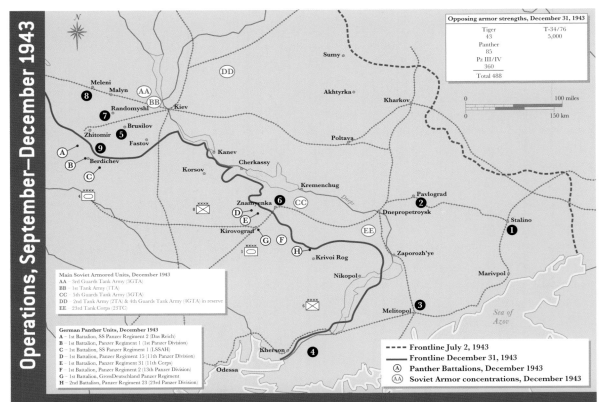

Opposing armor strengths, December 31, 1943

Tiger 43	T-34/76 5,000
Panther 85	
Pz III/IV 360	
Total 488	

Main Soviet Armored Units, December 1943
AA – 3rd Guards Tank Army (3GTA)
BB – 1st Tank Army (1TA)
CC – 5th Guards Tank Army (5GTA)
DD – 2nd Tank Army (2TA) & 4th Guards Tank Army (4GTA) in reserve
EE – 23rd Tank Corps (23TC)

German Panther Units, December 1943
A – 1st Battalion, SS Panzer Regiment 2 (Das Reich)
B – 1st Battalion, Panzer Regiment 1 (1st Panzer Division)
C – 1st Battalion, SS Panzer Regiment 1 (LSSAH)
D – 1st Battalion, Panzer Regiment 2 (13th Panzer Division)
E – 1st Battalion, Panzer Regiment 31 (11th Corps)
F – 1st Battalion, Panzer Regiment 2 (13th Panzer Division)
G – 1st Battalion, GrossDeutschland Panzer Regiment
H – 2nd Battalion, Panzer Regiment 23 (23rd Panzer Division)

- - - - Frontline July 2, 1943
——— Frontline December 31, 1943
Ⓐ Panther Battalions, December 1943
ⒶⒶ Soviet Armor concentrations, December 1943

1. September 4: One company of II/Panzer Regiment 23 arrives to bolster 6th Army defenses around Stalino but is surrounded near Mospino by Soviet attack. The company is rescued by a 17th Panzer Division counterattack.

2. September 11–21: Remainder of II/Panzer Regiment 23 (23rd Panzer Division) arrives in 1st Panzer Army area and participates in counterattacks near Pavlograd against the Soviet 23rd TC.

3. October 9–10: I/Panzer Regiment 2 (13th Panzer Division) arrives near Melitopol on October 2, and helps to hold Wotan Line against Soviet 4th GMC and 11th TC. This is the first Panther unit at the front with mostly Ausf. A models. On October 24, 2nd Company destroys 35 Soviet tanks near Kalinovka.

4. October 31: I/Panzer Regiment 2 participates in counterattack east of Kherson against Soviet 4th GMC that succeeds in preventing the 4th Mountain Division and Group Becker from being encircled and destroyed.

5. November 15–24: 1st Panzer Division and *Leibstandarte SS Adolf Hitler* (LSSAH), both moved in by rail for major counterattack by 48th Panzer Corps against Soviet 1st TA west of Kiev. Attack starts with about 65–70 operational Panthers and succeeds in defeating 5th GTC and 8th GTC at Brusilov.

6. December 5–8: I/Panzer Regiment 15 (11th Panzer Division) and I/Panzer Regiment 31 attempt to defeat 5th GTA advance upon Znamyenka with about 30 Panthers. Panthers are able to destroy several dozen T-34s from 18th and 29th TCs but cannot prevent fall of Znamyenka.

7. December 6–14: 1st Panzer and LSSAH continue attack toward Radomyshl and inflict another defeat on 1st TA.

8. December 16–23: 1st Panzer and LSSAH attempt to encircle three Soviet tank corps (4th GTC, 5th GTC, 25th TC) in Meleni Pocket. The Germans inflict another defeat upon 1st TA but are unable to close the pocket.

9. December 24–31: Soviet 1st TA and 3rd GTA launch major winter offensive that rips open 4th Panzer Army front. 48th Panzer Corps, with about 45 operational Panthers, is unable to stop Soviet armor from seizing Zhitomir, although they are able to inflict heavy losses.

in overrunning parts of the Soviet 60th Army, but the Germans lacked the strength to annihilate isolated units. Before the Germans could finish off the Soviet units around Radomyshl, a Soviet flanking move by the 25th Tank Corps at Meleni caused Balck to call off the attack. *Leibstandarte* and the 1st Panzer Division rapidly shifted to the west of Meleni and struck the 25th Tank Corps on December 19. In four days of tough fighting, the Soviets lost about 100 T-34s, but the two best German panzer divisions were reduced to only a few dozen tanks each, and the 48th Panzer Corps had to shift to the defense on December 23. Von Manstein believed that these series of spoiling attacks had destroyed about 700 Soviet tanks in November to December and would prevent the Soviets from breaking out of the Kiev bridgehead. However, von Manstein once again seriously underestimated the Soviet ability to regenerate combat power. German intelligence had missed the transfer of large Soviet armor reinforcements into the Kiev area, giving Vatutin's 1st Ukrainian Front a decisive advantage in numbers.

Vatutin's offensive began on December 24 and quickly overran the German infantry units around Brusilov. Balck was outnumbered 5:1 in armor and could only mount a series of delaying actions to slow the Soviet advance. Between December 24 and 31, Vatutin lost almost 200 T-34s, although Zhitomir fell on December 31.

* * *

The tank battles west of Kiev in November to December 1943 were one of the last major German counteroffensives on the Eastern Front, and they were ultimately unsuccessful. Although the Germans claimed these actions and further small successes around Anamyenka were tactical victories, the fact is that they did not destroy any major Soviet units or delay Vatutin's breakout offensive. The Panther units achieved isolated successes, which German propaganda emphasized, but there were just too few tanks operational to make a real difference. Furthermore, they had failed to successfully perform the breakthrough role for which they had been created. Indeed, the Panther actually performed better in a defensive role, picking off T-34s advancing over open ground, but this role surrendered the initiative to the fast-moving T-34 armies. Additionally, the Soviets had finally learned to use combined-arms tactics effectively by late 1943, and the integration of T-34s with supporting antitank guns and motorized infantry was a combination that the Panthers could not defeat.

STATISTICS AND ANALYSIS

Production

A total of 842 Panther Ausf. D and 908 Panther Ausf. A models were built in 1943. From May to December, an average of just over 200 Panthers were built each month. However, only 1,071 Panther tanks, or 60 percent of those built, actually reached the Eastern Front in 1943. The balance remained in training units and new battalions that were being formed. Thus, despite the efforts lavished on developing and establishing a robust manufacturing base, the fielding of the Panther tank in 1943 failed to achieve the goals necessary to regain a degree of superiority.

In contrast to the German problems in fielding the Panther, Soviet industry was able to produce 15,812 T-34 tanks in 1943. Monthly production of the T-34 was about 1,300 machines. Production of the T-34 was aided by a mature design that had been simplified for mass production. Indeed, by mid-1943, the Germans were being outproduced by almost 3:1. Despite their technical merits, Tiger and Panther tanks constituted only 41 percent of German tank production in 1943, with the Panzer IV remaining the backbone of panzer units. The commitment of so many industrial resources to an untried tank design at the expense of the proven Panzer IV only served to starve the frontline units of effective tanks when they needed them most. It was this fear of disrupting production that caused the Soviet GKO to defer introducing a successor to the T-34 until absolutely necessary. The Soviet decision to delay upgrading the T-34 was costly to Soviet frontline tankers in the Ukraine in 1943, but it ensured that Soviet generals would have the numbers to conduct sustained high-intensity operations.

Strength at the front, Ukraine, 1943

At the beginning of *Zitadelle*, Army Group South (AGS) had 91 Tigers and 200 Panthers (plus 1,010 Panzer III and Panzer IV tanks) opposing 3,600 T-34s. By December, AGS had only 54 operational Tigers and 80 Panthers (plus 350 Panzer

ORDER OF BATTLE
Soviet Tank & Mechanized Corps in Ukraine 1943 that fought Panther units

CORPS	TANK UNITS	NUMBER OF T-34s	ASSIGNMENT	COMMANDER	ACTION
3rd Mechanized Corps	1 GTB 49 TB 14, 16, 17 TR	195	1TA	MGN Semen Krivoshein	Syrtsev/Dubrova
6th Tank Corps	22, 112, 200 TB	148	1TA	MGN Andrei Getman	Verkhopen'ye Tomarovka
	86 TB (separate)	50	1TA	Colonel Agafonov	Verkhopen'ye
31st Tank Corps	100, 237, 242 TB	155	1TA	MGN Dmitri Chernienko	Verkhopen'ye Borisovka
5th Guards Tank Corps	20, 21, 22 GTB	150	6GA	MGN Andrei Kravchenko	Grayvoron
4th Guards Tank Corps	12, 13, 14 GTB	122	27A	MGN Pavel Poluboyarov	Achtyrka
1st Mechanized Corps	3, 4, 9 TR 219 TB	160	53A	MGN Mikhail Solomatin	Lyubotin Kolomak
5th Guards Mechanized Corps	51, 54, 55 GTR 24 GTB	160	5GTA	MGN Boris Skvortsov	Lyubotin
10th Tank Corps	178, 183, 186 TB	150	40A	MGN Vasilii Alekseev	Trostyanets
23rd Tank Corps	3, 39, 135 TB	150	3GA	MGN Efim Pushkin	Pavlograd
4th Guards Mechanized Corps	37, 38, 39 GTR 36 GTB	120	3GA	MGN Trofim Tanaschishin	Melitopol Kalinovka
20th Tank Corps	8GTB 80, 155 TB	171	61A	MG Ivan Lazarev	Melitopol
18th Tank Corps	110, 180, 181 TB	100	5GTA	MGN Boris Bakharov	Znamyenka
29th Tank Corps	25, 31, 32 TB	100	5GTA	MGN Ivan Kirichenko	Mishurin Rog Znamyenka
8th Mechanized Corps	116 TB 41, 83, 139 TR	100	5GTA	MGN Abram Khasin	Znamyenka
25th Tank Corps	111, 162, 175 TB	200	13A	MGN Fedor Anikushkin	Meleni
7th Guards Tank Corps	54, 55, 56 GTB	200	3GTA	MGN Kirill Suleikov	Fastov Brusilov
9th Mechanized Corps	47, 53, 74, 166 TR 59 GHTR	50	3GTA	MGN Konstantin Malygin	Brusilov

ORDER OF BATTLE
German Panther battalions in Ukraine in 1943

PANZER BATTALION	NUMBER OF PANTHERS ASSIGNED	DATE ARRIVED AT FRONT	ASSIGNMENTS	COMMANDER(S)
Pz. Battalion 51	96	July 1, 1943	*Grossdeutschland* PzGr. Division	Hauptmann Heinrich Meyer (Jan. 13–Aug. 19, 1943) **KIA**. Major Julius Pfeffer Sept. 15–20 Nov. 1943)
Pz. Battalion 52	96	July 4, 1943	*Grossdeutschland* PzGr. Division	Major Gerhard Tebbe (July 5–6, 1943). Hauptmann Georg Baumunk (July, 6–24, 1943). Major Karl von Sivers (July 22, 1943–March 1944)
I/SS Pz - 2	71	August 22, 1943	SS *Das Reich* PzGr. Division	SS-Haupsturmführer Hans Weiss
I/Pz. - 15 (redesignated Pz. Bn. 52)	96	August 24, 1943	11th Panzer Division	Major Karl von Sivers (July 22, 1943–March 1944)
II/Pz - 23	96	August 31, 1943	23rd Panzer Division	Major Fritz Fechner
I/Pz. - 2	71	October 2, 1943	13th Panzer Division	Hauptmann Bollert (Oct. 2–21, 1943) **KIA**. Hauptmann Georg Grüner (Oct. 22, 1943–Mar. 11, 1944)
I/SS Pz - 1	96	November 9, 1943	SS *Leibstandarte* Panzer Division	SS-Sturmbannführer Herbert Kuhlmann
I/Pz. - 1	76	November 11, 1943	1st Panzer Division	Major Ernst Phillip
I/Pz. - 31	76	December 5, 1943	XI Corps (15 Dec 43) 3rd Panzer Corps (27 Dec 43)	Major Hubertus Feldtkeller

III/IV tanks) to hold off about 5,000 T-34s. Thus, despite the destruction of over 14,000 T-34s in 1943, German armor strength versus the Red Army fell in the last six months of 1943. The critical weakness of the Panther was its poor operational readiness (OR) rate due to persistent mechanical problems. Other than the first two days of *Zitadelle*, the Panther frontline operational strength was usually well below 100 tanks. In fact, it was not until April 1944 that the Germans again had at least 100 operational Panthers on the Eastern Front. Only one out of eight Panther battalions sent to the Eastern Front in 1943 managed to keep at least half its tanks operational for one week. The I/Panzer Regiment 1 had an OR rate of 57 percent after nine days at the front but dropped to 38 percent after three weeks. In contrast, most Panzer IV battalions had around 65 percent readiness during the last half of 1943. While exact figures for T-34 readiness in specific units are unknown, overall numbers indicate that the T-34 usually had around a 90 percent OR rate before an offensive and about 50–70 percent during operations.

Losses

During 1943, the Red Army lost over 14,000 T-34 tanks, including about 6,000 lost fighting AGS from July to December 1943. During the last half of 1943, 493 Panthers were lost. Furthermore, over 50 percent of Panthers lost were destroyed by the Germans when forced to retreat. German crew losses in Panther units were not as severe as tank losses. The 51st Panzer Battalion suffered only 72 dead in July to August 1943, or slightly more than one death for each Panther destroyed. Soviet analysis indicated that 81 percent of hits on T-34s were on the hull and only 19 percent on the turret. Over half of all hits failed to penetrate the armor. During the fighting in July, 26 percent of T-34s destroyed were hit by 88mm guns, 40 percent were hit by 75mm guns, and 33 percent were hit by 50mm guns. Less than 1 percent of Soviet tanks knocked out by 75mm guns in 1943 were hit at ranges greater than 1,400m and less than 10 percent were hit beyond 1,000m. Roughly 60 percent of tank engagements occurred between 200–600m, and 10 percent were destroyed at 200m or less. Despite the supposed safety of diesel fuel, about 25 percent of T-34s that were hit caught fire. Soviet tank crew losses were extremely heavy, with only about 25–30 percent of tank crews surviving the destruction of their vehicles.

AFTERMATH

By the end of 1943, the German armored forces in the Ukraine were severely outnumbered by the Red Army. The introduction of the Panther tank had failed to reverse the situation. Indeed, the Panther was essentially an experimental design in 1943, and it was plagued with mechanical reliability problems long after its initial introduction at Kursk. Although the Ausf. D and A models were powerful gunnery platforms, the Panthers were so mechanically fragile that they could rarely move far from railheads, and more were lost from noncombat reasons than from action against Soviet units. The introduction of the Panther Ausf. G in March 1944 did resolve some of the more nagging problems, such as engine fires and weak final drives, but the Panther remained an expensive fuel hog and it became increasingly vulnerable to Soviet 85mm and 122mm tank guns by mid-1944.

Despite a major effort to mass-produce the Panther, the quantity of operational Panthers available in frontline armor units was fewer than 100 for most of 1943, and the Wehrmacht was unable to convert the Panther's theoretical potential into a real battlefield advantage. While on occasion, the small Kampfgruppes of Panthers bloodied the Soviet T-34 tank brigades in the Ukraine in 1943, these were tactical successes that did not translate into any real change in the Wehrmacht's deteriorating operational situation. The total number of T-34s knocked out or destroyed by Panthers in July to December 1943 was probably in the vicinity of 500, or about 8 to 10 percent of the total number lost in the Ukraine in that period. On the other hand, T-34s destroyed relatively few Panthers in 1943 – probably no more than several dozen – but they kept them on the run, which led to breakdowns. In spite of the Panther's advantage in firepower, the T-34's mobility and reliability advantages were more germane to actual battlefield necessities in the Ukraine in 1943, allowing the Red Army to gain and hold the initiative by maneuvering large tank formations across hundreds of kilometers of steppe.

In contrast the Red Army had fixated on a quantitative approach to tank warfare. It was not until mid-1943 that the Soviets realized that their heretofore qualitative advantages in tank warfare had disappeared as new German designs were introduced, and the decision to upgun the T-34 to an 85mm gun was made rather slowly, with production beginning in March 1944. Despite the shortcomings of the basic T-34 design by late 1943, Koshkin had provided the Red Army with a tank that could move hundreds of kilometers on its own tracks without breaking down, which could ford rivers or cross them on pontoon bridges, and which could operate for months with minimal maintenance. In designing the Panther, the Germans ignored many of the T-34's best qualities and bet their fortunes on an overly complicated and ultimately flawed design.

In late 1943, a Panther Ausf. D crew replaces two damaged track blocks on Panther "134." The tank has been towed back to a railhead after apparently receiving mine damage. Note the opened access panels on the hull rear for adjusting track tension. (Nik Cornish)

Tiger

NORMANDY 1944

The German Tiger heavy tank is today the most famous tank of World War II, if not one of the most famous tanks in history. Introduced in mid-1942, the Tiger featured extremely thick armor, providing it with what was at that time a formidable level of battlefield survivability. The Tiger also mounted a powerful long-barreled 88mm gun that could at normal combat ranges defeat virtually every enemy tank then in existence. Germany's Tiger tanks dominated the battlefields of Europe for at least the next two years, striking fear into those Allied crews unfortunate enough to encounter them on the battlefield; many such crews did not survive these invariably brief and bloody actions. Although few in quantity, the relatively small numbers of Tigers available allowed the German forces to slow down the rising tide of Allied battlefield success for longer than they would have been able to otherwise.

By late summer 1944, however, the mighty Tiger was nearing its swansong. This period was the last time that the famous Tiger spearheaded Germany's defensive battles in any significant numbers. In August 1944, Tiger production ended in favor

Sherman Firefly

of the even more formidable King Tiger, which featured better-sloped armor and an even more powerful, longer-barreled 88mm gun. With Tiger production halted, the inevitable attrition of combat meant that the Germans could only deploy the Tiger in decreasing numbers. This attritional process was speeded up that summer by the arrival on the battlefield of a new generation of potent Allied tanks that could, for the first time in the war, take on the Tiger and win. For this very task, the British had developed the Firefly, an upgunned variant of the standard American-designed M4 Sherman medium tank. Instead of the 75mm gun of the standard Sherman, however, the Firefly mounted a potent 17pdr gun that made it a deadly opponent for even the heavily armored Tiger at normal combat ranges. Outperforming the 88mm L/56 gun of the Tiger, the theoretical penetrative power of the Firefly's 17pdr only came close to being matched by the 88 L/71 gun mounted by the King Tiger, which was then only just coming into service.

This struggle for armored supremacy between the Firefly tanks deployed on the one side by the British, Canadian and Polish armies, and on the other by Germany's Tiger tanks, was demonstrated most obviously during the summer 1944 battle for Normandy. During the two months of bitter combat that followed the Allied D-Day landings on June 6, 1944, the Allies slowly and painfully fought their way inland in the face of fierce German resistance. Continued Allied offensive determination, however, gradually began to bear fruit during early August, as Germany's defensive resilience finally began to crumble. Indeed, by August 8, 1944, the fate of the entire German front in Normandy hung in the balance after powerful Allied offensives had torn it open in several places.

It was at one of these breaches, south of Caen, on the early afternoon of August 8, 1944, that the famous German Panzer ace SS-Hauptsturmführer (Captain) Michael Wittmann led his troop of four Tigers in a desperate charge north towards the Allied lines. Awaiting this scratch force was a mass of Allied armor, which included a number of Fireflies. Advancing north, Wittmann's Tigers blundered into a classic tank ambush. In the course of this brief, bloody engagement, the fire of just one Firefly accounted for three of Wittmann's Tigers. As Wittmann's tank exploded after being hit, the famed German Panzer ace, who had proved such a scourge to the Allies in Normandy, met the warrior's death that befitted his military career. This combat episode provides bountiful testimony to the awesome killing power of the Sherman Firefly, the Tiger tank destroyer extraordinaire.

THE TANKS

The Tiger

Introduced in mid-1942, the Tiger can trace its direct development back to 1941 and its indirect antecedents to 1937. During 1937–40, the Germans carried out development work on a tank heavier than their then-heaviest tank – the Panzer IV. By 1940, this program for a 29.5-ton tank – designated the VK3001 – had produced several prototype designs, named the Breakthrough Tanks 1 and 2 (DW1 and 2) and the VK3001(H). The DW1 chassis, developed by the German armaments firm of Henschel, sported 50mm-thick armor plates and was powered by a 280bhp Maybach ML 120 engine. Its suspension featured the typical German torsion bar suspension. During 1939 Henschel produced its DW2 design. This tank married a modified DW1 chassis to a Krupp-designed turret that mounted the 75mm KwK L/24 gun used in the Panzer IV. Finally, during 1940 Henschel produced the VK3001(H) design. This was a turretless chassis which incorporated a novel running-gear arrangement based on interleaved wheels. The 30-ton VK3001(H), which featured 60mm-thick armor plates, was powered by a 300bhp Maybach HL 116 six-cylinder engine and could obtain a maximum road speed of 34km/h.

During 1940, the Henschel firm also began work on the heavier VK6501(H) design – an enlarged, uparmored and larger-engined version of the Panzer IV designed to fulfil the Army's future 65-ton KV6501/Panzer requirement. This massive design was to be powered by a 12-cylinder 600bhp Maybach HL 224 engine. Developmental work on this design did not progress any further, however, because the Army Weapons Department was happy with the Panzer IV as its heaviest vehicle. Nevertheless, these design efforts influenced the subsequent work that would lead to to the production of the Tiger.

The rival armaments firm of Porsche, meanwhile, had begun to develop a heavy tank designated the VK4501(P) – seemingly at Hitler's request and without formal contracts from the Weapons Department. From spring 1941, Krupp began to collaborate with Porsche on this project, by supplying the latter with its recently

The Tiger through 360 degrees

SPECIFICATIONS:
Tiger (Vehicles 1–250)

General
Production run: August 1942–August 1944
   (24 months)
Vehicles produced: 1,349
Combat weight: 55 tons
Crew: five (commander, gunner, loader, driver,
   radio/bow MG operator)

Dimensions
Overall length: 8.24m
Hull length: 6.20m
Width (with battle tracks): 3.73m
Height: 2.86m

Armor
Hull front: 100mm (at 66–80 degrees)
Hull sides: 60–80mm (at 90 degrees)
Hull rear: 82mm (at 82 degrees)
Hull roof: 25mm (at 90 degrees)
Turret front: 100–120mm (at 80–90 degrees)
Turret sides: 80mm (at 90 degrees)
Turret rear: 80mm (at 90 degrees)
Turret roof: 26mm (at 0–9 degrees)

Armament
Main gun: 1 x 88mm KwK 36 L/56
Secondary: 2 x 7.92mm MG 34; 1 coaxial in turret;
   1 hull front; 2 x treble smoke dischargers (turret
   sides)
Main gun rate of fire: 15rpm

Ammunition stowage
Main: 92 rounds (typically 50 percent Pzgr 39 APCBC,
   50 percent Sprgr L4.5 HE; also few Pzgr 40 APCR,
   Gr.39HL HEAT)
Secondary: 3,900–5,100 rounds

Artwork by Jim Laurier, © Osprey Publishing

Communications
Fu-5 Ultra-short-wave transmitter/receiver; intercom

Motive power
Engine: Maybach HL210 P435 21-liter V12-cylinder gasoline engine
Power: 642 metric bhp at 3,000rpm
Fuel capacity: 534 liters
Power-to-weight ratio: 11.6hp/ton

Performance
Ground pressure: 1.05kg/cm²
Maximum road speed: 38km/h
Maximum cross-country speed: 20km/h
Operational range (road): 100km
Operational range (cross-country): 57km
Fuel consumption (road): 5–5.3 liters/km
Fuel consumption (cross-country): 9–9.3 liters/km

The mammoth symbol on the tank is the tactical symbol for the unit schwere Panzer Abteilungen 502 (s. Pz Abt 502) – Heavy Tank Battalion 502. This was the first heavy tank battalion to be formed during the summer 1942. It was also the first unit to see action on the Eastern Front at Leningrad in August 1942. It was an inauspicious start. Several of the tanks got bogged down in the marshy terrain or simply broke down. The unit was later posted to France where it saw action from July 1944 onwards. It was re-formed in early 1945 as S. Pz Abt 511 and refitted with King Tigers. The unit eventually surrendered to the Soviets in May 1945

The turret is lowered into place during the later stages of the production of a Tiger I, 1944. (Bundesarchiv Bild 101I-635-3965-05)

developed 88mm KwK 36 L/56 tank gun – a modified version of the famous 88mm antiaircraft gun. The long-barreled Krupp tank gun delivered an impressive antitank capability by achieving a high muzzle velocity for its rounds. The effort the Germans devoted to heavy tank design remained dilatory until 26 May 1941, when a meeting of experts chaired by Hitler reviewed future German tank development strategy. At this meeting, the Führer demanded that a well-armored German heavy tank be developed that would outgun any enemy tank it might encounter. Future development work should proceed on the basis of a vehicle that sported 100mm thick frontal armor and a gun that could penetrate 100mm of armor at a range of 1,500m. The Führer thus ordered that the work already undertaken by the firms of Porsche and Henschel should be accelerated so that each could construct six prototype vehicles by summer 1942.

These developmental programs received another major impetus during the second half of 1941, as the German Army reacted to the shock experienced when its Panzers encountered two unexpectedly formidable Soviet AFV designs – the T-34 medium and KV heavy tanks. These modern Soviet tanks outclassed all German tanks then in existence, including their heaviest vehicle, the Panzer IV. This realization prompted the Germans to begin developing new medium and heavy tank designs. Work commenced simultaneously on a number of designs during 1941–42, but eventually these efforts coalesced during 1942–43 to produce a new generation of heavier, more powerfully armed and better protected tanks – the Panzer V "Panther" and the Panzer VI Model E "Tiger."

During 1942, however, these reinvigorated German efforts to develop a new heavy tank remained dogged by controversy. Hitler wanted the future heavy tank to mount an 88mm gun – either the KwK 36 or a version of the new and yet more powerful Rheinmetall 88mm Flak 41. After experimentation, Porsche concluded that the latter weapon was not suitable for mounting in the turret it was then developing. The Weapons Department, on the other hand, felt that mounting such a large gun in a tank (which would need to be large to accommodate a turret with a sufficiently wide turret ring to house the gun) would render the vehicle too heavy and immobile. The Department felt that the future heavy tank should mount a smaller 60mm or 70mm tapered-bore gun. This was a gun with an interior bore to the barrel that narrows towards the muzzle. This narrowing squeezes the special tungsten-steel round into the rifling on the inside of the barrel, enabling the round to be fired with greater muzzle velocity and accuracy, but crucially from a smaller gun. Tungsten steel, however, was an alloy that was already scarce and in much demand within the German war economy. The wrangling associated with this dispute led to the simultaneous commencement of work on two separate prototype heavy tank programs.

The Germans contracted one project, designated VK3601(H), to Henschel based on a specification for a 32.7-ton vehicle that mounted a tapered-bore 60mm or 70mm gun. Meanwhile, Porsche finally received formal contracts to produce the heavier VK4501(P) design, which mounted Krupp's 88mm tank gun. By mid-1941 Henschel had produced seven prototype VK3601(H) tanks that featured thick frontal armor and interleaved road wheels. However, the Germans then concluded that such was the demand for and scarcity of tungsten steel, that the tapered-bore gun central to the Henschel project was no longer feasible. The only way that the smaller Henschel heavy tank could compete with its heavier Porsche rival in tank-killing capability was to employ tapered-bore technology; with this ruled out, Henschel had no choice but to abandon the VK3601(H) program. The Germans, however, did not wish to waste the valuable design work Henschel had put into this project. Consequently, the Weapons Department contracted Henschel to develop a 41-ton heavy tank, the VK4501(H). Henschel decided to develop an enlarged version of its VK3601 that would mount the same 88mm tank gun featured in the rival VK4501(P) design. By late 1941, therefore, both Henschel and Porsche were now working on rival 41-ton heavy-tank designs that mounted the same gun.

By April 1942, Porsche and Henschel had completed their first prototype VK4501(P) and VK4501(H) heavy tanks, now generally referred to as the Porsche-Tiger and Henschel-Tiger, respectively. These rival designs had certain common features; most notably they mounted the same Krupp-designed turret that featured the 88mm KwK L/56 gun and the coaxial MG 34 machine gun. Both designs also had a ball-mounted bow machine gun and sported heavy armor up to a maximum of 120mm thick on the turret mantlet. Moreover, both tanks weighed around 53.6 tons, markedly above the original specification, because the German hierarchy increased the project's required levels of armor during the design process. Beyond this commonality, however, the two rivals were quite different.

The VK4501(P) was powered by two air-cooled Simmering-Graz-Pauker 320bhp engines that drove the tank through a series of dynamos and electric motors; the vehicle's drive mechanism was thus of petro-electric type, a typical Porsche arrangement. The VK4501(P) also featured a novel suspension that comprised six steel double road wheels suspended in pairs from longitudinal torsion bars. Because of its high fuel consumption, however, the tank could only achieve a disappointing operational range of just 50km. The tank also featured a low squat chassis with the angular Krupp turret located well forward, which resulted in the long 88mm gun overhanging the front of the vehicle to a conspicuous degree. This made the design very heavy at the front end, and consequently the tank was prone to get bogged down in soft terrain. Nevertheless, during April 1942, before this design had even been evaluated, Porsche received contracts for 90 tanks to be delivered during the period January–April 1943.

Several features differentiated Henschel's VK4501(H) tank from its Porsche rival. The Henschel tank mounted the identical Krupp turret but in the center of the vehicle, not at the front. This arrangement reduced the degree to which the main gun overhung the front of the vehicle, rendering it less front-heavy. The Henschel tank's running gear featured the same novel interleaved road-wheel arrangement used in the earlier VK3001(H). Unlike the Porsche design, the Henschel tank's suspension was based on the typical German arrangement of lateral torsion bars. Moreover the tank's hull superstructure was also wider and more angular than that

of the Porsche tank. The VK4501(H) also featured a single, rear-located 642bhp Maybach gasoline engine, and its fuel tanks provided it with a marginally better cross-country operating range than its Porsche rival. The Henschel tank also featured a hydraulically-controlled preselected eight-speed Maybach Olvar OG40 gearbox and semi-automatic transmission.

The first of the Tiger experimental series, the VK4501(H) V1 is seen here at the assembly hall of Henschel's Kassel factory in April 1942. It differed only marginally from the subsequent production Tiger design. (The Tank Museum)

To evaluate which of the two rival designs was superior, the Germans held a field trial in front of Hitler and other top Nazi officials at Rastenburg on April 20, 1942 – the Führer's 53rd birthday. When this and subsequent competitive trials had been completed, the Army concluded – despite Hitler's prejudiced favoritism for Porsche – that the Henschel model was marginally better than the Porsche; the greatest advantages were Henschel's superior engine power, reliability, and vehicle mobility. The Weapons Department also concluded that the Henschel tank was better suited for mass production than its rival – an important consideration for an already hard-pressed German war economy.

Hitler demanded that the new tank be committed to action as soon as possible. In July 1942 the Weapons Department contracted Henschel to mass-produce this tank under the designation Panzer VI Model E Tiger (later simplified to Panzer VI Tiger). Simultaneously, the Department canceled the contracts already awarded to Porsche for its 90 Porsche-Tigers. Not wishing to waste these 90 partially constructed chassis, however, the Germans subsequently used them to produce an improvized heavy tank destroyer designated "Elephant," and nicknamed the "Ferdinand" after Ferdinand Porsche. In addition to its test vehicle (designated Experimental Series Panzer VI H1), the first two Tiger tanks Henschel produced in early August were two preproduction vehicles. Henschel then completed the first four tanks in the main production run on August 20. These were rushed off to the Eastern Front on August 29, 1942. Thereafter arriving on the battlefields of Europe in greater numbers, the Tiger soon earned a fearsome reputation that it maintained well into the second half of 1944.

The Sherman Firefly

The Sherman Firefly, in contrast, did not enter combat until June 1944, by which time Tiger production would shortly be terminated. By late 1943, the American-designed M4 Sherman had become the British Army's standard medium tank, equipping many of its armored brigades. The Sherman was the first effective dual-purpose Allied tank that could perform adequately both the infantry support role (which required a heavily armored tank) and the exploitation role (which required a fast and mobile, and thus lightly armored, tank).

The M4 Sherman was a five-man tank in the 31–35 ton range, depending on the mark, which in British service was designated Sherman I through to V. These tanks either mounted the 75mm American M3 gun, or the 76mm American M1 gun, together with one coaxial and one bow machine gun. The tank sported sloped frontal armor that was up to 76mm thick, together with 38mm side plates. Powered by a rear-located Chrysler, Wright, GMC or Ford engine that produced 400–443bhp, the Sherman could achieve a maximum speed of 36km/h on roads and 22km/h cross-country. The Sherman's running gear comprised three pairs of bogie road wheels, based on the Vertical Volute Spring Suspension (VVSS) arrangement. The Sherman also featured a five-speed synchromesh gearbox and clutch-and-brake transmission; this produced a rather crude steering system in comparison to the sophisticated (if fault-prone) twin-radius system employed in the Tiger.

However, combat experience in the Western Desert and Italy during 1942–43 had shown that British tanks were vulnerable to the latest Panzers. The long-barreled 75mm guns of the new Panzer IV Special and Panther inflicted heavy losses on British armor, as did the Tiger's even more potent 88mm gun. The latter could knock out British tanks at such long range that the Tiger remained impervious to return fire. This situation led the War Office to consider how to upgun their existing tanks so that they could knock out any German tank at a range of up to 1,300m.

This view of a Sherman Firefly, taken in Putanges, Normandy, on August 20, 1944, shows the sheer length of the tank's 17pdr gun barrel. (IWM B 9477)

The obvious weapon for this was the Royal Ordnance 17pdr antitank gun, which had an established track record as a tank-killer. Firing armor-piercing rounds, the gun could penetrate 172mm armor at 914m range – sufficient to penetrate even the Tiger's formidable gun-mantlet armor.

During late 1943, the British first attempted to mount this fearsome weapon on the Cromwell tank chassis. Entering service in March 1944, much later than expected, the resulting A30 Challenger tank remained an unsatisfactory expedient. The Challenger featured a tall turret, which was required to mount the gun's tall mechanism, as well as levels of armor protection inadequate for the battlefields of 1944. As the War Office's dissatisfaction with the delayed Challenger program grew during late 1943, its thoughts increasingly turned to the issue of whether the 17pdr could be successfully mounted in the Sherman. This latter possibility had been first entertained back in late August 1943, but no official action to investigate the matter was authorized until early October.

The Ministry of Supply's Tank Department remained sceptical that the gun could be mounted effectively in the standard 75mm-equipped Sherman. The existing 17pdr antitank gun featured large and cumbersome cylinders located both above and below the barrel to absorb the gun's powerful recoil; this made the gun too tall

The Firefly through 360 degrees

SPECIFICATIONS:
Sherman VC Firefly

General
Production run: January 1944–May 1945 (17 months)
Vehicles produced: Between 2,139 and 2,239
Combat weight: 34.8 tons
Crew: Four (commander, gunner, loader/radio operator, driver)

Dimensions
Overall length: 7.82m
Hull length: 6.5m
Width: 2.67m
Height: 2.74m

Armor
Hull front: 51mm (at 45–90 degrees)
Hull sides: 38mm (at 90 degrees)
Hull rear: 38mm (at 70–90 degrees)
Hull roof: 25mm (at 0 degrees)
Turret front: 38–76mm (at 85–90 degrees)
Turret sides: 51mm (at 85 degrees)
Turret rear: 64mm (at 90 degrees)
Turret roof: 25mm (at 0 degrees)

Armament
Main gun: 1 x 17pdr (76.2mm) ROQF Mk IV or Mk VII
Secondary: 1 x .30cal coaxial M1919A4 machine gun
Main gun rate of fire: 10rpm

Ammunition stowage
Main: 77 rounds (typically 50 percent APCBC/APDS, 50 percent HE)
Secondary: 5,000 rounds

Artwork by Jim Laurier, © Osprey Publishing

Communications
No. 19 Set transmitter/receiver

Motive power
Engine: Chrysler Multibank A57 30-cylinder gasoline engine
Power: 443 metric bhp at 2,850rpm
Fuel capacity: 604 liters
Power-to-weight ratio: 12.9hp/ton

Performance
Ground pressure: 0.92kg/cm^2
Maximum road speed: 36km/h
Maximum cross-country speed: 17km/h
Operational range (road): 201km
Operational range (cross-country): 145km
Fuel consumption (road): 3 liters/km
Fuel consumption (cross-country): 4.2 liters/km

A Firefly from the Sherman-equipped armored regiment 1 Northamptonshire Yeomanry. Led by Lt-Col D. Foster, the regiment fielded three squadrons – "A," "B" and "C." Most of the regiment's tanks bore distinctive names. "A" Squadron tanks were named after Soviet towns. This is tank No. 16 "Kursk."

to fit into the compact Sherman turret. The sheer force of the recoil would also take up a large proportion of the already limited available space in the Sherman turret. However, back in summer 1943 the Royal Armoured Corps Gunnery School at Lulworth had already undertaken some unofficial experiments with mounting the gun in a modified Sherman turret, which convinced them the proposition was both a feasible and economic one.

With the War Office won over by these arguments, it issued a contract for the design of a modified version of the 17pdr, designated the Mark IV, which would fit in the Sherman turret. This design was based on the earlier Lulworth Cove experiments, which had employed the expertise of a Vickers engineer, W. G. K. Wilbourne, who was attached to the Department of Tank Design. During late fall 1943, British engineers produced the redesigned gun, which featured a modified barrel base in front of the breech that shortened the weapon's recoil in its cradle. This redesign also left the gun with more suitably arranged recoil cylinders and a modified mount. During late December 1943, the new gun and mount were successfully tested. Such was the haste with which the War Office now embraced this project that within a few days of the trials being completed, the gun and mount were fitted into a modified Sherman V chassis. This vehicle is said to have been completed at Woolwich on December 31, 1943. On January 6, 1944, trials began on the new vehicle, now designated the 17pdr Sherman. This tank was differentiated from other variants with the suffix "C" after the mark, but did not use the the name Firefly. For whatever reason, the first units to receive the new tank used this name and since 1945 it has become the common designation for the tank.

By January 1944, the War Office was desperate to mount a more effective tank-killing weapon in the ubiquitous Sherman – not least because the Allied invasion of Nazi-occupied France was only a few months away. Fortunately, the War Office was entirely satisfied with the trials undertaken by the first Firefly in early January. The design offered a quick and easy-to-accomplish expedient that would deliver reasonable numbers over the ensuing months. The War Office immediately placed production orders with the Royal Ordnance Factories at Leeds, Cardiff, Woolwich and Hayes for an initial batch of several hundred Fireflies to be completed as soon as possible. The speed of the process by which the Firefly was designed, tested and manufactured owed much to the rapidly growing support at the highest political levels that emerged for the upgunning of the Sherman. On January 12, 1944, Prime Minister Winston Churchill accorded the Firefly program "the highest priority ... [within] the whole munitions programme."

TECHNICAL ASSESSMENT

The Tiger

The first 250 Tigers manufactured by Henschel's Kassel factory between August 1942 and April 1943 formed a distinct batch. The standard Tiger tank was a large and angular vehicle – an unimpressed Lieutenant Otto Carius described it as "plump" – not dissimilar to the smaller Panzer IV in appearance. Weighing 55 tons, the Tiger mounted the same potent long-barreled 88mm KwK 36 L/56 main gun as the prototype. Using an armor-piercing round, this accurate gun could penetrate the side or rear armor of a Sherman V or VC Firefly at a staggering 3,500m and puncture it frontally at 1,800m. In contrast, the standard 75mm-gunned Sherman could only puncture the Tiger's side

Here a mid-production Tiger has been knocked out in Normandy. In this photograph, taken on June 26, 1944 near Rauray, the ripple effect of the *Zimmerit* paste can be clearly seen, as well as the vertical glacis plate into which are set the driver's visor and the bow machine gun. The feet of a dead soldier can be seen in the left foreground. (IWM B6155)

Inside the Tiger

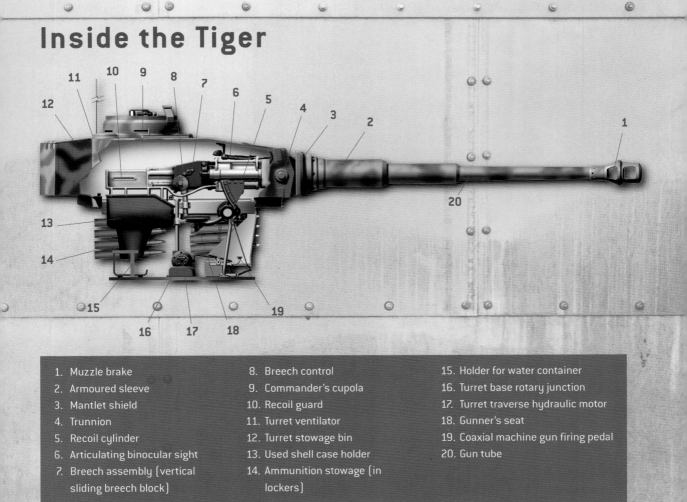

1. Muzzle brake	8. Breech control	15. Holder for water container
2. Armoured sleeve	9. Commander's cupola	16. Turret base rotary junction
3. Mantlet shield	10. Recoil guard	17. Turret traverse hydraulic motor
4. Trunnion	11. Turret ventilator	18. Gunner's seat
5. Recoil cylinder	12. Turret stowage bin	19. Coaxial machine gun firing pedal
6. Articulating binocular sight	13. Used shell case holder	20. Gun tube
7. Breech assembly (vertical sliding breech block)	14. Ammunition stowage (in lockers)	

armor at 100m, and could not even penetrate the Tiger frontally at point-blank range. The Tiger typically engaged an enemy tank at 800–1,200m range, although lucky kills at 2,000m were not unknown; the gun could even fire an HE round 8,000m. The Tiger carried 92 rounds for its main gun, usually a 50/50 mix of Armor Piercing Capped Ballistic Capped (APCBC) and HE rounds. Less commonly, the Tiger carried a few Armor Piercing Composite Rigid (APCR) and High Explosive Antitank (HEAT) rounds.

The Tiger possessed very thick high-quality homogenous armor that ranged from 120mm-thick mantlet armor to 80–82mm-thick side and rear plates. This armor provided excellent battlefield survivability, even if – in comparison with later tanks – it was not well-sloped. Manned by a crew of five, the tank was powered by a 642bhp

Inside the Firefly

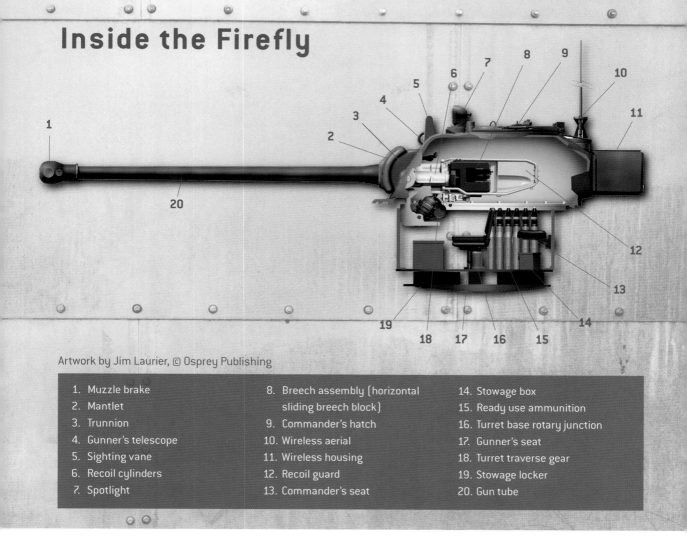

Artwork by Jim Laurier, © Osprey Publishing

1. Muzzle brake
2. Mantlet
3. Trunnion
4. Gunner's telescope
5. Sighting vane
6. Recoil cylinders
7. Spotlight
8. Breech assembly (horizontal sliding breech block)
9. Commander's hatch
10. Wireless aerial
11. Wireless housing
12. Recoil guard
13. Commander's seat
14. Stowage box
15. Ready use ammunition
16. Turret base rotary junction
17. Gunner's seat
18. Turret traverse gear
19. Stowage locker
20. Gun tube

Maybach HL210 gasoline engine. Yet despite its immense size, the tank developed a satisfactory degree of mobility, obtaining top road and off-road speeds of 38km/h and 20km/h, respectively. A surprised Lieutenant Otto Carius discovered that the Tiger "drove just like a car." The vehicle devoured gasoline, however, and thus its fuel tanks only enabled it to travel a paltry 57km off-road before it needed to refuel. It was able to move satisfactorily cross-country thanks to its unusually wide battle tracks, which ran on six interleaved layers of road wheels. When fitted with these battle tracks, however, the Tiger was too wide to be transported on a standard German railroad flat car. To solve this problem the Germans designed the Tiger to use a two-track system. When in action, the Tiger used its wide battle tracks. When it needed to be transported by rail, the crew removed these tracks and the outer layer of road wheels, and fitted narrower transport tracks. The Tiger was also too heavy to cross many European bridges, so it was fitted with wading equipment that allowed it to move submerged along the bed of a river.

In total, between August 1942 and August 1944, Henschel produced 1,349 Tigers, an unimpressive total for a 24-month production run. This low figure reflected the high cost and significant time – more than twice that needed for a Panther – that had to be expended to produce a tank as large, technically complex and well engineered as the Tiger. Yet the Tiger's combination of lethal firepower, superb battlefield survivability and adequate mobility meant that it dominated the battlefield during 1942–44. From summer 1944 onwards, however, it began to meet its match in better-armed and better-armored Allied rivals such as the Firefly, the Soviet IS heavy tanks and the American Pershing tanks.

The Tiger's undoubted battlefield prowess, however, did not mean that the design was without weaknesses. The tank's transmission was prone to break down if preventative maintenance was not carried out regularly; it needed a high level of general technical maintenance; ice tended to freeze on the interleaved road wheels; and it was extremely difficult to recover a disabled Tiger from the battlefield. Despite these flaws, the Tiger soon became the German tank most feared by Allied units. It continued to spearhead Germany's elite heavy-tank units until the latter half of 1944, after which it was increasingly replaced by the even more formidably armored and gunned King Tiger. Nevertheless, Tigers continued to give sterling battlefield service, albeit in dwindling numbers, until the end of the war in early May 1945.

Production-run modifications

Like all tanks, the design of the Tiger was regularly modified during the main production run. Indeed, this run can be divided into three main sub-categories – the "early-" "mid-" and "late-" production vehicles, although the transition from one category to another was by no means distinct. The "early" Tigers – the first 250 tanks – have been described above. The mid-production sequence commenced in late April 1943 with vehicle 251 and continued until chassis 824 in January 1944. All Tigers after vehicle 251 featured the more powerful 694bhp Maybach HL230 engine, as well as an improved transmission, which marginally improved the vehicle's off-road performance. Next, from vehicle 391 in July 1943, Tigers featured a redesigned turret commander's cupola with armored periscopes instead of visors. From September 1943 onwards (from vehicle 496), the design discontinued the expensive and little-used wading equipment, as an economy measure to boost delivery rates. Tigers completed after this date were also outfitted with *Zimmerit* paste to protect them from infantry-delivered magnetic mines.

Late-production modifications appeared during the last eight months of Tiger production (January–August 1944) and featured a varying combination of the following features. From January (vehicle 820) onwards, selected vehicles featured the multi-purpose Close Defense Weapon. From this time on, Tigers also began to feature resilient steel-rimmed road wheels in place of the previous rubber-tired ones. Next, from March (chassis 920 onwards), the turret roof armor was increased from 25mm to 40mm to help protect against plunging fire. Then from around chassis 1100 in April, Tigers featured the monocular TFZ 9c sight in place of the previous binocular TFZ 9b one. Other minor modifications introduced during this period included the addition of stowage brackets on the turret sides to hold five spare track links and the replacement of the two hull roof-mounted headlamps by a single one fitted onto the driver's front plate.

Tiger variants

The Germans only developed two specialized Tiger tank variants which were both command-tank designs.[1] Henschel produced 89 command Tigers – either the Sdkfz 267 battalion commander's tank or the Sdkfz 268 company commander's vehicle. Both of these were similar to the standard production Tiger tank except for the addition of a powerful radio transmitter. The Sdkfz 267 featured the ultra-long-range Fu-8 30-watt transmitter/medium-range receiver, while the Sdkfz 268 mounted the long-range Fu-7 20-watt transmitter/ultra-short-wave receiver. Both command designs possessed a second aerial to service their additional communication sets, and this enabled friend and foe alike to distinguish these vehicles from standard Tigers. Space was created for these radios by reducing main gun round stowage to 66 rounds and removing the coaxial machine gun.

The Sherman Firefly

Spurred on by the urgent need to upgun the Sherman prior to D-Day, the War Office accepted the Firefly for general production in early January 1944. Within days, the War Office placed contracts for the conversion of 2,100 Shermans to the new design in a limited time frame. To meet these contracts, the factories raced with an almost unseemly haste to mount all available 17pdr guns on any suitable available Sherman chassis. It was not deemed possible to modify the 76mm-gunned Sherman owing to its incompatible turret mantlet design, and so during early 1944 the only suitable Sherman chassis available was the Mark V. As the Firefly production program unfolded,

---

[1]   The only other significant Tiger variant was the Sturmtiger assault vehicle, developed during 1943–44 to engage heavily fortified enemy bunkers

other compatible Sherman chassis – the Mark I and the I (Hybrid), the latter with a cast-hull front – were used to create the Sherman IC and IC (Hybrid) Firefly.

The War Office later raised its orders to 3,414 Fireflies, of which the factories completed between 2,139 and 2,239 tanks – the documentation remains contradictory – during a 17-month production run from January 1944 to May 1945. This represented an impressive average delivery rate of 126–132 tanks a month, reflecting the fact that the Firefly was an easy-to-accomplish conversion based on an existing chassis and gun. By May 31, 1944, 342 Fireflies had been delivered, the vast majority to Montgomery's 21st Army Group for the D-Day landings. This was sufficient to provide one Firefly per troop, including those squadrons equipped with the Cromwell. Between D-Day and the end of the Normandy campaign in late August 1944, a further 562 Fireflies were produced, sufficient to replace those lost during the campaign. By February 1945, the factories had delivered 2,002 Fireflies, adequate to begin equipping the 21st Army Group with two Fireflies per troop. During spring 1945, however, three factors led to the program being wound down, with the last tank completed in May: the war in Europe was obviously coming to an end; the Firefly was not required for the Far Eastern theater, where Japanese tanks lacked the potent guns of the latest Panzers; and the expedient Firefly was being replaced by purpose-designed medium tanks like the A34 Comet. While the Firefly only saw action in British service during the 1944–45 Northwest Europe and Italian campaigns, the last confirmed Firefly action occurred during the 1976 clash between Christian Phalangist forces and other Lebanese paramilitaries.

The Firefly was externally similar to the standard Sherman mark upon which it was based. The glaring exception was the much longer barrel of the 17pdr, which overhung the front of the vehicle; this made the Firefly stand out among standard Shermans. The Germans soon learned to knock out any Fireflies they encountered first before engaging the standard Shermans. For British tank crews who received the tanks at short notice and with little training, this was often an unwelcome surprise. Trooper Joe Ekins of the 1st Northamptonshire Yeomanry (1NY) remained blissfully unaware of this enemy practice until a Panzer knocked out his Firefly on August 8, 1944. In response, the British attempted to disguise the tank by painting the end of the barrel in light colors or even fitting a fake muzzle brake half way along the gun.

The Firefly carried 77 rounds for its main armament, normally a mixture of armor-piercing and high-explosive rounds just like other tanks. Typically, the Firefly was supplied with up to five types of ammunition – the Armored Piercing Capped (APC), APC Ballistic Capped (APCBC), the rare AP Discarding Sabot Super Velocity (APDS-SV), and the two standard Mk I HE rounds. With armor-piercing rounds, the Firefly was a potent tank killer. In terms of textbook penetrative power,

Ammunition types

1. Tiger HE
2. Tiger APCBC
3. Tiger APCR

4. Firefly APDS (SV)
5. Firefly APCBC
6. Firefly APC

7. Firefly AP
8. Firefly practice round
9. Firefly HE

AP round: Armour Piercing. The basic design of a solid tank round with a pointed nose designed to penetrate thick steel armor of enemy tanks through kinetic energy.

APC round: Armour Piercing Capped. A variant of the AP round that featured a soft metal nose, which gave better penetration performance against sloped armor.

APCBC round: Armour Piercing Capped Ballistic Capped. A variant of the APC round that featured a brittle cap on top of the soft metal cap, designed to achieve good penetration against sloped armor.

APCR round: Armour Piercing Composite Rigid. A soft metal round with a small, high-density core; on impact the core is ejected at very high speed from the round, penetrating the target.

APDS round: Armour Piercing Discarding Sabot. A solid round fired via the medium of a sabot which is squeezed into the rifling and which falls away from the round once fired; enables the round to be fired with greater velocity.

HE round: High Explosive. A shell filled with explosive filler that explodes on impact to give a large blast area; used to engage "soft" (that is, unarmored or lightly armored) targets such as enemy soldiers, trucks, half-tracks, etc.

HEAT round: High Explosive Antitank. A conical round filled with explosive filler that penetrates armor through chemical effect (a thin jet of molten-hot metal pierces the plating).

Artwork by Jim Laurier, © Osprey Publishing

the Firefly with the rare APDS round outperformed the Panther, the Tiger and even the new King Tiger which began to reach the battlefields during spring 1944. Although these Panzers maintained an advantage in accuracy, particularly at longer range, at normal combat ranges the Firefly's APDS round could penetrate the Tiger's armor from any direction. This was the capability that transformed the Sherman from a satisfactory dual-purpose tank into a lethal tank-killer.

The Firefly's major drawback was that a blinding flash, which often threw up a cloud of fumes and dust, emanated from the muzzle brake when the gun was fired; a similar flash, combined with powerful back-blast, also filled the turret. No one warned Trooper Ekins about these occurrences when he fired his first Firefly round in training just prior to D-Day; the shock that ensued was so great that he later reported that he "nearly jumped out of the tank." These problems were particularly acute when the Firefly fired HE rounds. Given the velocity at which its rounds were fired, the brief flashes made it difficult for the momentarily blinded Firefly crews to observe the fall of their rounds, which had hit the target before the flash had died down or their sight

The entire crew of Corporal Snowden's 75mm-gunned Sherman of No. 3 Troop, "C" Squadron, 1NY, use the long barrel rod to clean the gun rifling of any impurities that could impair the accuracy of the weapon. This demanding chore had to be carried out on a daily basis. (IWM B 8795)

was restored. The flash also exposed their location to the enemy, forcing tank commanders to regularly move to new firing positions. Despite the technical measures intended to minimize this problem, it was never really solved. As three-quarters of all tank rounds fired were HE – generally against "soft" targets like infantry, antitank guns and trucks – the Firefly's inadequate HE performance was a serious problem. Given this, British tank squadrons were loath to accept more than two Fireflies per troop, as the standard Shermans were required for their better HE performance.

The Firefly also sported other differences from the typical Sherman tank from which it had been modified. In particular, the standard design needed minor modification to be able to mount the 17pdr Mark IV gun, including a redesigned turret mantlet. Other observable differences included the large box attached to the turret rear which housed the vehicle's radio and the lack a of hull machine gun. The absence of the latter allowed the crew to be reduced to four, freeing up space in the cramped interior for the large 17pdr rounds. The combination of the heavier gun and ammunition increased the Firefly's weight to 34.8 tons from the 31.8 tons of the Sherman V. The crew reduction in the Firefly meant that the loader had to double as the radio operator. In combat, loaders were so engrossed in loading the tank's main armament that they were hard-pressed to operate the vehicle's communications effectively. This made it more difficult for Fireflies to operate successfully as part of a larger tank unit.

In other respects, however, the expedient Firefly design was all but identical to the standard Sherman. The Firefly featured the same armor as that of the Sherman mark on which it was based; for the Sherman VC, this amounted to sloped frontal armor up to 76mm thick, and 38mm side plates. Thus, at normal combat ranges the Firefly was no more capable of withstanding the lethal fire of the Panzer IV, Panther or Tiger than the standard Sherman was, and if hit it was equally prone to burn. This propensity led understandably scared Firefly crew like Trooper Ekins to bale out as soon as their tank got hit, lest it "brewed up." The VC also had the same Chrysler gasoline engine as most Sherman Vs and this – despite the vehicle's slightly increased weight – provided it with the same performance and mobility as that of the standard Sherman.

Main-run modifications

Due to its relatively brief production run, the Firefly design witnessed fewer modifications than most tanks. Indeed, there was no significant variant to the design. One change that did occur during the production run was that increasing numbers of Sherman I or I (Hybrid) chassis were used for the conversion instead of the Sherman V. Sherman IC Fireflies differed externally to the VC in several ways:

ICs had vertical rear plates, not sloped ones; some ICs had an appliqué armor cheek fitted to the right side of the turret front, whereas VCs did not; other ICs had a pistol port in the turret side and open-spoked road wheels, features not generally present on the VC.

Other minor modifications introduced during the production run reflected attempts to reduce the firing flash and to improve its accuracy when firing APDS. Later Fireflies incorporated a slightly modified muzzle brake with an altered internal bore that enabled the tank to fire APDS rounds more accurately at longer ranges; REME teams carried out this modification on tanks already in-theater. Another such development was the introduction of improved HE rounds like the Mk.IIT Reduced Charge shell that reduced the round's muzzle velocity and thus the amount of blast created. The only other significant change made during the Firefly production run was the moving of the gun's travel rest – which was needed to protect the long barrel when the tank was being transported – from the center of the rear hull deck to the left side. This modification was designed to make it easier for the driver to escape quickly from the tank if it had started to burn after receiving an enemy hit.

THE MEN

To be able to fully understand the realities of this clash of rival armor that occurred in Normandy during mid-1944, one has to appreciate the realities of tank combat on the Western Front, including an understanding of the way in which Firefly and Tiger crews were trained, how these tanks were organized into combat units and what daily life was like for Tiger and Firefly crews both in combat and in the quieter periods in between actions.

Throughout the 1939–45 war, Panzer troops represented an elite arm that spearheaded German military operations. The Panzer arm received the best personnel, handpicked for their outstanding leadership and technical capabilities. These personnel were exposed to extensive specialized training to produce some of the finest tank crews of the war. Of course, as the war progressed the overall quality of Panzer troops inevitably declined as the standard of available German personnel and training declined. Nevertheless they remained an elite until the German surrender, and the small number of Tiger tank crews that existed represented an elite within this elite.

Training

All recruits for the German Army and Waffen-SS began their military service with a program of basic training as infantrymen. Only when this was completed would the recruits apply to undertake further training – either as other ranks or as aspirant officers – with the specialized branch of their choice – Panzer troops, mountain troops, engineers, signalers, etc. Only a proportion of those recruits and aspirant officers who put themselves forward for the popular branch of the Panzer forces were accepted for specialized training, invariably only those recruits who had excelled in basic training. To fill the role of tank commander, the branch sought to recruit exceptional leaders who could swiftly size up a complex tactical situation and execute a timely decision based upon this appraisal. The Panzer branch also required experienced mechanics and highly skilled technicians to serve as tank drivers, gunners and wireless operators. The tank loader was probably the least technically qualified member of the crew – but this physically demanding role was just as vital to the performance of the tank as the others. In practice, some Tiger commander's roles were filled by accomplished former gunners or drivers who had completed specialist refresher courses. It was less common for a loader to be promoted to command a tank, although this is precisely what occurred with Otto Carius, who went on to become one of Germany's leading Tiger aces.

Specialized Panzer arm training was undertaken at one of the many dedicated armored training schools located within the Reich. Personnel received extensive training in the tank-crew role for which they had been selected, as well as more superficial training in the other crew roles. Such training also sought to instil within a particular tank crew a smooth and efficient interaction between the various team members. Nowhere was this interaction more crucial than in the interplay between commander, gunner and loader in the drills performed for engaging enemy tanks. The crews honed these skills by regularly conducting live firing on the ranges and proving grounds located within the Reich; around 20 of the earliest Tigers had been allocated to the training schools for this purpose.

The basic German tank engagement drill ran as follows. Once a tank commander had spotted an enemy tank, he would indicate the bearing and order the crew to engage it. If necessary, the driver would move the Tiger to a better firing position.

Many experienced tank commanders (like Wittman and Sergeant Gordon) bravely eschewed the safety of going into action with the cupola hatches closed in order to gain that vital advantage of good observation of the battlefield – itself often the difference between survival and death. Here Sergeant S. Driver, MM, looks out from the open cupola of his 13th/18th Hussars' Firefly in southern England on May 30, 1944. (IWM H 38969)

Then, looking through his superb Zeiss gunsight, the gunner would calculate the range and lay the main gun onto the target, compensating for expected trajectory disturbances caused by strong crosswinds or the spinning of the round in flight. In the meantime, the loader had manhandled a long Tiger APCBC round into the gun's breech mechanism. Unless the target was at close range, most first antitank shots from a Tiger were regarded merely as an acquisition shot, expected to be more likely to land near the target rather than hit it. The gunner then corrected the range (by bracketing the range up or down in increments of 50m–200m), and/or the direction (by aiming off the target to allow for wind and round deflection in flight). With these compensations made, the crew then fired a second round. This shot – termed firing for effect – was expected to hit (and hopefully destroy) the target. German training taught crews to expect to be the first tank to hit an enemy target, rather than to be the first tank to fire in any given engagement.

In each military district the Commander of Panzer Troops controlled at least one school along with a host of Panzer training units, where the basic gunnery training took place. In addition to these basic gunnery drills, the training done at these schools covered the whole gamut of professional knowledge. The recruits received instruction and practical exercises in the science of ballistics, in the various drills associated with vehicle maintenance and effective use of the tank's communications devices. In addition, personnel received instruction in combat tactics and the tactics of Tiger tanks cooperating with other combat arms, notably the Panzergrenadiers, the antitank troops and the artillery. This all-arms capability was tested exhaustively during the final phases of specialized training, when various tank crews practiced operating as coherent tactical units – troops or companies– in a series of exacting field exercises. Personnel also participated in such exercises if they joined a Panzer regiment that was working-up, rebuilding or reequipping. Such exercises took place at armored maneuver areas, like that at Putlos, in northern Germany, and Senne, near Paderborn. Armored demonstration units were often attached to these grounds, where the experienced, high-caliber combat veterans employed in such units demonstrated the correct tactics to be employed by a Tiger unit. The caliber of these instructors is attested to by the fact that in July 1944, SS Tiger ace Michael Wittmann was offered a place at such a school; he turned the posting down on the grounds that his skills were desperately needed at the front. The importance the German military attached to this training is indicated by the fact that even in the last desperate weeks of the war, they largely resisted the powerful temptation of throwing half-trained Panzer units into the many breaches that had emerged in the German line.

The training regime of Firefly crews bore much resemblance, in a general sense, to that of Tiger crews. After basic training, those selected for service in the Royal

Armoured Corps (RAC) would join one of the its training regiments. Here recruits learned their specialist trade – commander, driver, wireless operator and loader. With a crew of just four – the Firefly had no hull machine-gun or wireless operator (the latter task was undertaken by the loader) – specialist training was by necessity modified from that for the standard Sherman. In addition, the often laborious work of general tank maintenance and field-care had to be done by just four individuals, rather than five in a Tiger. In addition to their specialist roles, RAC personnel also received instruction and training in the other roles of a tank crew. One RAC private, for example, recalled this approach at the 51st RAC Training Regiment in Yorkshire. In the morning the recruits received instruction in engine maintenance. Every other afternoon a group of three went off in an Austin Seven car to learn the art of navigating a vehicle by map and by communicating with higher headquarters; the individual who was the map reader on the first excursion would drive during the next outing, before acting as wireless operator on the third trip.

Like their German counterparts, the British Army also looked for tank commanders who could make good split-second decisions. Personally brave enough to observe out of the cupola while in action, a good commander had to respond instantly to the flash of an enemy round being fired towards his tank – supersonic tank shells would hit before the sound of it being fired was heard. The British Army also looked to recruit as drivers men who combined good mechanical skills with steely imperturbability; after all, drivers were the only members of a tank crew who could see a lot of what was happening, yet had to remain passive as the commander, gunner and loader slogged it out with the enemy. Tank drivers generally began their training on motor vehicles and progressed to out-of-date armored vehicles before commencing training in the type of tank they were to drive when they got posted to their slated operational unit. Moreover, drivers of Fireflies – like those of Tigers – had to be trained to drive with special attention to the long barrel overhang, otherwise a tank descending a bank or traversing in a narrow street could get the gun stuck. While embarrassing on maneuvers, making such an error in action could be fatal.

Towards the end of their training, the recruits found themselves receiving increasing amounts of instruction and undertaking exercises in unit tactics as well as participating in live-firing practice on the ranges. The personnel were trained in how to operate their individual vehicles as part of a wider tactical entity and introduced to the tactical realities of combat that now existed during this middle phase of the war. Operating as part of a Sherman unit was particularly difficult because the hard-pressed loader had to perform the key duty of wireless operator as well, which in part accounts for tank troop leaders preferring to operate from standard 75mm- and 76mm-gunned Shermans rather than Fireflies.

Otto Carius

One of the leading exponents of the art of effective combat with the Tiger was Lieutenant Otto Carius, who as reward for his total of over 150 enemy "kills" received the Oakleaves to the coveted Knight's Cross. Born on May 27, 1922, at Zweibrücken, Carius finally managed to voluntarily join the German Army in May 1940, having been previously turned down twice on the grounds that he was underweight. After basic training as an infantryman, Carius put his name forward for the much sought-after armored forces. Subsequently, he served as a loader in a Panzer 38(t) of the 1st Company of the 21st Panzer Regiment. Immediately on completing its training, the German High Command committed this regiment, as part of its parent formation 20th Panzer Division, to Operation *Barbarossa* — the 1941 invasion of the Soviet Union. During the *Barbarossa* campaign, the now Sergeant Carius was wounded in action, for which he was awarded the Wound Badge in Black. In late 1942 Carius underwent officer training before being posted to the 502nd Heavy Tank Battalion in April 1943. As a commander of a Tiger in the battalion's second company, Carius served during 1943–44 on the northern sector of the Eastern Front. It was during these battles, that Carius's mastery of the Tiger tank became evident. On 22 July 1944, Carius's Tiger, plus another Tiger, launched a bold counterattack on a Soviet armored spearhead that had advanced to the village of Malinava, north of Daugavpils in Latvia. Catching the enemy by surprise, the accurate fire of Carius's Tiger dispatched some 16 T-34s and one new IS heavy tank in a matter of 20 minutes. This stunning success ranks alongside Michael Wittmann's June 1944 victory at Villers Bocage as probably the most impressive Tiger action of the entire war.

In August 1944, Carius took command of the 2nd Company of the newly forming 512th Heavy Anti-Tank Battalion, which was to be equipped with the monstrous 65-ton Jagdtiger tank destroyer. By early 1945, this unit

was still in training with its new vehicles at Döllersheim near Vienna, as the Western Allies successfully advanced towards the Rhine. On March 8, 1945, the desperate German High Command felt compelled to commit the part-trained battalion to action on the Western Front near Siegburg. Despite Carius's tactical abilities, his 2nd Company could not prevent the American forces from overwhelming the flimsy German defensive screen thrown up along the eastern bank of the Rhine. Indeed, by mid-April, the battalion had been surrounded — along with most of Army Group B — in the Ruhr. Carius's unit surrendered to American forces alongside some 300,000 other German troops. Whether the mighty Jagdtiger would have withstood the Firefly's potent gun remains uncertain, as Carius's company only saw service against the Americans, who did not generally use 17pdr-equipped Shermans. After his release from American captivity, Carius went on to run a pharmacy named, rather appositely, Der Tiger Apotheke, and as of 2011 Carius was still active at the ripe old age of 88. Today he is still widely considered as one of the greatest tank commanders of the war.

Initially, the training of Firefly crews to an adequate standard proved problematic because British units only received Fireflies a few weeks prior to D-Day. Trooper Ekins of the 1st Northamptonshire Yeomanry, for example, got only one day on the firing ranges at Linney Head, during which he fired just five rounds. To enable Firefly crews to operate their tanks effectively, this training had to drill them in the effective handling of much heavier rounds within the confined Sherman turret. This training also drilled them in how to combat the effects of the back-blast and flash that erupted when the gun was fired. This led Firefly crews to practice the execution of a more complicated firing drill than was usual with the standard 75mm-gunned Sherman; this necessary drill inevitably slowed the rate of fire that could be obtained from the Firefly's gun.

First, the commander gave the order to engage a target. Next, the loader/radio operator – usually a physically strong individual – cradled the heavy and long round in both hands and edged it into the breech. The loader then tapped the commander on the legs to signal that the gun was loaded. Meanwhile, the gunner had acquired the target and the commander warned the crew that the gun was about to be fired with a "3-2-1-fire!" This gave the crew sufficient time to close their eyes, open their mouths and hold their hands over their earphones – all required to withstand the powerful shockwave and flash produced when the gun was fired. Looking out, the commander would attempt to spot the fall of the shot and size up the tactical situation before initiating the drill all over again if need be.

A Firefly crew have removed their tank's engine so that they can undertake major preventative maintenance on it. (IWM B 8893)

British and Canadian tank training also attached more importance to multi-role training than the Germans. In large part this was due to the long time – sometimes over two years – that some tank units spent in the UK training for D-Day. Thus, through a series of periodic training courses held during the war, many Allied tank crewmen became skilled in several roles. Trooper Ekins received extensive training in the roles of gunner, driver and wireless operator, although not on the Firefly. That many Allied tank crew possessed multiple professional skills meant that crew could be swiftly moved from role to role within the same tank or between tanks, to replace the inevitable casualties that occurred in combat. However, in comparison to battle-hardened German veterans, many Allied crews lacked real combat experience. Whatever the differences, British and German training ensured that when the Firefly clashed with the Tiger in Normandy, these actions were fought by crews that were as well-prepared as possible considering the circumstances.

Unit organization

During the 1944 Normandy campaign, each British/Canadian Sherman-equipped armored regiment theoretically fielded 59 Sherman tanks. The regiment fielded three squadrons (usually designated "A," "B" and "C") each with 19 Shermans, plus a Regimental HQ troop of two Shermans. Each armored squadron comprised four troops, which each fielded four Shermans, plus a headquarters troop of three Shermans. In Normandy, there were sufficient Fireflies to equip just one vehicle per standard troop of four. Thus, in theory, each full-strength squadron should have possessed four Fireflies and 13 Shermans, and thus a regiment ought to have 12 Fireflies and 47 standard Shermans. In armored regiments equipped with the Cromwell cruiser tank one Firefly also featured in each troop. A British/Canadian armored brigade fielded three regiments, and thus had a maximum strength of 36 Fireflies and around 145 other tanks. Four British armored brigades existed in Normandy as independent formations, while an additional three served in the three British armored divisions employed in Normandy. In addition, just prior to and during the Normandy campaign, each armored division's reconnaissance regiment was reequipped with Shermans (and thus Fireflies), turning into a de facto fourth armored regiment.

The precise role that the Firefly played within the troop varied to a degree between units. Many regiments gave command of a Firefly to an experienced NCO. This was the scheme employed by the 1NY in early August 1944, with all but three of its 12 Fireflies commanded by sergeants and the remainder by corporals. Fireflies tended not to be used as the troop commander's vehicle, however, because the smaller crew of four struggled to undertake the additional task associated with command of a tank troop.

Wilfred Harris

Although the British Army produced fewer tank aces during World War II than the Wehrmacht, this was not due to a lack of British service personnel who possessed the same degree of tactical acumen as the Tiger commanders such as Michael Wittmann. Rather, this dearth arose because for most of the war British tanks did not mount main armaments that outclassed the enemy. Even when a comparable gun was present – as with the Firefly – these tanks only served during the last 11 months of the war and then only in small numbers. Most German aces, moreover, served in Tiger tanks, whose massive armor provided their crews with a level of survivability not available to British crews.

Therefore it is all the more creditable that – despite these obstacles – a few British Firefly commanders demonstrated their combat prowess on the battlefields of Northwest Europe. Once such ace was Sgt Wilfred Harris. Born in 1911 in Walsall, Harris joined the 4th/7th Dragoon Guards during the interwar years. A stickler for maintaining standards, Harris's immaculate appearance earned him the sobriquet "Spit" – from that familiar British Army phrase "spit and polish." After leaving the regiment in 1935, he reenlisted on the outbreak of war. After serving with the Motor Troop of "A" Squadron during the disastrous 1940 campaign in France, Harris came through the evacuation from Dunkirk unscathed. Subsequently, he retrained as a tank commander, and by early 1944 was a much-respected veteran troop sergeant. In June 1944, the 4th/7th Dragoon Guards were committed to battle in Normandy as part of the independent 8th Armoured brigade. On the morning of 14 June, the regiment supported a successful attack launched by the 9th Durham Light Infantry (part of 50th Division) to secure the village of Lingèvres, near Tilly-sur-Seulles.

Subsequently, the three Shermans of No. 4 troop, "A" Squadron – plus Sgt Harris's attached Firefly – joined the infantry in assuming defensive positions within the village. Observing with binoculars from his Firefly's open cupola, Harris spotted two Panthers approaching Lingèvres from the east at a range of 800m. Harris's first round destroyed the lead Panther, while his second round disabled the other. Having moved to a new firing position on the other side of the village, Harris observed three Panthers approaching from the west. From this well-concealed flanking position, Harris's Firefly dispatched all three Panthers with just three rounds. In a spectacular display of shooting, Harris and his gunner, Trooper Mackillop, had destroyed no fewer than five Panthers with the same number of rounds. For this action, Harris received a richly deserved promotion to squadron quartermaster-sergeant and an award of the Distinguished Conduct Medal. After the war Harris served with the War Office police, before passing away in 1988.

During 1943–45, the principal German unit that deployed Tiger tanks was the heavy tank battalion. The German Army ultimately raised ten such battalions and the Waffen-SS three. When at full strength, these battalions each fielded 45 Tigers – organized in three companies of 14 tanks, plus three Tigers in the headquarters. Each company fielded three troops of four tanks, plus two in the company headquarters. Two other types of German unit also fielded Tigers. The three premier SS divisions and one select army division each possessed a single heavy Panzer company during some phases of the war. Finally, there were also four army heavy radio-controlled tank companies, in which Tigers operated alongside remote-controlled demolition vehicles. The German Army in the West (Westheer) only ever deployed one army and two SS Tiger battalions, plus one Tiger company, to the Normandy frontline.

Daily life in the Tiger and Firefly

Daily life for the crew of a Tiger or a Firefly was essentially similar to that of any tank crew in World War II. The tanker's world was a small one. The nucleus of his existence was the vehicle's crew – a small group of four or five individuals. With so much of the tanker's life spent in a cramped metal container, and with the shared experiences of mortal danger and adrenalin rush of combat, tank crews soon became tightly knit cohesive communities. Most individual tank commanders after all were "only" NCOs – only troop or larger unit commanders were officers. Given the hierarchical nature of military organizations a surprisingly egalitarian atmosphere often emerged within a tank. Trooper Ekins, for example, recalled that military discipline was all but non-existent in his tank. The crew called the NCO commander "Hog" and referred to one another by their first names. Many decisions taken outside of the heat of battle, Ekins recalled, were formed through democratic consensus.

That is not to say that the commander, whatever his rank, was not the center of the crew's world, for the crew's fate rested upon the speed of the commander's reactions and the correctness of his decisions. Yet, beyond this, the survival of the crew also depended on how well each crewman performed his own specialized role. No matter how quickly a keen-eyed commander spotted an enemy tank and ordered it to be engaged, the ability of the tank to hit its opponent first rested on the driving skills of the driver, the strength and dexterity of the loader and the marksmanship of the gunner; even the wireless operator played a part if supporting vehicles were required on the scene. Therefore, a particularly strong sense of functional interdependence developed within a tank crew, who were only as strong as the weakest man amongst them. Tank crews also developed a very personal relationship with their vehicle, in which they spent so much time. Crews soon grew accustomed to the nuances of the rumblings of the engine and the noise of changing gears. After all, their lives depended on such things working effectively. To many crews, therefore, the tank itself became a living thing that represented the fifth (in a Firefly) or sixth (in a Tiger) member of the crew. Often – and one might hypothesize all sorts of reasons for this – the tank was the only female in the group, identified with popular names such as "Betty" and "Mavis," or "Irma" and "Brunhilde."

Like most tankers, Firefly and Tiger crews spent much of their time out of combat, engaged in routine maintenance work. This was particularly true of the Tiger, which was a complexly engineered vehicle that needed constant attention to ensure that it functioned properly. When not at the helm, a Firefly or Tiger tank driver was invariably busy tinkering with the engine, fine-tuning its delicate mechanisms – mainly as a preventative effort. Similarly, the wireless operator would spend long hours cleaning and overhauling the mechanisms of the radio set. The other crew members would spend long hours inspecting the vehicle – checking for signs of leaks, scrutinizing the tracks for signs of damage and assessing whether the road wheels were adequately lubricated. Each day it would take at least three crew members to repeatedly ram the long cleaning rod down the gun barrel to remove any tiny impurities that had accumulated in the rifling.

The entire crew also mucked in with the tasks of checking that all their items had been stowed safely internally and externally. Everyone also helped out with the time-consuming fine art of camouflaging the tank. As Unteroffizier (Corporal) Westphal's crew in the Panzer *Lehr* Division discovered, this even involved replacing every twig that had slipped from its original position, or straightening every blade of corn squashed down by the tank's tracks, to stop it being observed by aerial reconnaissance. Though these tasks were tedious in the extreme, most crews – despite their ribald complaints – fully understood their importance; after all, a failure of just one of these systems could easily result in the death of them all. Thus many tank crews lavished the same degree of love and attention on their mechanical beast as did the cavalryman of old on his charger and the infantryman on his rifle.

In terms of combat tactics, Firefly and Tiger commanders were both trained to engage enemy antitank guns or tanks at 800–1,200m range. The powerful gun mounted on both tanks, however, could obtain a hit at distances up to and beyond 2,000m and – with some good fortune – disable or even knock out the enemy tank at such long ranges. Their training and combat experiences led Firefly and Tiger commanders to strive to attack the enemy's more vulnerable side or rear armor, whilst protecting their own less well-protected side and rear plates from enemy fire. This could be most readily achieved, if the battlefield situation was conducive, by assuming a concealed ambush position and knocking out the unsuspecting enemy

Trooper G. Aitken of Sussex, New Brunswick, Canada is seen in his Firefly during exercises in Italy. This shot shows the redesigned mantlet required to mount the 17pdr gun, with the coaxial machine gun visible. Note the unusual twin Vickers K guns mounted on the turret roof. (The Tank Museum)

from the flank or rear. One British Firefly ace, Sgt Wilfred Harris of the 4th/7th Dragoon Guards, managed to accomplish this with spectacular results near Villers Bocage on June 14.

A tank commander's ability to freely observe the battlefield was a crucial factor in determining a successful outcome to an encounter with an enemy tank. However, with the commander safely battened down in the turret with his cupola hatch closed, he could only see various parts of the battlefield – a series of compass points – through his armored visors or periscopes. Experienced Tiger and Firefly commanders like Wittmann and Gordon soon learned the value of going into action with their heads sticking up through the open turret cupola, providing a good field of vision for observation of the battlefield.

It was generally only through such a quick panoramic visual scan of the battlefield with the naked eye or with binoculars that a Tiger or Firefly commander could fulfil his doctrinal training: to be the first to get a round off in an engagement, or – more critically – to be the first to hit the enemy. To achieve this, both German and Allied tank training focused on two main things: getting the commander to appraise the situation and make a swift, correct decision, and, once an order to fire had been issued, to instil a smooth and rapid working relationship between commander, gunner and loader. Thus, good tank commanders usually went into battle with their heads exposed to enemy fire; some of them paid for their professional commitment through sustaining injuries – even death – that may have been avoided if they had sought the sanctuary of a battened-down turret. During the August 8 battle with Wittmann, for example, Sgt Gordon may have been concussed when a Tiger round apparently hit a glancing blow to his open cupola hatch, bringing the armored piece crashing agonizingly down onto his head.

While a tank commander at least had some opportunity to scan the battlefield if his cupola hatch was open, the rest of the crew enjoyed only very limited observation. The driver had the best field of vision through his relatively large driver's visor, while all the gunner saw of the outside world was through his small monocular or binocular gunnery sight. Throughout the war, the Zeiss optics fitted to German tanks, including the Tiger, were consistently excellent, and this contributed to the accuracy of the Tiger's 88mm gun, even at long ranges. The loader, of course, could see nothing of the outside world. Thus, while not the most technically challenging role in a tank, the loader needed to possess a certain personality. A loader required extreme stoicism to withstand the psychological pressures that derived from spending most of his time incarcerated in a metal box with no view of the outside world or of the enemy that threatened his life. While his survival undoubtedly depended on the rapidity and fluency

The best view of the battlefield came from an open hatch. (Bundesarchiv Bild 183-J05741/Ernst Schwahn)

with which he placed shells into the gun chamber, there was little else he could do to alter his fate, which rested in the hands of his crew mates.

A Tiger or Firefly crew, therefore, spent much of their time carrying out the often mind-numbingly tedious routine calls of duty that occurred between the few fleeting moments of intense action. These ranged from mounting guard, carrying out maintenance, observing the battlefield, refueling and taking on ammunition, to camouflaging the vehicle and undergoing refresher training. Beyond these routine duties, the tanker's world was dominated by thoughts of food, drink, sleep and – of course – women. Usually crouched behind their tank for protection from unexpected enemy fire, Tiger and Firefly crews utilized the issued gas-stove to warm up their rations. Most Firefly crews received "Compo Packs" – designed to provide sustenance for 14 men for one day. Each pack contained preprepared meal pouches, canned vegetables and fruit, cigarettes, powdered soup and 84 sheets of toilet paper. A lucky few occasionally received that famous invention, the self-heating soup can! To supplement these often tasteless offerings, Firefly crews often went "foraging" to "appropriate" or barter for local supplies: eggs, poultry, cheese and alcohol. Cigarettes and chocolate were the main currency of the barter system, but almost anything could be – and was – used in this unofficial world of commercial exchange.

Many a crewman awoke in the morning with a sore head after sampling the potent local Normandy farm cider. A warm cup of tea, of course, was crucial to the continued effectiveness of Firefly crews. Most found the issued "Compo" tea – premixed with powdered milk and sugar – extremely unpalatable. Much experimentation took place with additives and/or heating procedures to get the least awful brew from this unpleasant concoction. Luckily, in Normandy Firefly crews encountered hundreds of cows abandoned by their owners that provided much-welcomed fresh milk.

Whether the day had involved vicious and deadly action, or routine chores, by evening the thoughts of a Tiger or Firefly crew increasingly turned to the big question – getting some decent sleep. British armored regiments generally followed doctrine by withdrawing behind the front to leaguer for the night in an all-round defensive position. Designated crews took it in turns to remain on full alert, fully dressed in their tanks, whilst their comrades settled down to sleep on a rota basis. Some German units leaguered in much the same way, while others remained in the front – particularly when on the defensive – to support the infantrymen. Whatever the exact arrangement, sleep for a tanker could only be obtained after digging the essential foxhole or trench. Some crews dug their shelters under the tank to get extra protection, while others – fearful of the tank sinking slowly into the ground to crush them – dug theirs adjacent to their vehicle. Few got much sleep, disturbed as they were by the bustle of crews going on or returning from sentry duty, by harassing

A Tiger refuels. Note the
crewman in the background
taking the opportunity to
rearm the tank.
(Bundesarchiv Bild
146-1978-107-06)

enemy artillery fire, enemy aircraft flying overhead, or just the plethora of flies and
insects that assailed them during those short and warm Normandy summer nights.
Long hours of tedious maintenance and camouflaging, of sleepless anxiety-filled
nights, were periodically punctuated by a few brief and emotion-laden minutes of
action-packed encounters with enemy armor.

BATTLEGROUND: NORMANDY 1944

During spring 1944, the forces of General Bernard Montgomery's British 21st Army Group trained relentlessly for the Allied D-Day landings on the coast of German-occupied Normandy, which were finally initiated on June 6. Both sides knew that the outcome of these landings – and the ensuing battle for Normandy – held monumental significance for the course of the war. It was not surprising, therefore, that during this period the first Sherman Fireflies to be completed were rushed to the British and Canadian armored units then finalizing their preparations for D-Day. These units, which included the 1st Northamptonshire Yeomanry (1NY), held high hopes that the Firefly would enable them to defeat the enemy's most potent tanks, including the Tiger. Senior German commanders in turn held equally high expectations for what the Tiger would contribute to the imminent struggle, hoping that it would spearhead the defensive and the counteroffensive actions required to halt and even reverse the Allied invasion. This was a particularly tall order, as the Westheer typically deployed fewer than 80 operational Tigers. Nevertheless, battlefield events within a week of the landings showed that these grandiose German expectations were not unrealistic. On June 13, in a famous incident, a few Tigers led by Michael Wittmann mauled the British armored brigade that had thrust audaciously south to Villers Bocage.

But such isolated examples of successful German counterattacks were not sufficient to stop the gradual expansion of the Allied beachhead in Normandy. However, the Tiger's defensive prowess did help the Germans slow the Allied advance to a crawl, frustrating Montgomery's plan to create a sizable lodgement area bordered by the Loire and Seine rivers by early September. By mid-July the Tiger's capabilities had helped turn the Normandy campaign into a bloody attritional war of matériel. These hard-fought battles again demonstrated the vulnerability of the Sherman (and thus the Firefly) to German tank fire, as well as the Tiger's virtual invulnerability to 75mm-gunned Sherman fire. On July 18, during Operation *Goodwood*, for example, 11th Armoured Division lost 21 of its 34 Fireflies to enemy tank and antitank fire in just one day. Despite such setbacks, on numerous occasions

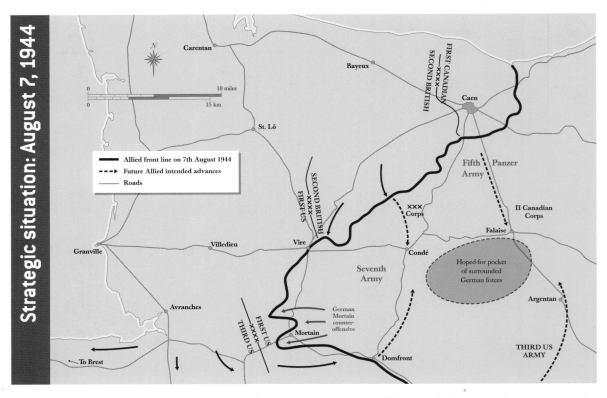

Strategic situation: August 7, 1944

Sherman and Firefly crews bravely engaged Tigers, with many of them paying the ultimate price for their gallantry. An unofficial dictum soon sprang up in British armored units – if a Tiger appeared, send out a troop of four Shermans (with its single Firefly) to destroy the Panzer, and expect only one to come home. Understandably, after such painful combat experiences some Allied tank crews became so concerned about the Tiger's capabilities that "Tiger-phobia" became evident. One brigadier recorded an extreme manifestation of this phobia, when a solitary German Tiger "fired for one hour … [and] then drove off unmolested … [because] not one tank went out to engage it."

Despite the disproportionate damage done by the few Tigers deployed in Normandy, the combination of Allied numerical superiority, offensive determination and the Firefly's lethal gun gradually wore down the Westheer's powers of resistance while Allied tank crews' confidence increased. For the bitter armored battles waged in Normandy showed that the Firefly's potent 17pdr gun could indeed take out even the much-feared Tiger. During a 96-hour period of the late-June *Epsom* offensive, British 11th Armoured Division Fireflies knocked out or disabled five Tigers in a series of bitter encounters. Aided by the Firefly's firepower, the repeated Allied attacks finally bore fruit in late July when LtGen Bradley's First US Army Cobra offensive broke through the German front around St-Lô. Just prior to this Montgomery's *Goodwood* offensive had advanced the Anglo-Canadian front to the Bourguébus Ridge, from where the *Totalize* offensive commenced on August 7–8. Between July 31 and August 6, American forces – having passed the bottom corner of the Cotentin peninsula and with the German line shattered – raced west into Brittany, south towards the Loire and east towards the Seine.

Hitler now blundered strategically by ordering the Westheer to counterattack the narrow corridor located behind the American breakout. Consequently, during 6–7 August, German armor attacked west towards Mortain. This ill-advised attack predictably failed and in so doing sucked German forces further west, pulling them deeper into a large encirclement that was beginning to form in the Mortain–Argentan area. For by August 8 – by which time *Totalize* had commenced – American forces had raced southeast to capture Le Mans, deep into the German rear. Meanwhile, the western part of the Allied front, manned by Montgomery's two Anglo-Canadian armies, had remained relatively static, from the coast to the Bourguébus Ridge and thence southwest to Vire, where the American sector began. By August 8, therefore, it now seemed possible that if the infant *Totalize* offensive could secure Falaise, its forces might then be able to link up around Argentan with the northwesterly

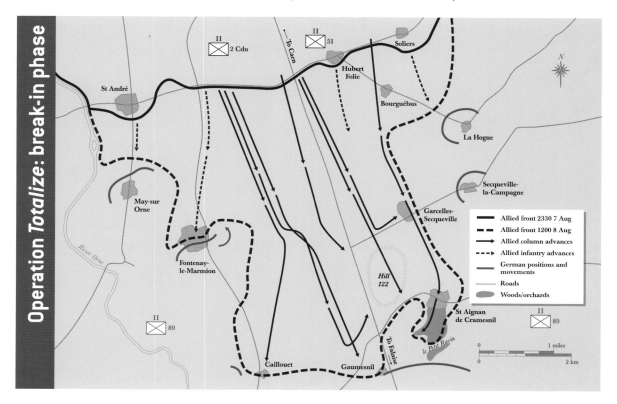

American advance beyond Le Mans. In so doing, the Allies would have encircled substantial German forces in a giant pocket.

Operation *Totalize*

LtGen Guy Simonds's II Canadian Corps' *Totalize* offensive aimed to advance 24km south from the Bourguébus Ridge to secure the high ground that dominated the town of Falaise. The offensive had originally been intended to aid the advance of British forces located further west. By the time it was launched on the night of August 7–8, however, *Totalize* had acquired greater strategic significance, as the precursor to the Allies being able to close the Falaise pocket, which had developed in the Falaise–Argentan area. First Canadian Army commander General Crerar had stated his expectation that *Totalize* would play a pivotal role in the campaign, by making "the 8th August 1944 an even blacker day for the German Armies than is recorded against that same date twenty-six years ago" – the World War I battle at Amiens.

Simonds's five divisions and two independent brigades would attack the defenses manned by the 89th Infantry Division (part of I SS Panzer Corps), while the 12th SS Panzer Division *Hitlerjugend* held reserve positions further south. During the offensive's first phase, two infantry divisions would attack south astride the main Caen–Falaise road in an initial surprise night break-in operation, aided by night-time heavy bombers. Seven mobile columns – formed of tanks and infantry embussed in armored vehicles – would spearhead the attack by audaciously infiltrating between the forward defensive localities (FDLs) to seize objectives deep in the German rear. Simultaneously, infantry would attack the FDLs the columns had bypassed.

Aided by surprise, during the night of August 7–8 this first phase of *Totalize* went extremely well. By mid-morning on the 8th, Simonds's forces had secured a 6km-deep rupture of the German front. According to the commander of *Hitlerjugend* – SS-Oberführer (Senior Colonel) Kurt Meyer – this advance had smashed the 89th Division, thus creating a yawning gap in the German front that remained undefended and unoccupied. Meyer commanded a unique German division. The *Hitlerjugend* had been raised during spring 1943 as part of Germany's general mobilization towards total war that followed the disaster at Stalingrad. The elite division mainly comprised 16- and 17-year-olds from the Hitler Youth movement who, despite being too young to join the armed forces, had nevertheless volunteered to enlist in this unique SS division. Many fought with great determination in Normandy, but the division's battlefield record was stained by the war crimes its personnel committed in murdering dozens of Allied prisoners of war.

During the late morning of August 8, Simonds's offensive began its second phase – the daytime break-in operation directed against the enemy's reserve defense line located between Bretteville and St-Sylvain. His two reserve armored divisions moved south of Caen, ready to move up to the front to spearhead this assault. Erroneously believing this second German position to be a formidable one, Simonds had arranged that a second bombing strike should smash the enemy line shortly after noon. That morning 681 American B-17 Flying Fortresses droned their way south from England towards the Falaise plain, striking six German targets between 1226 and 1355hrs. The late morning of August 8 thus witnessed a largely unavoidable lull in the Allied advance as Simonds's forces readied themselves for the second phase while waiting for the bombers to arrive. Perhaps rather unfairly, Kurt Meyer lambasted the German tactics during this period since they "transferred the initiative from … leading combat elements to timetable acrobats [back] at Headquarters." Unfortunately for the Allies, during this lull the enemy began recovering from the shock inflicted upon them by

The initial night-time break-in phase of Operation *Totalize* secured significant success. Here a Sherman has been knocked out during the attack that secured May-sur-Orne on the afternoon of August 8. (Ken Bell/PA-131352)

the successful night attack. Orchestrated by Meyer, the Germans now launched countermeasures against the Allied penetration.

Around 1135hrs that morning, Meyer was being driven north to Cintheaux when he encountered German infantrymen retreating south in disorder. Meyer stood "alone in the middle of the road … armed with just a carbine" and through much bravado rallied the fleeing troops. Subsequently, Meyer met up with SS-Sturmbannführer (Major) Hans Waldmüller and the two officers drove up onto the gentle rise situated northeast of Gaumesnil to reconnoitre the front. Shortly before noon, from the vantage point of a barn, the two officers observed the spearheads of Simonds's two armored divisions formed up behind the front, apparently ready to strike south. The two officers were hardened veterans, but this display of Allied offensive strength nevertheless took their breath away.

Meyer knew that if this armor struck south it would smash through the as-yet only thinly held German reserve line; if this transpired, "nothing could have prevented the Canadians from taking Falaise that evening." Meyer knew instinctively what such a crisis demanded – whatever meager forces were immediately available to him must act immediately to prevent the Allied armor thrusting south. The odds could not have been higher, for with Falaise lost, an entire German army might well be subsequently encircled in the Domfront–Falaise–Argentan area. After such a disaster, the German defense of Normandy would collapse and the entire course of the war could be decided. Meyer ordered that all *Hitlerjugend* units in the vicinity should counterattack north at 1230hrs. While this scratch force was woefully weak, it did nonetheless contain four or five of Wittmann's powerful Tigers, and it was upon these tanks that Meyer placed most of his slim hopes for success.

Would the awesome firepower and massive armor of a handful of Wittmann's Tigers prove sufficient to defy the massive odds stacked against them? Could Wittmann's desperate charge north towards the Allied lines prevent the seemingly imminent collapse of the German front north of Falaise? The scene was set for a classic clash of Fireflies vs Tigers.

THE ACTION

As *Hitlerjugend* commander Kurt Meyer and his subordinate Hans Waldmüller observed the battlefield from their vantage point near Gaumesnil, shortly before noon on August 8, 1944, they would have seen how Simonds's *Totalize* offensive had smashed in the German front during the previous night and his reserve armor was prepared to move forward that morning. Simonds's forces were ready to strike south as soon as the approaching strategic bombers had crushed the reserve German defense line. The situation was critical – if the Allied armor struck south it would rupture the still thinly manned German reserve position and charge south to capture Falaise. Simonds's forces might subsequently thrust south to link up with the northwesterly advance of American forces from Argentan, enveloping an entire German Army in what would become known as the Falaise Pocket. Meyer knew he had but one choice – to throw whatever meager forces he had in the vicinity into a desperate, probably suicidal, charge north into the Allied lines. Despite facing enormous odds, Meyer hoped that through the sacrifice of his forces, he might buy some precious time to enable other German units to move north and shore up the largely unmanned second defensive line. And so at around noon, Meyer ordered his forces to initiate an improvized counterstrike against the Allied line at St-Aignan-de-Cramesnil, a riposte he demanded commence in just 30 minutes' time.

Unfortunately for Meyer, he had few forces available in the vicinity to initiate this audacious impromptu response. Operating under Waldmüller's command, this scratch force was a composite of several units. The infantry component comprised 500 Panzergrenadiers from I Battalion, SS Regiment 25. The stiffening element for this force came from 20 tanks (mostly Panzer IVs) from SS Panzer Regiment 12. The vanguard of the counterstrike, however, was formed from four or five (one source suggests seven) Tigers from SS-Hauptsturmführer Michael Wittmann's 2nd Company, 101st SS Heavy Tank Battalion. Meyer placed most of his hopes that this desperate mission might achieve success through the lethal firepower and proven battlefield survivability of these few Tigers. Although the evidence concerning the composition of this Tiger force is contradictory, it is certain that most of the tanks were from

Senior *Hitlerjugend* officers discuss the battlefield situation on June 9, 1944; from right to left: the then commander of SS Panzergrenadier Regiment 25, Kurt Meyer; the then divisional commander Fritz Witt; and the leader of the division's Panzer regiment, Max Wünnsche. When Witt was killed by Allied naval gunfire on June 12, Meyer took command of the *Hitlerjugend* and directed the fanatical resistance the division offered during the Normandy campaign. A ruthless commander, Meyer was later convicted by an Allied military court of war crimes, after evidence was discovered that indicated that *Hitlerjugend* personnel had executed as many as 155 Canadian prisoners of war during early June 1944. (Bundesarchiv Bild 146-1988-028-25A)

Wittmann's own troop. However, a mass of Allied units faced this weak German strike force. In the La Jalousie–St-Aignan sector the Allies deployed three armored regiments and four infantry battalions, not to mention the spearhead of two armored divisions assembling behind them. Although only a small proportion of these tanks could bring their fire to bear on Wittmann's Tigers, his armored column was clearly about to charge north into an inferno of Allied tank, antitank and artillery defensive fire.

At the moment when Meyer ordered Waldmüller to initiate this ad hoc counterattack, Wittmann was in his Tiger, alongside three others, located in the Les Jardinets area, 600m east-southeast of Meyer's Gaumesnil vantage point. One of the major benefits to the Germans in their defensive role was their familiarity with the territory. Carefully camouflaged, the drivers had hidden their Tigers behind by a typical tall Normandy tree-hedge line; the row of low bushes running along the other side of this narrow dirt lane added to this concealment. At around 1205hrs, Wittmann heard that Meyer had urgently summoned him to a briefing at nearby Cintheaux. Wittmann's driver steered Tiger 007 west down country lanes for a few minutes to arrive at the village. Jumping down from his turret, Wittmann found Meyer and Waldmüller settling the final details of the counterstrike, outlining the part Wittman's Tigers would play in the action.

> " Wittmann's gunner:
> "They are behaving as if they'd won the war already."
> Michael Wittmann:
> "We're going to prove them wrong." "
>
> (Villers Bocage, Normandy, June 13, 1944)

Michael Wittmann

Born a farmer's son on April 22, 1914, Michael Wittmann rose to become one of Germany's leading Tiger tank aces. After service in the German Army as a private during 1934–36, Wittmann enlisted in the elite *Leibstandarte SS Adolf Hitler*. After service in the 1939 Polish campaign, Wittmann led a StuG III assault gun platoon during the spring 1940 Balkan war. Next, he participated in the invasion of the Soviet Union, during which he received the Iron Cross First Class and promotion to SS-Oberscharführer (Sergeant) for his outstanding performance as a destroyer of Soviet tanks. After officer training, SS-Untersturmführer (Second Lieutenant) Wittmann rejoined the *Leibstandarte* in December 1942. While serving with the division's Tiger-equipped 13th Heavy Company, he again performed well during the July 1943 battle of Kursk, thanks to his careful planning of actions and the "unshakable calm" he maintained during combat. This company then formed the nucleus of the newly raised 101st SS Heavy Tank Battalion, with which Wittmann continued to serve until his death on August 8, 1944. During January 1944, the newly promoted SS-Obersturmführer (Lieutenant) Wittmann received the Knight's Cross, and then the Oakleaves to this coveted award, for his tally of over 90 enemy kills. By the time he assumed command of the 101st Battalion's 2nd Company in March, Wittmann had also married Hildegard Burmester. Goebbels' propaganda machine now seized upon Wittmann's exploits and transformed this modest yet determined officer into a national hero.

On 13 June 1944, Wittmann joined combat in Normandy with the 101st Battalion. That day his Tigers inflicted a bloody repulse on the British 7th Armoured Division at Villers Bocage. Wittmann's Tiger was on reconnaissance when he observed the spearhead tanks of the British 22nd Armoured Brigade advancing through the hazy daylight near Villers Bocage. Wittmann's Tiger moved west behind the column while four other Tigers moved east to attack its spearhead.

Catching the column by surprise, the Tigers poured fire into it, leaving around 20 enemy vehicles burning furiously.

So far the Tigers had triumphed, but the second half of the action did not go as well for them. By the time that Wittmann, possibly supported by two other Tigers, headed west into Villers Bocage, the 22nd Brigade had established an effective defensive position. One Sherman Firefly, three Churchill tanks and a 6pdr antitank gun had deployed in the town's side streets, ready to ambush the Tigers with close-range fire against their more vulnerable side armor. As the Panzers moved through the main street, the antitank gun engaged and disabled Wittmann's Tiger, forcing the crew to flee on foot. Ultimately that day the Germans lost at least four Tigers in the actions that raged all day around Villers Bocage, while the Allies lost at least ten tanks and around 20 other vehicles. With this feat behind him, Wittmann served in the bitter defensive stands the Germans enacted in and around Caen during July. Yet on August 8 – by which time the now SS-Hauptsturmführer (Captain) Wittmann had claimed 139 combat kills – the Panzer ace met a warrior's end during a desperate counterattack launched against numerically superior Allied forces.

According to Meyer, a dramatic event then occurred that transformed the timeframe for the intended attack. The three SS officers observed a solitary Allied heavy bomber fly over Cintheaux, sending out colored flares. This was obviously an Allied Pathfinder designating the aim points for an impending strategic bombing strike. Given what Meyer already knew about Allied Pathfinder tactics from the earlier Normandy battles, he knew that the heavy bombers were already less than ten minutes away from his current location. It was obvious to all that the Allied armor assembling behind the current frontline had not commenced its assault south because they were waiting for heavy bombers to unleash a rain of destruction on the German forces below.

This realization merely confirmed Meyer's recent decision to strike north. If his forces remained where they currently were, they would be obliterated by hundreds of tons of high explosive. No doubt, as his dazed forces struggled to recover from this onslaught, the massed Allied armored formations would surge south to overwhelm them. The second German line would swiftly collapse and there would be nothing to stop an Allied advance to Falaise and beyond; the collapse of the already reeling German front in Normandy might ensue. Meyer again ordered them to launch the attack – but now to do so immediately. Despite the appalling odds facing his mission, Wittmann climbed into his tank and headed east back to his company's positions in Les Jardinets. Within minutes, his force of four Tigers had shaken off their camouflage and had begun to advance north across the open fields towards the Allied lines. A few hundred meters further east, a fifth Tiger (and possibly two others) also began to rumble north. Over the ensuing hour Wittmann and his Tigers bravely attempted to wrest an improbable victory from the jaws of defeat.

Advance to St-Aignan

One of the Allied units deployed in the La Jalousie–St-Aignan sector would play a key role in defeating Wittmann's riposte. The 1NY was a Sherman-equipped armored regiment in the independent British 33rd Armoured Brigade. Led by Lt Col D. Forster, the regiment fielded three squadrons – "A," "B" and "C," plus the regimental headquarters. Most of the regiment's tanks bore distinctive names; "A" Squadron's were named after Soviet towns, "B" Squadron's after American states, and "C" Squadron's after Northamptonshire villages. The regiment's authorized strength was 59 Shermans, including 12 Fireflies.

As part of the "Left British column," which also comprised the infantry of the 1st Black Watch (1BW), the 1NY had advanced 6km to St-Aignan during the early hours of August 8. Having assembled in a formation 50 vehicles deep by four

1NY tank crews complete preparations for the forthcoming *Totalize* offensive near Cormelles on August 7. In the foreground is a Sherman (Hybrid) while behind this the long barrel of the second tank identifies it as a Firefly. (IWM B 8805)

vehicles wide, the column's advance commenced around midnight. At 0130hrs, No. 2 Troop, "A" Squadron, which had detached from the rest of the column, stumbled upon four well-camouflaged enemy self-propelled guns (SPGs) and a fierce action ensued that demonstrated the Firefly's killing power. Four rounds hit Lt Jones's lead Sherman No. 5 "Brest-Litovsk"; one tore off the external blanket bin, another penetrated to lodge in the vehicle's transmission gear, the third gouged a groove out of the frontal armor before bouncing away, and the fourth smashed through to the engine. With the tank on fire, Sgt Burnett's IC (Hybrid) Firefly No. 8 "Balaclava" engaged the three SPGs. The Firefly dispatched two of them with three rounds, but not before the third SPG had knocked out the troop's two remaining standard Shermans. While the sole survivor – Burnett's Firefly – caught up with the column, the three dismounted crews endured the rest of the night pinned to the ground by machine gun fire. Lt Jones had previously written to his mother telling her not to worry, but during this ordeal he said out loud "… for goodness sake Mother start worrying now!"

Subsequently, the column rumbled on until, at 0325hrs, it reached a hedge situated north of its objective, St-Aignan. Accompanied by artillery fire, two Sherman squadrons pushed through gaps in the hedge and engaged the enemy, while the now-dismounted infantry stormed the village. After an hour-long battle, the column captured St-Aignan and began establishing firm defensive positions around it. As part of this process, "A" Squadron assumed defensive positions in the orchards located southwest of St-Aignan at Delle de la Roque. At this stage the regiment fielded 54 operational Shermans, including the 12 Fireflies, having lost four standard Shermans during the night advance; a fifth tank – Sgt Duff's No. 56 "Lamport" – ended up with the 144th RAC at Cramesnil.

Wittmann's death charge

At around 1220hrs, therefore, Wittmann's troop of four Tigers began to advance north from Les Jardinets. That day, Wittmann was not in his usual vehicle, Tiger 205, which was being repaired. Instead, he was using battalion commander Heinz von Westernhagen's command Tiger, number 007. Apart from Tiger 007, it is probable that the column comprised Ihrion's Tiger 314, Dollinger's 008, and Blase's tank – the exact composition of and the order within this formation remains unclear. The tanks rumbled north-northwest, one behind the other, on an axis parallel to, but around 150m east of, the main Caen–Falaise road. That Wittmann's column was in line ahead suggests that he expected enemy fire from the north around Hill 122. This deployment, however, left the Tigers' more vulnerable flanks exposed to fire from the northeast – from the orchards of Delle de la Roque, southwest of St-Aignan. Wittmann remained unaware that "A" Squadron, 1NY, was positioned in these woods.

Both Meyer and his medical officer, SS-Hauptsturmführer Dr Wolfgang Rabe, observed the initial stages of Wittmann's advance. The Tigers rumbled north through a hail of Allied defensive artillery fire. The tanks only stopped periodically in shallow gullies to fire at long range towards the northwest, engaging Sherbrooke Fusilier tanks located west of the main road. At a range of 1,800m, the Tigers knocked out several Shermans, whereas at this distance only the Canadian regiment's few Fireflies stood a slim chance of destroying the Tigers. Having observed the first phase of Wittmann's charge from the northern fringes of Cintheaux, Meyer's attention was now diverted to the northern horizon. Suddenly, the sky to the north began to darken as what seemed to be an endless stream of Allied bombers droned south towards the village. Meyer and the grenadiers dug in around him were rendered speechless by this display of vast Allied air power. "What an honour," remarked one, "Churchill is sending a bomber for each of us!" The SS grenadiers raced across the open fields located north of the village to escape the impending onslaught. Just in time, they witnessed the bombers pass over them and begin dropping their bombs onto the village behind them.

Deployed behind the cover provided by the tall tree-lined hedge that marked the southern border of the Delle de la Roque orchards, the four tanks of "A" Squadron's No. 3 Troop held the westernmost part of the 1NY defensive position. Led by

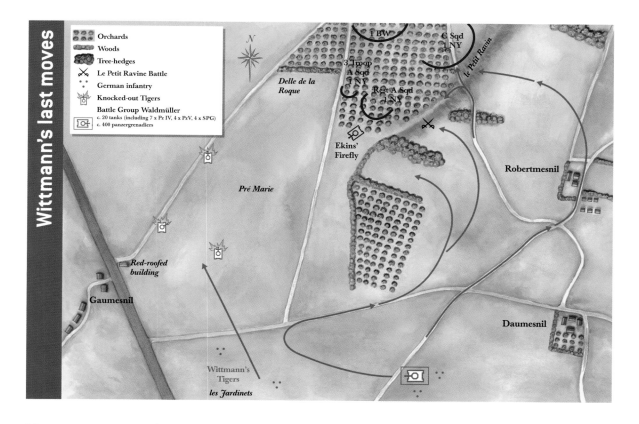

Lieutenant James in Tank No. 9, a standard Sherman, the troop also deployed two more standard Shermans – Sgt Eley's No. 10 "Vladivostock" and Cpl Hillaby's No. 11. The troop's last and most potent asset was Sgt Gordon's VC Firefly No. 12, according to some sources, named "Velikye Luki." Straining to see through the gaps in the tree-hedge, the Troop's observers peered south across the open ground towards the Les Jardinets area. Three Tigers were heading north-northeast in line ahead, on an axis just east of the main road. The range was 1,200m. Gordon reported this sighting via radio to Captain Boardman, the squadron second-in-command. Boardman claims that he then ordered Gordon to hold his fire until he could get there to direct the action. Why the captain did not instruct the squadron's three other Fireflies to reinforce Gordon's tank remains a mystery. Moving west through the orchard in his Sherman I, No. 18 "Omsk," Boardman soon arrived at the No. 3 Troop position. By this time rather random German artillery and mortar fire was landing in the general area of the orchard.

The British observed the advancing Tigers for a couple of minutes. The enemy seemed to be unaware of the British tanks' presence, as the Tigers still remained deployed in line ahead on a bearing north-northeast, which exposed their relatively less formidable side armor to No. 3 Troop's tanks. Convinced that they were undetected, the Troop calmly allowed the Tigers to advance until the range had closed to 800m, by which time the tanks had neared the vicinity of the isolated red-roofed building adjacent to the main road. At this range, Gordon's Firefly stood a good chance of penetrating the Tiger's side armor, although the other Shermans still stood virtually no chance at all. The time was now 1239hrs. According to Gordon's gunner, Trooper Joe Ekins, the sergeant now told the other Shermans to stay under cover while he courageously attempted to deal with the Tigers.

Gordon ordered his driver to move the Firefly forward a few meters to a position just in front of (that is, south of) the orchard's southern edge to obtain a better field of fire. Gordon remained with his head poking through the open commander's cupola during the ensuing brief action. Gordon selected his target – the rear Tiger of the three, as was normal practice; such a tactic hoped to exploit the fact that the leading tanks might not even know that their rear colleague had been hit. The reason why British accounts only mention three Tigers, when Wittmann's column may well have had four or five, remains unclear. Some of the Tigers may have dropped out of the column and were heading north-northeast on an axis to the left (west) of the others and may even have been obscured from view. The time was now 1240hrs. Looking through his sight, gunner Ekins was now very frightened because he believed that there "was no way" a solitary Firefly could take on three Tigers and survive. With "but one thought in my mind – to get the bastard before he gets you" – Ekins aimed the gun and fired two armor-piercing rounds at the rear Tiger. Despite having only fired six 17pdr rounds before, Ekins nevertheless had "a knack" at gunnery, and both rounds seemingly hit the target; within seconds, the Tiger was burning. Other Allied tanks, however, were also engaging the Tigers at this time. The Canadian Fireflies of the Sherbrooke Fusiliers were firing from their positions west of the main road at a range of 1,100m. Similarly, 144th RAC Fireflies, located on Hill 122, were engaging Tigers at a range of 1,300m. While it is not impossible that this longer-range fire hit and penetrated the Tiger at precisely the same as Ekins engaged it, the most likely explanation is that Ekins's rounds penetrated the tank and caused it to burn.

As soon as the Firefly had fired its second shot, Gordon followed doctrine by ordering the driver to reverse back into the cover of the orchard. As they did so, the second Tiger traversed its gun right towards the Firefly. Looking through his sight, Ekins recalled that the Tiger's 88mm gun "looked as big as a battleship" as it swung to face him. The Tiger fired a round at the Firefly as it began to reverse and then a further two rounds as the tank entered the concealment of the apple orchard. As the third round passed close by the tank, the flap of the open commander's cupola came crashing down onto Gordon's head, knocking him half-senseless. It is not clear if this was caused by the flap knocking into a tree-branch or because the Tiger's round had

actually hit it a glancing blow. The dazed Gordon clambered uneasily down from his tank and was immediately wounded by shrapnel, as the German artillery and mortar fire moved closer to the tree-hedge. All Ekins knew of this incident was that suddenly there was no commander in his tank!

Next, the commander of No. 3 Troop – Lt James – bravely jumped out of his tank and raced across to take command of the Firefly. James ordered the driver to move the tank to a new firing position. The tank reached this new position just before 1247hrs, according to the war diary entry. Moving out from cover, James now ordered Ekins to engage the second Tiger – the one that had fired at the Firefly. At 1247hrs Ekins fired one shot at the second tank, which hit it, causing it to explode in a ball of flame. As the tank Wittmann was believed to be in – command Tiger 007 – was found with its turret blown off, and German eyewitness reports recorded only one exploding tank, it seems likely that this was the precise moment at which Wittmann's prolific career was terminated. Next, Gordon's driver again reversed the Firefly back into the cover of the orchard. This success left intact just the lead Tiger and the mystery fourth and fifth Tigers, which the British accounts of the battle seem to have missed altogether.

At this juncture, it is claimed that some standard Shermans advanced south out of the woods to engage the remaining Tigers at such close range that they stood some chance of damaging them, but this inadvertently hampered the fire delivered by Ekins's Firefly, which had reemerged out of the orchard. The ensuing hail of

One of Wittman's Tigers knocked out on June 13, 1944, at Villers Bocage, photographed on August 5, 1944, after the Allies had captured the town. The ruined state of the place was typical of many Normandy towns liberated after D-Day. (IWM B 8635)

Tiger: in the gunsights

August 8, 1944, 1247hrs
On receipt of orders from the tank commander, Lieutenant James, the Firefly's gunner – Trooper Ekins – begins to lay the 17pdr gun on the target, Wittmann's Tiger.

+ 20 seconds
With the Tiger in the crosshairs, Ekins calculates the range – around 800m and the loader places an AP round in the breech. As James counts down "3 – 2 – 1 – fire!" the crew place their hands over their ears, open their mouths and close their eyes – all in preparation for the violent back blast.

75mm Sherman fire apparently fell upon the lead enemy tank. While these rounds failed to penetrate the tank's thick armor, the hail of fire caused the driver to veer off erratically to the west, seemingly out of control. According to the regimental historian this tank "was in a panic, milling around wondering how he could escape." Captain Boardman then claims that he engaged the veering Tiger with a 75mm armor-piercing round that caused it to stop. Ekins, however, states that "it was still moving when I hit him." Ekins fired two shots that caused the Tiger to burst into flames; from this inferno none of the crew escaped. The time was 1252hrs. The final successes of this action also went to the Firefly. Just eight minutes later, at 1300hrs, Sgt Finney's Firefly – Tank No. 4 "Orenburg" – spotted two Panzer IVs moving to the west side of the main road at the prodigious range of 1,645m. In a brilliant piece of shooting, gunner Trooper Crittenden fired two shots and brewed up both Panzers.

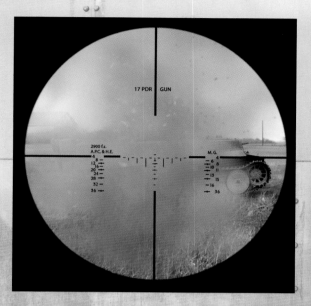

+ 30 seconds
The gun is fired and within a second the round has smashed into the Tiger. For a few seconds, however, this fact remains unknown to the Firefly crew, as they are momentarily blinded by the flash and back blast.

+ 50 seconds
Just a few seconds later, and the crews have adjusted to the now subsided blast. Looking through his gunsight, Ekins can see smoke rising from the Tiger. A few more seconds pass and then Ekins sees the Tiger erupt as its ammunition explodes.

Wittmann's death charge had been a remarkable action. As Ekins well knew, the chances of a solitary Firefly surviving a clash not with just one but with at least three (and possibly five) Tigers were extraordinarily slim. Yet in the space of just 12 minutes, Gordon's Firefly had dispatched three Tigers with just five rounds. In return, not only did the Tigers not even knock out a single enemy tank, but it seems as if not one of the rounds they fired hit its target. This astounding feat was one of the finest tank-versus-tank engagements seen during the entire Northwest Europe campaign. It seems odd, therefore, that none of his peers congratulated Ekins for this feat, even though the gunner maintains that he never expected it anyway. The accomplishment also deserves more recognition than the laconic note penned in the regiment's war diary: "Three Tigers in twelve minutes is not bad business." The combination of three factors – the regiment's use of terrain to ambush the Tigers, Gordon's "knack" at gunnery and the Firefly's awesome gun had turned the dispatching of one of Germany's finest aces from an almost impossible task into something "rather like Practice No. 5 on the ranges at Linney Head."

What then was Wittmann's fate? Dr Rabe had observed this short but bloody battle from the western side of the main road. He recalled that the four or five Tigers involved had come under enemy fire and that several had gone up in flames. He attempted to get closer to see if any of the crews had survived, but could not because of enemy fire. After waiting for two hours, not a single crew member had emerged from the battlefield, and so Rabe withdrew, assuming that all had been killed. Wittmann was officially listed as missing in action.

The battle for Le Petit Ravin

Shortly afterwards, a few hundred metres further east, another fierce tank-versus-tank action occurred. Although there were no Tigers involved, this action again attested to the increasingly value that the British could place on the potent Firefly. Around 1255hrs, "A" Squadron spotted 20 German tanks – mostly Panzer IVs but with some Panthers too – heading west across Les Jardinets towards the main road at a range of 1,200m. The tanks moved along the various tree-hedges in the area, which largely obscured them. Ekins fired one round at the leading tank. In another piece of superb marksmanship, the round hit, causing the tank to burst into flames. With other Shermans joining in, the Panzers scuttled into cover. Some then used the tree-hedges around Daumesnil to move north unobserved until they reached the eastern end of Le Petit Ravin, a steep-sided defile located south of St-Aignan. Some Panzers then infiltrated west along this narrow gully, while others advanced to the south of it, to attack elements of "A" and "C" Squadrons.

A fierce and confused battle now raged in and around the gully. Early on, Ekins's Firefly took a hit from a Panzer. Knowing the Sherman's tendency to burn, the crew swiftly baled out. A terrified Ekins, with fire erupting all around him, ran northwards towards the sanctuary of St-Aignan. Subsequently, a Panzer IV took up a well-concealed position in the ravine, with only its turret visible to the British, and quickly dispatched three Shermans. Major Skelton, the "A" Squadron commander, instructed Sgt Moralee's Firefly No. 16 "Kursk" to take out the troublesome tank by flanking round to the left. As Moralee attempted to locate the well-hidden Panzer, the latter fired twice and hit "Kursk," causing it to burn. Skelton angrily snarled, "we are not going to let this bastard pick off the Squadron one by one," and ordered Sgt Finney's Firefly No. 4 "Orenburg" to join him in a pincer movement. The Firefly bravely drew the Panzer's fire, being brewed up in the process, which allowed Skelton's No. 17 "Tomsk" to approach the German tank unnoticed from the other side and knock it out with a single close-range shot. The normally imperturbable Skelton, however, was so enraged by the casualties inflicted on his crews by the Panzer that he then ordered his gunner to pour a further six rounds into the stricken vehicle. This onslaught of hot metal obliterated both the tank and its entire crew.

A little later, the Panzer IV driven by SS-Sturmmann (Junior Corporal) Helmut Wiese, from the 5th Company, II Battalion, SS Panzer Regiment 12, was in the thick of the action near the gully. As they approached the British positions, Wiese described how the crew's nerves were stretched to breaking point as they experienced the violent rattle of British machine gun and rifle fire striking the tank. Spotting 1BW infantry moving an antitank gun into position in a nearby copse, the tank commander ordered the driver to reverse the tank at full speed, while the gunner unleashed several HE rounds towards the wood. Suddenly, an antitank round smashed into the tank, with a "bang as if a soda pop bottle had smashed into a stone floor." As flames consumed the stricken vehicle, Wiese baled out, his uniform on fire, but the loader and the gunner both perished in the inferno.

Next, Sgt Smith's Firefly No. 40 "New Jersey" engaged a Panzer IV located 1,500m away on the Robertmesnil Ridge. It took Trooper Coleman four shots to find the mark, however, but the end result was a burning Panzer. Smith then spotted and engaged another Panzer IV. Coleman's first round smashed through the tank's armor, causing it to burn and then explode as its ammunition went up; the tank promptly collapsed into "a junk heap of twisted, red hot, metal." By this time, the remaining German tanks and infantry were retreating in disarray. The combination of the fire from Firefly and ordinary Shermans, antitank guns, and supporting artillery had driven back the German counterattack. According to Allied accounts, 16 knocked-out German AFVs littered the battlefield around Le Petit Ravin, of which the Firefly had bagged seven. The upgunned Sherman had proved its ability to vanquish not just the ordinary Panzer IV, but also the most-feared German heavy tank, the Tiger. From this duel at St-Aignan – probably the last great clash of Firefly versus Tiger – the Firefly emerged triumphant.

That evening, a surreal epitaph to the day's events transpired. As darkness emerged, the surviving 1NY tanks gathered to leaguer for the night north of St-Aignan. Replacement 75mm Shermans and personnel moved forward to rebuild the badly damaged unit. Within "A" Squadron, Captain Boardman needed to find a wireless operator for one of the replacement 75mm-gunned Sherman. Luckily, a number of the surviving personnel were well trained in several disciplines. One gunner in particular was qualified as a wireless operator. And so that night, Boardman

"rewarded" Ekins for his spectacular gunnery achievements that day. The captain allocated Ekins to one of the new replacement 75mm-gunned Shermans – as its wireless operator.

The controversies of war

Many events that occur in battle are subject to different interpretations thanks to the inherent fog of war and the differing deductions made from the available evidence. Nowhere is this more evident than when famous wartime figures meet their death in battle. Given Wittmann's legendary status it should not surprise us that over the last three decades controversy has raged over which unit and which weapon actually destroyed his tank. For many years after 1945, however, no one on the Allied side even realized that Wittmann had been killed during the August 8 battle, which thus remained just one of hundreds of otherwise unremarkable, half-remembered wartime actions.

Once it became known on the Allied side that Wittmann had been a victim of this battle, the leading interpretation was that his demise had been caused by a high-explosive rocket fired from a RAF Hawker Typhoon aircraft. This interpretation was based largely on the circumstantial evidence that an unexploded rocket was found nearby, and on the specious logic that such a devastating explosion could only have been caused by such a weapon. As the doubts about this explanation mounted, a number of British and Canadian armored regiments deployed near Gaumesnil that afternoon claimed the distinction of dispatching Wittmann; of these, the claim of the 1NY stood out as being the one best supported by convincing contemporary evidence.

The long-held suspicions about the validity of the Typhoon explanation were vindicated in 2005 by Brian Reid's excellent book *No Holding Back*. Through careful examination of 2nd Tactical Air Force logs, Reid concluded that Wittmann "almost assuredly did not fall victim to an attack from the air." While accepting the strength of the 1NY claim, the Canadian historian went on to argue that Wittmann's tank may have been knocked out by a round fired from the west by a Firefly from a Canadian unit, the Sherbrooke Fusiliers. The justification for this interpretation relies on the accuracy of a brief description of Wittmann's tank made in late 1945 by a French civilian, which might be construed as indicating a hit fired from the west. Unfortunately, the Fusiliers' war diary was destroyed on August 8, so there is little contemporary evidence to support this interpretation, which accepts Major Radley-Walter's subsequent insistence that he had moved his Sherbrooke Fusilier squadron forward to Gaumesnil where they engaged some Tigers.

What this conjecture leaves us with is the few uncontested known facts from the time of the battle. As we have seen, the 1NY war diary recorded three Tigers being destroyed at the exact time when and in the general location where Wittmann's Tiger was destroyed. Furthermore, the unit's account of the battle was produced within a few weeks of the battle when no one in the regiment realized the significance of what they were describing. No other competing interpretation of how Wittmann came to be killed can remotely compete with the wealth of unequivocal impartial contemporary evidence that supports the claim of the 1NY. In all probability, it was a woefully inexperienced Firefly gunner, Joe Ekins, who dispatched the veteran SS panzer ace that afternoon. Even Reid accepts that Wittmann "may well have perished" at the hands of the 1NY, while in a newspaper article of June 2006, David Willey, curator at the Tank Museum at Bovington, UK, commented, "it is pretty much accepted now that Joe Ekins was the man who knocked out" Michael Wittmann.

After years of speculation as to the whereabouts of Wittmann's remains, in 1982 these were located and reinterred in the La Cambe military graveyard in Normandy. By then the Wittmann legend had become well-established and today the SS officer continues to stimulate huge public interest. In contrast, Ekins survived the war, and returned to Rushden, Northamptonshire, to live a quiet life. He worked in a shoe factory, married and had two children and for many years declined to enter discussions about what happened during the war. It now seems fitting that after all these years he has finally received some public recognition for his remarkable war service.

One of the 1NY's Fireflies in action. This photograph shows the Sherman IC Firefly No. 32 "New Orleans" of No. 2 Troop, "B" Squadron. The image was taken on July 17, 1944 in the Odon Valley sector of the front. (IWM B 7423)

BATTLE ANALYSIS

For analytical purposes, the climactic battle near St-Aignan on the early afternoon of August 8, 1944, can be divided into two actions; the death charge of Wittmann's Tigers, and the confused battle that raged around Le Petit Ravin. Finally, the approach march of the British left column during the previous night can be counted as a necessary precursor to these two actions. Like all battles, a degree of confusion and contradictory evidence exists regarding these actions, but this section attempts to analyze and quantify the known facts.

One obvious feature of the battle to be analyzed is the number of AFVs destroyed during these actions. Table 1 depicts the German losses suffered during these actions, according to British accounts.

TABLE 1: GERMAN AFV LOSSES, AUGUST 7–8, ACCORDING TO BRITISH ACCOUNTS

Type of AFV	Night march	Wittmann action	Le Petit Ravin action	Total lost
Panzer IV	0	2 [2]	7 [4]	9 [6]
Panther	0	0	4 [1]	4 [1]
Tiger	0	5 [3]	0	5 [3]
SPG	2 [2]	0	4 [2]	6 [4]
Unidentified	0	0	1	1 [0]
TOTAL	**2 [2]**	**7 [5]**	**16 [7]**	**25 [14]**

(Numbers lost to Fireflies shown in square brackets)
Sources: 1NY War Diary; Abbott; Neville; Taylor (see bibliography for full details)

We also possess detailed contemporary records, or secondary accounts, about the tank losses the 1NY suffered during the battle. The regiment started *Totalize* with a full complement of 59 tanks. During the night advance to St-Aignan, as Table 2 shows, the regiment lost the services of five tanks.

TABLE 2: 1NY TANKS LOST DURING NIGHT ADVANCE				
Vehicle #	Type	Trp/Sqd	Commander	Fate
2 "Odessa"	Sherman	1/A	Sgt Ryan	KO'd by Panzerfaust
5 "Brest-Litovsk"	Sherman	2/A	Griffith-Jones	KO'd by German SPG
6 "Bryansk"	Sherman	2/A	Sgt Jeffcoates	KO'd by German SPG
7 "Belgorod"	Sherman	2/A	Cpl Smith	KO'd by German SPG
56 "Lamport"				Became detached, ended up in Cramesnil

Sources: Abbott; Neville

During the battle for Le Petit Ravin, as Table 3 shows, the 1NY lost four Fireflies and nine standard Shermans, plus another Sherman seriously damaged but recovered. It is interesting to note that the regiment did not lose a single tank during the brief encounter with Wittmann's Tigers.

TABLE 3: 1NY TANK LOSSES DURING THE BATTLE FOR LE PETIT RAVIN			
	Lost to tank fire	Lost to antitank fire	Vehicle number/name
Sherman	8	1*	No. 11, 13, 14 "Kerch," 43 "Cottesbrooke," 47 "Sulgrave," 48, 55 "Lillingstone," 61 "Brixworth"; * No. 49
Firefly	4	0	No. 4 "Orenburg," 12, 16 "Kursk," 50 "Stony Stratford"
TOTAL	**12**	**1**	

Sources: 1NY War Diary; Abbott; Neville

Another aspect worth attempting to quantify is the personnel casualties suffered during these actions. German sources provide us with only fragmentary evidence on this issue, and one can only piece together a rough estimate based on various snippets of information, as shown in Table 4. This is particularly true of the Wittmann action. It seems that all of Wittmann's crew died when Tiger 007 exploded. We do not know how many of the other four Tigers' crews escaped, although it is reasonable to assume that the entire crew of the fifth (northernmost) Tiger escaped, as it was abandoned intact. One witness to the action – Dr Rabe – did not see anyone from the crew from the three Tigers destroyed by Ekins's Firefly successfully flee the battlefield. It is reasonable from this to assume that German tank crew casualties in the Wittmann action were at least 15 killed.

TABLE 4: ESTIMATED GERMAN PERSONNEL LOSSES DURING AUGUST 7–8 BATTLES

	Killed, wounded, missing, captured
Defense of approaches to St Aignan	60 (including 40 POWs)
Wittmann's death charge – tank crew	15+
Wittmann's death charge – Panzergrenadiers	30
Battle for Le Petit Ravin – tank crew	35+
Battle for Le Petit Ravin – Panzergrenadiers	50+
TOTAL	**190+**

Sources: 1NY War Diary; H. Meyer; K. Meyer; Neville

British sources are more detailed in giving the number of personnel casualties the 1NY suffered during these actions, as depicted in Table 5.

TABLE 5: 1NY PERSONNEL CASUALTIES DURING AUGUST 7–8

	Officers	NCOs/ORs
Killed	2	10
Wounded	11	40
TOTAL	**13**	**50**

Notes: These figures include at least one officer, one NCO killed, and seven NCOs/ORs wounded during the night advance, but excludes 1BW casualties during the night march.
Sources: 1NY War Diary; Abbott; Neville

If all this data is put together, an approximate summary of the respective losses suffered during the actions of August 7–8 can be calculated, as shown in Table 6.

TABLE 6: LOSSES DURING THE AUGUST 7–8 ACTIONS AROUND ST-AIGNAN

	Germans	1NY
AFV permanent losses	25	13
Personnel losses	190+	63

Sources: War Diaries; Abbott; H. Meyer; K. Meyer; Neville; Niemis; Taylor

THE AFTERMATH

Thanks to the Firefly, Wittmann's desperate charge north into the Allied lines near St-Aignan was repulsed and his Tigers either destroyed or abandoned. Allied Firefly and standard Sherman fire, augmented by antitank and artillery fire, also eventually forced back the other element of Meyer's counterattack force in the battle that raged in and around Le Petit Ravin. Meyer's audacious attempt to block the impending Allied armored onslaught in Phase Two of Operation *Totalize* had failed. The Allied armor commenced its attack south on schedule, after the bombing ended at 1355hrs. In these circumstances, the rest of August 8, 1944, ought to have been precisely the disastrous "black day" for the Germans that the Canadians had hoped it would be. Thanks to the Firefly, Meyer's fear that the Allies would successfully race south to occupy Falaise that day ought to have been realized.

But the spectre of disaster did not materialize. The two armored divisions of Lt Gen Guy Simonds's II Canadian Corps – both as yet unblooded into the horrors of combat in Normandy – advanced cautiously that afternoon, fearful of the long-range killing power of the handful of Tigers, Panthers, Panzer IVs and 75mm antitank guns still available to the meager German defending forces. The lethal firepower of such assets in such open terrain was soon demonstrated when the advancing Polish armor lost 40 tanks to German fire in the space of just 15 minutes. The defenders used the intervening time well to rush reinforcements to their severely depleted front on the Falaise plain. In fact it would take Simonds's forces another week to secure the high ground that dominated Falaise. Thus it was a combination of other factors, plus some good fortune – rather than the sacrifice of Wittmann's Tigers – that enabled the German forces to escape the debacle envisaged by Meyer that lunchtime on August 8.

This lucky escape, however, did not alter the fate that was about to consume the Westheer in Normandy – it merely postponed it by a few days. By mid-August, Simonds's forces had pushed forward beyond Falaise to link up with the Americans near Trun to close the Falaise Pocket. Undoubtably the Allies had won a great victory. The German's Seventh Army and the greater part of the Fifth Army had been destroyed with the loss of thousands of German soldiers. Although many German troops escaped with some armor and guns towards the Seine, no significant German forces remained to face the Allies after the loss of Normandy. In the ensuing weeks the Allies rampaged forward all the way to the borders of the Reich. There seemed a remote and fleeting opportunity that the war might be won during 1944. However, Allied logistical exhaustion and rapid German recovery ensured that the Allies would have to grind their way through Germany in a series of bitter battles that would rage into early 1945. By then – with nearly half the British spearhead armor being Fireflies and with very few Tigers still operational – the predictable German collapse ensued. On May 8 the Nazi regime surrendered unconditionally to the Allies.

So what did the summer 1944 battle for Normandy – and particularly Wittmann's death charge of August 8 – prove about the epic clash of Firefly versus Tiger? The Normandy campaign aptly displayed the weaknesses of the expedient Firefly design. With armor identical to the standard Sherman, the Firefly remained vulnerable to enemy tank and antitank fire. It took great bravery from Sherman crews to go into action against the latest generation of powerfully gunned Panzers,

This Tiger was knocked out at Tosters, France, on August 30, 1944. (Harold G. Aiken/Library and Archives/Canada/PA-114159)

especially given the Sherman's legendary tendency to burn when hit. Yet equally, the campaign – and the August 8 action in particular – showed that, in the Firefly, Allied armored units had finally got the "Panzer killer" they required. These battles showed that the Firefly could take on and defeat all of Germany's latest tanks, including the much-feared Tiger. The battle that raged near St-Aignan on August 8 represented the Firefly's finest hour. With careful concealment and courageous patience, the 1NY ambushed Wittmann's desperate charge north. In a matter of minutes, a single Firefly had dispatched three Tigers with just five rounds, in the process dispatching one of Germany's leading tank aces.

In August 1944, therefore, the Firefly and the Tiger were the dominant tanks on the battlefields of Northwest Europe. Yet this dominance was short-lived. While from the perspective of Normandy the Firefly emerged as the victor and the Tiger the vanquished, both at this time also shared a growing sense of approaching demise. With its production ended and the tank now outclassed by the King Tiger, the Tiger would appear on the battlefield in decreasing numbers until the end of the war. So too the Firefly; with production ended in May 1945, it was soon replaced by specifically designed medium tanks like the Comet that were better armed and armored. The Firefly was, after all, just an expedient – albeit an economical, effective and well-timed one. Without its lethal firepower, it is possible that the Westheer may have been able to maintain a coherent front in Normandy for much longer than they did. Sherman Fireflies were indeed, as reports at the time suggested, "battle-deciding weapons … everyone of which … will help materially to shorten the war."

M26 Pershing

KOREA 1950

The Korean War (1950–53) presents an intriguing opportunity to compare American and Soviet tanks of World War II. These erstwhile allies had developed their tanks in the 1943–44 period to fight German panzers, only to face one another unexpectedly on the new Cold War battlefield. Both the T-34-85 and the M26 Pershing were designed to combat the same foe, the new German Panther tank, which had appeared in action in the summer of 1943. The technical paths taken by the Americans and Soviets were quite different. The T-34-85 was an evolutionary change in the successful T-34 design, substituting a larger turret with an 85mm gun for the earlier smaller turret with its 76mm gun. There was no change in basic tank armor or in other major aspects of the design. As a result, the Soviet army received its first T-34-85s in early 1944, only about half a year after the program had been initiated. The M26, by contrast, was a fundamentally new design intended to replace the M4 Sherman. Compared to the T-34-85, the US Army's development of the M26 Pershing was quite protracted, the tank not appearing in service until March 1945, more than a year after its program start.

T-34-85

From a purely technical standpoint, a comparison of the T-34-85 against the newer and heavier M26 is not entirely fair. A more approriate comparison would be between the later Soviet T-44 and the M26, which were much closer in their developmental cycles and which were both new designs. But the T-44 and M26 Pershing never faced each other in combat, so the point is moot. To add a bit of balance to the comparison, however, we will more broadly examine the performance of the T-34-85 against all the major types of US medium tanks in Korea, including the M4A3E8, which was closer to the T-34-85 in size and performance.

Korea provides an excellent laboratory for tank warfare, since the major tank-versus-tank battles were compressed in time to only a few months in the summer and early fall of 1950. They also took place after the US Army had established a more elaborate operational research effort than had existed in World War II. As a result, there is a great deal of statistical analysis of the tank battles, which helps elucidate the relative performance of the North Korean and American tanks in this conflict.

These studies tended to confirm the results of Allied operational research in World War II. Although military buffs enjoy comparing the purely technical aspects of tank design, such as armor thickness and gun performance, operational research indicates that other factors are far more important in deciding which side prevails in a tank battle. The simplest condensation of the rule of tank fighting is "see first, engage first, hit first." Research in both World War II and Korea strongly indicated that the side which spotted the enemy force first had a marked advantage. Tanks in a stationary defensive position had an obvious advantage against tanks moving to contact, since the stationary tanks were more likely to spot the approaching enemy first. But regardless of the situation, target acquisition was central to victory in tank fighting.

Do technological advantages such as better armor and better guns affect the balance of tank battles? Korea provides some strong evidence in this debate, since the US side operated several tank types ranging from the M24 light tank and the M4A3E8 medium tank to the larger M26 and M46 tanks. Since crew performance in the US tanks would be similar if not identical, a comparison of the performance of these types in combat helps to provide an answer. The evidence strongly suggests that the newer and more powerful M26 and M46 did have appreciably higher combat effectiveness in the Korean War than the M4A3E8 Sherman. However, despite the M26 and M46's firepower and armor advantages over the M4A3E8, the smaller tank had mobility and reliability advantages over the newer tank types.

Yet it is also worth mentioning that the older and lighter M4A3E8 became the preferred US tank in the later phases of the Korean conflict. While this fact may seem to run against the technical performance issue, it is important to point out that the tactical dynamics of the battlefield changed in late 1950. The North Korean People's Army had a sizeable tank force in the summer of 1950, one that had a decisive influence on the battlefield, but the introduction of large numbers of US tanks quickly overwhelmed this force and essentially wiped it out. The Chinese intervention in late 1950 was not accompanied by a significant tank element, and as a result tank-versus-tank fighting became a rarity in the later war years; instead, US tanks were used primarily in the infantry support role in 1951–53.

THE TANKS

World War II tank development went through three major periods of transformation. The first was the result of tank combat in the Spanish Civil War of 1936–39, which demonstrated that the thinly armored, weakly armed tanks of the 1930s were not adequate when facing enemy 37–45mm antitank guns, nor were they suitable for tank-versus-tank fighting. These lessons led to the fielding of larger and more capable tanks, such as the German Panzer III, the workhorse of the Wehrmacht in the *Blitzkrieg* era from 1939 to 1942. They also resulted in the Soviet T-34 tank, which saw its combat debut in the summer of 1941 during the German invasion of Russia.

The T-34 was the premier tank of this generation, and it revolutionized tank design in the opening years of World War II. It established the benchmarks in the "holy trinity" of tank design: armor, firepower, and mobility. The T-34 used thick, well-sloped armor that was invulnerable to frontal attacks from German 37mm and 50mm guns. By contrast, its closest German counterpart, the Panzer III, used nearly vertical armor that was far more vulnerable to attack by the T-34. In terms of firepower, the T-34 employed an excellent dual-purpose 76mm gun that was useful for engaging both enemy tanks with armor-piercing projectiles, and enemy troops and equipment with high-explosive rounds. The 50mm gun on the Panzer III had mediocre antiarmor performance against the T-34 and equally mediocre HE firepower. T-34s also had substantially wider tracks than had been the norm in previous tank designs; these tracks were an essential feature in operations in Russia, where roads were poor and where wet or snowy ground could bog down other tank types.

The unexpected appearance of the radical T-34 design caused the second transformation in World War II tank design. The Wehrmacht responded to the T-34 in a two-step process, first improving the firepower of its existing Panzer III and Panzer IV tanks as a stopgap measure, while at the same time initiating the design of an overmatching adversary for the T-34. This new design eventually emerged as the Panther tank in 1943. The Panther raised the bar yet again by introducing even heavier frontal armor and a more powerful gun than the T-34.

It saw its combat debut in the battle of Kursk in the summer of 1943 and it set off the third transformation in World War II tank development, one that would result in the design of the principal tanks covered here – the Red Army's T-34-85 and the US Army's M4A3E8 and M26 tanks.

T-34-85 development

For the Soviets, the appearance of the Panther tank in the summer of 1943, as well as the more widespread use of the new Tiger heavy tank, led to a reconsideration of Red Army tank policy. The disastrous performance of the Soviet tank force in 1941 and 1942 had led to enormous losses in armored vehicles. As a result, in 1942 the Red Army adopted a strict policy to limit changes on the T-34 tank in order to maximize production quantity over quality. A large number of improvements had been proposed since 1941, including the substantially redesigned T-34M with torsion bar suspension, and the T-34-57 with better antitank firepower. The only changes that were permitted, however, were relatively minor ones, most often tied to production economies rather than tactical improvements. By the end of 1942, the Soviet main tank directorate was discouraging the development of an upgraded T-34 in favor of manufacturing a substantially more heavily armored version, the T-43, armed with the same 76mm gun. The appearance of the Panther at the battle of Kursk forced the Red Army to reconsider this policy.

Following Kursk, an assessment by the main Soviet tank research institute compared the combat effectiveness of the T-34 against its German opponents,

The ammunition stowed in the rear turret bustle made the T-34-85 prone to catastrophic propellant fires that blew off the turret roof. This wreck was inspected by a US Army survey team, which chalked markings on the three visible tank gun hits: one on the turret rear and two against the engine compartment. Judging from the size, they were probably 76mm HVAP projectiles. This particular tank was knocked out during the fighting near the Naktong River in late August 1950. (NARA)

assigning the baseline value of 1.0 to the current production version of the Panzer III. In this assessment, the T-34 rated at only 1.16, the Panzer IV at 1.27, and the Panther at 2.37. While the T-34 had been equivalent or superior to most German armored vehicles on the battlefield in 1942, this was no longer the case by mid-1943. Even the Panzer IV had seen significant improvements in armor and firepower, while T-34 improvements had been blocked. The most alarming trend was the increasing thickness of German frontal armor, which was making the Soviet 76mm gun increasingly ineffective in most combat situations.

As with the Germans in 1941, the Red Army selected a two-step process. While the improved armor of the T-43 was popular, switching to a new design would cut into production. Nor did the T-43 address the armament problem. A straightforward approach would be to substitute a more powerful gun on the existing T-34 as a short-term stopgap solution, but develop the new T-44 tank, with better armor and a better gun, as a final objective.

There were several contenders for a new gun for the T-34. In 1941, a small batch of "tank-hunter" T-34s had already been rearmed with a tank version of the ZIS-2 57mm antitank gun to improve its antiarmor performance. This design was revisited in the spring of 1943, and four T-34s were armed with the 57mm ZIS-4. In mid-August, three of these were dispatched to the front as Special Tank Company 100 under Capt Volosatov for field trials. The trials were successful enough for the Uralvagon Plant No. 183 in Nizhni-Tagil to create another batch of "tank-hunters" using 170 ZIS-4 guns. In the end, this program was stillborn due to other developments. The main drawback of using the 57mm gun was that its HE round was inferior to that of the existing 76mm gun. The Red Army was well aware that the vast majority of tank targets required the use of high-explosive ammunition, and improving antitank performance at the expense of the more versatile HE capability would be foolish.

The alternative solutions were an improved 76mm gun or a new tank created around the existing 85mm antiaircraft gun. The 76mm S-54 gun was an adaptation of the 3K 76mm Model 1931/38 antiaircraft gun. With a longer barrel than the

Soviet T-34-85 production					
Plant	Location	1944	1945	1946	Total
183	Nizhni-Tagil	6,583	7,356	493	**14,432**
112	Gorkiy	3,079	3,255	1,154	**7,488**
174	Omsk	1,000	1,940	1,054	**3,994**
Total		**10,662**	**12,551**	**2,701**	**25,914**

existing F-34 76mm tank gun, the S-54 had better antitank performance. This performance, however, was not superior enough to warrant its use. Indeed, Soviet tank designers generally disapproved of the German selection of the 75mm KwK 43 on the Panther, feeling that for its size and weight it was inferior to the 88mm gun on the Tiger I. The Soviet designers felt that the 88mm gun offered a better balance of AP and HE firepower, while the 75mm was optimized for antiarmor performance at the expense of the more commonly used HE round.

Aside from offering versatility in combat, with good antiarmor and HE performance, the Soviet 85mm gun had the added attraction that the ammunition was already in production for the widely used 85mm antiaircraft gun, as well as its armored-vehicle variants used on the SU-85 tank destroyer and KV-85 tank. The only drawback of this weapon was that the ammunition did not contain as much propellant as ammunition for the 75mm KwK 43 gun, so it offered about 87 percent of the muzzle energy of the Panther gun and correspondingly less penetration. Yet the Red Army recognized the need to balance technical perfection against economic realities, and so accepted the trade-off.

Having selected the 85mm solution, there were two other issues to be settled. Several design bureaus were assigned to a crash program to develop a suitable 85mm gun based on the existing ammunition. One of these resulting designs had to be selected, and there was also some debate regarding how the new gun would be mounted. Some advocated simply mounting it in the existing hexagonal 76mm turret, since this would obviously simplify production. Although the 85mm gun was successfully mounted in this turret, the configuration was extremely cramped and inefficient. By this stage of the war, the Red Army had come to realize that the two-man turret layout of the T-34 was one of the main causes of poor Soviet tactical performance on the battlefield. The tank commander had to split his responsibilities between commanding the tank and serving as the gunner. German tankers found that T-34 units were slow-witted in tank-versus-tank combat, as the Soviet commanders were distracted from their command responsibilities by having to hunt out targets and threats. While the Soviet 76mm gun had a high rate of fire on paper, in practice the German tankers often found they could fire three rounds for every one fired by their Soviet opponents. The solution to this problem had been addressed in the T-43 turret design by adding a third crewman in the turret as a dedicated gunner, and this solution migrated to the new T-34 variant when the T-43 turret formed the basis for the new 85mm turret. The new turret adopted a larger turret ring to accommodate the heavier recoil of the 85mm gun, and the basic turret armor thickness was also increased compared to the T-34.

In the rush to field an 85mm gun, the Red Army accepted the D5-T gun as a stopgap in a turret developed at Plant No. 112 in Gorkiy; this was the same gun used in the SU-85 tank destroyer and KV-85 heavy tank. Production began in late 1943. In the meantime, the development of a more refined gun, the S-53, was completed and this became the standard weapon for the T-34-85, entering production in parallel with the D5-T gun at Gorkiy Plant No. 112 in February 1944 and subsequently at Plant No. 183 at Nizhni-Tagil and Plant No. 174 at Omsk in March 1944. The serial production version of the S-53 gun was designated the ZIS-S-53 after its production plant (Zavod imeni Stalina No. 92). The T-34-85 Model 1944 with the ZIS-S-53 gun became the standard version and remained in production through 1947. The tanks used in Korea in 1950 were of this type.

The T-34-85 was first deployed with the Red Army in March 1944, and saw its baptism of fire in the battles around Kamenets-Podolskiy on the Ukrainian–Romanian frontier. They were in widespread service by the summer of 1944 during the great Red Army offensive that pushed the Wehrmacht out of the Soviet Union, and continued improvements were introduced through the production run. In August 1944, the turret casting was increased from 75mm (2.95in) to 90mm (3.54in) at the front. In January 1945, an enlarged commander's cupola with a single piece hatch was introduced. Also in early 1945, Plant No. 112 in Gorkiy began manufacturing a widened turret with greater internal volume; the new turret split the ventilator fans and placed one closer to the gun where it was most needed.

The T-34-85 was an adequate stopgap, since German Panther tank strength was so meager – in May 1944, the Wehrmacht had only 304 Panthers on the entire Eastern Front. T-44 design, however, was underway at the Uralvagon plant in Nizhni-Tagil. The most significant difference between the new tank and the T-34-85 was in the hull (the turrets of both tanks were very similar). The designers wanted to incorporate thicker armor able to resist the 75mm Panther gun without substantially increasing the weight of the tank. The only way to do so was to reduce the hull volume. While the substitution of torsion bar suspension for the bulky Christie spring suspension partially accomplished this goal, another important change was the decision to drop the redundant crewman in the right front hull station, who operated the hull machine gun. This function was not particularly necessary, and the space could be better used to stow ammunition. Prototypes were ready for testing in August 1944, a few months later than the closest American counterpart, the T26E3. The type went into production in late 1944, even though not all of the design problems had been solved. The T-44 represented the culmination of Soviet wartime design efforts, with an impressive mixture of simplicity and high combat effectiveness for a 32-tonne (35-ton) tank. It is interesting to note that the Soviets were able to come very close to the combat capabilities of the German Panther in a design that weighed only about 65 percent as much. Yet the T-44 never saw combat in World War II, as the first

The T-34-85 through 360 degrees

SPECIFICATIONS: T-34-85

Crew: 5
Combat weight: 32 tonnes
Power-to-weight ratio: 14.2hp/tonne
Hull length: 6.1m
Overall length: 8.1m
Width: 3.0m

Engine: V-2-34 4-stroke, 12-cylinder diesel, 500hp @ 1,800rpm
Transmission: Dry multi-plate clutch, mechanical gearbox, one-stage side drives with side clutches and strap brakes; four forward, one reverse gears
Fuel capacity: 545 liters internal, 270 liters external
Max speed: 54.8km/h
Cross-country speed: 30km/h

production batches had lingering mechanical problems, and it remained in training units. Production was quite modest by Soviet standards, with only 1,253 being manufactured in 1944–47.

No sooner was the T-44 completed than the Red Army recognized it was a dead-end. The 85mm gun was not adequate to compete against the growing firepower and armor of enemy tanks and an even larger gun was needed. Although the D-10T 100mm gun was tested on both the T-34 and T-44, the only practical solution was to develop an enlarged turret for the T-44, which led to the T-54 tank program in December 1944. Small-scale production of the T-54 began in 1947, but the design was not really mature until 1950. The limited production of the T-44 and the slow maturation of the T-54 in the aftermath of World War II meant that none

Artwork by Richard Chasemore, © Osprey Publishing

Range: 298km on road
Primary armament: ZIS-S-53 85mm gun L/54.6
Max gun range: 13.3km for HE indirect fire
Main gun ammunition: 55 rounds
Gun elevation: -5 to +25 degrees
Secondary armament: Hull-mounted and coaxial DTM
    7.62mm machine guns

Top: UBR-365K AP
Bottom: UBR-365P HVAP

	Soviet postwar medium tank production						
	Sep–Dec 1945	1946	1947	1948	1949	1950	Total
T-34-85	3,041	2,701					5,742
T-44	335	718	200				1,253
T-54			22	593	152	1,007	1,774
Total	**3,376**	**3,419**	**222**	**593**	**152**	**1,007**	**8,769**

of these more modern types was exported prior to the start of the Korean War. The most modern tank sent to allied armies was the T-34-85 and this type would form the basis of the North Korean tank force in 1950. Once T-54 production was well underway in the Soviet Union in the early 1950s, T-34-85 production began in both Poland and Czechoslovakia. However, all the T-34-85 tanks used during the Korean conflict were Soviet-made.

M26 Pershing development

The development of the M26 medium tank by the US Army was also prompted in large measure by the appearance of the Panther, but in a far less direct fashion. US tank development was managed by US Army Ground Forces (AGF), headed by LtGen Lesley McNair, a brilliant artilleryman who micromanaged most aspects of army organizational development. The AGF's weapons acquisition philosophy was dominated by battle-need and battle-worthiness. Battle-need was the concept that weapons would only be acquired if the troops in the field expressed a clear need for them; McNair wanted to avoid the "mad scientist syndrome," with engineers in the Ordnance Department dreaming up fanciful weapons that would simply clog up the supply chain without improving the Army's battlefield effectiveness. Battle-worthiness was a demand inspired by the Army's unhappy experiences in World War I, when many weapons and vehicles manufactured in the United States proved to be unreliable and lacking in combat durability. Of the two requirements, battle-need was the most problematic. It underestimated the tyranny of time, since once the deployed troops demanded a new weapon to meet a pressing need, it would take months if not years to develop the weapon, place it on the production lines, ship it to the field, and train troops in its use. This philosophy was not especially worrisome in more established classes of weapons such as small arms and field artillery, where technological change was less dynamic, but tanks were a relatively new weapon and the pace of technological change in World War II was brisk.

Through the summer of 1943, the US Army had relied on the M4 Sherman medium tank armed with a 75mm gun. While the US forces had encountered the German Tiger I heavy tank in Tunisia, Sicily, and mainland Italy in 1943, the threat initially did not have a major impact on the US Armored Force – Tigers were encountered in small numbers and seldom had a decisive influence on the battlefield. Allied intelligence learned of the appearance of the Panther from attachés in Moscow, and technical details were widely available by the fall of 1943. In spite of the appearance of this new tank, there was very little reaction in the US Army due to a fundamental intelligence mistake. It was widely presumed that the Panther was

The 90mm gun on the M26/M46 family underwent three iterations during production. The final version of the M3A1 used on the M46, as seen here, had the bore evacuator first used on the M26A1, but also introduced a new muzzle brake. The Marine 1st Tank Battalion was reequipped with M46 tanks after the spring 1951 campaign, to make up for its losses. Here, Co. A rearms for a fire mission on April 25, 1952. By this time, the unit had been moved to western Korea, south of Panmunjom, and was holding a defensive perimeter called the Jamestown Line. The 90mm ammunition was delivered in two-round wooden crates, while the rounds themselves were stored in black fiberboard tubes for added protection. (NARA)

simply another German heavy tank like the Tiger I that would be deployed in a limited number of heavy tank battalions at corps or field army level. In fact, it was designed as a medium tank to replace the Panzer IV. McNair and the AGF diligently sent teams into the field to inquire whether there was a need for a better tank with a better gun. The last such mission before the Normandy landings, the "New Weapons Board" sent to Italy in early 1944, came back to Washington with little sense of urgency about the need for an improved tank.

In contrast to the US Army's complacency, the British Army was intent on fielding a better gun on its tanks due to the general trend towards increased armor through the war years, and the 17pdr-equipped Sherman Firefly was the result. The US Army had been experimenting with a 76mm gun in the Sherman since 1942, but there had been little enthusiasm for the design, as it offered only marginally better antitank firepower, but inferior HE firepower, than the 75mm gun. In this respect, the US tank commanders echoed the Soviet viewpoint that a tank gun had to have a versatile combination of AP and HE firepower, and not be optimized for only one of the two criteria. The 76mm gun was half-heartedly accepted for production in the fall of 1943, but at the time of the Normandy landings in June 1944 none were in the hands of combat troops. As a result, when US tank units went ashore on D-Day in June 1944, they were equipped with versions of the M4 Sherman tank little different from the versions in service in November 1943 in Tunisia.

SPECIFICATIONS:
M26 Pershing

Crew: 5
Combat weight: 41.9 tonnes
Horsepower-to-weight ratio: 10.8hp/ton
Overall length: 8.63m

Width: 3.5m
Height: 2.77m
Engine: Ford GAF 500hp liquid-cooled,
    4-cycle gasoline engine
Transmission: Torquematic with three forward, one
    reverse gears
Fuel capacity: 692 liters

The US Army's Ordnance Department had been working on a follow-on tank for the Sherman since 1942, but with little sense of urgency. The most important innovation in the design was that the transmission was shifted from the front of the tank back to the rear engine compartment. This reconfiguration removed the need for a power-shaft though the center of the fighting compartment. The power-shaft in the Sherman took up considerable space and led to the Sherman's excessive height, so the new design had a lower, sleeker hull. Yet there was no consensus about what features were important, and the design went through numerous variations as the T20, T22, T23 and T25. These various designs examined different powerplants, different types of suspension, and different armaments. Ordnance favored the T23 design armed with a 76mm gun, but this vehicle was widely criticized by tank officers in the combat theaters, as it used a novel electrical transmission that promised to be a maintenance burden in the field. Even though there was little

Artwork by Richard Chasemore, © Osprey Publishing

Max speed: 40km/h
Cross-country speed: 32km/h
Range: 62km on road
Main gun: M3 90mm gun in M67 mount
Main gun ammo: 70 rounds
Max range: 19,568m, HE indirect fire
Gun elevation: -10 to +20 degrees

Top: M304 HVAP   Bottom: M82 APC-T

support from frontline commanders, production of 250 T23 tanks started in November 1943 and lasted through December 1944.

Because of Armored Force views, in May 1943 two more T20 derivatives entered development. The T25 was fitted with 75mm frontal armor, weighed 33 tonnes and was armed with a 90mm gun. The T26 was essentially similar but with 100mm frontal armor, and so weighed 36 tonnes. The pilots of the T25 and T26 were completed with the controversial electric drive, but recognition of the problems with this technology led to the substitution of mechanical torquematic transmission on the improved T25E1 and T26E1.

Once again, McNair and AGF solicited the advice of forward-deployed tank commanders, but there was little consensus on what type of tank would be needed in the future. With the invasion of France planned for the summer of 1944, the US Army began final steps to prepare its forces for combat in the main European theater.

Snow billows as an M46 of Co. C, US Army 6th Tank Battalion, fires its 90mm gun while supporting the 24th Infantry Division near Song Sil-li, Korea, on January 10, 1952. (NARA)

In the fall of 1943, LtGen Jacob Devers was commander of US forces in the European Theater of Operations (ETO), a place-holder position until Dwight Eisenhower's appointment at the beginning of 1944. Devers had previously headed the Armored Force and was well aware that US forces had encountered Tigers in Sicily and Italy in 1943. He wanted to make certain that the US Army could better deal with this threat. Devers requested that development of the T26E1 be accelerated and that 250 of these be manufactured as quickly as possible so they could be deployed in the ratio of one per five M4 medium tanks. Ordnance agreed, but also wanted to produce 1,000 of the despised T23 as well. The War Department forwarded these conflicting recommendations to the AGF for review. LtGen McNair flatly turned down the request on the grounds that there was no demand from troops in the field and that the new Sherman with its 76mm gun was perfectly adequate. Devers continued to press the case for the T26E1 and on December 16, 1943, the War Department issued a directive that authorized the production of 250 T26E1 tanks by April 1945. Devers' position was later ratified by Eisenhower, but the T26E1 was far from ready for production, even on a rush basis. A total of 40 T25E1 and ten T26E1 prototypes were completed at the Grand Blanc tank arsenal from February to May 1944.

The army's opinion about the need for new tanks changed abruptly after the Normandy landings in June 1944. Widespread encounters with the Panther in Normandy in June and July 1944 led to an outcry about the Sherman's poor armor and inadequate firepower. The standard 75mm gun on the Sherman was incapable of penetrating the frontal armor of the Panther, and even the new 76mm gun was not up to this task. As a stopgap, M4A3 Sherman (76mm) production was accelerated, along with the manufacture of new hyper-velocity armor-piercing (HVAP) ammunition, with a tungsten-carbide core. The improved horizontal volute spring suspension (HVSS) was introduced on the M4A3, producing the M4A3E8 version, which entered combat around Christmas 1944 in the Ardennes. This version was the ultimate type of Sherman fielded by the US Army in World War II, and was also used in large numbers in Korea in 1950. In most respects, it is the most direct equivalent of the Soviet T-34-85.

In spite of improvements to the Sherman, clearly a new tank with a much better gun was needed. Trials of the prototype T26E1 tanks in the summer of 1944 were successful enough that on June 15, 1944, the War Department decided that the 1945 tank production program would be changed to permit production of 6,000 T26 tanks. Nevertheless, the testing program uncovered a substantial number of significant modifications that would be needed before series production started. As a result, the series production version with the 90mm gun was designated the T26E3 heavy tank.

In the meantime, a tank-destroyer version of the Sherman tank armed with the 90mm gun, the M36 90mm Gun Motor Carriage (GMC), had already entered production and first saw combat in the ETO in October 1944. The new 90mm gun had been developed by Ordnance in 1943 for essentially the same reasons as the Soviet 85mm gun: because it could be developed quickly from an existing 90mm antiaircraft gun. Yet Ordnance showed little enthusiasm for the project due to a lack of corresponding requirement from the field until the summer of 1944, and specialized

M26 Pershings of the 1st Marine Tank Battalion in action on September 3, 1950. An observer is on the ground between the two tanks, but he would evacuate his position before they fired to avoid concussion from the muzzle blast. That day, the Marine tanks took part in fighting against the new NKPA 16th Armored Brigade, knocking out several T-34-85s near Yongsan.

antitank ammunition development was sluggish. When first introduced into combat in October 1944 on the M36, the 90mm gun was still unable to penetrate the Panther's frontal armor at normal combat ranges due to poor ammunition. This situation gradually improved with the advent of HVAP ammunition late in 1944.

By the end of 1944, a total of 40 T26E3 tanks had been completed. There was pressure to do something in response to the growing criticism coming from Europe; the fierce tank fighting in the Ardennes in December 1944 increased the volume of complaints. The head of Ordnance research, MajGen G. M. Barnes, suggested sending half of the new tanks to Europe for impromptu combat trials – Zebra mission – while the other 20 went to Fort Knox for the usual tests. The first batch of 20 T26E3s arrived at the port of Antwerp in January 1945 and were assigned to Gen Omar Bradley's 12th Army Group. They were split into two groups, with ten each going to the 3rd and 9th Armored Divisions. Training for the new tank crews concluded by late February 1945, and the new tanks went into action in March 1945. Those with the 9th Armored Division attracted the most attention when they took part in the capture of the Rhine river bridge at Remagen. Additional batches of T26E3 tanks arrived in late March and early April, and were issued to the 2nd Armored Division (22 tanks), the 5th Armored Division (18 tanks), and the 11th Armored Division (30 tanks). In the final weeks of the war, the T26E3 tanks saw little tank-versus-tank combat due to the collapse of the German armed forces. By the end of the war, 310 T26E3 had been delivered to Europe of which 200 had been issued to tank units. However, it was only the tanks supplied in February 1945 that saw extensive combat.

The T26E3 experience can best be summed up as "too little, too late." A postwar report by First Army assessed the combat trials of the Zebra mission. "Unfortunately for this test, the German armor had been so crippled as to present a very poor opponent and the cessation of hostilities so soon after forming these companies precluded the gaining of any real experience." In the wake of the war, the T26E3 was standardized as the M26 medium tank. Britain had been naming US Lend-Lease tanks after American generals, such as the "Sherman" for the M4 series. In 1945, the US Army adopted the British practice and the experimental T26E3 was accepted for service as the M26 Pershing, named in honor of Gen John "Black Jack" Pershing, who had commanded the American Expeditionary Force in France in World War I. Besides the basic gun version of the M26, the US Army also wanted an assault gun version armed with a 105mm howitzer to provide direct fire support, much as the M4 (105mm) Sherman. This armored vehicle was designed as the T26E2 and accepted for service after the war as the M45.

The June 1944 tank production plan for 1945 called for 7,800 medium tanks consisting of 2,060 T26E3 (90mm), 2,728 T26E2 (105mm howitzer), and

3,000 M4A3 (105mm howitzer). Furthermore, the British wanted 750 T26 (90mm) and 400 T26 (105mm howitzer). By December 1944, in the midst of the Ardennes tank battles, the US Army decided that the T26E2s with 105mm howitzers were less necessary than the standard 90mm tank version, so the 1945 objective became 4,716 T26E2 (90mm). In point of fact, 2,002 M26 and subsidiary variants were manufactured through August 1945 and only 37 M45 (105mm) howitzer tanks; eventually 185 M45 howitzer tanks were completed. A portion of the M26 fleet was modernized with the M3A1 90mm gun after the war; the gun added a bore evacuator to the barrel to reduce the fumes in the fighting compartment when firing. These were designated the M26A1 Pershing.

The main complaint about the M26 was that its automotive performance was sluggish compared to the M4A3E8 Sherman, since they both were powered by the same engine but the M26 was nearly 9 tonnes heavier. As a result, a program was undertaken after the war to examine better powerplants, and eventually the 740hp Continental AV-1790 engine and General Motors CD-850 cross-drive transmission were selected. Construction of ten M46, a modified M26 design with the upgraded elements just mentioned, was authorized in the 1948 budget and 800 in the 1949 budget. The Army eventually decided to convert most of its existing inventory of M26 and M45 tanks into the M46 configuration, in addition to new-construction tanks. The plan was to have 810 M46 tanks available by 1950, mainly through conversion, but this schedule slipped. As a result, all four of these tank types, the M26, M26A1, M45 and M46, saw combat service in Korea.

The M46 was a further elaboration of the basic M26 design, but with a new powertrain based on the AV-1790 engine and a new cross-drive transmission. It is most easily distinguished from the M26 by the new mufflers on the rear fenders, as seen in this example of a Marine 1st Tank Battalion M46 rearming during the fighting in Korea. (NARA)

TECHNICAL ASSESSMENT

Protection

The T-34-85 sat between the M4A3E8 and M26 in terms of armor protection. The M4A3E8 was the most weakly protected of the three tanks covered here, due to the basic armor as well as the armor layout. The T-34-85 actually had thinner front hull armor than the M4A3E8, but more effective protection due to its greater slope; likewise its side armor offered substantially greater protection due to slope rather than thickness. The turret armor of the T-34-85 was also better than on the M4A3E8. In contrast, the M26 offered significantly better frontal protection than the T-34-85, which is not altogether surprising since it was a later design and a significantly heavier tank. The table on page 174 shows the actual thickness of the major armor surfaces of these tanks, as well as effective thickness, a factor that addresses the angle of the armor. Effective thicknesses are only approximate, since they can vary widely according to the precise angle of shell impact, type of projectile, velocity of projectile, and other factors. The effective thickness figures, therefore, are presented here only to provide a rough comparison.

There were significant differences in armor hardness and tank manufacturing quality between the US and Soviet tanks. The Soviet tank armor tended to be of more erratic quality due to hasty manufacturing by inadequately skilled workers, and it exhibited poor welds by American standards. Soviet tank armor was generally heat-treated to very high hardness (430–500 Brinell) in order to achieve maximum resistance to certain classes of German antiarmor projectiles, even at the expense of structural integrity under ballistic attack. US tank design favored more conventional armor hardnesses (280–320 Brinell) based on US testing. In spite of the sloppy Soviet manufacturing standards, a 1953 report on Soviet ordnance metallurgy warned readers that:

> … although welds in Soviet tanks are inferior in quality and much more brittle than corresponding welds in American tanks, this condition has not been a major

factor in impairing the battlefield performance of Soviet armor. Poor joint fits, sloppy appearance, jagged and rough finishes should not divert attention from the fact that the Soviet tanks are rugged and battle-worthy and require many fewer man-hours of labor, precision machine tools, jigs, and fixture to construct than corresponding American tanks.

Armor data provides only part of the picture of a tank's protection. Other factors in assessing the vulnerability of a tank include the internal arrangement of fuel and ammunition. The T-34-85 is a clear example of the trade-off between the benefits and drawbacks of steeply angled protective armor. Although the T-34's sloped sides reduced the likelihood of the tank being penetrated by enemy projectiles, it also led to a decrease in internal hull volume. In the event that the T-34 was penetrated, the projectile was far more likely to produce catastrophic damage among the fuel and ammunition stored in such a small space. The side sponsons of the T-34's fighting compartment in particular contained fuel cells that if penetrated could lead to fire and the destruction of the tank. In contrast the US tanks, with their larger internal hull volumes, allowed segregation of the fuel cells in the rear of the tank where they were less likely to be hit and less likely to lead to crew casualties.

These are two of the three T-34-85 tanks of the 109th Tank Regiment knocked out in the fighting near the Obong-Ni Ridge, but pushed off the road after the skirmish. The tank to the left has suffered an ammunition fire in the turret, which has blown off the roof. (NARA)

Ammunition location poses a significant problem in tank design due to the trade-offs necessary between locating the ammunition away from areas most likely to be hit, while at the same time keeping the ammunition accessible enough to ensure a high tempo of fire. In this respect, the T-34-85's ammunition layout also decreased the survivability of the tank. The larger size of the 85mm ammunition forced the designers to place a significant portion of the tank's ammo load, 16 of 55 rounds, in the turret, where there was a high probability of being hit. The remainder of the rounds were stowed in the floor or lower hull walls near the loader. The American tanks, however, benefited from US armored combat experiences in 1942–43, which showed the vulnerability of the Sherman to catastrophic damage due to ammunition stowed in the hull sponsons. This situation led to a 1943 program that removed the majority of the ammunition from the sponsons and placed it into lightly armored stowage bins in the floor. This location reduced the likelihood of the ammunition being hit during a penetration, and so also reduced the possibility of devastating tank fires, which were usually caused by ignited ammunition. The lightly armored ammo bins were not well enough protected to prevent penetration by a direct hit, but they were adequate to reduce the vulnerability of the ammunition to ignition by spall or shrapnel from a penetration. The turret bustles on the American tanks were used for radio and machine-gun ammunition stowage rather than main gun ammunition stowage.

The consequences of these design decisions were very evident from combat statistics in Korea. American tanks hit and penetrated by T-34-85 gun fire on average suffered two casualties: one killed and one wounded. This was remarkably similar to World War II casualty statistics. Generally, the crewman in the path of the penetrating

Armor protection comparisons			
	T-34-85	M4A3E8	M26
Glacis thickness	45mm	64mm	100mm
Glacis effective thickness	~122mm	~118mm	~182mm
Hull side thickness	45mm	38mm	50–75mm
Hull side effective thickness	95mm	38mm	50–75mm
Mantlet thickness*	75mm	89mm	115mm
Turret front thickness*	90mm	64mm	102mm
Turret side thickness	75mm	64mm	76mm
Turret side effective thickness	~80mm	~70mm	~80mm

*Effective thicknesses not given for these surfaces since they are curved, and hence variable.

enemy projectile was killed and at least one crewmen near the point of entry was injured. If penetrated, a US medium tank was on average likely to incur 42 percent crew casualties (killed and wounded). About a third of US tanks that experienced a penetrating hit were recovered and put back into action. Yet in the case of the T-34-85 tanks penetrated by US tank gun fire, crew casualties were about double (82 percent) and nearly all were fatalities. Few if any T-34-85 tanks that were holed by US tank guns were recovered, a fact due to both tactical circumstances as well as the tendency of the T-34-85 to suffer an ammunition or fuel fire after penetration.

Firepower

In general, the firepower of the T-34-85 was close to that of the 76mm M4A3E8 in terms of antiarmor performance, but superior to the 76mm gun in terms of HE firepower. It was significantly inferior to the 90mm gun of the M26 in AP firepower, and slightly less effective in HE firepower.

The T-34-85 standard ammunition load in Red Army service was 55 rounds, consisting of 36 rounds of HE-fragmentation, five rounds of HVAP, and 14 rounds of AP. In view of the fact that the Republic of Korea Army had no tanks, the North Korean ammo load-out was five rounds of AP and 50 rounds of HE-fragmentation. The precise type of AP ammunition available in 1950 is not known, but at least some HVAP was available (US troops captured some examples). The basic tank-fighting ammunition was the UBR-365 round, which used the streamlined BR-365 AP projectile. In contrast to US AP ammunition in Korea, which had a blunt nose and ballistic cap (the shell was officially known as armor-piercing capped – APC), the BR-365 was streamlined with no ballistic cap. An in-service variation was the UBR-365K, which used the BR-365K with a blunt nose but no ballistic cap. Another difference between US and Soviet AP ammunition was that the latter included a small burster charge inside, which was intended to increase its lethality after penetration; the US projectiles had no charge. The 85mm BR-365 had armor-penetration performance similar to the 76mm M62 round, but it was markedly inferior to the heavier and higher-velocity 90mm APC round fired by the M26 Pershing. The most potent antiarmor projectiles available for US and Soviet tanks in Korea were the HVAP rounds, which were composite designs made of light metals such as aluminum with a heavier and denser tungsten-carbide core. The US assessment of the Soviet BR-365P was that it was based on older German arrowhead ammunition of about 1942 and had a relatively small sub-caliber core. Its performance was inferior to the American 76mm HVAP and markedly inferior to the 90mm HVAP.

Ammunition employed in tank-vs-tank fighting in Korea, 1950

	APC	HVAP	HE	WP	Total
M4A3E8	53	43	29	5	130
M26	96	35	33	1	165
M46	19	16	2	0	37
Total	168	94	64	6	332

The HE ammunition on the T-34-85 reflected Soviet preferences, with the O-365 projectile having a somewhat heavier steel case than comparable US rounds, favoring fragmentation over blast. The Soviet 85mm gun offered a good balance of HE performance and AP performance, while the US 76mm had mediocre HE qualities. Yet the 90mm gun was significantly better than the Soviet 85mm gun in both categories. It was capable of penetrating the frontal armor of the T-34-85 at normal battle ranges; the HVAP ammunition was so powerful that it would sometimes penetrate the front of the T-34-85 and exit out of the rear. The use of various types of ammunition in tank-versus-tank fighting in Korea was summarized in a US report, shown in the table above. HE and white phosphorous (WP) smoke ammunition was sometimes used after a T-34-85 was hit with AP rounds, in order to kill the escaping crew or to set the tank on fire.

In terms of fire control, the US tanks had a number of advantages. They had two sighting devices linked to the main gun. The first consisted of an M10F periscope in an M73 mount on the roof, with an integral M47A2 telescope. The periscope sight provided the gunner with good situational awareness, since it could be operated at 1x for general surveillance and then switched to 6x magnification, using the integral telescope for precision aiming. The Pershing also had one of two main telescopic sights fitted. Some used the older M71C with 5x magnification and a 13-degree field of view; others used the newer M83C which offered a variable 4x to 8x magnification.

In contrast, the T-34-85 relied solely on a telescopic sight for aiming. The gunner was provided with an MK-4 periscope, but it was only for general observation, and

First-round hit probability in Korean War tank-vs-tank fighting

Range: yards	0–350	351–750	751–1,150	over 1,150
USA	84 percent	63 percent	39 percent	16 percent
NKPA	50 percent	23 percent	25 percent	0 percent

not linked to the gun for aiming. So after identifying the target in the periscope, the gunner had to then switch to the telescopic sight, with the attendant problems of loss of vital time and the possibility of losing sight of the target. The US sights also offered higher magnification. All three tanks relied on stadiametric rangefinding to compensate for the ballistic fall of the projectile at longer ranges. The US tanks in Korea demonstrated a similar level of first-round accuracy in tank fighting: about 66 percent for the M4A3E8 Sherman and 69 percent for the M26 Pershing. Not surprisingly, first-round accuracy was very dependent on range. Data on North Korean T-34-85 accuracy were much less complete, but were also compiled in a US study, as shown in the table opposite. The average firing range in Korea was about 450 yards (411m).

Besides the observation devices available to the gunner, the commander's sights were also important in fire control, since he was responsible for identifying and selecting the target. In this respect, the US tanks had a decided advantage by offering the commander a more practical cupola better suited to obtaining situational awareness and target identification. Commanders of both the M4A3E8 and M26

One of the less satisfactory features of the M26 armament was the placement of the .50cal antiaircraft machine gun on a pintle mount behind the commander's cupola. In order to use it against ground targets, the commander had to exit the tank and fire it from outside while standing on the engine deck. Here, a tanker on an M26A1 Pershing of Co. D, Marine 1st Tank Battalion, takes aim at NKPA troops in the hills near Chochon-dong, during antiguerilla sweeps there on February 5, 1951.

Firepower comparison			
	M4A3E8	**T-34-85**	**M26**
Caliber	76mm	85mm	90mm
Type	M1A2	ZIS-S-53	M3
Tube length (calibers)	52.8	54.6	52.5
Tube length	4,159mm	4,641mm	4,718mm
Rate of fire (rpm)	20	3–4	8
Propellant charge weight	2.2kg	2.9kg	3.8kg
Ammunition stowed	71	55	70
Telescopic sight	M71D	TSh-16	M71C or M83C
Sight magnification	5x	4x	5x or 4x and 8x
AP projectile	M62 APC	BR-365 AP-HE*	M82 APC
AP projectile weight	7.0kg	9.3kg	10.9kg
Muzzle velocity	792m/sec	792m/sec	854m/sec
Armor penetration, @1,000m	109mm	102mm	147mm
HVAP projectile	M93	BR-365P	M304
HVAP projectile weight	4.3kg	5.0kg	7.6kg
Muzzle velocity	1,036m/sec	1,030m/sec	1,020m/sec
Armor penetration, @1,000m	178mm	130mm	250mm
HE projectile	M42A1	0-365	M71
HE projectile weight	5.8kg	9.5kg	10.6kg
HE projectile HE charge	0.39kg	0.775kg	0.952kg
HE projectile max. range	13.5km	13.3km	13.4km

*Soviet AP projectile is not capped, and has HE bursting charge

were provided with a vision cupola fitted with six 203mm (8in)-wide view ports, each protected by laminate glass, which gave 360-degree azimuth coverage as well as elevation coverage of -15 to +80 degrees. The T-34-85 commander's cupola was fitted with six smaller prismatic sights that offered a more constricted view of the surroundings. All three tanks also had the periscopic sights noted earlier, fitted to the cupola roof.

The combination of better observation devices and better training meant that US tanks tended to find the North Korean tanks first and engage them first, a critical ingredient in tank duels. Overall, US medium tanks were first to fire in 57 percent of Korean tank duels; in the case of M26 tanks, the figure was 60 percent. According to a US operational research study, by engaging first the US tank units increased their effectiveness in tank duels by a factor of 5.9.

In terms of machine guns, all three tanks had similar armament. Both US tanks had a .30cal coaxial machine gun in the turret, and a ball-mounted .30cal machine gun in the hull; the T-34-85 likewise had a 7.62mm coaxial machine gun and a hull-mounted 7.62mm machine gun. The main difference in machine-gun armament was that both US tanks were fitted with a .50cal heavy machine gun on the turret, ostensibly for antiaircraft defense. This weapon was very widely used against enemy infantry and unarmored targets such as trucks. The T-34-85 lacked a heavy machine gun.

Mobility

In terms of basic automotive performance, the T-34-85 had marginally better speed and range than its American opponents. All three tanks were powered by 500hp engines, but the T-34-85 used a diesel engine, while the American tanks were gasoline-powered. As the T-34-85 was lighter, it had a slightly better power-to-weight ratio than the M4A3E8, and a markedly better ratio compared to the M26. The ground-pressure of all three tanks was similar, with the M4A3E8 having the advantage. The T-34-85 carried significantly more fuel compared to the US tanks due to the use of three external 90-liter fuel tanks, and it had significantly longer range.

Although the T-34-85 had a number of advantages over its American opponents in basic automotive characteristics, it had some significant mechanical shortcomings that undermined its actual performance in the field. The T-34-85 transmission was located in the rear of the tank and was actuated by control rods running under

Performance characteristics			
	T-34-85	M4A3E8	M26
Weight, combat-loaded	32.2 tonnes	33.7 tonnes	41.9 tonnes
Power	500hp	500hp	500hp
Max. road speed	54.8km/h	41.8km/h	40.2km/h
Ground pressure	0.83kg/cm²	0.77kg/cm²	0.87kg/cm²
Fuel capacity	545 + 269 external liters (144 + 71 external gallons)	635 liters	692 liters
Road range	298km	62km	62km

the floor, a system that could prove to be problematic without considerable maintenance. The tank used rough clutch-and-brake steering, and the driver's job was awkward and fatiguing due to the use of spur-gear clash-shift transmission and a multi-disc dry clutch that made shifting difficult as well. T-34-85s had a number of design faults and manufacturing problems that also affected automotive performance. US inspection of T-34-85s captured in Korea found poor soldering of the radiator core fins, a problem that significantly degraded the tank's cooling performance. The single worst fault in T-34-85 engine design was a very deficient air cleaner, which could lead to early engine failure due to dust intake and resultant abrasive wear; several hundred miles of driving in the dusty conditions typical of the Korean summer would lead to severe engine power loss.

Of the two American tank designs, the M4A3E8 was definitely the fleeter of the two, in spite of the M26 Pershing's more sophisticated transmission, simply because they both used the same engine and the M26 was significantly heavier. In the later years of the war, after tank-versus-tank combat become a rarity, the M4A3E8 was the preferred tank type in Korea due to its better performance in the hill country. The M26 also had a number of automotive teething problems that had not been completely ironed out in 1945, such as weak fanbelts, that could lead to engine overheating. Of the three tank types compared here, the M4A3E8 was the most reliable and durable.

THE MEN

T-34-85 crew

The crew of the T-34-85 consisted of five men. In the hull was the driver/mechanic on the left side and a bow machine-gunner on the right side. The turret crew consisted of the gunner in the forward left side and the tank commander behind him; the loader was alone on the right side. The interior of the T-34-85 was very austere; crew ergonomics had never been a strong point of Soviet tank design. The T-34-85 lacked a turret basket, and the crew sat on seats suspended from the turret ring. Its interior was considerably more cramped than the M26 Pershing or M4A3E8 Sherman. Ventilation was not especially good in summer weather, and the air became foul very quickly once the main gun began firing. Transit across rough ground was hard on the crew since the suspension lacked any shock absorbers.

The commander was responsible for directing the rest of the crew. During combat actions, communication was by means of the vehicle intercom via the headsets in the canvas crew helmets. The commander communicated with other tanks in his platoon via the 9RS radio transmitter located on the left turret wall; some tanks had the 12 RDM radio, which was actually intended for self-propelled artillery. During combat actions, the commander would select the target to be engaged, and would direct the gunner while at the same time instructing the loader on the type of ammunition to be used.

The gunner operated the main 85mm gun and coaxial 7.92mm DTM machine gun. When not in action, the gunner could observe the terrain using the MK-4 periscope above and to the left of the telescopic sight; at his left shoulder there was also a small view port, which could be used in conjunction with a pistol port for self-defense. The gunner's position offered very poor visibility of the surrounding environment, and so he depended on instructions from the commander for locating the target. Once a target had been identified, the gunner swung the turret in the intended direction with the electro-mechanical turret traverse, using his left hand. The turret traverse was not precise enough for fine gun-laying, but would move the

Inside the T-34-85

turret quickly into the rough azimuth, at which point the gunner would do final corrections using the mechanical turret traverse. The gunner elevated and depressed the main gun with the mechanical elevation wheel using his right hand. He aimed the tank's main armament via the TSh-16 telescopic sight and used the stadia in the sight to estimate the range in order to introduce any necessary elevation corrections for either the main gun or coaxial machine gun. The gunner fired by using foot pedal controls, with the left foot pedal triggering the main gun and the right foot triggering the coaxial machine gun. There were also back-up triggers for both weapons.

Inside the M26 Pershing

1. M2 .50cal heavy machine gun
2. 90mm ammunition ready rack
3. Loader's seat
4. 90mm gun breech
5. Gunner's periscopic sight
6. Gunner's telescopic sight
7. Hydraulic turret traverse mechanism
8. Gunner's gun control yoke
9. Gunner's turret traverse lever
10. Turret azimuth indicator
11. Gunner's seat
12. Commander's seat

Artwork by Richard Chasemore, © Osprey Publishing

The loader had a simple seat suspended from leather straps between the turret ring and the gun trunnion. In combat this seat would be folded up out of the way and the loader would stand on the floor. The immediate source of main gun ammunition consisted of a few rounds stowed vertically in the right rear corner of the fighting compartment, and a rack of four ready rounds on the right rear wall of the turret. The turret bustle contained another 12 rounds of ammunition, and there were two more rounds stowed vertically behind the bow machine-gunner. Once all these rounds were expended, the loader would have to extract rounds from the six metal boxes on the floor that contained the rest of the tank's ammo supply. The gunner's job was made more difficult by the lack of an easy or safe means to dispose of spent shell casings.

The driver, as already noted, had one of the most demanding and exhausting tasks of any of the crew due to the relatively simple tractor-style driving controls and the need to activate the rear brakes via mechanical linkages running along the floor to the rear-mounted transmission. To make matters worse, the front driver's station was quite small and cramped, so drivers had to be both short and exceptionally strong to endure the rigors of the job. The driver was also responsible for the maintenance of the engine.

Adjacent to the driver on the right side of the hull was the bow-gunner, who operated the 7.62mm DT machine gun. This position was also relatively cramped and extremely claustrophobic, since the only view of the outside was via the 2x telescopic sight used to aim the machine gun. The lack of a vision cupola in this station made it unlikely that the bow-gunner could identify a target unless it was very obvious. The dubious utility of this weapon meant that this position was the first left vacant in the event that the vehicle was undermanned. North Korean People's Army (NKPA) prisoners indicated that this weapon was seldom used, and the coaxial machine gun was the preferred weapon against enemy infantry.

M26 crew

The crew layout of the M26 Pershing was conventional, like that in the T-34-85, with two men in the hull and three in the turret. One difference was the turret layout, with the tank commander and gunner in the M26 sitting in the right side of the turret rather than the left. In general, the interior of the M26 was significantly more spacious than in the T-34-85, and the configuration much more modern. Korean War tanker memoirs compared the two as "a rudimentary Ford Model T versus a 1945 Cadillac."

The M26 tank commander sat behind the gunner and to the right side of the main gun. He was responsible for directing the tank crew in combat, and also operated the radio, which was located in the bustle behind him. The tank commander had two seats, one at turret race level for riding inside the tank and a folding seat on the turret wall for riding outside the cupola. The "all-vision" cupola had six laminated-glass vision ports, and the hatch had a fitting for either the standard M6 periscope or a 7x periscopic binocular. In contrast to the T-34-85, the commander in the M26 had a remote control for the power turret traverse, which allowed him to swing the turret in the direction of a target to cue the gunner, providing faster reaction time in a tank duel. US tank commanders were issued

This Pershing crew trainer provides an interesting view of the turret interior. As can be seen, there was a ready rack of ammunition on the left forward side of the turret for the loader. (MHI)

M7 binoculars, which had a built-in stadiametric rangefinder that the commander used to estimate range. As in the T-34-85, the tank commander communicated with the rest of the crew via an internal intercom.

The commander also had a .50cal heavy machine gun mounted on a pintle behind the cupola. As we have seen, this gun was intended for antiaircraft defense, but it was used most often for defense against enemy infantry. It was poorly positioned for this role, however, as the commander usually had to exit the tank and stand on the rear engine deck to employ the machine gun in this role. A large percentage of tank commander casualties were the result of this ill-conceived mounting for the machine gun. Although the problem had been well understood at the end of World War II, nothing was done about it in the aftermath of the war.

The gunner sat immediately in front of the commander. He operated the gun elevation manually via a wheel with his left hand. Power traverse was by a joystick at his right hand, and firing could be done either by a trigger on the joystick or by a button on the floor next to his feet. The telescope was the preferred means of aiming the tank armament when engaging precision targets at long range, but the periscopic sight was preferred at close ranges.

The loader sat in the left side of the turret on a small seat that would be folded up in combat, since the loader needed to stand on the turret floor to get enough leverage to move the heavy ammunition. The Pershing had a ready-rack with ten rounds of ammunition stowed vertically in front and to the left of the loader. Once these were expended, the loader would have to extract ammunition from the stowage bins in the floor.

The hull crew consisted of the driver to the left and the assistant driver/bow-gunner to the right. Drivers in the M26 had a considerably easier time than their counterparts in the T-34-85. The Pershing used a more sophisticated torquematic transmission, which was much simpler and less exhausting to operate. Curiously enough, the assistant driver actually did have a set of redundant driving controls on his side of the tank, though there is little evidence that these were widely used. The main role of the assistant driver was to operate the bow gun, a ball-mounted .30cal machine gun. The bow-gunner's external vision in the Pershing was significantly better than in the T-34-85, by means of a periscopic sight mounted in the hatch above, though aiming the gun with any precision was difficult. Usually, the gun was aimed by observing the tracer ammunition, but when tracer ammunition was lacking, the gunner would usually aim at the ground and walk the machine-gun fire onto the target.

Training the North Korean armored force

The North Korean armored force began to be formed in 1948 with Chinese and Soviet assistance, following the formal creation of the NKPA on February 8, 1948. A small cadre of North Korean tank personnel was organized in China and trained on captured Japanese and American tanks, as well as a few Soviet T-34s. The Soviet army created a special training cadre from officers and NCOs of the Twenty-Fifth Army, which had liberated Korea from the Japanese in 1945. In 1948, the Soviets also formed the 15th Tank Training Regiment at Sadong, in the suburbs of Pyongyang. This unit had two T-34-85 tanks and instruction was provided by a team of about 30 Soviet tank officers. The regiment was commanded by Senior Colonel Yu Kyong Su, who had served as a lieutenant in the Soviet army in World War II and later commanded the North Korean 4th Infantry Regiment. His selection for the command of this important unit was helped by the fact that he was the brother-in-law of premier Kim Il-Sung's wife. The unit's original cadre came mainly from soldiers who had served in Korean infantry units formed since 1945; most of the officers had served earlier in the Soviet or Chinese armies. The initial training consisted primarily of technical instruction, the trainees stripping and reassembling the two T-34-85 training tanks on hand.

In May 1949, the 15th Tank Training Regiment was reorganized and its cadets became the officers of the new 105th Armored Brigade. This formation was intended to serve as the shock force in Kim Il-Sung's invasion of South Korea, so no

T-34-85: through the gunsights

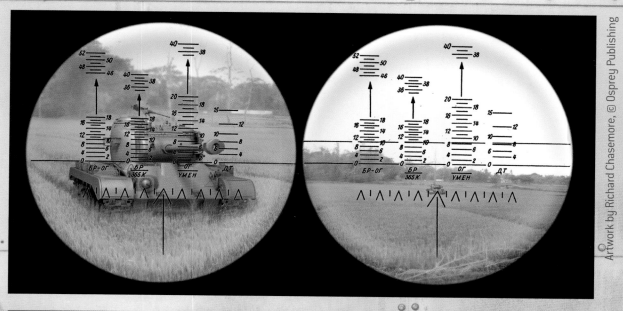

Artwork by Richard Chasemore, © Osprey Publishing

The T-34-85's TSh-16 sight was a 4x power telescope with a simple stadiametric rangefinder configured into the reticle. The four vertical bands are for providing ballistic corrections for the four main types of ammunition (from left to right): armor-piercing (AP), hyper-velocity armor-piercing (HVAP), high-explosive (HE), and the DT machine gun. The lower lines, consisting of upside-down Vs and dashes, provide a stadiametric scale, with the width of the center V roughly equivalent to the length of a tank when viewed at 1,000m. The horizontal line bisecting the image represents the elevation of the gun. In the view on the left, the gun is at 0 range.

The view through the sight on the left shows the gunner's aim when dealing with a point-blank target, such as encountered during the duel at Obong-Ni Ridge. At a range of under 100m, no super-elevation of the gun is necessary as there is essentially no ballistic drop for the projectile.

The view to the right shows an engagement with a Pershing at a range of 1,000m. In this case, the gunner compensates for the range by adjusting the elevation of the gun upwards, as represented by the horizontal line in the reticle. Since the commander has instructed the crew to use BR-365K HVAP shot, the gunner would adjust the horizontal line to the second set of vertical bands, placing it over the "10" line, which represents 1,000m.

efforts were spared to prepare it for combat. Since hardly 20 percent of Korean men were literate, recruitment for the tank force was more select than for the infantry.

The brigade was based around the 107th, 109th and 203rd Tank Regiments. It received its full complement of T-34-85 tanks in October 1949, with each regiment receiving 40 T-34-85 tanks. The brigade also included the 308th Armored Battalion with 16 SU-76M assault guns and the truck-mounted 206th Motorized

T-34-85 number 800, which belonged to the commander of the 16th Armored Brigade, knocked out in the Naktong fighting on September 4, 1950. This newly formed unit, only a few companies in strength, was prematurely committed to the September 1 offensive against the Pusan perimeter, where it was decimated.

Infantry Regiment. The brigade went through intensive training through the spring of 1950. The training tasks of the former 15th Tank Training Regiment were shifted to the newly formed 208th Tank Training Regiment under the command of Colonel Kim Chol Won, a Chinese People's Liberation Army veteran.

One of the main problems facing the Soviet instructors was the shortage of translators. Few Russians had any knowledge of the Korean language, and most of the Korean soldiers who had served in the Red Army in World War II were earmarked for command slots in the NKPA, not for employment as translators. Indeed, many of the higher-level command documents were written in Russian. The brigade never trained to operate as a unified unit; rather, it was intended for use in its component parts for infantry support, with the individual tank regiments attached to infantry divisions in the offensive.

With its full complement of equipment on hand, the component elements of the brigade were dispatched to separate bases for further training. The 107th Tank Regiment, commanded by Colonel Choe U Sik, along with the brigade's infantry, motorcycle, and training regiments remained at the original Sadong base. The 109th Tank Regiment, commanded by Colonel Kim Tae Ryon, was shipped to Chorwon, where the troops worked through December 1949 creating their own barracks. The 203rd Tank Regiment, led by the former commander of the 1st Battalion, 15th Tank Training Regiment, Colonel Choe Ul Suk, was sent to Namchonjom.

The training in early 1950 consisted of instrument familiarization, operation of the tank radio and intercom system, operation of the 85mm gun and 7.62mm machine gun, and driving instruction. The crew members were taught only the skills needed for one position in the crew; there was no cross-training. Gunnery instruction was limited by parsimonious allotments of practice ammunition, and in general there was little or no practice in tank-versus-tank fighting, since it was presumed that no enemy tanks would be encountered. Captured prisoners indicated that they had only fired two rounds of live main gun ammunition in prewar practice. Although North Korean tanks did carry AP ammunition, the standard crew drill stressed the use of HE ammunition, which was the principal type used in the 105th Armored Brigade. Most of the units conducted three-day, battalion-level exercises prior to the start of the war. Further details of North Korean tank crew training are scant due to the severe losses suffered by the units in combat.

At the time of the North Korean invasion of South Korea in June 1950, the NKPA possessed 242 T-34-85 tanks, about half of them in the 105th Armored Brigade, including the 20 tanks with its 208th Tank Training Regiment. The remainder were intended as replacements or for new armor units. In contrast to the extensive training provided to the 105th Armored Brigade, the follow-on units received only hasty training (often as little as a month), mainly from the North Korean cadre. The 41st, 42nd, 43rd, 45th, and 46th Tank Regiments were actually understrength battalions seldom with more than 15 tanks each. Two more tank brigades were also being formed, the 16th and 17th, but they only reached tank regiment strength (about 40–45 tanks) by the time they were committed to action for the September 1 offensive on the Naktong River.

As well as the T-34-85 tanks, there were 176 SU-76M assault guns and 54 BA-64 armored cars. Besides their employment in the tank units, the SU-76M assault gun battalions were also attached to several of the frontline North Korean infantry divisions for fire support. They were sometimes called Samouth by the NKPA troops, a corruption of the Russian *samokhodnaya ustanovka* ("self-propelled carriage").

Training the US tank force

The US Army and Marine Corps underwent a substantial demobilization after the end of World War II. The Army's size fell from eight million men in late 1945 to about one million in 1947, and of that figure nearly 400,000 belonged to the newly independent US Air Force. Major armored forces deployed overseas amounted to only three US Constabulary brigades in occupied Germany and four tank companies attached to the occupation divisions in Japan, equipped with the M24 Chaffee light tank. Worsening relations with the Soviet Union encouraged the US government to halt the military decline and to begin a gradual rebuilding of Army strength. This program eventually included the conversion of the three Constabulary brigades in

Germany into armored cavalry regiments, the creation of the 3rd Armored Cavalry Regiment in the United States, and the strengthening of the 2nd Armored Division. On paper, each infantry division was supposed to have an organic tank battalion, but as will be seen later, this had not necessarily taken place by 1950.

The US Army wrote off a large number of tanks immediately after the end of hostilities due to age or damage, and by the end of 1945 was down to about 29,000 tanks. Of these, 6,426 were disposed of by the end of June 1949, some via foreign aid contributions and further demilitarization. The table on page 192 shows the holdings at the end of June 1949, broken down into holdings in the US Zone of the Interior (ZI) and overseas. These total holdings were far in excess of the US Army's actual force structure requirements, so in 1949 the Army Field Forces prepared a report for a "Balanced Tank Program," which planned to cut the inventory by more than half, some of the tanks being transferred as further foreign aid, and others converted as recovery vehicles.

US Army tank crew training remained centered on the Armored School at Fort Knox. However, the miniscule size of the armored force in the postwar years led to a greatly shrunken program. During the Korean War, the US Army depended heavily on veteran tank crews who had been in uniform since World War II, or reservists called up after the outbreak of the war. So, for example, the commanders of the first four US Army tank battalions deployed to Korea were all experienced tank commanders. The 6th Tank Battalion was led by LtCol John S. Growdon, who had served in the headquarters of the 9th Armored Division; the 70th Tank Battalion was commanded by LtCol William Rodgers, who commanded a tank battalion in the Pacific theater in World War II; the 73rd Tank Battalion was led by LtCol Calvin Hannum, who had served in the wartime headquarters of the 2nd Armored Division; the 89th Tank Battalion was commanded by LtCol Welborn Dolvin, who commanded the 191st Tank Battalion in World War II. Indeed, the combat experience of the US tankers would be a major factor in the success of US tank units in action against the North Korean tank force in 1950. While most enlisted men in both the Army and Marine Corps were recent inductees, tank units had a disproportionate share of NCOs, many of whom were World War II veterans. In the case of the Army tank battalions, many of the NCOs had served in training units.

Although the individual skills of US tankers were considerably better than those of their North Korean counterparts, any organizational advantages were almost entirely lacking. The first units to see combat were separate tank companies of the four infantry divisions in Japan. These were equipped with M24 light tanks, which were incapable of dealing with the T-34-85 and were brushed aside while incurring heavy casualties. In the wake of the disastrous pummeling of American and South

M26 Pershing: through the gunsights

Artwork by Richard Chasemore, © Osprey Publishing

The M26 gunner could aim the main gun either using the M10F periscope or the M73 telescope. This set of views shows the use of the M10F periscope in order to highlight the value of such a sight. Its main advantage over a telescopic sight was that it provided the gunner with better situational awareness by allowing him to observe the terrain at low (1x) magnification, and then switch to high (6x) magnification for precise aiming. The periscopic sight was generally preferred when dealing with short-range targets or during engagements when rapid response was needed. The telescopic sight was preferred for engaging long-range targets, as it offered better resolution at longer ranges and tended to keep bore-sight better than the periscopic sight, which was knocked out of alignment more easily by vibration or other impacts.

The center lines capped by a "+" sign are the main aiming axis. The horizontal lines provide the necessary ballistic correction for engaging targets at longer range and are gradated in 400-yard intervals. So the "8" represents 800 yards, the "12," 1,200 yards, etc. At a relatively short range of 400 yards, such as seen here, the unitary power view can be used. The view to the right shows the view when switched to higher 6x magnification. Although the reticle here could be used for simple stadiametric rangefinding, US practice was for the tank commander to determine range through binoculars that incorporated a rangefinding reticle. The commander would then instruct the gunner on which target to engage and would provide him with range data at the same time. The gunner would then adjust the horizontal line within the "aiming +" to the proper range.

Korean units in early July, the US Army began mobilizing tank units to rush to Korea. There were very few tank battalions near strength. The 6th Tank Battalion had been reactivated on January 31, 1949, and was equipped with the new M46 medium tank. Two more training battalions were also available: the 70th Tank

Battalion, which was the training battalion at Fort Knox with M4A3 and M26 tanks, and the 73rd Tank Battalion with M26 tanks from the infantry school at Fort Benning. As well as these three battalions, the Eighth Army in Japan managed to scrape together 54 rebuilt M4A3E8 Shermans and form them into the 8072nd (later the 89th) Medium Tank Battalion. The first company from this unit arrived in Korea in late July and was committed to combat on August 2, 1950. The Marine Corps activated Co. A of the 1st Marine Brigade, and reequipped it with M26 Pershing tanks replacing the previously-equipped M4A3(105) howitzer tanks. This company was attached to the 1st Marine Provisional Brigade. Later in the summer, the entire brigade was dispatched to Korea to serve under the reactivated Marine 1st Division. These tank units began to reach the embattled Pusan perimeter at the southeastern tip of the Korean peninsula in early to mid-August 1950.

The experiences of the 70th Tank Battalion illustrate the haste with which the units were mobilized. LtCol Bill Rodgers received a phone call on Monday morning, July 8, 1950, and was told that he had been placed in command of the battalion and that it would depart for an unspecified foreign assignment that Friday, five days later. Tank Cos. A and C had 22 M4A3E8 Shermans each, and Co. B had 22 M26 Pershings, all old and beat-up tanks used for training. The companies were being used by the Armor School at Fort Knox for gunnery, driving, communications, and recovery training, as well as for tank–infantry team demonstrations. To bolster tank

US tank postwar inventory, 1945–50					
	Dec 31, 1945 total	1949, ZI	1949, OS	1949 total	1950 plan
M22, M5A1 light tank	4,337	964	0	964	0
M24 light tank	4,962	3,379	454	3,833	3,833
M4 (75mm) medium tank	6,933	5,455	156	5,611	0
M4 (76mm) medium tank	6,582	5,635	65	5,700	3,688
M4 (105mm) howitzer tank	3,731	2,886	97	2,983	0
M26 medium tank	1,918	1,523	378	1,901	0
M45 (105mm) howitzer tank	185	183	0	183	183
M46 medium tank	0	18	0	18	810
Other 90mm tank	0	49	0	49	47
Flamethrower, other tanks	n/a	151	0	151	149
Total	**28,648**	**20,243**	**1,150**	**21,393**	**8,710**

strength, some M26 tanks that had been parked as monument tanks around the base were hastily sent through maintenance, and Rock Island Arsenal dispatched additional Shermans to the port of embarkation to make up for the worn-out tanks. All the tank companies were short-staffed, and tank crews were hastily dispatched from various units at Fort Campbell, Fort Meade and Fort Knox to bring the unit up to strength.

The battalion departed Fort Knox, Kentucky, on July 17 by train cross-continent, arrived at Camp Stoneman, California, on July 20, departed Fort Mason by transport ship on July 23 and arrived in the Pusan perimeter on August 7. LtCol Rodgers later remarked: "We sailed on a ship with two other tank battalions, the 6th and the 73rd, whose men had the same kind of hectic stories to tell. We landed at Pusan and went straight into combat, a complete bunch of strangers with no training." The battalion began to deploy towards Taegu on August 13, a little over a month after mobilization. One of the unit's enlisted men recalled that "Many of the men had stayed in the Army following World War II, and other like myself had joined the peacetime army but never thought we would be called on to go to war, certainly not in Korea. But here we were on this little train headed north from Pusan to Taegu where we would unload and soon be tested in the fire of combat."

The situation with the US Marine tanks was essentially the same. In July 1950, the USMC mobilized its 1st Marine Provisional Brigade to rush to Korea. The brigade's armor attachment, Co. A, 1st Tank Battalion, was the only active-duty Marine tank company on the west coast. It was commanded by Capt Gearl M. English, a veteran World War II tanker, like his Army counterparts. He had crewed an M2A4 light tank with one of the early Marine tank deployments (Co. A, 2nd Tank Battalion) in 1941 in Iceland and served through much of the war as an instructor at the Marine Tank School at Jacques' Farm. In 1944, he was assigned as a platoon leader

The first Pershing tanks to see combat in Korea were found in Tokyo depots and hastily shipped to Korea. They were used to form a provisional tank company, but during their first engagement at Chinju against the NKPA 6th Infantry Division on July 28, all were lost due to mechanical breakdowns. This photo of the unit was taken during training at Taegu on July 20, 1950. There is an M24 Chaffee and an M8 armored car in the background.

On arrival at Pusan harbor in early August, Co. A, Marine 1st Tank Battalion, was loaded on flatcars for shipment to the front. The deployment was so hasty that the tank guns were bore-sighted from the flatcars against neighboring hills. (USMC)

with Co. C, 4th Tank Battalion and saw combat on Roi-Namur, Saipan, and Tinian, and earned the Silver Star during the violent fighting on Iwo Jima in 1945.

Co. A was normally equipped with M4A3 tanks, but for deployment to Korea it drew M26 Pershings from the Barstow Marine tank depot. The Marine Corps had obtained 102 Pershings from the Army, but most Marine units, including Co. A, continued to use the M4A3 (105mm) howitzer tank for peacetime training. The only Pershing tanks in the battalion prior to Korea were in the HQ and Services Company, but it had been battalion practice in 1948–49 to rotate tank crews through this unit to acquaint them with the new tank. Conversion to the Pershing was not overly difficult, as the fire controls and engine were the same as the M4A3. As in the case of the Army tank battalions, the company was brought up to full strength on the eve of its deployment by calling in Marine tankers from posts scattered around the United States. The company had just one day on the tank ranges to become familiar with the new tank, and each gunner/loader team was able to fire only two rounds of 90mm ammunition. Although the company had a nominal strength of 22 tanks, five extra tanks had been dispatched for the tank platoon attached to the Marine regiment, at least on paper, and these were manned by the company headquarters staff.

The company arrived at Pusan on August 2, 1950, and was immediately dispatched to the front line. Time was so short that the company completed its first gunnery practice and gun bore-sighting from the railroad flatcars moving them to the front. As will be recounted later, this company was the first of the Stateside replacements to encounter the T-34-85 in combat.

BATTLEGROUND: KOREA 1950

K orea had been occupied by US and Soviet forces in 1945, with the Red Army north of the 38th Parallel, and the US Army to the south. With the onset of the Cold War, both areas set up their own rival governments, with promises to unify the country under each government's respective control. The US Army largely abandoned South Korea in 1949 except for small training detachments. Although the Republic of Korea (ROK) had begun to set up its own ROK Army (ROKA), the US government was reluctant to provide it with offensive weapons more powerful than small arms because of concerns that the Syngman Rhee government would attempt to reunify the country by force. The Soviet Union and China in the meantime had equipped the NKPA with the full understanding that the Kim Il-Sung government had the same ambitions. Feckless US diplomacy led Stalin and Mao to conclude that Korea was outside the US sphere of influence after the 1949 troop withdrawals, and so gave the North Koreans the green light to initiate the war. War planning was conducted with Soviet assistance. Under the cover of peace negotiations, on June 12–23, the NKPA moved seven infantry divisions and the 105th Armored Brigade to within 10–15km of the 38th Parallel separating the two zones. The plan was based on a marked superiority of the NKPA over the ROKA, with a 2:1 advantage in troops and rifles, a 7:1 advantage in machine guns, and a 13:1 advantage in submachine guns. The ROKA had no significant field artillery or tanks. The June plan, completed with Soviet assistance, expected that the NKPA would advance 15–20km per day and that the campaign would last 22–27 days.

While the NKPA tank force seems puny by today's standards, in 1950 this was the most formidable force in Asia except for that of the Soviet army. Japan's armored force had been destroyed in the war, and China's force was a motley collection of captured Japanese and American tanks. The US Army had no substantial tank force in occupied Japan beyond four companies of M24 Chaffee light tanks, and had withdrawn the medium tanks used in the occupation of South Korea in 1949. South Korea had no tank force and its only armored vehicles were 37 M8 armored cars and a small number of M3 half-tracks of a cavalry regiment

The North Korean invasion: June 25–August 4, 1950

Sariwon

XX 10

Yesong River

XX 13

P'yonggang

Kumhwa

XX 15

x 3BG

XX 6

XX 1

XX 4
Ch'orwon

XX 3

XX 2

XX 12

x 1BG

Yangyang

Haeju

II 203   II 107   II 100

38th Parallel

Kaesong

ROK Capitol (-)

ROK 1

XX ROK 7

Ch'unch'on

XX ROK 6

XX ROK 8
Kangnung

Uijongbu

SEOUL

Inch'on

Suwon

Hon River

Samch'ok

Osan

Ch'ungju

Ulchin

XX ROK 8

XX ROK 6

ROK 7

Kum River

Remnants Cap., 1, 2

XX ROK 3

Yongdok

US 2   Taejon

Uisong

Kunsan

Kumch'on

P'ohang-dong

Chonju

Waegwan

TAEGU

Naktong River

Chinju   Masan

Kwangju

PUSAN

Makp'o

Posong   Yosu

TSUSHIMA

N

0   40 miles
0   40 km

◄···· North Korean attacks
◄--- North Korean attacks
◄— North Korean attacks
◄····· North Korean attacks
······· The Pusan Defense Perimeter, evening August 4, 1950

of the 1st Capitol Division in Seoul. Antitank weapons were poor and consisted of 140 ineffective 57mm antitank guns – an American copy of the British 6pdr – and about 1,900 2.36in bazookas.

The NKPA planned to use the 105th Armored Brigade as the spearhead of its invasion of South Korea. Korea is an extremely mountainous country, particularly along its eastern coast. The traditional invasion route has been along the western coast, as the mountains gradually give way to a coastal plain. Equally importantly, the South Korean capital of Seoul was located in this area, so it was the natural destination of the 105th Armored Brigade. Contrary to Soviet doctrine, the brigade did not fight as a single unit, but its regiments were doled out to support NKPA infantry divisions.

North Korea's ally, the People's Republic of China, sent combat troops to Korea in late 1950. PLA T-34-85 units were first deployed to Korea in February 1951 and saw limited combat. After being decimated in the summer fighting, the PLA 3rd Tank Regiment was withdrawn to China for rebuilding and took part in the 1953 National Day Parade in Tiananmen Square in Beijing to honor its service.

THE ACTION

The lead NKPA tank unit was the 109th Tank Regiment, commanded by Colonel Kim Tae Ryon, which was attached to the NKPA 3rd Infantry Division. These formations were the first across the border at 0500hrs on June 25, 1950, near Sachang-Ni in the westernmost section of South Korea. This unit overran the ROK 17th Infantry Regiment, and other NKPA units soon followed. Colonel Choe Ul Suk's 203rd Tank Regiment was attached to the NKPA's 1st Infantry Division, and attacked along the Kaesong–Seoul "Unification" highway. The 107th Tank Regiment led by Colonel Choe U Sik overran the ROK 12th Regiment of the 1st Infantry Division at Kaesong and the 13th Regiment near a ford over the Imjin River near Korangpo. South Korean troops claim to have knocked out 11 T-34 tanks during the Imjin fighting, but later interrogations of NKPA tankers revealed that none had been lost, although several had been damaged. The 107th Tank Regiment, supporting the NKPA 4th Infantry Division, attacked along the Yonchon–Seoul road, to the east of the other two tank regiments. It crushed several units of the ROK 7th Infantry Division.

Most South Korean troops had never seen a tank before, and the ineffectiveness of their 57mm guns and 2.36in bazookas was demoralizing. Several Korean infantry units attempted to stop the tanks with improvised satchel charges or TNT blocks wrapped around grenades, at high cost – some 90 soldiers of the 1st Division alone were killed using these desperate tactics. The helplessness of the South Korean infantry at the hands of the North Korean tanks led to "tank panic," which eroded the ROK's resistance.

After overcoming the remaining defenses of the ROK 7th Infantry Division, the NKPA 107th and 109th Tank Regiments met up on June 27 at Uijongbu, which served as the staging point for the main attack on Seoul. Following the capture of Seoul on June 28, the brigade moved to the Han River. In panic, the ROK Army prematurely blew the main railroad bridge over the river, with heavy ROK traffic still on it, killing several hundred soldiers and civilian refugees. This catastrophe left significant elements of the ROK Army trapped on the northern side of the Han River, along with most of their heavy equipment, and they were quickly overcome.

The NKPA engineers now needed several days to improvize means for the tanks to cross the river. The first tanks were not across until July 3, and the 109th Tank Regiment took part in the capture of the port of Inchon the same day.

In the meantime, the US Army began mobilizing forces to rush to Korea, and won United Nations (UN) approval for a multinational campaign. The first source of troops was units stationed on occupation duty in Japan. Task Force Smith from the 24th Infantry Division was the first to arrive, consisting of about 400 infantrymen. On July 5, the NKPA had its first encounter with Task Force Smith near Osan, when the US infantry unit was attacked by 33 T-34-85 tanks of the 107th Tank Regiment. US 105mm howitzers began engaging the tanks with HE ammunition, which killed many NKPA infantry riding the tanks Soviet-style but failed to stop the tanks themselves. A 105mm howitzer battery, however, waited until the tanks were within 500 yards (457m) and managed to knock out the two lead T-34-85 tanks using high-explosive antitank (HEAT) ammunition. Yet there were only six HEAT rounds available, which were quickly exhausted. US troops also fired on the tanks with two 75mm recoilless rifles, which proved useless. The battalion's main antitank weapon, the 2.36in bazooka, was equally ineffective, and no fewer than 22 rockets were fired without effect. The Task Force managed to disable only four tanks before being forced to retreat. Task Force Smith lost about 150 men, over a third of its strength, in the one-sided battle.

The principal antitank weapon of the ROK Army was the towed 57mm antitank gun, an American copy of the British 6pdr. This gun had limited capability against the T-34-85, except against the side armor. This ROK Army 57mm gun is being towed by a ¾-ton truck during the evacuation of Suwon airbase in 1950. (NARA)

The 34th Infantry was the first large US unit to arrive at the battlefront, and deployed around Chonan. When attacked by T-34-85 tanks on July 8, the regimental commander, Col Bob Martin, attempted to rally his dispirited troops in the street fighting. After grabbing a bazooka, he faced down a T-34-85 tank in the town, but the rocket failed to stop the tank. He was blown in half by tank fire at close range; the US positions disintegrated against the relentless tank assaults.

On July 9, the NKPA's 105th Armored Brigade, recently given the honorific title of 105th Seoul Tank Division, was united near Suwon for further operations. Up to this time, the brigade had only lost two tanks to mines and two more in the fighting with Task Force Smith. The NKPA's heaviest armor losses occurred on June 28, when seven of the brigade's 16 SU-76M assault guns were knocked out by counterbattery fire from the 105mm howitzers of the ROK 6th Infantry Division near Chunchon. By now, the UN operation to thwart the NKPA invasion was beginning to take shape, but American air actions against the armored spearheads in early July were ineffective, contrary to pilots' claims.

The four US Army divisions with the Eighth Army in Japan – the 7th, 24th, 25th Infantry, and 1st Cavalry – nominally each had an attached tank battalion, respectively the 77th, 78th, 79th, and 71st Tank Battalions. But because of the narrow roads and delicate bridges in Japan, they in fact only had a single company from each battalion, equipped with the M24 Chaffee light tank. These were rushed to Korea.

The first of these units to see combat was Co. A, 78th Heavy Tank Battalion, which supported the 21st Infantry Regiment of the 24th Infantry Division at Chonjui on July 10. The M24s were hopelessly outclassed by the Korean T-34-85s; they scored several direct hits on the enemy tanks, but only disabled one. Two M24s were lost in the first day of fighting when their poorly maintained gun recoil systems malfunctioned, wrecking the guns and the turrets. Three more M24s were lost the following day. The M24 was vulnerable not only to the T-34's 85mm gun, but also the NKPA's 14.5mm PTRS antitank rifles, which the American tankers labeled "buffalo guns." The poor performance of the M24 against the T-34-85s demoralized the crews, and the tankers proved to be very skittish in supporting the infantry in the ensuing battles for the Kum River line, even without NKPA tank opposition. By August, only two tanks of the original 14 in the company were left. The other two tank companies were also roughly handled: Co. A, 71st Tank Battalion, lost most of its tanks by early August, and Co. A, 79th Tank Battalion, suffered in several unequal skirmishes with T-34-85s. US Army commanders soon lost confidence in tank support and pleaded instead for better antitank weapons. Supplies of 3.5in "super-bazookas" were airlifted to Korea in mid-July.

NKPA infantry from the 3rd and 4th Divisions overcame US resistance along the Kum River without tank support in mid-July. The 107th Tank Regiment moved across

The only US tanks available in Japan at the start of the Korean War were M24 Chaffee light tanks, which were completely inadequate against the T-34-85. This is an M24 of the 24th Reconnaissance Company, 24th Infantry Division, in the Pusan perimeter on August 17, 1950. (NARA)

the river around July 16 to support the assault on the surviving elements of the US Army 24th Infantry Division at Taejon. The battle of Taejon was the first time that 3.5in bazookas were available, and they were first used in action on July 20, knocking out two T-34-85 tanks in the first encounter. Through the course of the day, tank-hunting teams destroyed or disabled several more T-34-85s in the streets of Taejon. They included a team led by the divisional commander, MajGen William F. Dean. Dean took the personal lead in an urban tank-hunting mission to convince his troops that the new bazookas could destroy the previously invincible T-34 tanks, especially in the close confines of a town. The NKPA lost about 15 tanks in the fighting for Taejon, its heaviest armored losses to date. Seven of these were due to bazookas and five were caused by air attacks. Nevertheless, the 24th Infantry Division suffered about 30 percent casualties in the fighting, including Gen Dean, and Taejon was lost.

On July 20, 1950, during the hasty defense of Taejon, the commander of the US 24th Infantry Division led a detachment to prove that the newly arrived 3.5in bazooka could stop a T-34-85. This is one of two tanks knocked out by Dean's group that day, the first small victory against NKPA armor. (NARA)

The Pusan perimeter

With the fall of Taejon on July 20, US and South Korean forces pulled back over the Naktong River to the Pusan perimeter at the southeasternmost tip of Korea, there to await further UN reinforcements. The main cause of North Korean tank casualties in late July was the poor road conditions in the mountainous country leading towards the Pusan perimeter. The tanks began to show the first signs of wear caused by the intensive actions of the previous weeks of fighting and by the harsh terrain; some tanks had to be cannibalized for parts. More heavy losses were suffered at Kumchon on July 23, when several tanks were destroyed in minefields and several more knocked out by bazookas during a bloody battle with the "Wolfhounds" of the 27th Infantry. This was the first time an NKPA armored attack had been stopped by US infantry and proved the effectiveness of the new 3.5in bazookas in the hands of determined troops. The minefields and infantry resistance delayed the NKPA tank advance, and on July 28 the UN airstrikes finally began to take effect, when at least five tanks were knocked out by rocket and napalm attacks. By early August, the operational strength of the North Korean armored brigade was down to only about 40 T-34-85 tanks, with many others waiting by the roadside for repair. Although the air attacks did not destroy the number of tanks claimed, they did disrupt the supply of spare parts and replacement tanks.

The air attacks led the North Korean armored brigade to change its tactics, and large-scale movements were confined to night to avoid the UN aircraft. Attempts to cross the Naktong River were rebuffed at least twice by US aircraft, which claimed another five tanks. In the meantime, another US tank action took place. Three broken-down M26 Pershing tanks had been discovered at the Tokyo Ordnance Depot and were quickly refurbished and shipped to Korea. They formed a provisional tank platoon alongside a small number of M24 Chaffees, and were used in attempts to defend Chinju from the NKPA 6th Infantry Division on July 28. However, they broke down during the fighting and were abandoned.

The Marine Corps' Co. A, 1st Tank Battalion, was the first of the Stateside units to arrive in Pusan, on August 2, 1950, and the first to be sent into combat. The four US Army tank battalions mobilized in July 1950 also began to reach the embattled Pusan perimeter by mid-August. The first Army medium tank unit in action was the 89th Tank Battalion, equipped with three companies of M4A3E8s and one of M26 Pershings; the surviving M24s of the 79th Tank Battalion were attached as a fifth company. The battalion's introduction to combat was not auspicious. A tank company of M4A3E8 Shermans led an attack near Masan on August 2, and were ambushed by an NKPA 45mm antitank platoon, which knocked out eight tanks in quick succession. The battalion saw no further tank fighting in early August, but was extensively and successfully used in support of local infantry actions.

The standard US Army and Marine infantry support weapon in the Korean War was the M20 75mm recoilless rifle. This was often used in encounters with North Korean tanks, but was seldom effective, as its HE projectile had little armor-penetrating power. (NARA)

As US Army and Marine tank strength began building up in the Pusan perimeter, the UN forces began to conduct a more vigorous defense, including some local counterattacks. The tide was beginning to turn very slowly in favor of the UN and the US Army was regaining its confidence in its tank units.

The NKPA 105th Armored Brigade finally made it across the Naktong River and took part in the attacks on Taegu on August 12, 1950. The 2nd Battalion of the 109th Tank Regiment was decimated by severe UN air attacks on Chonjui around August 13, with the regiment losing 20 tanks and having several more damaged. The surviving tanks of the 105th Armored Brigade were dispersed, and they supported NKPA infantry assaults on towns all along the Pusan perimeter rather than being concentrated for one major blow. Finally, on August 15, an independent tank battalion with 21 T-34-85 tanks from the Sadong tank training center arrived to make up for the losses of the previous weeks of fighting. During the crossing of the Naktong River near Waegwan, the brigade was again subjected to merciless air attack.

Duel at Obong-Ni Ridge

US Marine tanks were the first to defeat the invincible NKPA T-34-85s. By mid-August 1950, the North Korean offensive was running out of steam in the face of increasing resistance from US and ROK forces. The first US/ROK efforts to break out of the Pusan perimeter had begun on August 17, 1950, with attacks towards the Naktong River. The 5th Regiment of the 1st Provisional Marine Brigade was assigned to seize the Obong-Ni Ridge, better known to the Marines as "No Name Ridge," a mile-long series of hills averaging about 350ft (107m) in elevation. On the northern flank was the US Army's 9th Infantry Regiment. The infantry were supported by a platoon of four M26 Pershing tanks of Co. A, Marine 1st Tank Battalion, led by Lt Granville Sweet. Opposing them was the NKPA 4th Infantry Division, supported by the 2nd Battalion, 109th Tank Regiment.

The fighting that day was dominated by infantry actions, with the American assault supported both by artillery and airstrikes. By early evening, the 5th Marines and the US 9th Infantry began to set up defensive positions for the night. Around 2000hrs, Lt Sweet received the radio message "Flash Purple," the Marine code for imminent tank attack. The Pershing tanks were in the process of refueling, and they moved forward individually as they completed this task. Up to this time, the T-34-85 tanks had proven invincible, but Sweet was determined that his platoon would halt the North Korean drive, if only by blocking the road through a narrow defile with the hulks of their tanks. The 1/5th Marines had set up a tank ambush, though there was little confidence that it would do much good against the North Korean tanks.

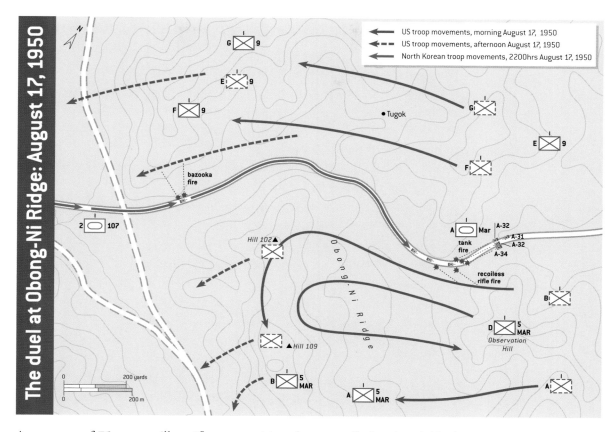

A company of 75mm recoilless rifles was positioned on a small elevation dubbed "Observation Hill," with a clear field of fire towards the road. Marine positions forward of the tank platoon had deployed their 3.5in bazooka teams on Hill 125, which covered the road on the north side. The North Korean column was first hit by an air attack by Marine F4U Corsairs, which stripped away some of the accompanying infantry; the Marine pilots also claimed to have damaged one T-34-85 tank.

The platoon of four T-34-85 tanks of 2nd Battalion, 109th Tank Regiment, advanced down a road between the positions of the US Army 9th Infantry Regiment to the north, and the 5th Marines to the south, and threatened to cut behind American lines. Bazooka and recoilless rifle teams fired on the tanks, setting their external fuel tanks on fire but failing to stop them.

When the first T-34-85 turned around the corner of the hill, it was confronted by a solid steel phalanx of M26 tanks blocking the road. Three of the Pershings were arranged in a line from left to right, consisting of TSgt Cecil Fullerton's A-34, Sgt Gerald Swinicke's A-33, and Sgt Basilo Chavarria's A-32, with Sweet's tank (A-31) behind them. Sweet's tank had a problem with the gun elevation mechanism, and so would take no direct part in the duel.

Fullerton's tank spotted the first North Korean tank to round the bend and began engaging it with HVAP ammunition. After the first three rounds were fired, Fullerton complained to his gunner, Sgt Stanley Tarnowski, "You missed, Ski!" Tarnowski replied "I don't miss, Sergeant Fullerton." Tarnowski had a reputation in the unit as a crack shot, and it would be hard to miss at point-blank range. In fact, the HVAP was such an overmatch for the T-34-85 glacis armor at such short range that the rounds had passed through the tank.

The first round had struck the glacis near the hull machine gun, killing the gunner and killing or wounding the loader before punching through the rear plate. Marines on a neighboring hill thought they themselves were under fire when the three rounds impacted near them. Curiously enough, the Marine tanks then burst into flames, though not from enemy action. In the haste to finish refueling, a considerable amount of gas had been spilled on the decks of some of the Pershings. The initial gun blasts ignited the gasoline fumes; these were extinguished by the subsequent gun blast, only to be ignited by the next shot in a curious pyrotechnic display.

The second T-34-85 foolishly continued past the stalled lead tank and was hit by a volley of fire from the Marine tanks. One round struck the turret, which swung uncontrollably to the left, firing its gun into the banking. The third T-34-85 attempted to fire back past the wrecks of the two other tanks, but was soon pummeled by seven rounds of APC and HVAP. Three of the crew escaped from the stricken tank, but were killed by small-arms fire. The Marines kept pouring fire into the tanks to set them ablaze, until ordered to stop by Lt Sweet. The skirmish had lasted less than ten minutes. Accounts of the action vary, with some reports claiming that the NKPA tanks repeatedly fired back at the Pershings, but the brigade after-action report states that the NKPA tanks fired only two rounds. The fourth NKPA tank, that of the 2nd Battalion commander in tank 314, escaped down the road, but was knocked out by an army bazooka team from the neighboring F Co., 9th Infantry.

The Marines later surmised that the North Koreans had continued to advance because they thought they were only facing the puny M24 tanks encountered over the previous weeks. The lead T-34-85 tanks did not burn when first hit, so the following tanks did not realize the danger they faced. Assuming, therefore, that they were impervious to the 75mm guns of the M24, they continued to advance, only to be blasted by the 90mm guns.

The official Marine history later recalled that the duel had "shattered the myth of the T-34 in five flaming minutes." The T-34-85, once dreaded as invincible, was now derisively called the "Caviar Can." The NKPA attack had employed careless tactics. Until this point in the war, the T-34-85 had had nothing to fear from any weapon, so the Korean tankers were overconfident. The Marine tankers were surprised that the T-34-85s continued to advance around the corner, even after the first tank had been hit. Nor were the Marines impressed with North Korean gunnery skills. The NKPA tank crews seemed unprepared for action and failed to respond quickly enough once the firefight began.

The duel near the Obong-Ni Ridge also reinforces a conclusion of operational research on tank-versus-tank fighting in World War II: the tank that sees the enemy first and fires first is the most likely winner of the duel. A study of US tank engagements in Korea concluded that the M26 had an effectiveness rating of 33.1 when firing first, but only 0.5 when firing second in tank duels (combat effectiveness was assessed as the ratio of tank losses versus tank kills along with the relative number of enemy and friendly tanks). Not surprisingly, tanks in a defensive position consistently had a significant advantage in tank duels since they tended to locate and engage first against an approaching opponent. Overall, tanks firing from defensive positions tended to be three times more effective in the US case, and two times more effective in the case of the North Koreans.

The NKPA partly redeemed its fumbling attack a few weeks later on September 5, 1950, when two more T-34-85s supported by a pair of SU-76M assault guns and a company of infantry attacked the same location. The M26 tanks of the 1st Platoon rushed forward, but with their turrets facing in the wrong direction; both were hit by 85mm fire and knocked out. The NKPA armored vehicles, however, were also all knocked out with bazooka fire.

The "Bowling Alley"

The next heavy tank action took place further north near Tabu-dong, where the US Army 27th Infantry Regiment was attacking to relieve pressure on Taegu. Co. C, 73rd Tank Battalion, was assigned to support the infantry. On the night of August 27, 1950, the NKPA began its last major tank action down a valley, with elements of the 107th Tank Regiment reinforced by some new tanks and crews from the Sadong tank school. Tracer fire came barreling down the road through the center of the valley, leading to its nickname the "Bowling Alley." The NKPA attack was stopped by the infantry and Pershing tanks, and in two days of fighting the North Koreans lost 13 T-34-85 tanks and five SU-76M assault guns.

After the tank skirmishes, it became increasingly risky for the NKPA to mass its armor, as the UN air forces had become much more prevalent over the Pusan perimeter and tanks were a high-priority target. The end of August saw the final commitment of the NKPA tank force. An assortment of partially formed tank

On the night of August 27, 1950, the NKPA 107th Tank Regiment began its last major tank action down the "Bowling Alley" near Taegu against the US Army 27th Infantry. It was stopped by tank fire from Pershings of Co. C, 73rd Tank Battalion. Here, after the fighting, an M26 Pershing drives past some of the North Korean wrecks. (NARA)

regiments and brigades were sent south for an offensive intended to smash the Pusan perimeter, starting on September 1, 1950. In total, about 150 T-34-85 tanks had been committed to the initial assault on South Korea, and this second wave totaled about 100 tanks, but the crews were far more poorly trained than those of the elite 105th Armored Brigade.

The North Korean infantry, almost as poorly equipped as the ROKA as far as antitank weapons were concerned, would often try to overwhelm American tanks by massed infantry attacks, hoping to pry open a hatch. It was a costly tactic, but sometimes worked, especially at night or in close terrain. While the bulk of the NKPA attention was focused on the Pusan perimeter and the September Naktong offensive, a far more serious threat was about to strike the NKPA from behind.

The Inchon landings

By September 1950, the UN forces in the Pusan perimeter had gained numerical superiority over the NKPA forces besieging them. The area outside the perimeter was very mountainous, however, and the UN commander, Gen Douglas MacArthur, opted for a bolder approach to turn the tide against the North Koreans. In a brilliant gamble, X Corps was assigned to stage an amphibious landing behind the main NKPA forces at the port city of Inchon on the Yellow Sea coast west of Seoul. MacArthur hoped that the sudden appearance of a strong UN force at Seoul, deep in the NKPA rear, would cause the enemy to go into headlong retreat.

The X Corps assault formation for the Inchon landings was the 1st Marine Division, supported by the 1st Marine Tank Battalion, followed by the US Army 7th Infantry Division with its 73rd Tank Battalion. The landings began on September 16 using LVT-3 amtracs, since the coastal mud in the beach area was too thick for the Marines to wade ashore from landing craft. The assault forces landed in three areas: in the early morning at Green Beach on the Wolmi-do peninsula and in the afternoon at Red Beach and Blue Beach on either side of Wolmi-do. The ferocious tides in the approaches to Inchon and the limited resources did not permit a simultaneous landing. Yet the only North Korean armor encountered in the initial landing at Wolmi-do was a BA-64 armored car, which was blown apart by a 90mm round from a Marine M26 Pershing.

The North Koreans had been warned of the planned landing by Soviet intelligence, based on information from British spies. Kim Il-Sung, however, ignored the warnings and concentrated instead on renewed attacks on the Pusan perimeter. The North Korean leader believed a collapse of the Pusan perimeter was imminent, and that the amphibious assault on Inchon and Seoul would be preempted by the need to rescue surviving US forces at Pusan. Instead, the US forces in Pusan were on the verge of breaking out, and Seoul was only weakly defended.

The NKPA only had the inexperienced 42nd Mechanized Regiment, with 18 T-34-85s, in the Seoul area. Yet once news arrived of MacArthur's assault, the 105th Armored Brigade was ordered to withdraw back north, and the new 43rd Tank Regiment with 10–15 T-34-85s was transferred from Wonson. A company of fewer than ten T-34-85 tanks of the 42nd Mechanized Regiment tried to intervene during the late afternoon of September 16, but three were knocked out by airstrikes, and three more by Marine M26s. On September 17, 1950, six T-34-85 tanks, their crews still munching on their breakfasts, stumbled into the 5th Marines who were moving on Kimpo airbase. The Marines were supported by M26 Pershings of the 1st Marine Tank Battalion, and all six T-34-85s were destroyed in a storm of recoilless rifle and tank fire without loss to the Marines. A short time later, the burning NKPA column was passed by Gen MacArthur, who commented "Considering that they're Russian, these tanks are in the condition I want them to be!"

Most of the NKPA tanks in Inchon and Seoul were destroyed by Marine bazooka teams. A total of 24 T-34-85s were destroyed between September 16 and 20, eliminating the 42rd Mechanized Regiment. Another 12 T-34-85s from the

43rd Tank Regiment were knocked out on September 25, at least seven by Marine tanks. The main task of the Pershings in the Seoul fighting was providing close fire support during the street combat. The NKPA had erected barricades across most of the major streets, and the Marine tanks were used to help break up these defenses in savage street actions.

On September 20, Co. B, 73rd Tank Battalion, was supporting a drive by the 31st Infantry, but ran the gauntlet of North Korean defenses along the Suwon road, losing one M4A3E8 to Korean tank fire, but destroying eight T-34-85s. A portion of the unit later repulsed a North Korean tank attack near the airstrip, destroying three more T-34-85 tanks after they ran over four scout jeeps. In the final tank action by the battalion near Seoul, Co. A entered Suwon from the western side of the town, and knocked out four more T-34 tanks. The column, in support of Task Force Hannum, continued south towards Osan, where four more T-34-85s were encountered and destroyed.

Breakout from the Pusan Pocket

While MacArthur was landing at Inchon, plans were underway for the Eighth Army to begin a breakout from the Pusan perimeter. The North Koreans had been reinforced opposite the pocket, prior to the beginning of the September 1 Naktong offensive, by the newly raised 16th and 17th Armored Regiments. The offensive, although very costly to both sides, had failed, and the NKPA was near breaking point. Its units were decimated and its troops exhausted and on the brink of starvation.

The Eighth Army counteroffensive was scheduled for a day after the Inchon landings (September 17), hoping to take advantage of panic amongst the North Korean troops after word of the Inchon landings reached them. The broad offensive was indeed aided by news of the Inchon landings arriving at NKPA headquarters, and, as expected, a general retreat northwards commenced. The North Korean units were ordered to fall back on Seoul, but many soldiers instead headed into the mountainous country along the eastern coast, realizing that the US forces were less likely to follow them there. By this time the 105th Armored Brigade was already withdrawing, based on previous orders. There were large numbers of T-34-85 tanks that had broken down during earlier offensives. Many of these vehicles had functional weapons, so they were moved into defensive positions along key routes in the hope of acting as improvized pillboxes to stop the UN advance.

The commander of the Eighth Army, Gen Walton Walker, had served with George Patton in World War II, and he decided to use a mobile force to spearhead the link-up between the Pusan perimeter formations and MacArthur's X Corps in

Seoul. He chose a battalion from the 7th Cavalry Regiment reinforced with seven M4A3E8 tanks from Co. C, 70th Tank Battalion. The spearhead was called Task Force Lynch.

The task force set out late on the night of September 21, with the objective of seizing the Naktong-Ni ferry crossing site 56km north of Tabu-dong. The motorized unit moved very quickly against light resistance. With tanks in the lead, the column was finally halted at Naksong-dong, when the two lead M4A3E8 tanks were knocked out by an emplaced 76mm gun. The gun position was overcome by infantry, however, and shortly afterwards Task Force Lynch encountered the rear elements of the retreating NKPA. An enemy ammunition train soon fell victim to tank fire, and a further 20 artillery pieces, 50 ex-US Army trucks, and four T-34 tanks were captured. An NKPA infantry column was caught in the middle of the Naktong River and decimated.

As the Korean War went into stalemate along the 38th Parallel the role of tanks changed, and they were often used for artillery fire support. Here, some M4A3E8s from the 72nd Tank Battalion provide fire support for the 23rd Infantry, 2nd Infantry Division, north of Pia-ri on the east-central front on September 18, 1951.

The success of the Task Force in taking its objective led Gen Walker to order it to continue its lightning advance to the northwest. In the lead was the 3rd Platoon, Co. C, 70th Tank Battalion, under Lt Robert Baker. Baker's column linked up with X Corps' 73rd Tank Battalion near Suwon around midnight, September 26/27 – the first contact between the Pusan perimeter troops and MacArthur's Inchon force. Task Force Lynch had covered 164km in only 11 hours. Baker's tank platoon, however, had lost contact with the other elements of Task Force Lynch, which were still behind him. Later that night the task force was attacked by about ten T-34-85 tanks. The remaining tanks from 2nd Platoon, Co. C, 70th Tank Battalion, moved forwards from the rear of the task force to engage them. Two Shermans were quickly knocked out by two dug-in T-34-85s, but the third M4A3E8 moved forward and destroyed these. Another T-34-85 slipped into the infantry truck column and crushed about 15 jeeps and trucks, before finally being destroyed by a 105mm howitzer at a range of around 10m. Four other T-34s were destroyed by bazooka teams. That afternoon, two surviving T-34-85s were chased through the villages of Habung-Ni and Pyongtaek, where they were finally hit from the rear by tank fire from the 70th Tank Battalion. This encounter was the largest tank-versus-tank engagement during the break-out.

The best-equipped US Army tank unit, the 6th Tank Battalion, had the new M46 tanks, but saw very little tank fighting until October 22, when Co. A encountered eight T-34-85s and one SU-76M and knocked them all out in a brief and one-sided firefight. Eight other T-34-85s were found shortly afterward, all abandoned by their crews.

Final tank battles

The heaviest tank-versus-tank fighting of the Korean War took place from August to October 1950. There were hardly any encounters with North Korean armor after November 1950, although the US Army and Marine Corps continued to make extensive use of tanks for infantry support for the remaining two years of the conflict. Other UN forces also employed tanks during the fighting, including British Centurion, Churchill, and Cromwell tanks, and Canadian Shermans. The only British tank duel of the war was fought between a Centurion and a Cromwell tank that had been captured by the Chinese.

The NKPA received some tank reinforcements from the Soviet Union in 1951 after the Chinese intervention. Also in 1951, the 105th Tank Division was reorganized as the 105th Mechanized Division, the 17th Mechanized Brigade was given divisional status, and the 10th Mechanized Division was formed though not

equipped. A number of separate tank and assault gun battalions were also formed on paper. However, Soviet resupply was completely inadequate to equip these units, and in 1951 the NKPA armored force numbered only 77 T-34-85 tanks and 63 SU-76M assault guns. By 1952, the NKPA decided to drop the pretense: it disbanded the 17th and 105th Mechanized Divisions and converted the 10th Mechanized Division back to an infantry unit. The vehicles and crews on hand were used to form six separate tank/assault gun regiments. By war's end, the NKPA armor units mustered 255 T-34-85 tanks and 127 SU-76M assault guns, yet these saw little if any combat in the final years of the war.

The Chinese People's Liberation Army (PLA) had very little tank support during its intervention in 1950. At the end of the Chinese Civil War in 1949, the PLA had a force of 349 tanks, consisting mainly of Soviet-supplied Japanese Type 95 light tanks and Type 97 medium tanks, as well as smaller numbers of American M3A3 Stuart light tanks and M4A4 Sherman medium tanks captured from the Nationalist Kuomintang army during the war. These tanks were nominally organized into the 1st and 2nd Armored Divisions and two independent tank regiments.

By May 1950, the PLA tank force had been increased modestly to 410 tanks, mainly by combing the civil war battlefields for abandoned or damaged vehicles. Few of the tank units were fit for combat, so in August 1950 the existing units

M46 tanks of the newly arrived 64th Tank Battalion take up defensive positions at Kagae-dong in support of the 3rd Infantry Division, in an attempt to stem the tide of the Chinese advance on December 7, 1950. The 3rd Infantry Division had moved into the Hamhung–Wonsan area in November to relieve the 1st Marine Division, which was moving forward towards the Chosin reservoir area. (NARA) were consolidated into three tank brigades, with a remainder used to form tank training centers. In the meantime, the Soviet Union agreed to a major increase in arms sales, intended to support the Chinese involvement in Korea. In October 1950, ten Soviet tank regiments moved into northern China. Over the next three months, the Soviet crews instructed their Chinese counterparts on using the tanks, which were then turned over to the PLA. So, for example, two Soviet tank regiments deployed to Xuzhou, where they transferred their equipment to the 3rd and 4th Tank Regiments of the PLA's 2nd Armored Division; a similar process was undertaken with the 1st Armored Division and the two independent regiments. Each Chinese regiment received 30 T-34-85 tanks, six IS-2 heavy tanks, four ISU-122 heavy assault guns, and various items of support equipment (by 1953, the Soviet Union had sold the PLA a total of 278 T-34-85s, 38 IS-2s, 48 SU-76M light assault guns, and 27 ISU-122s).

In February 1951, the Chinese People's Volunteer Army (CPV) in Korea was reinforced with four tank regiments: the 1st and 2nd from the 1st Armored Division, the 3rd Tank Regiment from the 2nd Armored Division, and the 6th Separate Tank Regiment. These did not fight as unified bodies, but were usually spread out to support Chinese infantry formations. So, for example, the 3rd Tank Regiment was split between the Thirty-Ninth and Forty-Third Armies during the June 1951 fighting. It took part in 18 engagements and claimed to have knocked out two US tanks. However, the unit was almost wiped out in the process, and was withdrawn to China in the following July. It was replaced in June 1952 by the division's 4th Tank Regiment. A tank of this unit, number 215, claimed five tank kills along with numerous bunkers and other targets destroyed, and was honored as a "People's Heroic Tank" and displayed at the PLA museum in Beijing. The Chinese tank interventions in Korea were extremely small-scale, and were so minor that most US accounts assert that no Chinese tanks were encountered in the 1951–53 fighting.

ANALYSIS

Although the North Korean armored force had substantially outnumbered its US equivalent at the beginning of the war, by August 1950 the US Army began to enjoy the numerical advantage in armor. By the end of 1950, US tank units in Korea had received 1,326 tanks, consisting of 138 M24 Chaffees, 679 M4A3E8 Shermans, 309 M26 Pershings, and 200 M46 Pattons.

A 1954 operational survey concluded that there had been 119 tank-versus-tank actions during the war, 104 involving US Army tank units and 15 involving the 1st Marine Tank Battalion. On the US side, the tanks that were involved were the M4A3E8 in 59 actions (50 percent); M26 in 38 actions (32 percent), M46 in 12 actions (10 percent), and M24 in 10 actions (8 percent). Most of the tank battles were on a very small scale, and only 24 engagements involved more than three North Korean tanks. A total of 34 US tanks were knocked out by North Korean T-34-85 tanks or SU-76Ms, of which only 15 were totally lost; the rest were repaired and returned to action. The US tanks knocked out 97 T-34-85 tanks, and claimed a further 18 as probable. Not surprisingly the M24, with its thin armor, proved the most vulnerable to enemy tank fire. At least four M24s were knocked out by the T-34-85's 85mm gun.

Notwithstanding the M24, the T-34-85 was generally less able to resist hostile tank fire than the US tanks. It could be penetrated by the fire of any of the US medium tanks, while it had difficulty punching through the M26 or M46 armor. The M26 and M46 were indeed a clear overmatch for the T-34-85, with thicker armor and heavier firepower. The T-34-85 and the M4A3E8, however, were on fairly equal terms. Although the M4A3E8 had a gun of smaller caliber, the widespread availability of HVAP ammunition made it quite capable of penetrating the T-34-85's armor. Likewise, the T-34-85 had no particular problem penetrating the armor of the M4A3E8 at normal combat ranges. US operational research concluded that the M26 was about three times more effective than the M4A3E8.

If the T-34-85 was penetrated, its crew was far more vulnerable to injury. A US inspection of T-34-85s found that 75 percent of the crews were killed when hit by tank fire, compared with only 18 percent in the case of US medium tanks hit by T-34 fire. This imbalance was in part due to the US tankers' practice of hitting a tank repeatedly until it burned to make certain that it was knocked out. In general, the study concluded that the T-34-85 was an excellent tank, but that the North Korean crews were not as well trained as their American opponents. The US lost 136 tanks in 1950, but the main source of loss (69 percent) was mines. In contrast, a total of 239 T-34-85 and 74 SU-76M wrecks were counted by UN intelligence in October 1950, surprisingly close to the figure of 258 T-34-85s initially supplied by the Soviet Union. A total of 296 T-34 hulks were identified as of April 1952.

In 1950, the US Air Force claimed to have destroyed 857 tanks in air attacks, several times the number actually present, and about eight times higher than actual results. Through June 1952, the Far East Air Force also claimed 1,256 tanks destroyed and 1,298 damaged; there were also 123 kill claims by Marine Corps and allied land-based aircraft, and another 163 tanks were destroyed and 161 damaged by Marine Corps and US Navy carrier-based aircraft. Of the original 239 T-34-85 wrecks surveyed by US intelligence, 102 were attributed to aircraft (60 percent of these to napalm) and 13 to bazookas; a later assessment downgraded the confirmed air kills to only 29, though many of the unknown kills were likely due to napalm air attacks. The excessive kill claims by aircraft are similar to assessment issues in

NKPA tank losses by cause, July–November 1950			
Cause	Destroyed	Damaged	Total
M24 light tank	1		1
M26 medium tank	29	3	32
M4A3E8 medium tank	41	4	45
M46 medium tank	18	1	19
Tank sub-total	89	8	97
Artillery	20	8	28
Bazooka	11	11	22
Recoilless rifle	9	4	13
Land mine	1		1
Grenades	3		3
Aircraft	27	2	29
Unconfirmed	63		63
Total	**223**	**33**	**256**

Tempo of T-34-85 losses to US tanks, August–November 1950					
	August	September	October	November	Total
M24				1	**1**
M4A3E8	2	23	20		**45**
M26	3	21	8		**32**
M46		4	5	10	**19**
Total	**5**	**48**	**33**	**11**	**97**

World War II. Part of the problem stemmed from aircraft repeatedly hitting the same tanks, as well as the difficulty of distinguishing tanks and trucks when making high-speed passes in poor weather conditions. The US Navy was credited with 12 tanks destroyed by naval gunfire. The table above is based on a second and larger survey of the tank wrecks.

The opinion of US tankers about the various types of US tanks changed in 1951 once the T-34-85 threat disappeared. The M26 Pershing was undoubtedly the most sought-after type in 1950, when the tank fighting was still intense. But once the tank fighting declined after 1950, the M26 was shunned due to its automotive shortcomings, particularly its sluggish performance on hills and its sloppy transmission. Those tankers with experience in the M4A3E8 preferred it over the M26, since it was more reliable, easier to maintain, and far more nimble to drive. Its automotive performance in the hilly Korean countryside was far superior to that of the M26, and its firepower was perfectly adequate against the now rarely encountered T-34-85. The M46 cured many of the problems encountered with the M26 due to the introduction of a new engine and cross-drive transmission, and so was preferred over the M26.

Centurion

GOLAN HEIGHTS 1973

The tank was the dominant weapon in land warfare during World War II, supported by a myriad of other armored fighting vehicles adapted to meet the demands of total war. Together with the essential infantryman, the tank was the basic component of every offensive from the deserts of North Africa and olive groves of Italy to the hedgerows of Normandy and jungles of the Far East. It was however on the Eastern Front that armored battles occurred on an unprecedented scale between the forces of Nazi Germany and the Soviet Union. It was a clash of titans as thousands of tanks and other AFVs fought from the gates of Moscow to the heart of Berlin. As the war progressed, the Germans produced a series of outstanding tank designs such as the Tiger and the Panther but they were over-engineered and therefore expensive to produce. As such, they were manufactured in relatively small numbers. The Soviet Union on the other hand produced a series of simple but effective designs that could be produced in vast numbers. Although its tanks destroyed a disproportionate number of Allied AFVs, Nazi Germany was defeated by the mass of war matériel arraigned against

S T-55

it, with the ubiquitous T-34 at the spearhead of every offensive from the East and the American M4 Sherman from the West.

It was a lesson that became ever more significant as the postwar world devolved into mutual mistrust between the antagonistic camps of the Western Powers and the Soviet Union as codified by the North Atlantic Treaty Organization (NATO) and the Warsaw Pact. Like the T-34, the Soviet Union would produce the T-54/55 series of tanks on a scale that the West could not possibly match. NATO therefore adopted a policy of designing tanks of superior capability to counter the Soviet advantage of numbers. Since the armored doctrine of the Red Army remained based on the concept of an overwhelming offensive against Western Europe through the use of thousands of tanks, NATO was faced with a huge challenge. In the early 1950s, the only tank being manufactured in Western Europe was the Centurion. Originally conceived at the height of World War II, the design allowed for it to be repeatedly upgraded with heavier armor and more powerful main armament to maintain its qualitative lead over the T-54/55. But the fundamental question remained whether qualitative superiority could ever match quantitative superiority on the battlefields of Western Europe, when the only real example was the experience of the Wehrmacht during World War II.

Fortunately, it was never put to the test in Northwest Europe but both the Centurion and the T-54/55 were sold in large numbers to client states in the continuing Cold War between East and West. During the 1960s and 1970s, one of the main arenas of superpower rivalry was the Middle East. The first major confrontation between the Centurion and the T-54/55 occurred during the Six Day War of 1967. Due to a flawed strategy and inept commanders, the Egyptian forces were totally outfought by the Israelis and no true comparison could be drawn between the tanks. In the following years, the Israelis upgraded the Centurion with a new engine and transmission for better automotive performance, as well as many other improvements, to become the Shot Cal.

It was this model that faced the Syrian army on the Golan Heights in October 1973. Equipped with a vast array of Soviet weapons, the Syrian army was trained in the classic Soviet military doctrine of "shock action" with a total of 1,400 T-54, T-55 and T-62 tanks poised for action along a border area some 35 miles long by 15 miles deep. Beyond lay the nation of Israel. Against this massive force, the Israelis mustered just 177 Centurions divided into two armored brigades, the 7th and 188th Barak. When battle was joined on the afternoon of 6 October 1973 this was not just another round in the cycle of Arab-Israeli wars but the ultimate test in battle of two opposing philosophies in armored warfare – of East and West, of quantity versus quality. It was also a duel to the death of the Centurion and the T-55 that epitomized those conflicting doctrines. This is an account of one of the most extraordinary defensive battles ever conducted as 177 Israeli tanks fought for four long days against overwhelming numbers for the survival of their country.

THE TANKS

At the outbreak of World War II, the British Army possessed just 977 tanks across the whole of the far-flung British Empire. Worse still, only 77 of these tanks mounted any weapon larger than a machine gun. The great proportion of the army's tank inventory was made up of "tankettes" or light tanks as these were much cheaper to produce than true tanks and more suitable for garrison duties in Britain's overseas territories or combating hill tribesmen on the North-West Frontier. After a period of innovative exercises in the practice of mechanized warfare in the late 1920s, British tank design and armored doctrine languished due to political and financial constraints. The torch of innovation passed to the Soviet Union during the 1930s, together with Nazi Germany. Ideologically wedded to the offensive doctrine in warfare, the Red Army conceived the doctrine of "deep operations" that was conceptually similar to *Blitzkrieg* as devised by the Wehrmacht. Both doctrines envisaged a rapid offensive based on the integrated combination of tanks, ground attack aircraft and motorized infantry, as well as paratroopers to land in the enemy's rear areas and disrupt lines of communication. Prior to World War II, Germany and the Soviet Union produced large numbers of tanks of increasingly effective designs.

When Britain began rearmament in face of the growing Nazi threat, it lacked both the design capability and the manufacturing capacity to produce tanks in quantity. In consequence, the British Army entered World War II with a series of generally ineffective designs configured for a variety of roles on the battlefield. These included infantry tanks to support infantry attacks and cruiser tanks for mobile operations once a breakthrough had been achieved. It was a doctrine that harked back to World War I rather than the age of *Blitzkrieg*. Most of the Army's tanks were lost during the battle of France in May 1940, so Britain had no choice but to continue building the same types despite their known deficiencies because of the immediate threat of invasion and its widespread overseas commitments, particularly in North Africa. It was patently unrealistic to expect commercial companies to turn their hands to the design and construction of complex AFVs and produce battleworthy models without years of experience. Conversely, the Soviet Union was producing tanks in vast quantities due to its wide industrial base. Thanks to ambitious Five Year Plans throughout the 1930s, equipment had been guaranteed as a priority for the Red Army. At the outset of Operation *Barbarossa* in July 1941, it possessed 24,000 tanks; more than the rest of the world put together. Among them was a model that was to influence many subsequent designs during World War II – the T-34.

The T-34 was a simple, rugged and highly mobile tank with greater firepower than most of its contemporaries. It was well suited to mass production but suffered some significant design flaws in the early versions. Nevertheless, the T-34 came as a rude shock to the Germans as they had nothing comparable to its excellent combination of firepower, armor protection and mobility – the three fundamental design parameters of any successful tank. In the first two months of Operation *Barbarossa*, the Red Army lost over 5,000 tanks in combat including most of the modern T-34s and KV-1s. When the frontlines stabilized at the gates of Moscow in December 1941, the Red Army possessed only 4,495 tanks of which 2,124 were stationed in the Far East. Just as the British kept building inferior tank designs after the battle of France, so the Soviets were obliged to continue producing existing models to compensate for the massive losses of 1941. No modifications, however necessary or desirable, were tolerated if they interfered with production quotas until the German invasion was fully contained. Accordingly, the T-34 did not see any radical improvements until after 1943 when the battle of Kursk revealed the urgent need for a more heavily armed version of the tank to counter the much-feared Tiger and Panther tanks.

An improved model of the T-34 armed with a 85mm D-5 gun was accepted for production on December 15, 1943, and the first T-34-85 entered service with the Red Army in March 1944. Production of the T-34-85 was soon running at 1,200 per month at a time when there were only 304 Panthers on the whole Eastern Front. The T-34-85 was at the forefront of the climactic battles of Operation *Bagration* in the summer of 1944 that led to the destruction of Army Group Center in the greatest defeat suffered by the Wehrmacht in World War II. Meanwhile, plans for a successor to the famed T-34 series were underway at the Alexsandr Morozov design bureau at Nizhni Tagil under the project codename Obiekt 136. The new tank was designated the T-44 and it was undoubtedly an impressive design, although early models suffered the recurring problem of many Soviet tanks of a troublesome transmission. It displayed excellent ballistic protection, with the armor of the hull and turret up to 120mm thick, with good mobility. In fact, the T-44's combat capabilities were on a par with the Panther but it weighed only two-thirds as much at just 32 tons. However, there is no record that the T-44 saw combat during the Great Patriotic War.

By 1943, the British were at last producing a worthwhile tank in the Cromwell, which featured an adequate 75mm main armament and high mobility. However its armor protection was barely adequate by contemporary standards. Coupled with the widespread use of the American M4 Sherman, it allowed the newly formed Department of Tank Design to start with a completely clean sheet. On September 8, 1943, the General Staff issued the requirement for a new cruiser tank under the designation A-41. In the intractable debate in tank design as to how to combine the three basic elements of firepower, protection and mobility, the British opted for the first two, although agility across country was considered of more importance than a high road speed. The main armament of a 17pdr gun had to be capable of defeating the Tiger and Panther at normal combat ranges. Conversely, the A-41 was required to provide sufficient armor protection against the dreaded German 88mm. This was to be achieved by incorporating a well-sloped front glacis plate similar to the T-34 and Panther. The final specification for the A-41 was considered by the Tank Board on February 23, 1944, when they gave their full support to the project and ordered the production of 20 prototypes. The first A-41 prototype was delivered in April 1945, and in the following month six prototypes were rushed to Germany as part of Operation *Sentry* to test the new tank under combat conditions. They arrived just too late to see action but the trials continued and the men of the Royal

A fundamental aspect in the design of the T-54/55 series was its ability to negotiate rivers by means of a snorkel device with the minimum of preparation so as to maintain the momentum of the advance. The OPVT snorkels on these Polish T-55s are fitted in place of the loader's periscope with the top half of the device folded during an approach march and then raised for an operational crossing of a river. (The Tank Museum)

The T-55 was the first main battle tank designed to operate on the nuclear battlefield and fight under conditions of NBC contamination. It was also able to operate in the severest of climatic conditions; here, a formation of T-55s undergoes winter maneuvers during the 1970s; a scene so reminiscent of its illustrious predecessor the T-34 fighting on the Eastern Front during the Great Patriotic War. (The Tank Museum)

Armoured Corps enthusiastically endorsed the new tank, now named Centurion, although they did note that it did not represent any real qualitative improvement over the Panther that had been introduced in 1943. Production of the Centurion began in early 1946 and the first tanks were issued to troops in Germany in December 1946.

Although a highly promising design, the T-44 still retained the same 85mm gun as the T-34-85. Attempts to install a larger weapon were not overly successful because of the cramped turret interior. Accordingly, the development of a larger turret mounting a D-10T 100mm gun began in 1945. It was fitted to a revised hull of the T-44 under the project codename of Obiekt 137. The first prototype was completed in late 1945 and it was accepted for service in April 1946 as the T-54. Production began in the following year but the original version suffered such serious teething troubles that production was suspended. Furthermore, the greater bulk of the 100mm ammunition meant that only 34 rounds were carried in the T-54-1 as compared to 60 in the T-34-85. Yet another turret was designed displaying a distinct similarity to the excellent ballistic shape of the IS-3 Heavy Tank with its hemispherical configuration. The new turret was accepted for service in 1949 although it still had unsatisfactory shot traps at the rear. Series production of the T-54 resumed as the T-54-2 or T-54 Model 1949 to differentiate it from the earlier model. A third and definitive turret design was introduced in 1951 with its classic bisected egg shape, the narrow end pointing forward and mounting the D-10T 100mm gun in a narrow mantlet. This version was known as the T54-3 or T-54 Model 1951.

TECHNICAL ASSESSMENT

The Centurion

Both the Centurion and the T-54/55 were the synthesis of each respective country's wartime experiences of armored warfare. For the British, the employment of different types of tanks for armored operations was by now largely discredited. All had proved to be chronically undergunned and inadequately armored as the technological race for tank superiority accelerated throughout the war. While Germany was invariably at the forefront, both Britain and the Soviet Union proved superior in the field of mass production. Britain alone built more tanks than Germany during World War II, while the Soviet Union produced three times as many T-34s as all the German tanks manufactured from 1941 to 1945. A sea of steel swamped Germany as thousands of AFVs invaded the country from both the East and West. For the Red Army, the employment of separate medium and heavy tanks had proved successful with hordes of T-34s at the forefront of "deep operations" while the IS series of heavy tanks provided direct fire support in the assault while their powerful 122mm guns proved devastating against German armor: hence their nickname of "Animal Killers" for destroying Panthers and Tigers. For the British Army there was little consolation as, to the end, the majority of its tanks lacked the firepower to counter the latest generation of German tanks. Fortunately, the latter were few and far between in the final days of the war. Lurking antitank guns, self-propelled guns and handheld infantry weapons such as the Panzerfaust caused the majority of tank casualties. Nevertheless, the perception remained that British tank crews were at a distinct disadvantage in any tank-versus-tank duel. It was a sentiment that gave rise to the determination never to allow British tank crews to enter battle with inferior firepower or armor protection to a potential enemy.

To this end, the Centurion had been undergoing many improvements following its entry into service with the British Army. Like the T-54, the Centurion was fitted with a new turret design of improved ballistic protection and better layout for the crew in the Mk II version. More importantly, the revised turret was able to mount the new 20pdr (83.4mm) gun that was superior in performance to the D-10T

The Centurion Shot Cal through 360 degrees

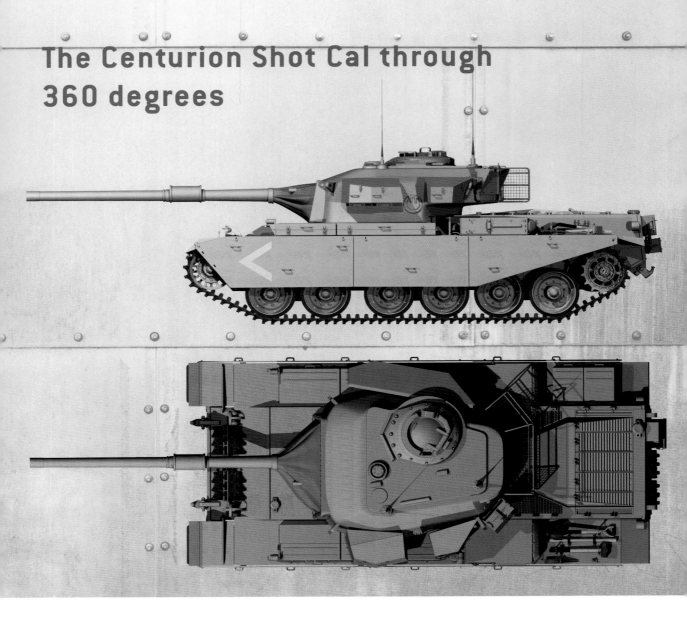

100mm main armament of the T-54, particularly when firing the new APDS ammunition. Introduced in 1948 as the Centurion Mk III, this was the definitive early model of the Centurion.

The Centurion Mk III was of conventional layout with the driving compartment at the front, the driver on the right and the main armament ammunition stowage to his left. The fighting compartment was in the center of the hull with the rest of the four-man crew – the commander, gunner and loader/radio operator – in a fully rotating power-operated turret containing the main armament and coaxial machine gun, together with the radio equipment. To the rear behind a dividing bulkhead

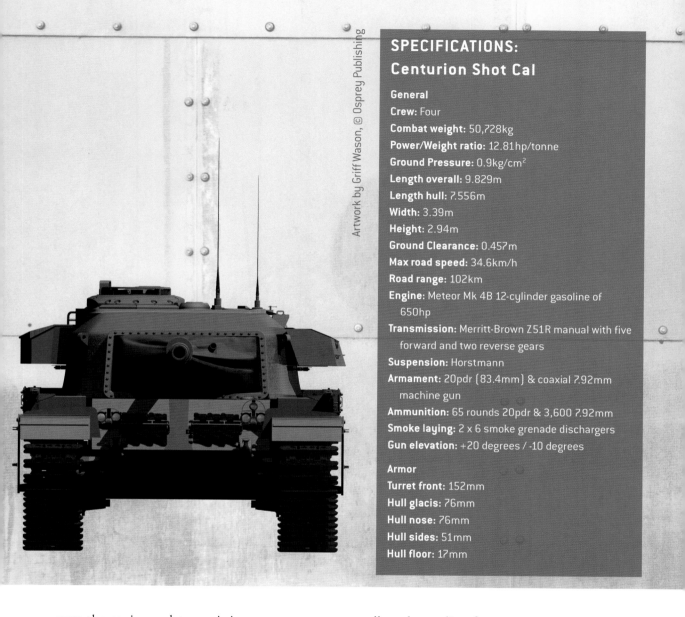

SPECIFICATIONS:
Centurion Shot Cal

General
Crew: Four
Combat weight: 50,728kg
Power/Weight ratio: 12.81hp/tonne
Ground Pressure: 0.9kg/cm²
Length overall: 9.829m
Length hull: 7.556m
Width: 3.39m
Height: 2.94m
Ground Clearance: 0.457m
Max road speed: 34.6km/h
Road range: 102km
Engine: Meteor Mk 4B 12-cylinder gasoline of 650hp
Transmission: Merritt-Brown Z51R manual with five forward and two reverse gears
Suspension: Horstmann
Armament: 20pdr (83.4mm) & coaxial 7.92mm machine gun
Ammunition: 65 rounds 20pdr & 3,600 7.92mm
Smoke laying: 2 x 6 smoke grenade dischargers
Gun elevation: +20 degrees / -10 degrees

Armor
Turret front: 152mm
Hull glacis: 76mm
Hull nose: 76mm
Hull sides: 51mm
Hull floor: 17mm

were the engine and transmission compartments, as well as the cooling fans. With a fully laden combat weight of 50 tons, some 44 percent of the Centurion consisted of armor, 11 percent armament and ammunition, 5 percent for the engine, 30 percent for the transmission, suspension and tracks while the remaining 10 percent was made up of the crew, stowage and other items such as fuel.

The driver sat on the right-hand side of the front hull with his two viewing periscopes in the access hatches in the hull roof above his head when driving closed down. The driving controls comprised the clutch, brake and accelerator pedal arranged conventionally left to right with the long gear-change lever mounted centrally. To each side of his seat were the steering levers. As one was pulled backwards so the relative speed of the tracks altered and thus the direction of travel of the tank. As all the controls were linked to the engine and transmission by mechanical rods, the Centurion demanded much physical exertion and constant concentration to ensure a smooth passage to the rest of the crew across broken country. With thorough training, a good driver was able to achieve a sustained cross-country speed of some 15mph with minimal crew discomfort, ensuring that they arrived at a point of contact in a fit state to fight. The driver's duties included undertaking first-line maintenance of the tank such as cleaning air filters and tightening tracks.

The crew commander was situated at the rear of the turret on the right-hand side with a vision cupola above his position providing all-round observation from under armor. He was also provided with a X10 binocular periscope for precise target acquisition. Forward of him was the gunner's position with his gun controls, periscope sight and range gear to his front and right. The Centurion was the first tank to be equipped with a full stabilization system for the main armament and coaxial machine gun in both azimuth and elevation. Previous systems such as fitted to the M4 Sherman were only stabilized in elevation. For the first time this allowed the tank to fire on the move with both the gunner and commander having full control in this mode. It is particularly effective when firing the coaxial machine gun in a prophylactic manner against entrenched infantry when advancing at speed. When engaging enemy armor, it was quite feasible to track a tank accurately while

The first Centurion prototype was completed in April 1945 and six prototypes were despatched to Germany the following month for combat trials, but the war ended before their arrival. From the Mk II onwards, the Centurion featured a cast turret with a welded roofplate. Shown during crew training with the 8th Royal Tank Regiment in Yorkshire during 1948, these are Centurion Mk IIIs with the more powerful 20pdr gun. (Author's collection)

on the move but it was often better to then stop and make final adjustments to the lay of the gun to maximize the chances of a first round hit: a process known as "firing from the short halt." Once the target was struck, the Centurion then moved off at speed while the commander acquired another target.

The Ordnance Quick Firing 20pdr Tk Mk I and the coaxial 7.92mm Besa machine gun were both served by the loader/operator positioned to the left of the main armament. By contemporary standards and the T-54 in particular, the internal volume of the Centurion was more than adequate to allow the crew to undertake their tasks efficiently. All the rounds of ammunition were stowed below the level of the turret ring to increase survivability. Statistical analysis of tank casualties of World War II showed that 60 percent of tanks that stowed ammunition in the turret suffered catastrophic fires when penetrated and that 60 percent of all tanks penetrated were struck in the turret. In addition, British designers opted for an all-electrical turret traverse system since this was safer than those powered by hydraulics, although it is more bulky and somewhat slower. Unlike Soviet tanks where the commander operated the radios, the loader fulfilled this function in the Centurion, hence his title of loader/operator. This allowed the commander to concentrate on his specific duty of directing the tank and any others under his command. The loader/operator also had the vital function of supervising the "boiling vessel." This device, peculiar to British tanks from the Centurion onwards, provided a constant supply of hot water for the endless cups of tea demanded by tank crews and for the warming of ration packs in the field. It also provided a modicum of heat in the turret during winter exercises on the bitterly cold north German plains.

The engine compartment was divided from the turret by a fireproof bulkhead. The Meteor Mk 4B V-12 gasoline engine developed 650bhp giving a top speed of 34km/h and, thanks to its high torque, commendable agility across country. Power from the main engine was transmitted via the clutch to the Merritt-Brown Z51R gearbox. The transmission comprised a combined steering and braking mechanism that drove the rear-mounted sprockets. The complete powerplant was highly reliable, if used regularly, although it did suffer from high fuel consumption. This gave rise to the major criticism of the Centurion with its inadequate range of approximately 80km before refueling was necessary. The vehicle featured a Horstmann-type suspension with three units, each of four road wheels, per side. Being externally mounted to the hull, these did not encroach on the internal space of tank as torsion bar systems did and were easier to replace following mine damage. The suspension units and the hull sides were protected from infantry handheld antitank weapons by three detachable skirting plates that gave the Centurion its distinctive profile, as did the stowage bins around the turret.

Inside the Shot Cal Centurion

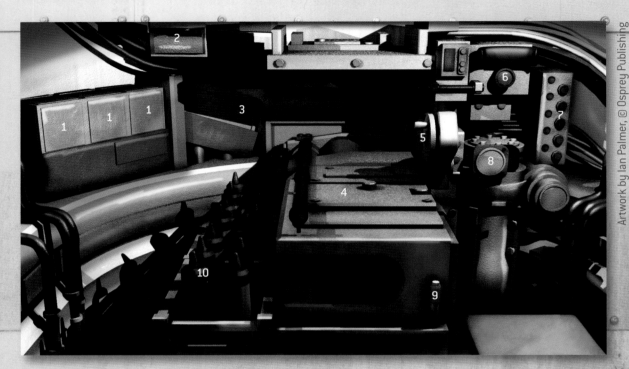

1. Spare boxes 7.62mm ammunition
2. Loader/operator's periscope
3. Coaxial machine gun and ammunition box
4. Breech of L7 105mm main armament
5. Elevating handwheel
6. Gunner's sight
7. Gun control equipment
8. Turret traverse indicator
9. Breech opening lever
10. 105mm ready ammunition rounds

Operational experience in West Germany and during the Korean War had shown the need to increase the radius of action of the Centurion, since in heavy going across country the range on one filling of fuel was as little as 50km. As an interim measure improvized fuel drums were mounted on the rear hull plate followed by a less successful mono-wheeled fuel trailer holding 200 gallons (909 liters). In late 1952, a comprehensive redesign of the Centurion hull was undertaken to increase the amount of fuel stowed under armor. Production of the Centurion Mk 7 began at a new Ministry of Supply factory run by Leyland Motors in 1954. In the following year, the decision was taken by NATO to standardize on the .30cal or 7.62mm caliber for small-arms ammunition. This led to the replacement of the

7.92mm Besa coaxial machine gun of the Centurion with the M1919A4 Browning. With this modification, the tank became the Centurion Mk 5. A Mk 4 had been planned, mounting a 95mm close-support howitzer, but it was never produced. Meanwhile, a new turret was under development with a revised mantlet featuring resiliently mounted gun trunnions and improved gun control equipment, as well as a new commander's contra-rotating cupola that allowed faster target acquisition and incorporated a double leaf hatch to give overhead "umbrella" protection to the commander while allowing him direct vision of the battlefield: a device subsequently adopted by the Israelis as the "Tal cupola." When this new turret was eventually mounted on the revised hull with its extended range, the model became the Centurion Mk 8 in 1956.

From 1959 onwards, the Centurion underwent an uparmoring and upgunning program whereby an extra 2in (51mm) of armor were added to the glacis plate to give greater immunity against the 100mm main armament of the T-55. This involved the substitution of the 83.4mm 20pdr with the L7 105mm gun that, because of its outstanding performance, became the de facto standard main armament within NATO. When both these modifications were applied retrospectively to previously built models, the Centurion Mk 5 became the Mk 6 while the Mk 7 and the Mk 8 became the Mk 9 and Mk 10 respectively. New-build vehicles had these features incorporated during production. The final two modification programs for the Centurion in the British Army were the fitting of IR night-fighting equipment and a coaxial-mounted .50cal ranging gun together with a thermal sleeve for the 105mm barrel. The Centurion hull also became the

After the Yom Kippur War, the Shot Cal was progressively improved with new fire control and turret traverse systems and subsequently with Blazer reactive armor panels to disrupt infantry HEAT antitank weapons such as the RPG and Sagger ATGM. The Blazer armor system is shown to advantage on this Shot Cal C with its gun barrel being cleaned near Beirut during Operation *Peace for Galilee* on June 16, 1982. (IGPO)

Jordanian tank crews of the 40th Armored Brigade prepare their Centurion Mk 7s for action prior to the battle of Ramtha on September 22, 1970, against the Syrian 67th and 88th Armored Brigades of the Syrian 5th Infantry Division that invaded Jordan in support of the Palestine Liberation Organization. In the first encounter between Centurions and T-54/55s of Arab armies, the Syrians lost 62 tanks out of a force of some 300 T-54/55s as against 19 Centurions knocked out in action. (Author's collection)

basis for a series of special purpose variants to undertake a variety of roles on the battlefield, including an armored recovery vehicle, various bridge layers, an assault vehicle for combat engineers mounting a 165mm demolition gun and a version for use on amphibious beach landings. Together they showed the great versatility of the basic Centurion design but, interestingly, the Israeli Armored Corps (IAC) did not procure such variants in any quantity as gun tanks were deemed to be paramount and the defense budget did not extend to such luxuries on the battlefield.

Shot Cal – the scourge of the T-55

Even before the 1967 Six Day War, the IDF Ordnance Corps was addressing the deficiencies of the Centurion, which it had begun acquiring in 1959. In particular, its limited operational range and low speed were deemed to be the main disadvantages, although its firepower and armor protection were greatly admired and appreciated. Many parents of sons entering the IAC demanded that they be assigned to Centurion units, as it was believed that they would have a greater chance of survival in battle. The ageing Meteor engines had to be repeatedly rebuilt, while ease of maintenance and engine replacement times in the field were long and arduous in the Centurion and overburdened the repair facilities. The auxiliary assemblies, particularly the cooling system, posed frequent maintenance problems. In the desert, radiators became clogged with sand and oil while pulleys and drive belts failed with increasing regularity. The original air filters proved to be only partially effective in the Negev Desert unless they were flushed with fuel and filled with fresh oil daily or in extreme conditions after every four hours of operation.

To overcome these problems, the Ordnance Corps devised an upgrading program to improve its performance and reliability following its experience with the M50 and M51 Sherman conversions. In the words of the official publication by the Ordnance Corps on the project:

> What prompted the IDF, after having used the British Centurion Mk 5 for a number of years to perform such an extensive operation and to completely reshape the old "battle horse"? The answer can be summed in one sentence: the necessity to bring the Centurion Mk 5 which was built in the early 1950s to the first line of the tanks of the 1970s in regard to performance, reliability, maintainability [sic] and ease of operation.

The primary requirement was to replace the gasoline-powered Meteor engine with a more fuel-efficient diesel powerplant. The choice of engines suitable in terms of power, speed and operational range was limited to six, but none of these would fit in the existing engine compartment. During the course of development, three different engines were tested. Although all three alternatives were successfully installed and trialed, the Teledyne Continental AVDS-1790-2A air-cooled diesel was selected primarily due to standardization with the M48A2C Pattons that were being similarly modified in a separate upgrading program. The adoption of this diesel engine had a number of further advantages including its ready availability on the international market, its lower fuel consumption by a factor of 1.7 and reduced fire risks in combat. At the same time, the Merritt-Brown Z51R gearbox was replaced by the Allison CD-850-6 automatic transmission that greatly eased the task of driving, particularly across country, and simplified driver training.

As the selected power pack was too large for the existing engine compartment, the rear hull had to be enlarged. Even so, the engine was installed at an inclination of 3.5 degrees, front side up, giving the characteristic hump shape of the back decks. Because of the increased fuel capacity requirements, intricately shaped fuel cells were developed to utilize all available space. Among the numerous other modifications were a more efficient oil-cooled braking system; fire extinguishers in the engine compartment of greater capacity, with a ten-second delay on actuation to allow the cooling fans to stop so that they did not disperse the extinguishing agent before it took effect; and increased ammunition stowage of 72 rounds, with more of them readily accessible to the loader. In all, it took three years to develop the upgraded Centurion at the former British Army barracks of Sarafand, later the IDF Ordnance Corps depot at Tel HaShomer, near Tel Aviv. The tank was given the name Shot Cal or "Whip" in Hebrew and earlier versions were designated Shot Meteor until such time as they were upgraded as well. The first Shot Cal entered service with the IAC in May 1970 and it soon saw combat during border incidents with Lebanon and Syria and during the War of Attrition along the banks of the Suez Canal. Within just one month of entering service, the Shot Cal fought its first major action when the 188th "Barak" Brigade conducted a raid into Syrian territory in June 1970 during a four-hour battle with a Syrian tank brigade in which 36 T-55s were destroyed. But the Shot Cal was to fight its most desperate battles during the opening hours of the Yom Kippur War of October 1973 – once again in the hands of the Barak Brigade.

The T-55

After its unhappy debut, and once the problems with the transmission were resolved, the T-54 proved to be a worthy successor to the T-34 series that had been largely instrumental in achieving victory on the Eastern Front and the eventual triumph over the remaining forces of the Third Reich in the battle of Berlin. Starting in 1949, the T54/55 series was built in greater numbers than any other postwar battle tank with over 50,000 rolling off the production lines. The T-54 entered series production in 1953 and the T-54A was introduced in 1955. The T-54A had a revised D-10TG 100mm main armament that featured stabilization in the vertical axis with the STP-1 Gorizont or Horizon system. The D-10TG also had a fume extractor near the muzzle fume, based on the bore evacuator design of captured American M26 and M46 medium tanks from the Korean War. This model was also manufactured in Czechoslovakia, Poland and in China as the T-59. Two years later, the T-54B appeared with full stabilization for the main armament that was now designated D-10T2S. The system was known as the STP-2 *Tsiklon* or Cyclone. In April 1959, infrared (IR) night vision and fighting equipment was introduced for the commander, gunner and driver. Intriguingly, the Centurion featured full stabilization from its earliest models in 1947 whereas the T-54/55 series achieved it only in 1957. Conversely, Soviet tanks were fitted with IR night-fighting equipment several years before their NATO counterparts. Total production of the T-54 series was approximately 24,750 in the Soviet Union with 5,465 in Warsaw Pact countries and a further 9,000 in China under the designation T-59.

In October 1955, a comprehensive improvement program for the T-54 was initiated under the designation Obiekt 155. The principal innovation was the introduction of protection against Nuclear, Biological and Chemical (NBC) contamination on the nuclear battlefield that Soviet planners now deemed to be inevitable in any future conflict. The new design was accepted for service in May 1958 and production ran from June 1958 to July 1962 in the Soviet Union and

Inside the T-55

Artwork by Ian Palmer, © Osprey Publishing

1. Commander's sight
2. Turret traverse handle
3. Gunner's sight
4. Gun control equipment
5. Breech of D-10T2S 100mm main armament
6. Gun recuperators
7. Coaxial machine gun
8. NBC filtration system
9. Breech opening lever
10. Turret traverse indicator

subsequently in Czechoslovakia and Poland. The T-55 was of conventional layout with a four-man crew. Like the Centurion, the wartime practice of a five-man crew with a hull machine gunner, such as the T-34 or Cromwell tanks, was dispensed with in the interests of extra ammunition stowage, given the increased size of the main armament ammunition. However, the crew positions were reversed to those in the Centurion and, indeed, most Western tanks. The driver was situated in the left-hand side of the hull front while the commander and gunner were positioned to the left of the D-10T gun and the loader to its right.

The most striking aspect of the T-55 was its compact dimensions with a height to the turret top of just 2.39m although the loader's roof-mounted heavy machine gun did somewhat compromise the low profile: in comparison, the M48 stood 3.13m tall and the Centurion 2.94m. However, the superb shaped turret did markedly reduce the internal volume of the tank and make it extremely cramped for the crew. This inevitably affected their performance when fighting closed down over extended periods of time. It also significantly reduced overall ammunition stowage, with just 43 rounds as against 65 for the Centurion. Nevertheless, such a compact tank was difficult to hit and the armor configuration made it more likely for shells to ricochet off the turret or glacis plate without penetrating, while the limited amount of ammunition carried was compensated for by the sheer numbers of Soviet tanks committed to any offensive. For these reasons, Soviet tank crews were chosen on account of their short stature with anyone over 1.68m in height being uncomfortably too tall for the task.

The hull was constructed of welded rolled armor plate with vertical sides and a well-sloped glacis plate with interlocking joints for increased ballistic integrity. The "driver/mechanic" in Soviet terminology sat in the left-hand side of the hull front with an access hatch in the hull roof and an escape hatch in the floor behind his position. Like the Centurion, the T-55 required considerable effort to drive with its basic mechanical controls and five-speed gearbox that required repeated gear changes when travelling over broken terrain. Such simplicity was typical of Soviet tank designs as it reduced procurement costs but at the price of reliability, often due to clutch failures. To the driver's right were the vehicle batteries, a fuel tank for the diesel engine and ammunition stowage for main armament rounds. As Soviet tanks had to operate over a vast temperature range including in the depths of a Siberian winter, the T-55 was equipped with a compressed air starter for the engine with an electrical system as a back up.

The V-55V 580bhp liquid-cooled V-12 diesel engine was mounted transversely at the rear and power was transmitted to the drive sprocket at the rear with the idler at the front. The T-55 featured a torsion bar suspension system with five double rubber-tired road wheels per side with a distinctive gap between the first and second road wheel stations. With a power-to-weight ratio of 16bhp per ton (as against 13 for the Centurion), the T-55 had a speed of 50km/h on roads and up to 30km/h across country. It had a range of 500km on its integral tanks with a further 200km when fitted with the external fuel drums at the rear, below which the tank usually carried a wooden unditching beam. Following World War II experience and the many river crossings that the advance into Germany entailed, the T-55 could be readily fitted with a snorkel for deep wading. Two types were developed, a thin one for operational use and a wider one for training exercises that allowed the crew to escape in an emergency. The OPVT fording equipment allowed the crossing of rivers up to 5m in depth and 700m wide with navigation by an onboard gyrocompass. Such a device was very much in keeping with the Soviet doctrine of the offensive, whereas no Western tank designs had this feature except on an experimental basis.

The commander and gunner were positioned to the left of the D-10T2S 100mm gun with its breech mechanism filling a large proportion of the turret interior. The ready-rack of ammunition rounds on the rear wall compounded space limitations and there were further rounds on the hull walls as well as under the gun and floor. The gun featured full stabilization of the main armament and electro-hydraulic traverse of the turret. By Western standards, the gun control equipment and sighting devices were rudimentary, with the commander acquiring a target through his TPK-1 designator sight. He then traversed the turret in line with the target and gave the gunner an estimation of the range by the graticule pattern of his stadiametric sight, while giving the loader the ammunition selection depending on the type of target. The gunner then made the final fine lay on the target with his TSh 2-22 sight with a magnification of 3.5x or 7x. He fired when ordered to do so by the commander. The main armament was capable of firing AP (Armor-Piercing), APC-T (Armor Piercing Capped Tracer), HEAT (High Explosive Antitank), HE-Frag (High Explosive Fragmentation) and subsequently APDS (Armor Piercing Discarding Sabot). The usual ammunition load was two-thirds HE and derivatives and one-third AP.

Meanwhile, the loader was trying to manipulate another round, weighing in the region of 25kg, into the opened breech as the tank bucked across country. His position was so cramped that most loaders had to ram home the projectile with their left fist, which made the task even more difficult. The loader was also responsible for the coaxial machine gun in the turret; originally the 7.62mm SGMT and subsequently the 7.62mm PKT machine gun. Like the T-54, the early production models of the T-55 featured an SGMT fixed rigidly in the center of the glacis plate and fired by the driver: a legacy of the wartime bow-gunner of the T-34. It proved to have limited tactical value and the driver/mechanic was usually too busy to bother with it. Accordingly, it was discontinued from the T-55 onwards and the space saved taken up with a further six rounds of 100mm ammunition. The T-55 was also the first model to have a fully rotating turret floor that made the loader's tasks somewhat easier in the confines of the turret. Undoubtedly, one of the most significant tactical disadvantages of the compact configuration of the T-55 was the lack of depression of the main armament, at just -4 degrees rather than the typical -10 degrees of Western designs. This meant that it was extremely difficult for a T-55 to obtain a satisfactory hull-down firing position with just the turret roof and gun barrel visible to the enemy, but again, as Soviet doctrine stressed the offensive, this shortcoming was deemed to be acceptable. A further serious limitation of such poor ergonomics was that the loader was hard pressed to load more than four rounds a minute when a proficient NATO tank crew was expected to fire

The T-55 through 360 degrees

the same number within the first 15 seconds of an engagement. In one demonstration, the crew of a Centurion Mk 5 armed with a 20pdr gun fired 15 rounds in 43 seconds at 15 different targets and hit every single one at ranges between 800 and 1,000 yards. These fundamental design differences were to have a significant effect during the fighting on the Golan Heights in October 1973.

As with most successful designs, a range of special-purpose variants was built on the T-54/55 chassis; in particular, a number of armored recovery vehicles that could also assist in deep-fording river crossing operations. Other variants included the

Artwork by Ian Palmer, © Osprey Publishing

SPECIFICATIONS:
T-55

General
Crew: Four
Combat weight: 36,000kg
Power/Weight ratio: 16.11hp/tonne
Ground Pressure: 0.81kg/cm²
Length overall: 9m
Length hull: 6.45m
Width: 3.27m
Height: 2.4m
Ground Clearance: 0.425m
Max road speed: 50km/h
Road range: 500km

Engine: V-55 V-12 diesel of 580hp
Transmission: Manual with five forward and one reverse gears
Suspension: Torsion bar
Armament: 100mm (20pdr) & coaxial 7.62mm machine gun
Ammunition: 65 rounds 20pdr & 3,600 7.62mm
Smoke laying: Diesel fuel injected into exhaust system
Gun elevation: +17 degrees / -4 degrees

Armor
Turret front: 203mm
Hull glacis: 97mm
Hull nose: 99mm
Hull sides: 79mm
Hull floor: 20mm

bridge-laying vehicles also modelled on the T-54/55 chassis. As part of its offensive armored doctrine, the Soviet army also employed several mine-clearing devices for the T-54/55 series by fitting gun tanks with rollers or ploughs to disable antitank mines. Typical systems included the PT-55 mine roller and the KMT-4 mine plough or a combination of them both with the KMT-5 system. The KMT-5 or Kolesniy Minniy Tral was the standard mine-clearing system in the Soviet army from the late 1960s. It was this type together with the MTU bridgelayers that spearheaded the Syrian offensive on the Golan Heights in October 1973.

COLD WAR COMBATANTS

By 1953, both the Centurion and the T-54 were in full-scale production. However, the volume of production was hardly in the same league. In Britain, the Centurion was manufactured at ROF Barnbow in Leeds and at Vickers-Armstrongs at Elswick, near Newcastle-upon-Tyne, at the rate of 11 a week. In the Soviet Union, the 1951–55 Five Year Plan authorized the production of no less than 11,700 T-54s for the Red Army or 44 a week from the Nizhni Tagil UVZ Tank Plant No. 183 in the Urals and the Kharkov No. 75 Tank Plant in the Ukraine. It was to be a keynote throughout the Cold War. The ability and determination of the Soviet Union to produce scores of thousands of tanks based on offensive doctrine could only be countered by the Western Powers through tanks of technological superiority: it was to be an unproven equation of quality versus quantity in a contest of the highest stakes between the NATO powers and the Warsaw Pact. In microcosm, the Cold War was reduced to a duel between individual tank crews exemplified by the Centurion and the T-54/55. Both tanks were to see combat in every corner of the world except in the region for which they were originally designed to fight – Northwest Europe. Many of these conflicts across the globe were but a projection of the prolonged Cold War between East and West and their respective ideologies. The most dangerous crucible of superpower rivalry was to be in the Middle East, where the Centurion and the T-54 were to fight their fiercest battles.

The Centurion first saw action during the Korean War of 1950 to 1953 in terrain and temperatures that were to test the tank's agility to the full. As part of the UN forces deployed to respond to the communist invasion of the Republic of Korea, an armored regiment of 45 Centurions manned by the 8th King's Royal Irish Hussars supported the British Army contingent. It was at the battle of the Imjin River in April 1951 that the Centurions of the 8th Hussars won lasting fame when their tanks covered the withdrawal of the 29th Infantry Brigade in heroic fashion in the face of the overwhelming Chinese spring offensive. Once the fighting became static, the Centurions proved their worth on many occasions when they acted as direct fire support to the infantry units facing human wave assaults from the Chinese army. The reputation it gained in Korea for its combination of firepower, armor protection and agility in such difficult conditions led to the procurement of the Centurion by several NATO nations through the US Mutual Defense Assistance Program, including Denmark and Holland with further sales to Australia, Canada, Egypt, India, Iraq, Israel, Jordan, Kuwait, New Zealand, South Africa, Sweden and Switzerland.

While the Korean War was still raging, the Centurion saw action in the Suez Canal Zone in 1952 to quell Egyptian insurgents and armed militia fighting for independence from the British. In a similar vein, but on a far greater scale, the T-54 first saw operational service during the Hungarian Uprising of 1956. The revolt began on October 23 and lasted until November 10, coinciding almost exactly with the Suez Crisis and the Second Arab-Israeli War. On October 24, Soviet tanks surrounded the Parliament building in Budapest but fighting soon erupted between armed Hungarian militia and the hated ÁVH secret police. On November 3, the Soviet army launched Operation *Vikhr* (Whirlwind) and invaded Hungary with some 17 Soviet divisions, occupying Budapest in force the following day. During the fighting, Hungarian freedom fighters captured a T-54 and it was inspected by the military attaché from the British Embassy. He was able to glean such vital information as the thickness and inclination of the armor configuration and many aspects of its interior that had previously eluded Western military intelligence. Intriguingly, the US Army deployed an "A" Team of Green Beret special forces to the Austrian border ready to capture a T-54 that had been identified just 28 miles inside Hungarian territory, but the operation was never authorized.

The Centurion first saw combat during the Korean War of 1950–53 in a completely different theater of operations for which it was designed. It proved highly effective despite the appalling cold weather and the mountainous terrain. Here a Centurion Mk 3 of A Squadron, the 8th King's Royal Irish Hussars, transports Australian infantry across the Imjin River in April 1951, where the Centurions of the 8th Hussars won lasting fame in the decisive battle that thwarted the Chinese spring offensive. (Author's collection)

Both the Centurion and the T-54/55 were primarily designed for high-intensity warfare in Northwest Europe but the closest they ever came to combat in that operational theater was during the Berlin Crisis of 1961. Following World War II, some 15 million people fled Soviet-occupied Eastern Europe to the West. To stem such an exodus, the Inner German Border was created in 1952 as a real manifestation of the Iron Curtain, with barbed wire fences and armed patrols. Thereafter, the main route for East Germans to escape to the West was through Berlin. By 1961, almost three and a half million East Germans or 20 percent of the entire population had fled to the West. On Sunday August 13, East German troops began the construction of a barrier to divide the city, which became known as the Berlin Wall. Soviet tanks were massed on the border to discourage interference by the Western Powers or riots on the streets. Tension rose in the coming months, culminating in a confrontation between fully-armed M48 and T-54 tanks at the Soviet checkpoint on Friedrichstrasse on the afternoon of October 27. Both sides had orders to open fire if fired upon. Centurion tanks of the Berlin Brigade were also placed on high alert and deployed on the streets of the city. Overnight negotiations between the White House and the Kremlin produced a face-saving formula. On the next morning, one Soviet tank followed by one American tank each reversed some five meters until the streets were clear and the troops returned to barracks.

The next major conflict fought by the Centurion was with the Indian army during the Indo-Pakistan War of September 1965. But the first major confrontation between Centurions and T-54/55s occurred during the Six Day War of June 1967. The T-54/55 was employed once more by the Soviets to crush another Warsaw Pact country when tanks of the 6th Guards and 35th Motor Rifle Divisions entered Czechoslovakia on the night of 20/21 August 1968 to suppress the "Prague Spring" under the guise of "fraternal assistance." Centurions went to war again with the 1st Australian Task Force in South Vietnam between February 1968 and January 1971. In the same year, Centurions fought in the Indo-Pakistan War of 1971, as did the T-54/55. India was equipped with the T-54A and the T-55 while the Pakistani army fielded the T-54A and the T-59, the Chinese license-produced version of the Soviet T-54A. However, there were no tank-versus-tank battles between Centurions and T-54/59s. During the Jordanian Civil War of September 1970, the Centurions of the 40th Armoured Brigade countered a Syrian invasion by the 5th Infantry Division reinforced by two armored brigades and a brigade of the Palestine Liberation Army. On September 20, 1970, at the battle of Ramtha, the Syrians lost 62 tanks out of a force of some 300 T-54/55s, mainly to the 20pdr guns of the Centurion Mk 7s and some to Hawker Hunter fighter-bombers of the Royal Jordanian Air Force. But the greatest confrontation between Centurions and T-54/55s was to occur in October 1973 during

the Yom Kippur War on the Golan Heights, only a short distance from Ramtha. Here this great test between the classic tanks of the Cold War era would be determined ultimately by the superior abilities of individual crews.

Tank crew training

In the 1970s, the induction of civilians into the IDF was the responsibility of the General Staff Manpower Branch. It was implemented by an Induction Administration whose task was to turn callow teenagers into soldiers to fill the ranks of all services of the IDF. There were four periods of induction each year, in February, May, August and November, once a person, male or female, reached the age of 18. The conscript's first experience of the IDF was at a reception center to the east of Tel Aviv where he or she spent four days being interviewed by placement officers from each of the constituent corps of the IDF. The recruit was allowed to specify three choices for assignment in order of preference, but the final decision lay with the IDF in all cases. Recruits were then assigned to a specific arm or corps where they underwent further medical and psychological examinations to determine their suitability for placement depending on a designated profile. Thus, the top percentile of 97 and above was assigned to the IDF elite formations such as fighter pilot units within the Israeli Air Force. The infantry did not admit anyone under a score of 80 and those wishing to join the paratroopers needed much higher, while the Israeli Armored Corps required a minimum of 72.

The first occasion when the Centurion and the T-55 met in hostile confrontation was during the Berlin crisis of October 1961, following the construction of the Berlin Wall. These tanks are a mixture of T-54 and T-54A models at the Friedrichstrasse checkpoint at the height of the confrontation on October 25. (Getty Images)

Those with technical qualifications were assigned to specific units, such as air traffic control, as the IDF deemed fit. In the IAC, the recruit then underwent four months of basic training in the Armored School before being sent to a regular tank unit to undertake his three years of service, or two for a female. It was during basic training that each recruit showed particular aptitude or not, whether it be as driver, loader or gunner. In general, those with the greater hand/eye coordination were chosen as gunners since tank gunnery was paramount within the IAC. Once the arcane skills of tank gunnery had been mastered, a crewman became eligible to qualify as a tank commander. In this way, there were always two gunners in a tank crew in order to maximize the benefits of multiple crew skills. It was in the field of tank gunnery that the IDF excelled and crews regularly trained to engage targets out beyond 2,000m range. Furthermore, IDF tank crews possibly fired more rounds of live ammunition than any other army at the time thanks to their rigorous gunnery training, which was implemented in the years immediately preceding the Six Day War. It was this that gave them the qualitative edge over their opponents.

While the IDF was a citizen army and serving a civic duty, the Syrian army was based on mass conscription of all males from the age of 18 for three or four years, depending on their given task within the armed forces. Many high school graduates and those from families with influence obtained deferment or exemption from military service, thus diluting the skills base within the armed forces at a time of 60 percent adult literacy for males and just 20 percent for females. Once conscripted, all Syrian recruits underwent a severe regime of 14 weeks' basic training before they were allocated to units by drafts rather than aptitude. Those assigned to tank units were often allocated to crew tasks based on their physical stature and strength, given the ergonomic drawbacks of Soviet tank designs; thus someone short but strong would be made a loader. By choice, most Syrian tank crew trainees wished to be trained as drivers since this gave them a particular skill and qualification in civilian life after leaving the army. While the majority of its modern weapons were of Soviet manufacture, the process of translating Russian technical and tactical manuals into Arabic was never fully implemented by the Syrians and was anyway mostly futile for an army of largely illiterate conscripts. Training was done by rote and on the most simplistic level: for instance, tanks crews were required to stop to engage the enemy and then fire only two rounds before proceeding with the mission. Live firing of tank ammunition was the exception rather than the rule and tactics were largely based on "follow the leader." Tactical flexibility was lacking at all levels. Nevertheless, what might have been lacking in finesse was more than made up for by mass, illustrating that Syria had imported Soviet doctrine as well as Soviet tanks.

BATTLEGROUND: THE MIDDLE EAST 1956–73

The 100 Hours War

Prior to the Yom Kippur War of 1973 Israel and her Middle East neighbors had engaged in a number of conflicts. In many cases armor had been the key to the decisive battles and in the decades prior to 1973 there had been a protracted arms race throughout the region fueled by the Cold War. Immediately before the Second Arab-Israeli War of 1956, the IAC was painfully aware of the limitations of its principal tank, the M4 Sherman. This was exacerbated by the massive arms deal of 1954 between Egypt and the Soviet Union that saw numerous AFVs being introduced into the inventory of the Egyptian army. Among them was the powerful IS-3M that could not be penetrated by the IAC's most numerous tank, the standard M4A1 armed with a 76.2mm gun that was known as the M1 Sherman in Israeli service. As soon as the Israel Defense Forces (IDF) learned of the Soviet arms deal, they approached the French for a means to upgun the M1 in a similar manner as the Sherman Firefly of World War II fame. By 1955, a prototype vehicle was produced by the Atelier de Bourges arsenal. It mounted the French CN 75-50 75mm gun, as fitted to the AMX-13, in a heavily modified Sherman turret on an M4A4 chassis. A modification program began during early 1956 in Israel: it was to be the birth of a fledgling Israeli tank industry. The first new M50 Sherman was delivered to Company Bet of the 82nd Tank Battalion of 7th Armored Brigade for user trials and it saw combat during Operation *Kadesh* in the Sinai. The M50 also equipped two tank companies of the 27th Reserve Armored Brigade during the assault on the Gaza Strip on November 1, 1956.

The 100 Hours War that resulted in the conquest of the complete Sinai Peninsula was undertaken in collusion with Britain and France. Both countries wished to regain control of the Suez Canal after it had been nationalized by President Gamal Abdel Nasser of Egypt. The Israeli invasion of the Sinai was used as a pretext for an

During its early service with the Israeli Armored Corps, the Centurion gained an unenviable reputation because of its complexity compared to the M4 Sherman and its tendency to break down in the dusty conditions of the Negev Desert. Following the implementation of strict maintenance procedures and its first combat experiences in the Water War against Syria, the Centurion or Shot, meaning "Whip" in Hebrew, became a firm favorite within the IDF. (Author's collection)

Anglo-French amphibious landing at Port Said at the northern end of the canal with the intention of occupying the whole Suez Canal Zone. As part of the Order of Battle, the British Army included a complete armored regiment – the 6th Royal Tank Regiment – equipped with Centurion Mk 5s. The initial assault landing of November 6, 1956, was supported by C Squadron, 6RTR, whose Centurions were fitted with deep wading equipment and came ashore with the first wave of Royal Marine Commandos. The Centurions of 6RTR were intended to thwart any Egyptian army counterattack with its recently supplied Soviet T-34-85s and IS-3Ms or even the Centurion tanks supplied by the British in 1954. In the event, only a few SU-100 self-propelled guns were encountered and no armored engagements ensued, although the Centurions of 6RTR gave invaluable fire support to the Commandos throughout the day until a ceasefire was imposed by the United Nations at the instigation of the United States. Under intense political pressure, the Anglo-French forces departed Port Said by December 10, 1956.

Similarly, Israel was forced to evacuate the Sinai Peninsula and Gaza Strip by February 1957 at the insistence of the United States and Soviet Union. Nevertheless,

the 100 Hours War brought about a fundamental change in the IDF perception of armored warfare. No longer were tanks to be used largely for infantry support. Now due to their firepower and mobility, they were to become the main striking force during offensive operations in a combined-arms division-sized formation designated *ugda*, that differed in configuration depending on the tactical situation or the task in hand. To this end, more capable and modern tanks than the Sherman or even the M50 were required to fulfil the new armored doctrine of the Israeli Armored Corps.

For political reasons, the Israeli government wished to procure M48 Pattons from the United States to aid the formation of a "special relationship" between the two nations, although America had resisted such an arrangement for many years. Even so, permission was granted for M48A2C Pattons of the Bundeswehr to be transferred to Israel as part of German reparations for the Holocaust. A total of 250 Pattons were shipped to Israel between 1960 and 1964 including a quantity directly from the United States on a clandestine basis. Since much of the IDF's equipment including tanks and aircraft were produced in France, Israel wanted to diversify her arms suppliers as she did not fully trust any European government to be constant in the face of Arab political pressure, particularly in the provision of vital ammunition. Accordingly, Israel also approached Britain with the wish to procure Centurion tanks as a quid pro quo for her involvement in the Suez campaign. After protracted negotiations, the first shipment of Centurions arrived in Israel in late 1959.

The Water War

The Centurion was the first modern main battle tank (MBT) to enter service with the IAC. At 50 tons, it was much heavier and more complex than previous tanks. From the outset, problems were encountered with the tank, particularly when operating in the training areas of the Negev Desert. The abrasive dust caused air filters to clog, leading to engines overheating and on occasions catching fire, while brake failures were commonplace. Within a short period of time, the Centurion gained a woeful reputation within the IAC as temperamental and unreliable, reportedly "more suited to English garden lawns than the Negev Desert." However, many of the problems were due to inefficient maintenance procedures, particularly in the field, plus poor driving and inadequate training. An added difficulty was that many of the Centurions bought from Britain were second-hand and in need of refurbishment and rebuilding, but at that time the Israeli Ordnance Corps did not have the facilities to undertake such major work. The majority of the Centurion models procured were the Mk 5 version armed with a 20pdr gun. When the Egyptian and Syrian armies began to receive the T-54 in significant numbers from

1962 onwards, the IAC sought a more powerful gun for its Centurions and Pattons. The answer was found in the outstanding British L7 105mm gun. It was simplicity itself to exchange the 20pdr of the Centurion with the 105mm gun, as well as new graticule sights and ammunition stowage racks, since the British Army had undertaken this modification in large numbers. It was somewhat more difficult with the M48A2C Patton, as this required a more complex conversion. Accordingly, priority was given to the upgunning of the Centurion, which began in February 1962. By now the Centurion was called Shot in Israeli service, the name meaning "Whip" in Hebrew. It first saw action along the Syrian border in November 1964 against dug-in World War II Panzer IV tanks and artillery weapons dotted along the dominating Golan escarpment that fired down on the Israeli settlements in the Huleh Valley and Finger of Galilee below. These encounters showed the need for improved gunnery procedures and the new commander of the Israeli Armored Corps, Brigadier Israel Tal, rigorously imposed these. Thereafter, the Syrians tried to divert the headwaters of the Jordan River in order to deprive Israel of a large proportion of its fresh water supplies. In what became known as the Water War, tanks were employed to destroy Syrian engineering equipment engaged in the diversion project. In time, the 105mm-armed Shots proved capable of hitting targets as small as a bulldozer, at ranges out to 11km (7 miles). It became the Tal credo of "first shot, first kill, one shot, one kill" using the L7 105mm gun or "Sharir." Such proficiency among the tank crews of the IAC was to prove decisive in the next major Arab-Israeli war as well as the conflict of 1973.

The Six Day War

Although the Arab attempts to divert the headwaters of the Jordan River failed, incidents continued unabated along the Syrian border. Under Soviet encouragement, Syria persuaded Egypt to sign a mutual defense pact against Israel. Tensions rose during the spring of 1967, as Arab rhetoric demanded the eradication of the Jewish state. In May, President Nasser expelled the UN peacekeeping personnel from the Sinai and heavily reinforced the Egyptian forces stationed in the peninsula. When Iraq and Jordan joined the defense pact with Egypt and Syria, belligerent and hostile neighbours surrounded Israel. In a further flagrant act of aggression, Nasser closed the Straits of Tiran to Israeli shipping. On June 5, 1967, the IDF launched a devastating preemptive strike against the Arab air forces and effectively eliminated them in the first 24 hours. At the same, three *ugdas* of the IDF poured into the Sinai Desert to strike the six Egyptian divisions, including the 4th Armored Division equipped with T-54 and T-55 tanks, that were threatening Israel's border.

In the north, the 84th Armored Division or "Ugda Tal," under the command of Brigadier General Israel Tal, attacked the heavily fortified Egyptian positions at Khan Yunis and Rafah Junction. Ugda Tal was spearheaded by the elite 7th Armored Brigade comprising 88 Centurions of the 82nd Tank Battalion together with the 66 M48A2C Pattons of the 79th Tank Battalion. There were also Centurion battalions in the 200th Armored Brigade of Ugda Yoffe and in the 14th Armored Brigade of Ugda Sharon. The heavily armored Centurions were invariably used to assault Egyptian positions frontally while the more mobile Pattons and Shermans maneuvered around the flanks through the difficult sand dunes to mount attacks from unexpected quarters. One by one, the Egyptian defensive localities were attacked

The first combat between the Centurion and the T-54/55 occurred during the Six Day War of June 1967. Due to the inept strategy of the Egyptian high command it was hardly a fair comparison between the two tanks, with the Centurion proving vastly superior due largely to the outstanding performance of the L7 105mm gun and the standard of tank gunnery in the Israeli Armored Corps. (IOP)

and overrun in a classic example of maneuver warfare while the great majority of Egyptian tanks were dug-in and immobile. By now the Israeli Air Force was pounding the hapless Egyptian ground forces as the tanks of the IAC surged westwards. In the first major tank battle between Centurions and T-55s, the Soviet tanks of the 4th Armored Division were severely mauled by 20 Centurions of the 200th Armored Brigade at the Bir Lahfan crossroads where 32 T-54s and T-55s were destroyed. Time after time, the 105mm gun of the Centurions proved devastating against the T-54/55, particularly at long ranges where the simple stadia sights of the Soviet design proved far less effective.

In five days of fighting, the Egyptian army lost almost 80 percent of its tanks during the Sinai campaign including 291 T-54s, 82 T-55s, 251 T-34-85s, 72 IS-3Ms, 29 PT-76s, 51 SU-100s, 50 assorted Shermans and some 30-odd Centurions. By comparison, Israeli losses were 122 tanks of all types. Israeli Centurions also served in small numbers on the Jordanian and Syrian fronts during the Six Day War. Intriguingly, both the Egyptians and Jordanians were equipped with Centurions, albeit the Egyptians in small numbers, but there is no evidence that there were any encounters between the Centurions of the opposing sides nor any combat between IDF Centurions and Syrian T-54/55s on the Golan Heights. It must be said that the stunning Israeli victory during the Six Day War was as much to do with the incompetence of the Arab officer corps as it was to Israeli prowess in battle. The tactical handling of armor by the Egyptian army was uniformly inept and the T-54/55 was hardly given the opportunity to prove itself on the battlefield. Hundreds of usable AFVs were captured by the IDF and many scores of T-54/55s were pressed into service with the IAC under the designation of Ti-67 or Tiran. These were progressively upgraded over the years but they never proved popular with Israeli crews because of their cramped interiors.

After the war, the commander of the 200th Armored Brigade, Colonel Yissacher "Iska" Shadmi, had some illuminating comments to make about the campaign and his Centurion tanks:

When I ask myself how it is possible that against the might of the Egyptian army, which my armored columns had to face while continuously changing on the move, I was able to destroy 157 enemy tanks while our losses were almost nil – well, how did it happen? I have to give the following explanations. First of all, I agree with what has been said by the others before [regarding the superior training and tactical handling of the Israeli army]. Second, the air force. Third to my mind it was proved that the Centurion tank is by far superior to the T-55 and T-54 Russian tanks and especially in one aspect which gave our boys their self-confidence – the additional 20 tons [sic] of armor steel. And the point which in my opinion shows more than anything else how we did it were the stories about tanks that got five, six, seven hits – and there was one with 12 direct hits – and which continued to fight. But let me just tell of a few incidents. Two tanks which participated until half way through the battles, limping along on half their tracks. They were hit by mines and damaged so they shortened their tracks and were able, at a slow pace, to continue the fight. One tank was hit by a direct 120mm [mortar] shell and its turret became immobile. The officer in command decided to keep this tank at the rear and so it advanced. At the battle of Jebel Libni this tank is credited with hitting two enemy tanks.

THE ACTION

The defense of the Golan Heights

The stunning victory in the Six Day War of June 1967 greatly extended the borders of Israel, with the capture of the Sinai Peninsula and the Golan Heights together with the West Bank and the Gaza Strip. For the first time in its history Israel now enjoyed the luxury of defense in depth. The speed and scale of the Israeli victory sent shock waves through the Arab world. Israel had drawn the teeth of its bitterest enemies and its demonstration of military prowess had garnered respect around the world. Israel's position now seemed secure. However, Arab hostility remained implacable. The Khartoum conference of Arab leaders in August 1967 declared that there would be "no recognition, no negotiations, no peace" unless Israel unilaterally withdrew from the territories occupied during the Six Day War. However, these very same conquered territories now gave Israel defensible frontiers and the IDF was loath to lose them without firm guarantees of lasting security. Furthermore, Israeli public opinion was in no mood to allow the spoils of this spectacular victory to be cast aside as had happened after the Sinai campaign of 1956.

Within weeks, however, the Egyptians resumed hostilities along the Suez Canal with heavy artillery barrages against Israeli positions. To reduce the casualty rate, the IDF were obliged to construct a static line of field fortifications on the eastern bank of the canal that fatally compromised the recently gained advantages of strategic depth for defense. It also negated Israel's superiority in maneuver warfare, as tanks were now required to come to the aid of the field fortifications that became known as the Bar Lev Line. The bitter War of Attrition that ensued continued until August 1970, but even after it ended the IDF strategy vacillated between a mobile defense of the Sinai Peninsula and a forward defense to protect the forts and occupants of the Bar Lev Line. The dilemma was never fully resolved prior to the Yom Kippur War of 1973, with dire consequences.

On the Golan Heights, the IDF faced different problems. The Israeli-occupied Golan Plateau was only 27km deep at its widest so a strategy of forward defense was essential, as it was not feasible to trade space for time: time to allow IDF reservists to be mobilized and deployed to stem any Arab offensive. Fortunately, the volcanic terrain strewn with impassable lava flows of basalt rock favored the defenders as only a few roads crossed the region. In addition, its numerous *tels* or extinct volcanic cones, up to 200m in height and overlooking the Damascus Plain where the bulk of the Syrian forces were stationed, made excellent vantage points for observation and firing positions. Only in the south was the terrain really suitable for tanks. The Israeli defenses were based on the "Purple Line" that ran from the Jordanian border in the south to the slopes of Mount Hermon in the north: the Purple Line took its name from the color on UN maps that marked the zone of separation between the two belligerents following the Six Day War. Again, as along the Suez Canal, the ceasefire was repeatedly broken with the Syrians bombarding Israeli positions with artillery. Accordingly, the Israelis constructed a series of 12 infantry strong-points called *Mutzavim* along the Purple Line. Each Mutzav was invariably on high ground with wide fields of view to allow constant observation of Syrian dispositions and movements. The Mutzavim were not intended as true fighting positions but primarily to direct artillery fire and close air support against any enemy incursion.

Over time, the Syrians adopted a prolonged campaign of harassment by artillery fire, coupled with infiltration by infantry units to capture specific Israeli positions in order to inflict debilitating casualties upon the Israeli troops. On occasions, these escalated into full-blown attacks that became known as "battle days" as they rarely lasted more than 24 hours. To counter such assaults on the Mutzavim, the IDF Northern Command, which was responsible for the defense of the Golan Heights, constructed tank-firing ramps beside the individual strong-points. These firing ramps dominated the surrounding terrain and allowed tanks to engage targets to well beyond 2,000m range. A deep antitank ditch protected by mines was dug along the Purple Line to deter encroachment by Syrian AFVs but such measures were alien to IDF armored doctrine, which advocated that the best form of defense was offense. In time of war, it was axiomatic that the IDF would take the battle onto enemy territory and field fortifications did not sit comfortably with this strategy.

Following the Six Day War, the IDF had been seduced into the conviction that the tank was the primary weapon of ground warfare, supported by an all-powerful air force that would guarantee air supremacy. With a limited defense budget and the air force taking priority in all expenditure – 52 percent of the total in 1973 – it was impossible to meet all the demands. In the army, the armored corps took precedence over the other arms and so more tanks were procured at the expense of mechanized infantry vehicles or self-propelled artillery weapons. At the time of the Six Day War there were 338 Centurions in service with the IDF. Many more were subsequently purchased on the international arms market – 90 in 1967, 100 in 1968, 120 in 1969, 120 in 1970, 120 in 1971 and 100 in 1972. Armored brigades were now configured with up to three tank battalions but with no integral mechanized infantry component. A tank battalion comprised three companies with three platoons of three tanks plus two more in company headquarters for a total of 11 in each company. With three tank battalions of 36, a fully organized brigade had 111 tanks including three in brigade HQ. Mechanized infantry was to be allocated depending on the mission within the overall *ugda* or divisional plan.

Facing the Israeli forces deployed on the Golan Plateau was a Syrian standing army of three infantry divisions and two armored divisions stationed within striking distance of the Purple Line. To the north was the 7th Infantry Division deployed from the foothills of Mount Hermon to Kuneitra where it linked up with the 9th Infantry Division, which in turn linked up with the 5th Infantry Division at Rafid. These were infantry divisions in name only since each was composed of two infantry brigades, each with an integral tank battalion of T-54/55 tanks, together with one mechanized and one armored brigade. There were therefore 180 T-54/55 tanks in each infantry division while the armored divisions were each equipped with 230 of the more modern T-62 tanks armed with the 115mm smoothbore gun. In addition, there were 400 T-54/55s in independent armored brigades to give a grand total of 1,400 tanks. These were supported by 115 batteries of artillery ranging from 85mm to 203mm, with a total of 950 guns with 70 to 80 guns per kilometre at the designated breakthrough points. Although impressive by any standards, this was still only half that stipulated by Soviet doctrine. The Syrian strategy was to attack in overwhelming force and recapture the Golan Plateau within 36 hours, as this was the time thought to be available before the Israeli reserves could be mobilized. Time was therefore of the essence for both sides. The Syrians had to complete their offensive before the reserves were deployed onto the Golan Heights while the Israelis had to fight a delaying action long enough for the reserves to be mobilized.

In the fall of 1973 there was just one armored brigade deployed on the Golan Plateau, facing some 1,400 tanks. The 188th Barak Armored Brigade – "Barak" is Hebrew for "Lightning" – was a regular formation of two tank battalions with just 69 Shot Cal upgraded Centurions. It was an absurd disparity of forces but the Israelis were the victims of their own hubris. Since the end of the War of Attrition, Israeli military intelligence, AMAN, was convinced that Egypt would not go to war until such time as its air force was a match for the Israeli Air Force and that would not be until 1975 at the earliest. Furthermore, Syria would not fight Israel without Egypt and therefore there was no possibility of all-out war for the foreseeable future. It was a concept born of arrogance and an abiding contempt for the fighting abilities of the

Defenses of the Purple Line

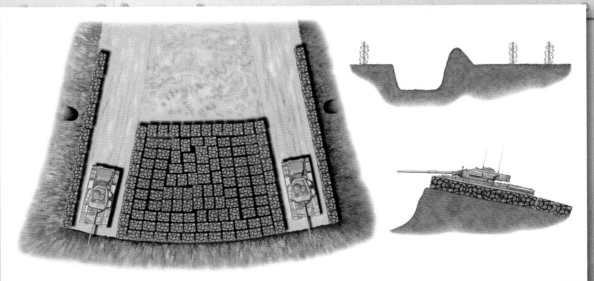

Artwork by Peter Bull, © Osprey Publishing

Dotted along the Israeli defences of the Purple Line were 16 strong-points or *Mutzavim* to protect infantry units from Syrian artillery fire. These were underground bunkers with a top covering of basalt rock bundles to absorb high explosive rounds. These Mutzavim were supported against enemy ground attack by firing positions for up to a platoon of three tanks.

The firing ramps were also intersperced between the Mutzavim on high ground to dominate all likely approaches of Syrian armor and to cover the antitank defences along the Purple Line. The antitank ditch was some 5m wide and 3m deep with a minefield to each side. The firing ramps were constructed to provide a hulldown position for the tank that optimised the -10 degree depression of the 105mm gun of the Shot Cals, so that just the barrel of the gun and the forward slope of the turret top were visible to the enemy and thus an extremely difficult target to hit. By reversing a few meters down the ramp even this part of the tank became invisible while the commander was still able to observe to his front from his cupola. At the bottom of the ramp, the tank was almost completely invulnerable to artillery fire with basalt rock bundles protecting the tracks and suspension. These simple firing ramps were fundamental to the successful defense conducted by the IDF in the opening days of the Yom Kippur War on the Golan Heights.

Arab armies, particularly Syria. Accordingly, the IDF high command remained unconcerned that the force ratio on the Golan Heights was approximately 20:1 since some 70 Shot Cal tanks were deemed sufficient to deal with any "battle day," given that there was no real chance of war. Even in the most unlikely of circumstances that major hostilities broke out, AMAN had promised that it would provide at least 48 hours warning: more than enough time to mobilize the reserves. Anyway the Israeli Air Force was on hand to support the ground forces and stem any assault from

During the desperate early hours of the Yom Kippur War, IDF reservists rushed to their depots to prepare their equipment before climbing the Golan Heights to join battle with the advancing Syrian army. A Shot Cal follows a line of Shot Meteors showing the differences of the rear hull, turret basket and stowage position of the Xenon searchlight. (IGPO)

the outset. On 13 September 1973, Israeli F-4E and Mirage IIICJ fighters were escorting a photoreconnaissance mission by RF-4E Phantoms tracking Soviet arms shipments to the port of Tartous. Syrian MiG-21 fighters were scrambled to intercept them but in the ensuing aerial combat 13 Syrian aircraft were shot down with just one Israeli loss. It was the pretext that allowed the Syrians to move their forces forward and adopt an offensive posture, which the Israelis interpreted as purely a public response to the catastrophic air battle. However, it prompted Minister of Defense Moshe Dayan to visit the Golan Heights on September 25, together with General Eli Zeira, the head of AMAN, and inspect the Israeli defenses. On a tour of the frontlines, he was briefed by Major Shmuel Askarov, the deputy commander of the 53rd Tank Battalion of the Barak Brigade. At just 24, Askarov was the youngest deputy battalion commander in the army with a rising reputation. He stated unequivocally: "War is certain." Dayan turned to Zeira for his comments only to be told blandly that there would not be a war for another ten years.

Nevertheless, after consultation with Major General Yitzhak "Khaka" Hofi, the GOC Northern Command, Dayan authorized the deployment of a single tank battalion of the famed 7th Armored Brigade from its base at Beersheba in the Negev Desert to the Golan Heights as reinforcement to the Barak Brigade. The 77th "Oz" Tank Battalion traveled northwards on the eve of Rosh Hashana, the Jewish New Year, and was equipped with Shot Cals held in reserve by Northern Command. By 1 October, the battalion, under the command of a dynamic Yemenite, Lieutenant Colonel Avigdor Khalani, was deployed on the Golan Heights with 22 tanks. The odds were now 15:1. General Hofi was now thoroughly alarmed by the Syrian

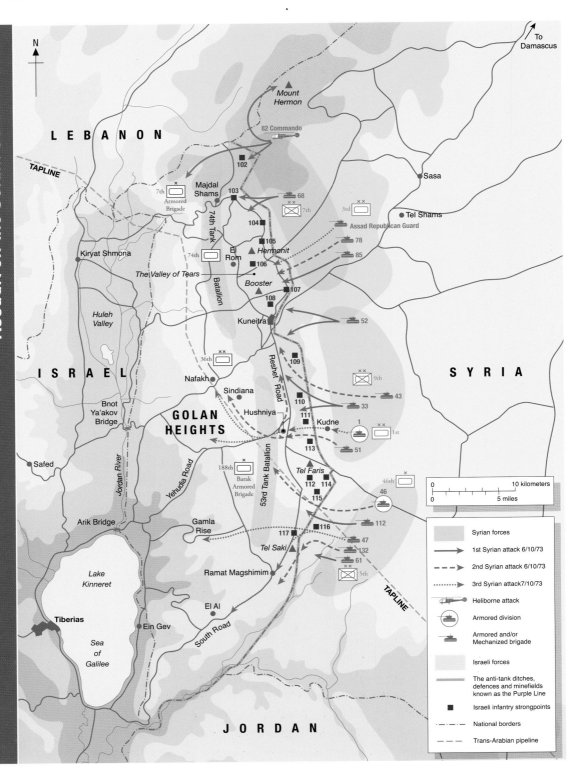

N

To Damascus

Mount Hermon

82 Commando

LEBANON

TAPLINE

Sasa

102

Majdal Shams

7th Armored Brigade

103

68

7th

3rd

Tel Shams

104

Assad Republican Guard

74th Tank

105

El Rom

Hermonit

78

74th

106

The Valley of Tears

Booster

85

Kiryat Shmona

Batallion

107

Huleh Valley

108

Kuneitra

52

ISRAEL

36th

109

Nafakh

SYRIA

Sindiana

Reshet Road

110

9th

Hushniya

43

Golan Heights

111

Kudne

33

Bnot Ya'akov Bridge

1

1st

Safed

113

51

Jordan River

188th

Barak Armored Brigade

53rd Tank Batallion

Tel Faris

112 114

46th

Yehudia Road

115

46

Arik Bridge

Gamla Rise

117

116

112

Tel Saki

47

Ramat Magshimim

132

61

Lake Kinneret

El Al

5th

TAPLINE

Tiberias

Sea of Galilee

Ein Gev

South Road

JORDAN

0   10 kilometers

0   5 miles

Syrian forces

1st Syrian attack 6/10/73

2nd Syrian attack 6/10/73

3rd Syrian attack 7/10/73

Heliborne attack

Armored division

Armored and/or Mechanized brigade

Israeli forces

The anti-tank ditches, defences and minefields known as the Purple Line

Israeli infantry strongpoints

National borders

Trans-Arabian pipeline

build-up and he issued orders for the antitank ditches to be widened and deepened, as well as for the sowing of thousands more mines, and for further tank firing ramps to be created on the hill features of Hermonit and Booster Ridge that dominated the Kuneitra Gap. It was here that Northern Command believed the Syrians would launch their main offensive if war broke out, as it would give them the shortest axis of advance to the main Israeli military base and headquarters on the Golan at Nafakh and from there onwards to the Bnot Ya'akov Bridge across the Jordan River. As a further precaution, Hofi replaced the reserve infantry battalions in the Mutzavim with hardened troops of the Golani Brigade in the strong points to the north of Kuneitra and paratroopers of the 50th Parachute Battalion in those to the south.

The Syrians were well aware of the dispositions of the Israeli forces on the Golan Plateau and made their plans accordingly, with the help of their numerous Soviet advisors. While the 7th Division was to tie down the Israeli forces to the north of Kuneitra, the main attack was to be made by the 9th Division through the Kudne Gap via Hushniya to Nafakh and on to the Jordan River. Meanwhile, the 5th Division was to break through the Rafid Gap and exploit southwestward down the South Road to El Al, blocking any Israeli reinforcements climbing up the escarpment from the Sea of Galilee. Waiting in the wings were the powerful 1st and 3rd Armored Divisions, ready to exploit any success with their potent T-62s and brand new BMP-1 mechanized infantry combat vehicles. This formidable force was supported by a vast array of artillery weapons including FROG ground-to-ground rockets capable of striking Israeli population centers. Helicopter-borne commandos were poised to land deep behind Israeli lines to capture key crossroads and choke points in order to disrupt supplies or reinforcements from reaching the frontline units. Like the Egyptians along the Suez Canal, the Syrians now believed they had the answer to the fearsome Israeli Air Force in the shape of the innovative SA-6 "Gainful" antiaircraft missile system combined with the highly mobile ZSU-23-4 Shilka self-propelled antiaircraft gun. The plan was well conceived and had every chance of success given the complacency of the enemy. The scene was set for an armored battle of epic proportions.

Countdown to war

The Israeli forces on the Golan Plateau were part of the 36th Armored Division under the command of Major General Rafael "Raful" Eitan, with his headquarters at Nafakh. In the opening days of October, they remained wholly inadequate in the face of the threat. On Friday October 5, the IDF Chief of Staff Lieutenant General David Elazar ordered a Gimel alert that canceled all leave and warned staff officers to prepare for the immediate mobilization of reservists. The personnel of the other two tank battalions of the 7th Armored Brigade, the 71st and 83rd, were flown north and rapidly equipped with Shot Cal tanks before joining the 77th on the Golan Heights. The 7th Armored Brigade was the most prestigious armored formation in the IDF, having been formed during the War of Independence. The brigade was commanded by Colonel Avigdor "Yanosh" Ben-Gal, a lanky 38-year-old who had risen through the ranks of the IAC. When his family was killed in the Holocaust, Ben-Gal arrived in Palestine in 1944 from Poland via Siberia, India, Teheran and Egypt: in his own words: "I joined the army in 1955. The army was my home. I was born again. My second birth was in a tank." Despite his unkempt appearance, he was a consummate professional soldier and a skilled proponent of armored warfare. His battalion commanders were similarly highly experienced, with Lieutenant Colonel Meshulam Rattes as OC 71st Tank Battalion and Lieutenant Colonel Haim Barak, OC 82nd Tank Battalion. The brigade also included a Sayeret reconnaissance unit mostly mounted in jeeps and armored personnel carriers (APCs). In addition, the 75th Armored Infantry Battalion commanded by Lieutenant Colonel Yos Eldar was attached to the brigade with their M113 APCs and M3 half-tracks.

In time of war, the 7th Armored Brigade was part of Southern Command and deputed to lead any counteroffensive across the Suez Canal. To this end, one of its tank companies of the 82nd was assigned the specialized role of towing bridging equipment across the desert to prepared crossing points on the banks of the Suez Canal. But even before Minister of Defense Moshe Dayan had ordered the 77th to the northern front, Colonel Ben-Gal had had a premonition of the prospect of war on the Golan Heights. On September 23, he organized a familiarization tour of the Golan Heights for his brigade staff and battalion commanders. Their newfound knowledge of the difficult terrain was to be of inestimable value in the forthcoming battles. Days of frantic

A force of Shot Cals advances across the rock-strewn ground of the Golan Heights with every commander standing high in the turret for a better view of the battlefield. This graphically illustrates why tank commanders suffered such high casualties during the Yom Kippur War from artillery fragments or strikes from Sagger ATGM and RPGs. (IGPO)

preparation followed as the other battalions of the 7th Armored Brigade requisitioned tanks and equipment from the depots of Northern Command before deploying onto the Golan Heights. The Shot Cals were taken out of storage, tested and loaded with ammunition and equipment before the guns were zeroed. Meanwhile, company and platoon commanders were criss-crossing the Golan Heights to familiarize themselves further with the terrain. Throughout the night of Friday October 5, tank transporters and supply trucks groaned up the escarpment to the Golan Heights with large stocks of ammunition. Northern Command had authorized an extra 200 rounds per tank as well as more 155mm shells for the 11 batteries of M109 self-propelled howitzers: just 45 guns as against the 930 of the Syrians, but it was the only M109 regiment in service. The 7th Armored Brigade was directed to complete its deployment to its assembly positions on the Golan Heights by noon on October 6, 1973, the Day of Atonement or Yom Kippur. There were now 177 Shot Cals in place on the Golan Heights: the odds were down to 8:1.

Yom Kippur was the day chosen for the simultaneous offensive by Egypt and Syria against Israel. It is the holiest day in the Judaic calendar, but the state of the tides in the Suez Canal and the amount of moonlight were more important to the Egyptians, while Syria wished to attack before the winter snows arrived. Egypt was determined to break the diplomatic logjam in order to reclaim the Sinai Peninsula while Syria sought to regain the Golan Heights by force of arms. The Arab armies fielded some 4,480 tanks and AFVs with 4,300 APCs while Israel possessed 2,000 tanks and 4,000 APCs. Almost all were committed to battle in the Sinai Peninsula and on the Golan Heights. The total number of AFVs was greater than those at the battle of Kursk and they fought in a smaller geographical area than the Kursk salient. With separate but simultaneous attacks from north and south, the parallels between the two offensives were remarkable. At 1345hrs, Israeli observers on Mount Hermon noticed the camouflage netting being removed from the hundreds of Syrian gun positions on the Damascus Plain. At 1356hrs, a thunderous artillery barrage fell upon the Israeli positions on the Golan Plateau that lasted 50 minutes without pause. Simultaneously, MiG-19 ground attack aircraft swooped down to bomb and strafe the headquarters at Nafakh. At that precise moment, Colonel Ben-Gal was giving his last-minute briefing to his battalion commanders and their company commanders at the base. He immediately gave a single, simple order: "Everyone to your tanks!"

Lightning strikes

At that moment, Major Shmuel Askarov, the deputy commander of the 53rd Tank Battalion, was in his office at the Hushniya base of the 188th Barak Brigade. His Shot

Cal was parked outside his door with the crew within hailing distance. As he had indicated to General Moshe Dayan ten days earlier, he was certain that war was imminent. Throughout the night, the command elements of the brigade had been in conference revising plans and preparations. The commander of the 188th Barak Brigade was the Turkish-born Colonel Yitzhak Ben-Shoham. The brigade was composed of just two battalions with the 74th Tank Battalion commanded by Lieutenant Colonel Yair Nafshi deployed in the north from the slopes of Mount Hermon to near Mutzav 109 to the south of Kuneitra and the 53rd Tank Battalion commanded by Lieutenant Colonel Oded Erez from Mutzva 109 southwards. There were just 69 Shot Cals scattered along some 43 miles of front bordering the Purple Line, giving an average of one and a half tanks per mile of front. Nevertheless, Ben-Shoham had received no indication from Generals Hofi or Eitan that the Syrians were likely to launch anything besides another "battle day." The radio net of the brigade was designated "Toffee" and it immediately despatched the codeword – "Capital." It was the signal for the tanks of the brigade to move to their assigned positions on the firing ramps beside the various Mutzavim. Major Askarov was in his tank within moments and heading eastwards at high speed through the heavy artillery barrage to Mutzav 111 overlooking the Kudne Gap. As his Shot Cal mounted the firing ramp he could see nothing but churning clouds of dust due to the intensive shelling. Eventually, there was a lull and the dust settled momentarily. He was dumbfounded when he saw hundreds of Syrian T-54 and T-55 tanks emerging from the dust cloud in dense columns spearheaded by specialized bridge-laying and mine-clearing variants.

All along the Purple Line, the tank platoons of the Barak Brigade were under fire as they maneuvered into their preassigned firing positions. In the northern sector, the 74th Tank Battalion was deployed with Company Het under the command of Captain Eyal Shaham with its three platoons guarding Mutzavim 104, 105 and 107 with the company commander and two tanks at Mas'adeh. Company Alef under the command of Major Zvi Rak was stationed in and around Kuneitra as it was thought to be a Syrian priority objective for a "battle day." Company Bet under the command of Major Avner Landau was held in reserve at Wasset Junction, while the battalion commander Lieutenant Colonel Nafshi stationed himself on the commanding heights of Booster Ridge overlooking the Kuneitra Gap. At 1415hrs, an observation post on Hermonit reported the advance of an armored force of T-54/55s proceeded by bridging and mineclearing tanks, but Nafshi immediately implemented a coordinated fire plan of tanks and artillery that stopped the enemy before they reached the antitank ditch. But the pressure was mounting by the minute. The Syrian 68th Infantry Brigade with an attached tank battalion of T-54/55s launched an assault

Golan Heights: through the gunsights

Artwork by Ian Palmer, © Osprey Publishing

Israeli tank gunners were uniformly superior to their Syrian counterparts, thanks in part to the superior optical sights of the Centurion. Here a T-55 is hit at close range, viewed through the gunner's Sight Periscopic No.30.

The TSh 2-22 gunner's sight has a magnification of 3.5x or 7x but in the final battles of the Syrian offensive the tanks were so close that range assessment was unnecessary and opposing AFVs often filled the gunner's field of view — but only if they left the safety of the firing ramps.

between Mutzavim 104 and 105, but Nafshi promptly despatched Company Bet to the threatened area and caught the enemy in the flank as the MTU-20s were trying to deploy their bridges over the antitank ditch. A further attack by the Syrian 85th Infantry Brigade to the north and south of Mutzav 107 was similarly halted by the 74th, as was an attack by the Syrian 52nd Infantry Brigade to the north of Mutzav 109. The Shot Cals on the firing ramps were exacting a fearful toll of the swarming enemy T-54s and T-55s while the few mobile reserves moved from one threatened point of penetration to another. The general feeling at the outset was that this was just another "battle day" but now the frontline units were reporting that yet more tanks were approaching. Equally serious was that the Shot Cals were running short of ammunition. Even now they were obliged to retire so that the crews could access the rounds stored in the bowels of the tanks.

The antitank defenses along the Purple Line proved crucial in stalling the Syrian offensive for sufficient time to allow the reserve units to reach the Golan. The antitank ditch was 5m across and 3m deep with the spoil heaped up on the Israeli side to make bridgelaying operations more difficult. Antitank mines were laid on each side of the ditch and a maintenance road ran along the Israeli side. Such an obstacle is only effective if covered by fire and the IDF constructed a series of firing ramps on higher ground some 1,500 to 2,000m to the west of the ditch. From these dominating positions, the Shot Cals were in hull-down positions with just their gun and turret tops showing, which made them extremely difficult targets from the front. They in turn were able to engage and destroy Syrian tanks out to a distance of 3,000m, such as these ones with a group of T-62As and BTR-152 APCs in the foreground, a T-54A in the ditch and a T-55A(M) toppled off the bridge of an MTU-20. Note how the ditch has been levelled by Caterpillar bulldozers that breached the antitank ditch under the cover of darkness. This part of the Purple Line was in the northern sector of the 7th Armored Brigade. (IGPO)

South of Mutzav 109, the 53rd Tank Battalion was under even more intense pressure as the 5th and 9th Infantry Divisions mounted the main Syrian attacks through the Kudne and Rafid Gaps. Company Zayin under the command of Captain Uri Avika was deployed from Mutzav 110 to 114, together with Major Askarov, covering the Kudne line. Immediately to their south was Company Gimmel under the command of Captain Uzi Arieli, although three of his tanks were detached to protect brigade HQ. The company's task was to guard the Tapline Road with a platoon of tanks at Juhader close to Mutzavim 114 and 115. The Trans Arabian Pipeline or Tapline extended some 1,200 miles from Arabia to the Mediterranean coast in Lebanon and ran diagonally across the Golan. It was to prove crucial in the campaign. As soon as the attack began, reports came in of a Syrian probe along the road bordering the Tapline and Captain Arieli despatched a platoon as reinforcements commanded by Lieutenant Oded Beckman. On arrival at Mutzav 115, his defending force numbered just five Shot Cals. To his front was a Syrian tank battalion of 41 T-54/55s of the 112nd Infantry Brigade, giving a ratio of 1:8. Although his limbs seemed to be shaking uncontrollably, Beckman's mind was crystal clear. He noticed an MTU-20 bridgelayer at the head of the column and allowed it to lay its bridge across the antitank ditch and withdraw. Only when a T-54 gun tank maneuvered onto the bridge and was halfway across did he open fire. He destroyed a second T-54 as it tried to push the first one aside, effectively blocking the crossing site entirely. He then engaged a second MTU-20 before it reached the antitank ditch, stalling the whole Syrian attack. All along the Purple Line, the specialized T-54/55 variants – the

MTU-20 bridgelayer and the mineclearing PT-54s fitted with mine-rollers – were the priority targets for Israeli gunners, since their primary role was to breach the antitank ditch and the minefields. Standard operating procedure dictated that these vehicles were engaged at the maximum effective range of 2,500m.

Finally, there was Company Vav under the command of Captain Avi Ronis with five tanks near Tel Juhader, a platoon at Mutzav 114 and a platoon under the command of Lieutenant Yoav Yakir at Mutzav 116, the most southern post on the Purple Line. Its role was to block both the Tapline Road and the South Road to El Al. In the more open rolling terrain of the southern Golan Plateau, this was an impossible task for so few tanks.

The stand of the Barak Brigade

At the command headquarters at Nafakh, confusion reigned since many of the senior officers were absent including General Khaka Hofi, his deputy, chief of staff and the commander of the resident 36th Armored Division, Major General Raful Eitan. At noon, Hofi had flown to Tel Aviv in his Piper Cub leaving Colonel Ben-Shoham in command of the Golan: a fact he failed to convey to Colonel Ben-Gal. Accordingly, the latter baulked at being given orders by his equivalent in rank to move two of his battalions to the Wasset Junction. He returned to Nafakh to clarify the situation only to find the command bunker packed with personnel sheltering from the artillery bombardment. Finding it impossible to talk to Ben-Shoham, he informed the Northern Command operations officer, Lieutenant Colonel Uri Simhoni, that he was going to move the 7th Armored Brigade toward Kuneitra. Ben-Shoham himself was frantically busy communicating with his two battalion commanders as they fought their desperate battles along the Purple Line. Realizing the problem in the chain of command, Shimoni took it upon himself to assume the authority of the GOC Northern Command. Thus, a mere lieutenant colonel assumed command in the opening hours of Israel's most critical battle. Crucially, both the full colonels, Ben-Gal and Ben-Shoham, were willing to take orders from a subordinate in rank as the representative of Northern Command.

Shimoni's first decision was to have far-reaching consequences and effectively set the course of the battle for the next four days. Within the first hour of battle being joined, he ordered Ben-Gal to move two of his battalions to the sector north of Kuneitra and one to the southern Golan. The tanks moved out of their assembly points around Nafakh and headed eastward along the various tracks and roadways but still carefully trying to avoid running over the irrigation pipes of the Golan kibbutz farmers. Under withering artillery fire, the 7th Armored Brigade deployed along the high ground some two and a half miles from the Purple Line, acting as an immediate reserve to the Barak Brigade now heavily engaged along the whole of the 43-mile frontlines, giving an average of just one and a half tanks per mile of front. This meant there were to be three tank battalions north of Kuneitra and two to the south. His decision was based on the information he was receiving from the front. The 53rd Tank Battalion's initial reports indicated that they were containing the Syrian attacks in the southern sector. But in the north the observation posts on lofty Mount Herman and the tall *tels* were able to see the magnitude of the overall offensive from their elevated positions, a facility denied to the 53rd. It also reinforced the mindset of Northern Command that was convinced that the Syrians would attack through the Kuneitra Gap following repeated wargames by the Israelis. Critically at this juncture, there were no more reserves to be had as the general mobilization of the IDF had only just been set in motion. Yet, with no intelligence to the contrary, Colonel Ben-Shoham was still convinced that this was just another "battle day" whereas Ben-Gal realized this was general warfare on two fronts. By mid-afternoon, Ben-Gal decided to visit the frontlines to see for himself and organize his brigade accordingly while Ben-Shoham remained in the command bunker at Nafakh and directed his brigade by radio.

At Mutzav 111, the deputy commander of the Barak Brigade was perched on a firing ramp in his Shot Cal opposite the Syrian fortification on Tel Kudne. To his front, the ground was still shrouded in dust and smoke as the Syrian artillery bombardment continued unabated. When the barrage lifted, Major Shmuel Askarov saw scores of tanks pressing forward in columns four abreast astride the Kudne Road as the 33rd Infantry Brigade launched its assault. Five MTU-20 bridgelayers were in the van. In his crew, Askarov had the finest gunner in the brigade, Yitzhak Hemo. Within minutes, three of the bridgelayers were in flames but Askarov suddenly realized that he was fighting alone. His accompanying tanks were sheltering behind the ramps from the fearsome artillery fire. Askarov immediately called up his fellow tank commanders by radio but got little response. Ordering his driver to reverse, he drew up beside the closest Shot Cal and jumped across. Drawing his pistol he pointed it at the commander's head and ordered "Get up there or I shoot," indicating the firing ramps. The other tanks quickly mounted the ramps and began firing methodically up and down the long lines of T-54/55s but still they kept advancing. With a display of cold courage not seen before by the Israelis, the Syrian tanks simply bypassed the burning victims of the devastating Israeli fire and pressed on, pausing occasionally to return fire.

Where the terrain permitted, groups detached themselves from the advancing columns and engaged the Shot Cals on the ramps with volley after volley of armor-

piercing shot, despite the difficulty of hitting such small targets. Inevitably, rounds struck home and one by one the tanks on the ramps were hit and most of their commanders killed, since the Israeli commanders fought with their heads outside of the cupolas for better vision. Askarov's Shot Cal was hit four times but remained operational. Within the first two hours, his crew destroyed 35 T-54/55s and numerous APCs, thanks to the superb gunnery of Yitzhak Hemo, who achieved a remarkable hit rate of one enemy AFV for every one and half rounds fired. Each Shot Cal carried 72 rounds. But still the Syrians advanced and closed on the ramps. Soon after 1600hrs, Hemo hit a tank to the left of his ramp at a range of just 50 yards but by now there were others even closer. Akarov swung the turret to the right to allow Hemo to engage another T-54 at 30 yards range but the two tanks fired simultaneously. Askarov was blown out of his commander's cupola with serious wounds to the throat and head. As dusk fell, the Kudne Road was now open.

To the north of Kuneitra, the fighting was bitter and intense around Mutzav 107 as the Syrian 52nd Infantry Brigade attacked in force with scores of tanks along the Damascus Road. Facing them were just the three Shot Cals of Lieutenant Shmuel Yakhin's platoon of Company Alef, 74th Tank Battalion. The three tanks were perched on the firing ramps several hundred yards apart on each side of the strong-point that was manned by men of the 1st Golani Infantry Brigade. They opened fire at 2,000

A graphic illustration of the dreadful and numbing intensity of the Syrian artillery bombardment as a pair of Shot Meteors maneuvers under fire with the tank commanders ducked down inside to escape the lethal shell fragments. Even the fittings on the turret tops, such as antennae bases, were blown off by the blast, as well as displacing optical devices. (IGPO) yards' range inflicting numerous casualties among the enemy. Volley after volley of APDS rounds crashed into the advancing AFVs until the ammunition ran low. The company commander, Major Zvi Rak, arrived with seven tanks to add their firepower to Yakhin's platoon. Burning wrecks and exploding vehicles now dotted the landscape until the column veered to the south and out of range. Major Rak sent his deputy, Captain Oded Yisraeli, with a platoon of tanks in pursuit. He soon discovered a company of T-54/55s crossing the antitank ditch over a bridge laid by an MTU-20. The enemy were lined up like ducks at a fairground and all the tanks were destroyed within minutes. A mile further on, Yisraeli encountered another company attempting to cross but the Syrian tanks returned fire with determination. Syrian combat engineers had found the answer to the antitank ditch and were now filling it in with an unarmored Caterpillar bulldozer. Captain Yisraeli called his company commander for reinforcements. Leaving Yakhin's platoon at Mutzav 107, Major Rak and his four tanks moved southwards in support but he suddenly heard an explosion and found himself covered in blood. It took some moments before he realized it was not his own but that of his loader, who had been decapitated by an rocket-propelled grenade (RPG). His headless torso slumped down into the turret spurting arterial blood around the interior. Both the gunner and driver became hysterical at the sight of their comrade's body. Rak slapped them and doused them in water until they calmed down. He then returned to Kuneitra to extricate the body and change to another Shot Cal. Such deaths occurred regularly during the first few days of the campaign. Although it was a relatively simple matter for Ordnance Corps personnel to clean the interior of the turret of blood, it did not take long for the residue to become malodorous, much to the discomfort of subsequent crews. The answer was found by wiping the interior walls of the turret with diesel oil as its smell masked the stench of the blood or decaying flesh. Furthermore, so many tank crewmen, especially tank commanders, were being

Shot Cals advance carefully towards the skyline in case of Syrian troops and tanks lying in ambush positions. This terrain and road is very similar to that which Lieutenant Zvi Greengold fought over during his heroic defensive action along the Tapline Road on the night of October 6/7. (IGPO)

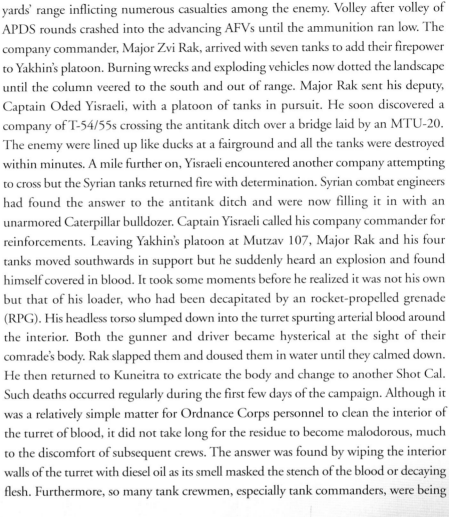

decapitated that crews were ordered to wear their dog tags around their ankles since they were often lost from a headless body.

Far to the south, a platoon of Company Vav under the command of Lieutenant Yoav Yakir had been fighting a lone action all afternoon. Although assigned to support the southernmost strong-point of Mutzav 116, he had fought an action near Tel Saki against a force of some 25 T-54/55s trying to cross the Purple Line along an old Roman road that once led to Damascus. Together with his first sergeant Nir Atir, Yakir destroyed most of them by accurate, long-range tank fire. Around 1600hrs, the Syrian 47th Tank Brigade attached to the 5th Infantry Division was observed advancing on the antitank ditch opposite Mutzav 116. The strong-point's commander, 2nd Lieutenant Yossi Gur of the 50th Parachute Battalion, immediately radioed to Lieutenant Yakir for support as his position was being blanketed in artillery fire. Yakir's platoon hurried north to Mutzav 116 where the Syrians had deployed bridges across the antitank ditch and tanks were streaming across. The three Shot Cals engaged the 60 T-55s of the 47th Tank Brigade from open terrain at ranges from 200 to 1,000 yards. They were joined by two tanks from a neighbouring platoon but these were soon knocked out: the gallant platoon was once more fighting alone. As darkness fell, they fought on by the light of flares fired from Mutzav 116 until 2300hrs, by which point two of Yakir's tanks had fired all their ammunition and the other had just five rounds left. Lieutenant Yakhir sought permission to withdraw and be resupplied with ammunition but the situation was so desperate that he was ordered to continue the action with just machine-gun fire to try and dissuade the Syrians from advancing in the dark. A few minutes later, Yakir was killed and Sergeant Nir Atir assumed command of the platoon. Realizing the hopelessness of the situation, Colonel Ben-Shoham ordered Atir to withdraw for more ammunition. The platoon had been fighting for seven hours without respite but, just as it fell back, the very first reinforcements were finally arriving on the Golan Heights, albeit just ten tanks of a ready reaction battalion. The Barak Brigade and its 69 Shot Cals had destroyed scores of Syrian T-54/55s and numerous other AFVs but the battle was to continue long into the night.

7th Brigade enters the fray

Major General Khaka Hofi arrived at the Nafakh headquarters at 1630hrs in company with Major General Mordechai "Motti" Hod, the former head of the Israeli Air Force and the architect of the preemptive strike in the Six Day War of 1967: a stratagem denied to the IDF in October 1973 by the government. He immediately concurred with Colonel Shimoni's disposition of forces but he divided the front into two separate commands. The 7th Armored Brigade was to assume responsibility for the northern sector and absorb the remnants of the 74th Tank Battalion into its command. The southern sector was now the responsibility of the 188th Barak Brigade, comprising its own 53rd Tank Battalion and the 82nd Tank Battalion, transferred in from the 7th Armored Brigade. The latter was now deployed along the high ground some two miles behind the frontlines with the 71st Tank Battalion in the north, and the 77th Tank Battalion in the center covering the Kuneitra Gap from the hill feature of Booster down to the deserted town of Kuneitra itself. Between them was the 75th Armored Infantry Battalion, reinforced by Company Humous under Lieutenant Emi Palant from the 77th Tank Battalion. The 82nd Tank Battalion had moved south to support the 188th Armored Brigade and was now positioned in reserve but unfortunately Lieutenant Colonel Oded Erez had not been informed of their presence. During the afternoon's fighting, the 53rd had lost 12 tanks, a third of its total. Two company commanders had been killed and the battalion deputy commander, Major Shmuel Askarov, wounded. He was now in hospital at Safed. Following an operation on his throat and for his other injuries, he was told he must remain in hospital for at least two weeks to recover. The 74th in the north had lost seven of its 33 tanks but had contained every Syrian attack so far. The crews were exhausted by their exertions and the fearful concussion of exploding artillery shells. Although the crews were relatively immune inside their tanks to artillery fire, the red-hot fragments sheared off radio

A mortally wounded tank commander is lifted from the turret of a Shot Cal after being struck in the throat by fragments from a Sagger missile. During the Israeli counteroffensive, the Sagger ATGM was used in large numbers and some tanks were festooned with the missiles' guidance wires. (IGPO)

antennae, damaged optical sights and ignited camouflage nets or bedding on the exteriors, rendering the vehicles deaf and blind until repairs could be made. Such artillery fire was also deadly to crew commanders standing with their head and shoulders exposed in their cupolas for better vision of the battlefield.

Around 1700hrs as dusk fell, the Syrians resumed the offensive with major attacks by a further two brigades in the northern sector and three more in the south against the hard-pressed Barak Brigade. Thanks to the intelligence gained during previous "battle days," the Syrians knew the dispositions of all the Mutzavim and the firing ramps. In the failing light, tanks and infantry infiltrated through the gaps in the Israeli defenses in large numbers. Infantry tank-hunter teams now moved among the frontline positions. T-54s and T-55s were pouring through the Israeli lines in the southern sector with approximately 140 in the Kudne area, some 60 advancing along the Tapline Road towards Hushniya and another 150 breaking through around Mutzavim 115 and 116. The 53rd Tank Battalion had just 15 tanks left fighting these hordes of T-54/55s along the Purple Line. The Syrians were now exerting intense pressure along the entire Israeli defensive line from Mount Hermon to Tel Saki.

The 53rd was desperately low on ammunition but it was virtually impossible to withdraw and reload since the Syrians would have quickly overrun the firing ramps. Lieutenant Colonel Erez radioed for more supplies to be brought forward. At 1830hrs, Colonel Ben-Shoham decided to leave Nafakh and join his brigade. In his M3 half track command vehicle, he took with him his operations officer, Major Benny Katzin, while his deputy Lieutenant Colonel David Israeli, remained at Nafakh. But as it neared Hushniya it came under such intense artillery fire that Ben-Shoham radioed for his Shot Cal to be brought to him. When it arrived, the crew informed him that they had passed many tanks in the darkness. Since the Barak Brigade was fighting along the Purple Line some four miles further east, the realization began to dawn on Ben-Shoham that the Syrians must have broken through in force. Belatedly, the 82nd Tank Battalion of Lieutenant Colonel Haim Barak was ordered forward to support the remnants of the Barak Brigade. The 82nd was composed of three companies of which two were made up of recent conscripts only halfway through their basic armor training course. On the other hand, Company Alef commanded by Captain Eli Geva was a veteran unit and considered among the best in the IAC. Company Bet under the command of Captain Yaacov Chessner was despatched to the Kudne sector at Mutzav 111, where it arrived with seven tanks, having lost four en route. Company Gimel was sent to support Mutzav 116 but was ambushed on the way, losing seven tanks in its first action. Captain Geva and Company Alef fought a successful battle in the darkness along the patrol road running north–south behind the Purple Line, destroying some 30 tanks for the loss of just one.

The Syrians exploited their success in the south by committing the 1st Armored Division through the Rafid opening following the successful attack of the 46th Tank Brigade while the 15th Mechanized Brigade of the 3rd Armoured Division expanded the breach in the Israeli line at Kudne. A strong column of AFVs from this formation turned north towards Kuneitra with the intention of striking the southern flank of the 7th Armored Brigade and dislodging it from its dominating fire positions.

All the Syrian armored divisions' tanks, from the T-54 to the T-62, were fitted with infrared headlights and projectors to aid night driving and illuminate targets at night with beams of light that were invisible to the human eye without special viewing devices. It gave the Syrians a distinct tactical advantage over the Israelis since their tanks had no such equipment. In the past, night-fighting had been an IDF speciality and they did not believe that the Arabs would continue operations under the cover of darkness. For the same reason, the IDF had too few artillery illuminating rounds and flares as previously the Syrian "battle days" had invariably ended by nightfall. The failure to equip Israeli forces adequately for night-fighting was to prove costly in the coming hours. Aided by their infrared equipment, Syrian tanks were now infiltrating up the wadis and tracks between the Israeli positions in the northern sector where the Shot Cals of the 74th Tank Battalion had broken the Syrian tanks. Under the cover of darkness, Syrian combat engineers were filling and levelling the antitank ditch with bulldozers in numerous places.

Soon after 2100hrs, the renewed Syrian offensive struck the 7th Armored Brigade in the center at the Hermonit hill feature that was defended by the 75th Armored Infantry Battalion. With clattering tracks and belching diesel exhaust fumes, the

A Shot Cal lies rent asunder by an internal explosion during the fighting of October 7 near Nafakh. Statistically, every Israeli tank employed on the Golan was hit 1.5 times and approximately 100 were completely destroyed, such as this one. (IGPO)

Syrian tanks were almost invisible in the dark. The battalion commander Lieutenant Colonel Yos Eldar called for flares to illuminate the battlefield but demands along the front quickly exhausted supplies. It was another glaring tactical and logistical failure by the IDF because they had believed the Syrians usually ended their "battle days" before nightfall, so flares were deemed unnecessary in large quantities. The Israeli tank crews were now fighting blind. Only some of the tank commanders had special binoculars capable of detecting infrared radiation. On Booster Hill to the south, Lieutenant Colonel Avigdor Kahalani witnessed the Syrian assault and quickly mounted a counterattack. As his tanks approached Hermonit, he heard over the radio that Yos Eldar had been wounded and evacuated so he took command of the battle. It was the first major Syrian incursion across the Purple Line of the day on the 7th Armored Brigade front. With no parachute flares to guide them, the Israeli gunners engaged targets by the light of burning hulks in the valley below. The battle raged for three hours as the Syrian 7th Infantry Division tried repeatedly to overwhelm the 7th Armored Brigade. At one point, Kahalani put his IR-sensitive binoculars to his eyes only to see his own tank bathed in light, but when he lowered them he could see nothing. Realizing his tank was being targeted by a T-55 just a few dozen yards away, he ordered his driver, Yuval Ben-Ner, to reverse down the slope immediately. The fighting died down after midnight and the exhausted crews took turns sleeping fitfully not knowing what the morning held.

During the day of Yom Kippur, the Syrians had committed some 720 tanks to battle and despite heavy losses had broken through the Israeli defenses in the southern Golan, although their timetable was now frustrated and delayed by the gallant defense of the 188th Barak Brigade. Over 300 tanks were now advancing into the heart of the Golan Plateau. The 132nd Mechanized Brigade was heading southwestwards towards the religious settlement of Ramat Magshimim. The 43rd Tank Brigade began a two-pronged attack with the major thrust towards Nafakh while a secondary force turned northwards up the Reshet Road towards Kuneitra. The last remnants of the Barak Brigade under the command of Lieutenant Colonel Oded Erez were still fighting rearguard actions against appalling odds. Gradually they were forced backwards and the survivors, including three from the 82nd Tank Battalion and three from Sergeant Atir's platoon of the 53rd that had run out of ammunition, withdrew to the relative safety of Tel Faris where they formed a night leaguer with some paratroopers, support troops and dismounted tank crews. During the night more stragglers arrived but the position was now completely cut off by the Syrians. Worse still, the 51st Tank Brigade with some 100 T-54/55 was now advancing along the Tapline Road towards the Israeli command headquarters at Nafakh and there was not a single Israeli tank in their path. Disaster loomed, but was to be averted by the indomitable courage of a solitary lieutenant, Zvi "Zvika" Greengold. This 21-year-old lieutenant fought for 20 straight hours, changing tanks six times as they were shot out from under him, and is credited with an astonishing 40 enemy tanks, although he himself would claim only 20.

At 0300hrs on October 7, the column of tanks and AFVs of the 43rd Tank Brigade was spotted moving northwards towards Kuneitra by the tank commander of a disabled Shot Cal. He reported his sighting to Colonel Ben-Gal. The role of the 43rd Tank Brigade was to strike the southern flank of the 7th Armored Brigade and dislodge it from its dominating fire positions. If this attack succeeded, the Israeli defense of the northern Golan would be shattered just as it had been in the south. Ben-Gal immediately ordered his Tiger Company under Captain Meir Zamir to meet the threat. Zamir carefully selected an ambush site with his ten tanks on both sides of the Reshet Road but positioned well back in hulldown positions. Since the Israelis did not possess any night sights on their tanks, they turned off their engines and waited in silence. Soon they heard the rumble of the approaching armored column. When most of the tanks were in the killing zone, one Shot Cal switched on its searchlight to illuminate the area. Within short order, some 40 T-54/55s were destroyed and the advance northward halted. While some of the survivors retreated, others turned westward, taking the line of least resistance toward the IDF headquarters at Nafakh.

Around midnight, the full gravity of the situation on the Golan Heights finally began to impinge on the senior officers of Northern Command at Nafakh. Against a background of artillery fire, Generals Hofi and Hod decided to return to the Northern Command headquarters at Safed beyond the Bnot Ya'akov Bridge at 0100hrs after passing command of the Golan to Brigadier General Raful Eitan. Hofi called up IDF Chief of Staff David Elazar and expressed doubts that the Golan Heights could be held but ended by saying that only the Israeli Air Force could stop the Syrians. And for that daylight was necessary. But the air force was committed to a major operation at daybreak against the Egyptian missile screen along the Suez Canal under the codename "Tagar" that had been in preparation since the War of Attrition. "Tagar" was canceled and the air force was ordered north as this threat to Israel was realized to be immeasurably greater.

After losing several of their aircraft in the opening hours of the war, the A-4 Skyhawk squadron at Ramat David airbase was now called upon to stem the Syrian armor on the southern Golan. But Syrian SA-6 missiles quickly found their mark. The ground troops vowed not to call for any further air support. In the first two days of the war, the Israeli Air Force lost 35 aircraft and close air support missions were largely suspended. Despite flying around 500 sorties a day over the Golan, the air force was committed to degrading the Syrian antiaircraft defenses as the priority

Overleaf: The Golan Heights

On the night of October 6 and long into the next day, Lieutenant Zvi "Zvika" Greengold fought one of the most remarkable individual tank battles in the annals of armored warfare. Unattached to any particular unit as he was on a company commander's coursel, he hitchhiked to Nafakh at the outbreak of war, where he took command of a pair of Shot Cals and set off down the Tapline Road at 2100hrs in the dark with absolutely no knowledge of the whereabouts of the enemy. For the next 20 hours using the callsign "Force Zvika" to disguise the size of his unit, he fought to stem the advance of the Syrian 51st Armored Brigade, mainly on his own but occasionally with other tanks. Singlehandedly, he destroyed some 40 Syrian tanks (but claims only 20) while having to change tanks six times due to battle damage. Although wounded, he fought on and disrupted the final Syrian assault on the IDF headquarters at Nafakh. Burnt and bloodied, the 21-year-old finally climbed down from his Shot Cal and collapsed saying simply – "I can't anymore." For his extraordinary gallantry, Lieutenant Greengold was awarded the Medal of Valor. (Artwork by Howard Gerrard, © Osprey Publishing)

mission. The reality was that the tank platoons and companies were on their own without air support and with only limited artillery assets to stem the Syrian offensive. The deciding factor remained the tank crews themselves and the 105mm guns of their Shot Cals. As one platoon commander later recalled: "It became clear in the first hour that the battle had been left to the company and platoon commanders and individual tank commanders. The adrenalin rush was tremendous. Orders from some officer in the rear didn't matter much. We were alone and we made the decisions." No more so was this true than in the epic stand of the 7th Armored Brigade.

In fire they will come

At 0400hrs, Lieutenant Colonel Avigdor Kahalani of the 77th Tank Battalion woke in the light of a chilly dawn. Using the callsign "Shoter" or "Policeman," he contacted his company commanders and ordered their crews to start their engines. The Shot Cals burst into life and black exhaust smoke filled the air. Some 2km to their front, scores of T-54/55s were doing the same. It reminded Khahalani of the roar of lions ready to pounce on their prey. He ordered the battalion forward on to the firing ramps overlooking the valley between Hermonit and Booster – the fabled Kuneitra Gap. As the Shot Cals took up their hull-down positions, the Syrians began to advance in serried ranks with all the crew hatches closed. All along the line, the Shot Cals engaged the enemy out to ranges of 1,500m; each crew fighting their own private war for survival. Numerous Syrian tanks were hit but the 77th was taking casualties as well. The commander of Vespa Company, Lieutenant Yair Swet, was killed as were seven other tank commanders, mostly from artillery fire as they stood exposed in their cupolas. One Shot Cal was deputed to evacuate the wounded to the

The Syrian tank crews displayed great determination and considerable courage during their initial offensive. They continued to advance despite fearful casualties and they came within a hair's breadth of victory on Sunday October 7. These T-54A tanks were reputedly destroyed by the Shot Cals of the 77th "Oz" Tank Battalion of Lieutenant Colonel Avigdor Kahalani in the area that became known as the Valley of Tears. The Arabic numerals on the nearest tank show the callsign 300. (IGPO)

medical teams that had moved as close to the front as they could in their vulnerable M3 half-tracks. Similarly, the Ordnance Corps Forward Repair Teams were working non-stop to repair any battle-damaged tanks and return them to the fighting troops. But they were inhibited by a lack of armored recovery vehicles and their half-tracks were not powerful enough to tow the victims, so combat engineers on unarmored bulldozers answered the call despite the devastating enemy artillery bombardment. With grim determination, attack followed attack at 0800hrs; at 0900hrs and again at 1300hrs. Khahalani marvelled at the courage of the Syrians: unseen in previous wars and so all the more unexpected.

The same was not the case in the southern Golan where the 53rd Tank Battalion had just 12 tanks left clustered in a defensive position at Tel Faris. During the night, Colonel Ben-Shoham had been forced back westwards by the relentless Syrian advance. His last order to Oded Erez had been to retire to Tel Faris with the words: "All we can do now is hang on until the reserves come up. We've done our bit." At dawn, the first Syrian tanks arrived at Ramat Magshimim. From there, they drove on unopposed towards El Al and halted some 700 yards short. At Mutzav 111, the radio operator intercepted a transmission from the Syrian unit: "I see the whole Galilee in front of me. Request permission to proceed." But the request was denied. The opportunity of victory was slipping away as even now the first 25 tanks of

Colonel Ran Sarig's 17th Reserve Armored Brigade were crossing the Arik Bridge and climbing the Golan escarpment. The Israeli mobilization was ahead of schedule. In contrast, the Syrian timetable was falling behind due to the tenacious defense of the Shot Cals. The whole weight of the Syrian offensive was still directed towards Nafakh despite the gallant defense of "Force Zvika" along the Tapline Road through the night. Colonel Ben-Shoman's command team now joined "Force Zvika." However, the T-62s of the Syrian 1st Armored Division were advancing along Yehudia Road threatening to outflank "Force Zvika" fighting the 51st Tank Brigade on the Tapline Road. On learning of this new threat to his headquarters, Brigadier General Eitan ordered Ben-Shoham to return immediately to Nafakh. With the sun now high in the sky, Ben-Shoham turned his Shot Cal towards Nafakh, standing upright in the turret together with Benny Katzin. As they passed a disabled T-54, they were killed outright by a burst of machine-gun fire. Ben-Shoham's deputy, Lieutenant Colonel David Yisraeli, was also dead, killed in action just moments before. The redoubtable 188th Barak Armored Brigade now ceased to exist.

But its sacrifice had not been in vain as the Centurion tanks of the 679th Reserve Armored Brigade under the command of Colonel Ori Orr was now reaching Nafakh from the west. By nightfall, the attack on Nafakh had been contained but the 1st Armoured Division was still moving inexorably westwards towards the Bnot Ya'ackov Bridge, which was even now being readied for demolition as the Israeli defense line in the central Golan was still far too thin. Accordingly, Northern Command dictated that all reinforcements be directed to the central and southern Golan. Originally, the 679th Reserve Armored Brigade was sent to support the 7th Armored Brigade but was diverted to Nafakh. The 7th Armored Brigade was on its own. After the battle with the Syrian 78th Tank Brigade throughout the morning of Sunday October 7, the 7th Armored Brigade had destroyed 71 enemy tanks but the Syrians were now biding their time until darkness, when they had the advantage of night-fighting equipment. However, the actual infrared equipment was rudimentary and only truly effective for engaging targets at ranges below 500 yards. Furthermore, the driver's IR periscope provided a flat two-dimensional monochromatic image that inhibited depth perception. On the Golan, with its innumerable boulders and ditches, this was a serious problem. Many T-54/55s were immobilized on large rocks beneath their belly plates, or shed tracks after slipping into unseen depressions. Unlike the Israelis, there was limited recovery or repair facilities for stranded Syrian AFVs so even those with minimal damage became booty for the IDF.

During the evening the Sayeret reconnaissance unit was conducting an intelligence-gathering mission in the valley facing the 7th Armored Brigade under the cover of darkness, when it encountered a large formation of Syrian armor in its forming-up position. The Sayeret beat a hasty retreat while informing Colonel Ben-Gal of their discovery. On their heels came the largest Syrian assault so far against the 7th Armored Brigade, with a force of some 300 tanks. The battle raged until 0100hrs when the Syrians withdrew, leaving scores of tanks burning or abandoned. There were now 130 knocked-out Syrian tanks and numerous other AFVs in front of the 7th Armored Brigade's positions in what the Israeli crews called "the Graveyard"; later it was to be known as the "Valley of Tears." But this respite came at a cost. One by one the Shot Cals withdrew to refuel and rearm with ammunition. Medical teams moved forward to evacuate the dead and wounded from the tanks hit on the firing ramps, closely followed by the forward repair teams to retrieve the damaged tanks and return them to service as quickly as possible.

On Monday October 8, the third day of the war, the 77th Tank Battalion made a sweep through the Graveyard to harass the enemy and prevent him from recovering any AFVs or equipment. For the first time, they encountered the Sagger ATGM as well as the usual heavy artillery, with one tank being hit by a Sagger and another by an artillery shell that killed the commander, Sergeant Zelig Haberman. Thereafter, the Shot Cals returned to their firing ramps to wait for the next Syrian offensive. During the afternoon, the injured Lieutenant Colonel Yos Eldar arrived at the brigade against doctors' orders. Both he and Shmuel Askarov had escaped form the hospital in Safed to return to their units. To Askarov's horror the 188th Armored Brigade no longer existed but he immediately began collecting crews and tanks to raise the Barak from the ashes. Meanwhile, following the death of Colonel Ben-Shoham and his senior staff, the remnants of the 82nd Tank Battalion joined the 7th Armored Brigade. Similary, Captain Chessner of Company Bet followed suit and together with their 17 tanks set off for the 7th Armored Brigade logistic depot at Wasset Junction. Reinforcements were now pouring on to the Golan including the 146th Reserve Division of Brigadier General Moshe "Musa" Peled and the 240th Reserve Division of Brigadier General Dan Laner. But, apart from the stragglers from the 82nd Tank Battalion, there were still no reinforcements for the 7th Armored.

On the afternoon of October 7, the Syrian high command held a fateful meeting at Katana some 25 miles behind the Purple Line. The decision was taken to halt the advance of all units on the southern Golan to allow them to reorganize and await reinforcements before a final offensive was launched on Tuesday. Only in the north was the offensive to continue with the 7th Infantry Division to attack that evening followed by the 3rd Armored Division as soon as they arrived at the front. Thus, the Syrians were reinforcing failure in the north rather than their success in the south.

Avigdor Kahalani

Avigdor Kahalani was born on June 16, 1944, at Nes Ziona in Palestine to a family of Yemenite extraction. On induction into the IDF, he wished to become a paratrooper but flat feet dictated otherwise and he joined the Israeli Armored Corps in 1962. He was assigned to the 82nd Tank Battalion and served as a gunner on a Centurion tank. After becoming an officer in 1964, he was posted to the Syrian border during the Water War and was then sent to Munsterlager in West Germany to learn about the M48A2C Patton that was being procured by the Israeli Armored Corps. On his return to Israel, he helped to set up the first tank battalion equipped with the Patton within the 7th Armored Brigade.

It was with the 79th Tank Battalion that Kahalani fought in the Six Day War when he was critically wounded during an action at Sheikh Zuweid. His burn injuries were so severe that he was not expected to live but after 16 operations and many months of recuperation he returned to service as an instructor at the Armored Corps School. In 1972, he was sent to the Command and Staff College and then served as deputy commander of the 77th Tank Battalion within the 7th Armored Brigade. In early 1973, Kahalani assumed command of the 77th or "Oz" Battalion – the number 77 is the numerical equivalent of the Hebrew letters OZ meaning Valor. It was a name he certainly lived up to during the Yom Kippur War during the bitter fighting on the northern sector of the Golan Heights and during the IDF incursion into Syria. He is photographed here posing for the camera after a quick shave, soon after the decisive battle in the northern sector of the Golan with the Valley of Tears in the background, where his comrades in arms destroyed over 500 Syrian AFVs during some 81 hours of intensive combat. For his outstanding courage and leadership during the war, Lieutenant Colonel Avigdor Kahalani was awarded Israel's highest decoration for heroism – Itur HaGvura, or the Medal of Valor.

After the war, he became the deputy commander of the Armored Corps School and then took over a reserve training base deep in the Negev Desert. In December 1975, he assumed command of the 7th Armored Brigade as a full colonel. Three years later, he attended the Command and General Staff College at Forth Leavenworth in Kansas, USA. In January 1980, he was promoted to brigadier general and was given command of the 36th Armored Division on the Golan Heights. Nicknamed the Basalt Division because of the rocky terrain of the Golan, it took part in Operation *Peace for Galilee*, the incursion into Lebanon, in June 1982. After the Lebanon campaign, he became the commandant of the Command and Staff College. His final posting in the IDF was as deputy commander of the newly formed Ground Corps Command. On leaving the army, he entered politics and was elected to the Knesset parliament in 1992, later becoming the Minister of Internal Security.

IGPO

At dusk fell the tanks of the 7th Infantry Division formed up for yet another assault against the 7th Armored Brigade. The GOC of the division, Brigadier Omar Abrash, was well forward with his troops readying his armor for the attack when an Israeli shell killed him. The attack was postponed until the following morning. It gave the 7th Armored Brigade a welcome respite to repair many of their battle casualties and for the tank crews to rest before the next battle. Tuesday was to be the decisive day in the war on the Golan Heights, since the Syrians were committing their elite units in a final bid for victory.

The Valley of Tears

At dawn on October 9, the Syrians attacked in great force. Once again, the assault was directed through the valley between Hermonit and Booster. The Shot Cals were already in hull-down positions on their firing ramps but under intense artillery fire. To the north between Hermonit and Bukata were the depleted ranks of the 71st Battalion under the command of Lieutenant Colonel Meshulam Rattes, with just seven serviceable tanks and to the south was the 77th near Booster with the remnants of the 74th and 82nd covering Kuneitra: a total of 34 tanks in all. As battle was joined and the enemy intentions became apparent, Colonel Ben-Gal ordered Khahalani to deploy his seven remaining tanks close to brigade headquarters at Yakir-Kirton as a second line of defense. The Seventh was in a vice. To their front, the valley floor was now inundated with some 100 T-62s of the 81st Tank Brigade from the 3rd Armored Division. The fighting was desperate on the central sector where the Shot Cals were being inexorably whittled away by artillery damage and APFSDS-T rounds – hyper-velocity fin-stabilized tungsten bolts – that ripped through armor plate with deadly effect. Such was the intensity of fire that Ben-Gal allowed the tanks to withdraw from the ramps to escape the worst of the shelling. The intention was that when the barrage lifted, the tanks would resume their positions on the ramps but the Syrians were advancing relentlessly, within yards of their own bombardment. Their tanks had every chance of getting there first. Yos Eldar and his vunerable APCs were obliged to fall back further because of the massive artillery barrage.

Realizing the danger, Ben-Gal ordered Kahalani to advance towards the ramps. The fighting was now at close quarters and any tank hit at such ranges was sure to be destroyed, usually exploding in ball of flame. Survival was dependent on quick reactions and the ability of the crews to acquire targets, load the correct type of ammunition and fire with accuracy in the shortest possible time. Throughout the four days of battle, Israeli crews proved far more proficient in tank gunnery than their Syrian counterparts, often firing ten rounds a minute in the Shot Cal as against four in the T-54/55 or T-62.

Kahalani and his crew alone succeeded in destroying five T-62s in five minutes. Yet still the Syrians advanced with great fortitude. From his position, Kahalani was able to see down into the valley where he could see hundreds of tanks massing. These tanks belonged to the elite Republican Guard commanded by Rifaat Assad, brother of the Syrian President Hafez Assad. Both sides realized that this was the last throw of the dice and victory or defeat was now at hand.

For the 7th Armored Brigade, it was critical to regain these dominating firing ramps if the Syrians were to be stopped. The tank crews were emotionally drained and exhausted after almost four days of fighting, without proper sleep or food and under constant bombardment from artillery and air attack. The Shot Cals had survived numerous duels with T-54/55s but now in the final hours of the war, it seemed as if they would be overwhelmed by the hordes of T-62s. For the last four days, Colonel Ben-Gal had led his brigade with the surest touch, encouraging and cajoling his men calmly yet firmly, while always retaining a reserve of tanks, however small. These were fed into battle at critical moments and then another reserve was immediately formed from other assets in the brigade. In reality, companies or battalions no longer meant anything, as platoons moved here and there as the situation demanded, plugging into a different radio net as directed for however long before redeploying to another sector or unit. It was a measure of the professionalism and flexibility of the crews and their commanders. Coupled with the Herculean efforts of the forward repair teams, battle-damaged Shot Cals were quickly returned to service since the brigade was denied any reinforcements at all. Similarly, the wounded or dead were never left on the battlefield but were evacuated to the hard-pressed medical staff as soon as possible. All the while, logistics personnel drove their unprotected trucks through shot and shell to ensure a constant supply of fuel and ammunition. Ammunition was the key. The tanks

A pair of T-55s and a BMP-1 infantry fighting vehicle lie abandoned on the Golan Heights where some 867 Syrian tanks were lost in the fighting out of a total force of 1,400. Many intact T-54/55 tanks were captured by the Israelis and they were modified for service with the Israeli Armored Corps as the *Tiran*. According to Israeli sources, no BMP-1s managed to cross the Purple Line in the northern sector, so this suggests these vehicles were lost to the 188th Barak Brigade. (United Nations)

had fired so many rounds that their gun barrels were shot out and were no longer accurate at long range, but the engagement distances were now measured in scores of yards at most.

Refused permission to withdraw, some reinforcements did arrive thanks to Major Shmuel Askarov who had discharged himself from hospital, together with Yos Eldar, on Monday morning. Once back on the Golan, he gathered tanks and men from a variety of shattered units. He was joined by Lieutenant Colonel Yossi Ben-Hanan, who had been the commander of the 53rd Tank Battalion until a month ago. The 53rd Tank Battalion of the Barak Brigade was born again. With the codename "Morning Exercise," the patchwork force moved off to help the 7th Armored Brigade in its desperate plight. In the meantime, the remaining tanks resisted attempts to position themselves on the ramps. One sergeant did offer to move forward but he was already out of ammunition. Realizing that direct orders were having no effect, Kahalani resorted to shaming his men into action:

> Shoter stations. This is the battalion commander. Look at the courage of the enemy mounting the position in front of us. I don't know what's happening to us. They are only the enemy we have always known. We are stronger than them. Start moving forward and form a line with me. I am waving my flag. Move!

Slowly the Shot Cals began to stir, gathering pace until a solid line was formed with just the heads of the tank commanders visible in the turrets. A T-62 loomed over the ramp but was instantly hit. The line of Shot Cals weaved their way around the burning wrecks of friend and foe alike until they reached the firing ramps. The Shot Cals opened fire with precisely aimed, rapid fire. Geva's tanks soon arrived on the firing ramps and added their weight of fire and were then joined by Lieutenant Colonel Ben-Hanan's forces. Topping the next rise, Ben-Hanan saw a T-55 just 50 yards away. Shouting to his driver to stop, he ordered his gunner to fire. The Barak Brigade was back in the war. Battle was joined at close quarters with Israeli and Syrian tanks hopelessly intermingled but gradually the Syrians were forced back and the attack was broken, but at a cost. Both Ben-Hanan and Askarov were injured; Askarov critically with a gunshot wound to the head. Shortly afterwards, an observer in Mutzav 107 reported that the Syrian column of vehicles across the Purple Line was turning round and AFVs were falling back from the "Valley of Tears." The battle was over. The 7th Armored Brigade and the 188th Barak Armored Brigade had prevailed against overwhelming odds. As the battle subsided, the commander of the 36th Armored Division, Brigadier General Raful Eitan, came on the 7th Armored Brigade radio net and announced: "You have saved the people of Israel."

AFTERMATH

By midday on Wednesday October 10, 1973, the Israeli counterattack in the central sector forced the last remaining Syrian units back across the Purple Line. The defense of the Golan Plateau in the opening days of the Yom Kippur War was undoubtedly the IDF's most difficult campaign since the War of Independence in 1948–49. For the first time, the ground forces had fought without air superiority or close air support from the Israeli Air Force; enduring repeated sorties by Syrian ground attack aircraft. The scale of casualties in men and matériel was unprecedented, with the Israeli Armored Corps suffering most. Almost 75 percent of the tank crewmen in the 7th Armored Brigade were either killed or wounded in the first four days of the war: many of them tank commanders. At its lowest ebb, it possessed just nine tanks but, within 24 hours of the final battle overlooking the Valley

The IDF captured large numbers of T-54/55 tanks during both the Six Day and Yom Kippur Wars. Although never overly popular in the IAC because of their cramped interiors, they were pressed into service and modified over the years. They were named *Tiran* or Dictator with those based on the T-54 designated Tiran 4, those on the T-55 being Tiran 5, while captured T-62s were Tiran 6. (Getty Images)

of Tears, the brigade strength rose to 100 tanks with many replacement crews drawn from the reservists. The 188th Barak Armored Brigade suffered even more casualties in men and machines, yet it too grew like a phoenix out of the ashes and burnt-out tank hulks dotted along the Purple Line to fight again. After lengthy deliberations throughout Wednesday afternoon, the Israeli government decided that the IDF must cross the Purple Line and capture a swathe of Syrian territory before the imposition of any ceasefire. The attack was to be launched on Thursday October 11 and the two units to lead the assault were to be the 7th and 188th Armored Brigades. It is axiomatic that any military unit that suffers more than 33 percent casualties in any given battle is fit for future operations only after a period of rest and recuperation, yet the 36th Armored Division led the Israeli counteroffensive into Syria after just 18 hours of reorganization. Within three days, Israeli forces and long-range artillery were threatening the outskirts of Damascus. It was a remarkable testament to the fortitude, flexibility and motivation of the IDF and the men of the Israeli Armored Corps.

It was these attributes that allowed a force of just 177 Shot Cals to resist the concerted offensive of 1,400 Syrian tanks over a period of 81 hours without reinforcement and with hardly any sleep or respite under an incessant artillery bombardment. There is no doubt that the IDF high command was highly remiss in allowing such a disparity of forces to exist on the Golan Plateau, yet this was also due to the masterly deception plan mounted by the Egyptians and Syrians in order to gain strategic surprise for their joint offensive against Israel. In the final analysis, it was the courage and resolve of the individual tank crews that determined the outcome of the defensive battle rather than any contingency planning by the IDF. Similarly the Syrian tank crews, mostly in their T-54/55s but also T-62s, fought with a grim tenacity never witnessed before by the Israelis. However, they too were let down by their high command. The Syrians were well aware of the Israeli dispositions on the Golan Plateau and intended to swamp the defenses with overwhelming numbers of tanks on a broad front along the entire length of the Purple Line. Nevertheless, the lack of tactical flexibility at the brigade and regimental level did not allow for any deviation from the overall plan, whether it was to bypass particularly determined Israeli defenses or capitalize on the superior night-fighting capability of their Soviet tank designs. The greatest mistake remained the failure to reinforce the success of the attack in the southern Golan rather than continuing to batter the 7th Armored Brigade in the north. The fault lay with requiring the field commanders to leave the frontlines for consultation with the high command at Katana some 25 miles away. The time lag between a decision being taken and then implemented at the front did not match the unfolding events on the ground.

Conversely, the Israeli command and control system was flexible and rapid, once the initial shock of the massive offensive was overcome. At the brigade level, Colonel

Yanosh Ben-Gal kept close behind his fighting units and was in constant communication with them. At all times, he attempted to maintain a reserve force, however small, to be committed at critical points and junctures as the situation demanded. Furthermore, he quickly recognized the scale of the Syrian offensive and the indecisive response of Northern Command on the first day. Accordingly, he did not allow any of his units to be diverted elsewhere, despite orders from above to do so to ensure as much cohesion as possible. There were simply not enough tanks to allow any further dispersal and throughout the battle he sought the recall of the 82nd Tank Battalion to his command: a move that was to prove critical on the morning of October 9 in the final battle of the Kuneitra Gap. On the southern sector, Colonel Yitzhak Ben-Shoham was not informed by the high command of the likelihood of a full-scale Syrian offensive on Yom Kippur. Instead, he remained at the command headquarters at Nafekh trying to conduct a different type of battle and thus separated from his frontline units. When he attempted to join them in the early evening, the Syrians had already broken through and so he was unable to link up with his brigade. Whether he could have done anything differently given the disparity of forces is debatable and the gallant officer paid the ultimate sacrifice in the defense of his country.

The GOC of Northern Command, Major General Yitzhak Hofi, came in for criticism of his handling of the campaign in the opening days of the war. He had been concerned about the disparity of forces on the Golan for sometime and voiced his dismay to the General Staff. He was particularly worried by the threat posed by the Syrian mobile antiaircraft batteries of SA-6 missiles. He feared that the air force would be unable to provide the essential close air support to the ground troops in the event of attack. But like the Israeli General Staff he did not believe that there was any real prospect of all-out war. Nevertheless, he authorized the extension and refurbishment of the antitank defenses along the Purple Line as well as the creation of more tracks across the Golan to allow easier provision of supplies to the frontlines by wheeled vehicles. Crucially, he also authorized the construction of more firing ramps on the Hermonit and Booster hill features overlooking the Kuneitra Gap. These simple earth mounds, together with those already built beside the infantry strong-points, were to prove of decisive importance during the defensive battle. Hofi's fears prompted General Moshe Dayan to request the deployment of the 7th Armored Brigade to the Golan Heights on the eve of Rosh Hoshana.

The role of Israeli artillery, whose sustained barrage helped to break the will of the attackers, was crucial to her defense but it was the crews of the Shot Cals and the T-54/55s that bore the brunt of the war on the Golan. Israeli casualties on the Golan were 772 dead and 2,453 wounded, mostly from the armored corps. The Syrians lost 3,500 dead and 5,600 wounded together with 348 prisoners of war.

The battlefield was also littered with hundreds of Syrian AFVs. Of the 1,400 tanks committed to battle, 1,181 were disabled during the war, as were 50 Iraqi and 20 Jordanian tanks. Of these 867 were left on the Golan Plateau, including 627-T-54/55s and 240 T-62s. Many of these were abandoned by their crews and were recovered intact by the Israelis and pressed into IDF service after modification as the "Tiran." Of those that were knocked out in battle, 80 percent were destroyed by 105mm tank fire, 10 percent were disabled by the antitank obstacles, mines, artillery or airpower with a further 10 percent by guided weapons and HEAT projectiles. The T-54/55, as well as the T-62, tanks featured remarkably thick armor for such a compact design and their excellent ballistic shape made them difficult to penetrate at the ranges favored for engagement by Israeli tank crews. The specialized AFVs such as the bridgelayers and mineclearing tanks were the priority targets and engaged at between 2,500 and 3,000 yards. However, 70 percent of all engagements were below 2,000 yards. Overall of those tanks hit by 105mm tank fire, 50 percent were penetrated, of which most caught fire. The combination of fuel and ammunition stowed in the front hull beside the driver proved particularly vulnerable to fire when hit by APDS rounds, even without full penetration.

Conversely, IDF statistics reveal that 680 Centurions were deployed on the Golan of which two-thirds were Shot Cal and the remainder Shot Meteor. Of the 200 Shot Cals engaged in the first few days, each was hit on average one and a half times by ordnance of various types and of those struck by 100mm and 115mm projectiles, 29 percent were penetrated of which 25 percent caught fire. During the course of the war on the Golan, 250 Shot and Sherman tanks were knocked out but of these 150 were returned to service after rebuilding and refurbishment.

During the defensive battle in the northern sector, the 7th Armored Brigade destroyed some 500 AFVs of which 260 were T-54/55 and T-62 tanks. Ammunition expenditure was huge. Each Shot Cal carried 72 rounds of main armament ammunition but after each battle day, 45 percent of tanks had fewer than 10 rounds left and the remainder fewer than 20. But it was superior gunnery techniques that proved ultimately decisive: the true legacy of General Israel "Talik" Tal. The close coordination between the average Shot tank crew, few of whom were over 20 years of age, allowed a sustained rate of accurate fire, particularly when perched on the dominating firing ramps. Israeli crews consistently enjoyed a range advantage of 500 to 1,000 yards thanks to superior training and sighting equipment. Coupled with better leadership and high motivation given the perceived threat to Israel's existence, the Israeli Armored Corps performed in an outstanding manner and by the end of the war their tanks were threatening both the Arab capitals of Cairo and Damascus. Those who stopped the Syrian onslaught were not volunteers from elite units but ordinary tank crews who represented a cross-section of society. The nation proved strong enough to survive the failures of its leadership. Similarly, the Shot Cal proved strong enough to resist the T-54/55 in combat and triumph in arguably the greatest defensive battle in the annals of armored warfare.

OPPOSITE
The last occasion that the Centurion fought the T-55 was during the protracted Angolan civil war in 1987–88 in southwest Africa. Manned mainly by Cubans, the T-55s were once again comprehensively outclassed by the modernized Centurions that are called Olifant in the South African Defence Force. Like Israeli Centurions, the Olifant Mk IA features a Continental V-12 750hp diesel engine and a semi-automatic transmission with a locally produced version of the L7 105mm gun as well as a new fire control system and passive night sights. This Olifant Mk IA or "Elephant" in Afrikaans is shown in the typical harsh bush terrain of Namibia and Angola during the final stages of the war against the FAPLA and their Cuban allies in June 1988. The SADF currently employs the Olifant Mk IB that remains a formidable main battle tank in the early 21st century: a remarkable testimony to a design that originated in 1943. (William Surmon)

M1 Abrams

DESERT STORM 1991

The Cold War never turned hot in Europe, so the intriguing question of how NATO tanks would have stacked up against their Warsaw Pact equivalents remains unanswered. However, other conflicts, fought away from the main theater, may hint at the answer. Operation *Desert Storm* of February 1991 provided a fascinating example of modern US versus Soviet-built tanks in action. This conflict was by no means a perfect surrogate for a 1980s NATO–Warsaw Pact clash, since the Warsaw Pact had better tanks than the Iraqi T-72M1 and their crews were also probably better that the average Iraqi tank crews. Nevertheless, close examination of these tank battles provides an intriguing look at the state of tank technology and tank warfare at the end of the Cold War.

The American M1A1 Abrams, German Leopard 2, British Challenger, and Soviet T-72 and T-80 were the ultimate tank designs of the Cold War years, and still have not been replaced by a new generation of tanks. Indeed, there is some question whether they will be replaced in the foreseeable future, since they continue to be viable battlefield contenders so long as they are well maintained and regularly updated.

T-72

In recent years the focus has instead been on the adoption of a new generation of lightly armored wheeled vehicles that are more economical for peacekeeping operations rather than high-intensity combat.

Several features distinguished the M1A1/T-72 generation from previous generations of tanks. In terms of firepower, these tanks represented the final switch to the use of APFSDS (armor-piercing, fin-stabilized, discarding-sabot) ammunition (simply termed "sabot" in the US Army) for tank fighting. While APFSDS had already been used by previous generations of tanks, HEAT ammunition had remained the predominant type in NATO and Warsaw Pact use through the 1970s. APFSDS began to attract serious attention due to its extensive use by Syrian and Egyptian T-62 tanks in the 1973 Yom Kippur War. The final triumph of APFSDS was due in part to advances in ammunition technology, but also to improvements in fire-control systems that gave APFSDS a level of accuracy resembling that of rivals such as guided tank projectiles. Both the M1A1 Abrams and the T-72 relied on APFSDS as their primary tank-fighting ammunition at the time of Operation *Desert Storm*.

The greatest disparity between the M1A1 Abrams and the T-72M1 was not in actual gun performance but rather in gun fire-control. The Abrams used a far superior FLIR (forward-looking infrared) thermal-imaging sight while the T-72 relied on the older and less versatile active infrared technology for night vision. The ultimate rule in tank fighting has always been "see first, fire first, hit first." It was the thermal sights on the M1A1 that provided the crucial combat edge in Operation *Desert Storm*, since US tanks could spot and engage Iraqi tanks before the US vehicles could be seen. Iraqi tanks suffered another significant disadvantage in 1991 in that they were supplied with inferior ammunition – a generation behind that used by the Russian army of the time.

In terms of armor, the M1A1/T-72 generation marked a distinct turning away from homogenous steel armor towards laminate armor. Laminate armor had been used since the 1960s in the glacis plates of Soviet designs such as the T-64, but it had taken some time for armies to be convinced that laminate armor was worth the trouble compared to conventional steel armor. The M1A1 and T-72 provide some important clues to the advantages of the new generations of armor and their value on the modern battlefield. In this respect, the M1A1 held a critical edge over the export T-72M1, which had armor inferior to that of the Red Army's contemporary T-72B tank.

There was also an important contrast between the T-72 and M1A1 in terms of propulsion. At the time of these tanks' design there was heated debate about the relative value of conventional diesel engines against the new generation of gas-turbine engines. In the Soviet case both engine types were utilized – the T-72 had a diesel engine, the T-80 a gas-turbine one. The US M1A1 was powered by a gas turbine, but this remained one of the most controversial features of the tank. Operation *Desert Storm* did not silence this debate, despite the outstanding performance of the Abrams.

The M1 Abrams and T-72 Ural offer a curious contrast in terms of design and development paths. The M1 Abrams program constituted an entirely new effort aimed at producing the best tank possible, albeit within a tight budget. The T-72, on the other hand, was a reinterpretation of the existing T-64A, arising from industrial rivalries within the Soviet Union.

Despite the vehicles' relative technical merits and flaws, the outcome of the tank battles of *Desert Storm* hinged as much on tactics, terrain, and crew capabilities as on the machines themselves. The Iraqi army was a mass conscript force that had become oversized as a consequence of recent wars; the army sacrificed quality for quantity in a bid to overcome Iran. The US Army had gone through a decade of reform and was now a lean professional force that had been honed to a sharp edge for potential combat in central Europe. By far the greater disparity between the two armies lay in their quality of troops than in the quality of technology.

THE TANKS

M1A1 Abrams

In the 1970s, the US Army tank force was based on the M60A1, with some of the older M48A3 Pattons still in service with National Guard units. Both tanks were evolutionary descendants of the M26 Pershing tank of 1945. An attempt to replace the Patton series with the more radical T95 design failed by 1959 as did the subsequent American–German MBT-70 program in the 1960s. Frustrated by cost overruns and poor performance, the US Congress killed the remnants of the MBT-70 program in 1971 and instructed the Army to make another fresh start. In the meantime, the M60A1 soldiered on through evolutionary improvements as the M60A3 (TTS), with important innovations including a laser rangefinder, thermal-imaging nightsight, and a new generation of ammunition.

In contrast to previous tank development programs, which had relied on the US Army's Tank-Automotive Command to undertake most of the design work, the new XM1 program was competitively developed by US industry. In 1972 General Motors and Chrysler received contracts to produce pilots of the XM1. The Army did not want a repeat of the situation with the overly complicated MBT-70, and the price per unit was capped at $500,000; by way of comparison, at the time a single M60A1 tank cost $339,000. Due to time constraints, the Army decided to stay with the existing 105mm gun instead of the more powerful German 120mm gun being developed for the Leopard 2, with provision for the 120mm weapon to be adopted at a later date.

One of the main innovations in the M1 Abrams design was the incorporation of laminate armor. The US Army had been studying various types of advanced armors since the 1950s, and in 1972 the British government agreed to share details of its breakthrough Burlington special armor – often referred to as "Chobham" armor, since it was developed by the Fighting Vehicle Research and Development Establishment at Chobham. The primary aim of laminate armor was to defeat shaped-charge HEAT warheads which had become a principal tank-killer through their widespread use in antitank missiles as well as projectiles fired by tank guns. With conventional high-explosive warheads the explosive energy is released in all directions. In contrast, a shaped-charge warhead is built around a hollow metal cone and when detonated, the explosive crushes the cone and forms it into a hypervelocity stream of metal particles which can penetrate a significant depth of armor. Experiments had shown that the penetration effect of shaped-charge warheads could be weakened using laminates. As the hypervelocity stream penetrated the layers it tended to break up or be diverted, lessening penetration. In the case of the M1 the protection objective was to shield the front of the tank against both the Soviet 115mm APFSDS projectile and a US 5in (127mm) HEAT warhead comparable to that used in Soviet antitank missiles.

The XM1 designs also began to explore other methods of protecting the crew besides the armor package. The primary cause of catastrophic tank loss in combat is the ignition of main gun ammunition propellant. Since World War II, tank designers had advocated transferring the ammunition to the floor of the tank where it was least likely to be hit, in order to minimize this hazard. However, this configuration does not guarantee that the ammunition will not be hit since mine damage or ricocheting projectile fragments inside the tank can still set it on fire. Furthermore, the floor location makes it difficult for loaders to reach and handle the ammunition – especially in view of the growing weight and size of modern tank ammunition. The US Army began to explore the idea of moving the ammunition into a bustle at the rear of the turret. The ammunition compartment would be separated from the fighting compartment by sliding blast-doors, and only open for a short time when the loader extracted a round. Should the ammunition be set on fire, the blast-doors would protect the crew long enough for the men to escape, and in many cases would slow or prevent the spread of a catastrophic fire into most of the tank.

One of the most controversial features of the XM1 was its propulsion. In the 1960s the Army had sponsored the development of a gas-turbine tank engine – the AVCO-Lycoming AGT-1500, originally considered for the MBT-70 – in place of more conventional diesel engines. The Army's enthusiasm for the gas-turbine option stemmed from the revolutionary improvements in gas-turbine propulsion in Army helicopters. A gas turbine is a form of jet engine, but with the power output through a transmission rather than a jet exhaust. Gas turbines were significantly smaller and lighter than contemporary piston engines of comparable power. In helicopters, their simplicity resulted in lower maintenance demands and greater reliability. However, some notable challenges did arise in adapting gas turbines to tanks. A major one was their voracious consumption of fuel and air. Unlike conventional piston engines, which can be slowed to idle to conserve fuel when the tank is not moving, the gas turbine operates near peak power all the time, consuming fuel. In addition, the engine requires a substantial flow of air – a more significant problem in a land-combat environment than in the case of helicopters, due to the presence of dust which can erode engine parts. In the end, Chrysler selected the more controversial turbine for its XM1 design while General Motors stuck with an AVCR-1360 diesel. Although both engines were rated at 1,500hp, the actual amount of power available from the turbine was greater since only about 30hp had to be diverted to engine cooling compared to about 160hp for the diesel. Both tank designs were subjected to extensive testing during 1976, but neither emerged as a clear winner. The Army originally favored the General Motors design, but at the same time wanted the AGT-1500 turbine. However, a plan to award the contract to General Motors with instructions to reconfigure the tank for the AGT-1500 was rejected by the Secretary of Defense. As a result, the contract was rebid with General Motors being pressured to modify the design to accommodate the AGT-1500 and both potential contractors were instructed to modify their turret design to accommodate the German 120mm gun.

The M1A1 Abrams tank represented the culmination of a number of technological trends in the 1960s and 1970s, which included the introduction of a new generation of digital electronics. This provided substantially better accuracy at long range, the ability to fire on the move, and significantly improved capabilities to see at night and through smoke and fog. (GDLS)

The M1A1 Abrams through 360 degrees

SPECIFICATIONS:

M1A1 Abrams

General
Crew: Four
Overall length: 9.8m
Hull length: 7.9m
Width: 3.7m
Height (to top of machine-gun): 2.9m
Ground clearance: 0.49m
Track contact: 4.6m

Track width: 0.64m
Gunner's night vision: Hughes thermal-imaging sight
Driver's day/night vision: Day periscope/image
  intensification night vision
Commander's day/night vision: Periscopes, optical
  elbow to gunner's primary sight
Fire protection: Automatic halon
Procurement cost: $1,624,000 (1988)

Chrysler's efforts at cost reduction paid off, and the full-scale engineering-development contract was awarded to the firm in November 1976. Low-rate initial production was approved in May 1979 and the first production tank was delivered in February 1980. The new tank was named after Gen Creighton Abrams, who had commanded M4 Sherman tanks in World War II, had been Army chief of staff in the later years of the Vietnam War, and was an ardent advocate of the new tank. The new AFV was formally type-classified as the M1 in February 1981 and full production was authorized with a procurement objective of 7,058 tanks. During the course of production, Chrysler's defense division was purchased by General Dynamics, becoming General Dynamics Land Systems (GDLS).

Artwork by Jim Laurier, © Osprey Publishing

Motive power
Engine: 1,500hp Avco-Lycoming gas turbine
Fuel capacity: 1,912 liters

Performance
Maximum road speed: 66km/h
Fording capacity: 1.2m without kit, 2.3m with kit
Obstacle clearance capacity: 1.2m
Power-to-weight ratio: 23.1hp/ton
Ground pressure: 1.0kg/cm²

Armament
Main armament: 120mm M256 smoothbore gun
Main gun rate of fire: 6rpm
Main gun stabilization: Azimuth in turret, elevation in line-of-sight
Main gun elevation: -10 to +20 degrees
Secondary armament: M240 7.62mm coaxial machine gun
Antiaircraft defense: .50cal Browning heavy barrel machine gun; M240 7.62mm
Smoke dischargers: Grenade launcher

No sooner had the M1 entered production than the Army decided to press ahead with the M256 120mm gun – a simplified copy of the German Rheinmetall weapon. By this time it was obvious that the 105mm gun would be inadequate to deal with the newer generation of Soviet tanks such as the T-64B and T-80B. The first M1E1 pilots with the 120mm gun were delivered in March 1981; these pilots incorporated a variety of other improvements, most notably an improved armor package. Details of the latter package remain confidential, but a Soviet report assessed the armor protection for the M1A1 against APFSDS as equivalent to 600mm RHA (rolled homogenous armor) compared to 470mm for the M1, and 700mm against HEAT compared to 650mm for the basic M1. These features, minus the 120mm gun, were incorporated into the M1 production line with the confusingly named IPM1 (Improved-Performance M1); 894 of the latter were delivered between October 1984 and May 1986. The 120mm version of the Abrams was type-classified as the M1A1 in August 1984 and the first production tanks were completed in August 1985. Priority for the new version went to US Army Europe (USAREUR), which had begun receiving them in large numbers by 1988.

During the late 1980s development of laminate armor packages for the Abrams continued, including a configuration using depleted uranium – that is, metallic uranium consisting of isotopes that emit little or no radiation. The principal advantage of uranium is its weight and density, which is about double that of lead. Depleted uranium was employed in a third generation of armor on the M1A1, leading to a variant dubbed the M1A1HA (HA standing for "Heavy Armor"). Besides being incorporated into new production tanks – starting in October 1988 – the heavy armor package could also be retrofitted to existing tanks. The M1A1 and M1A1HA were the principal types of Abrams used in the 1991 Gulf War.

T-72M1 Ural

The dynamics of the T-72 program were fundamentally different to those of the M1 program, and it was arguably less successful. A primary focus of Soviet tank development since the mid-1950s had been the Aleksandr Morozov design bureau's development of a new-generation tank at the tank plant at Kharkov (now Kharkiv in the Ukraine). This bureau had been associated with the legendary T-34 design, and before Kharkov was overrun by the Wehrmacht in 1941 the plant and associated design bureau were moved out of reach to Nizhni-Tagil in the Urals. There, the bureau was given responsibility for the next generation of Soviet tanks: the short-lived T-44 and the more successful T-54. The Morozov bureau returned to Kharkov in 1951 and began work on another new-generation tank, Obiekt 430. A small engineering team remained behind at the Uralvagon plant in Nizhni-Tagil to manage further evolution of the T-54 tank, starting with the T-55. This latter kernel would in the 1950s grow into a separate tank design bureau, headed by L. N. Kartsev, which would begin to rival the original Kharkov bureau.

Morozov's dream was to repeat the success of the T-34 with a revolutionary new tank that would match NATO tanks in firepower, armored protection, and mobility while remaining significantly lighter and more economical. The latest design went into production on a small scale in October 1963, as the T-64 tank. The T-64 incorporated a host of novel features including laminate armor in its glacis plate and an autoloader for its main gun. However, the design was plagued by problems, especially the poor reliability of its opposed-piston diesel engine. While Morozov was trying to cure the problems with the T-64, Kartsev's Uralvagon bureau had stretched the T-55 to accommodate a 115mm gun like that on the T-64. The resulting T-62 tank, while not offering the armored protection or sophistication of the T-64, was much more economical to build and much more dependable. As a result of the continuing tribulations of the T-64, the simpler and less expensive T-62 became the more widely manufactured tank of the 1960s.

Morozov continued to work on solving the problems with the T-64's powerplant as well as improving its combat performance by incorporating a more powerful 125mm gun. The improved T-64 went into production in May 1968 as the T-64A. However, while reliability had improved over the dismal T-64, the mean time between engine failures was still only about 300 hours. The Soviet army had hoped to standardize on the T-64A as its new standard tank (*osoboviy* tank), a concept that combined the heavy armor and firepower of heavy tanks with the size and weight of medium tanks.

In the meantime, the Kartsev bureau at Uralvagon had continued to plan the evolution of the T-62. The team investigated using a new type of suspension with smaller road wheels and return rollers, and also began work on an autoloader for either a 115mm or 125mm gun. These features along with other design innovations were incorporated into the Obiekt 166 and Obiekt 167 tanks. On August 15, 1967, the Uralvagon plant was informed that it would transition from the manufacture of the T-62 tank to the T-64A tank in 1970. Two variants were envisioned: the basic

The first of the T-72 export variants was the T-72 Model 1975, like this example from the Iraqi 3rd Saladin Armored Division, captured in 1991 by the US Marine Corps and subsequently displayed at Quantico, Virginia. The most characteristic feature of this version is the use of a coincidence rangefinder with the optical port in the protrusion in front of the commander's cupola. (Author's collection)

SPECIFICATIONS:
T-72M1

General
Crew: Three
Overall length: 9.53m
Hull length: 6.86m
Width: 3.59m
Height to turret roof: 2.19m
Ground clearance: 0.49m
Track contact: 4.29m
Track width: 580mm

Gunner's night vision: TPN-1-49-23
Driver's day/night vision: TNPO-168 and TVNE-4B (active IR/passive II)
Commander's day/night vision: TNP-160 and TKN-3
Commander's searchlight: OU-3GKM with IR filter
Fire protection: Automatic freon system, nine detectors
Unit price: $1,200,000; $1,800,000 with ammunition and spares (1992 export)

Motive power
Engine: V-46-6 12-cylinder diesel, 780hp at 2,000rpm
Fuel capacity (internal + external): 705 liters plus 495 integral; plus 400 liters in two fuel drums

T-64A with the troubled 5TDF diesel engine, and a "mobilization" version using a normal diesel engine from the T-62, which was intended as a low-cost alternative in the event of war. Kartsev hoped to develop a rival to the troubled T-64A, but was firmly rebuffed by Moscow. The political chief of the defense industry, Dmitriy Ustinov, continued to back the elegant and futuristic T-64A as the way of the future. In spite of Ustinov's continued preference for the Kharkov option, the Minister of Defense Industry, S. A. Zverev, had been impressed by a demonstration of the Uralvagon autoloader, and on January 5, 1968, instructed Kartsev's bureau to

Performance
Maximum road speed: 60km/h
Fording capacity: 1.2m without
  preparation, 5.0m with preparation
Slope-handling capacity: 30 degrees
  gradient, 25 degrees side-slope
Obstacle-handling capacity: 0.85m
  vertical, 2.9m trench
Power-to-weight ratio: 19.8hp/ton
Ground pressure: 0.9kg/cm²

Armament
Main armament: 2A46M (D-81TM) 125mm smoothbore gun
Main gun rate of fire: 8rpm (autoloader), 2rpm (manual)
Main gun stabilization: 2E28M electro-hydraulic, two-axis
Main gun elevation: -6 to +14 degrees
Secondary armament: Coaxial PKT 7.62mm machine gun
Antiaircraft defense: 12.7mm NSVT *Utes* machine gun
Smoke dischargers: Type 902A Tucha; 12 cover 300m² for two
  minutes
Crew self-defense: AK-47S assault rifle, ten F-1 grenades

continue working on a mobilization version of the T-64A tank with the bureau's own autoloader and the improved V-45 diesel engine. This version, designated Obiekt 172, comprised a T-64A hull and turret reconfigured for the new autoloader and cheaper powerplant. Two examples were completed by the late summer of 1968. Comparative testing during 1969 uncovered a number of design flaws, but the results of trials had been sufficiently promising for Uralvagon to be authorized to build 20 prototypes. The delicate running gear of the T-64A remained a source of mechanical problems.

The rivalry between factions in the industry and the army supporting Kharkov and Nizhni-Tagil continued unabated in the late 1960s. The preference of senior army commanders for the simpler and more reliable Uralvagon approach counterbalanced the influence of Ustinov and the Kremlin bureaucracy. In the midst of the controversy, Kartsev was transferred from Uralvagon to an army tank research institute and his place was taken by V. N. Venediktov. On May 12, 1970, a state decree on standardizing the T-64A gave Uralvagon permission to develop a further elaboration of the Obiekt 172 which took it even further away from the T-64A configuration by permitting incorporation of the new suspension from the Obiekt 167. This version was designated Obiekt 172M, and a prototype was ready by the end of 1970. Curiously enough, a similar battle was being waged in Leningrad over plans to convert the plant there to T-64A production. The alternative approach here was to go one better than Kharkov and adopt a more powerful gas-turbine engine, a decision that would prove every bit as problematic as the opposed-piston 5TDF. In the event, by 1971 the Soviet tank industry had three new "standard" tanks on hand – the original T-64A, and two derivatives, ready for trials, Obiekt 172M (T-72) and Obiekt 219 (T-80).

A preproduction batch of 15 Obiekt 172Ms was completed by the summer of 1972 and subjected to a grueling field trial in June–October 1972. Overall, the army was very impressed by the durability and firepower of the Obiekt 172M. Ustinov continued to oppose production of the Uralvagon tank, but the army continued to press for its manufacture due to lingering reliability issues with the T-64A and the immaturity of the new Obiekt 219 (T-80). To settle the matter, the Kremlin ordered the creation of a special commission under the First Deputy Minister of Defense, Marshal I. I. Yakubovskiy. By this stage a second preproduction batch of Obiekt 172Ms had been completed, in which most of the problems found in the 1972 trials had been rectified, so the commission recommended production. On August 7, 1973, Obiekt 172M was accepted for army service as the T-72 standard tank; in 1975 it was named the T-72 Ural after its birthplace in the Ural mountain region. The initial production series of 30 vehicles was completed by the end of 1973, with 220 more completed in 1974.

In April 1976 Defense Minister Marshal Andrei Grechko died and his place was taken by Ustinov, who had never favored the T-72 and referred to it as a "step backwards in Soviet tank development." Since the production debates of 1970–72, his support had shifted from the troubled T-64 to a new champion – the gas-turbine-powered T-80, developed by a consortium of Leningrad concerns with powerful political connections within the Kremlin. As a result, Ustinov put a cap on T-72 advances. The T-64 and T-80 would serve as the premier Soviet standard tanks with forward-deployed units facing NATO in Germany and would receive priority for technological innovations in fire-control and advanced protection, while the T-72 would be used for second-line units in the Soviet Union as well as for export.

The T-72 underwent continual evolution during production. The second production series, Obiekt 172M sb-1A, incorporated several modest changes and can be distinguished from tanks of the early production series by the shift of the Luna infrared searchlight from the left side to the right side of the gun. This version, sometimes called the T-72 Ural-1 Model 1976, was in series production at Nizhni-Tagil from 1975. A command-tank version, the T-72K Ural-K (Obiekt 172M sb-2), was next in the development cycle, and was similar to the T-72 Model 1976 except for the added radio and navigation system.

The original T-72 versions through 1977 used laminate armor in the glacis plate, but had a conventional "monolithic" cast-steel turret. The laminate glacis plate comprised an initial layer of 80mm high-carbon steel armor, followed by 105mm of GRP (glass-reinforced plastic or stekloplastika) about a quarter of the density of the steel, and finally a 20mm layer of high-carbon steel. The contemporary T-64 variant, the T-64A, also used laminate glacis armor but instead of the monolithic steel turret was fitted with a special-armor turret which had a large cavity in the front that was filled with aluminum. The monolithic steel turret of the T-72 was

The T-72M1 was by no means equivalent to the best Soviet tanks of the early 1990s. The best T-72 variant at the time was the T-72B with *Kontakt* reactive armor; pictured is an example of the T-72S export version, on display at the Nizhni-Novgorod Yarmark arms show in September 1996. Iran subsequently bought this version, which had substantially better armor than the T-72M1 as well as better ammunition. (Author's collection)

about two percent better at resisting APFSDS attack while the T-64A turret was about ten percent better against shaped-charge attack. However, firing tests discovered that the T-64A's apparent advantage was less than it seemed because after a single hit the cavity tended to deform and lose its protective advantage. The next generation of special armor used a Combination K (K for *korundum*, or ceramic) layer in the turret. The original configuration developed by NII Stali (the State Research Institute for Steel) used ceramic balls in an aluminum matrix. Although this went into production for the T-64A in 1975, it was difficult to manufacture and was soon replaced by a modified version using ultra-porcelain (*ultrafarforov*) ceramic rods instead of balls, also sometimes called "sandbar armor."

The new turret special armor with ceramic-rod filler was first used on an interim version of the T-72 series, the T-72 Model 1978 (Obiekt 172M sb-4), which entered production in 1977. Besides the new turret armor, this version also incorporated a switch from an optical-coincidence rangefinder to the TPD-K1 laser rangefinder. However, this version was relatively short-lived, being supplanted by the T-72A Model 1979 (Obiekt 172M sb-6, later Obiekt 176) which represented the first substantial redesign of the T-72 family. This used the new ceramic-rod turret filler and TPD-K1 sight, but also incorporated improved glacis laminate armor, new anti-shaped-charge sideskirts, an improved suspension with more travel for the road wheels, the improved 2A46 gun, and the Tucha smoke dispensers. This version was accepted for service in June 1979. The next production series, the T-72A Model 1983, introduced antiradiation cladding on the turret roof and several other changes, including the 16mm glacis appliqué mentioned below. This version was in production through early 1985.

The third generation of the T-72, the T-72B (Obiekt 184), introduced a substantially improved form of turret laminate armor as well as improvements in the glacis plate armor. This was prompted in large measure by lessons from the 1982 Lebanon war. Syria provided the Soviet Union with some captured Israeli tanks and ammunition, and an Israeli M48A5 with the new M111 APFSDS ammunition was sent to the Kubinka proving ground near Moscow for firing trials against a T-80. The Soviet engineers were shocked to discover that the M111 could penetrate the multi-layer glacis armor. This led to a series of improvements to the armor on the T-64, T-72 and T-80, as well as a crash program to retrofit a steel appliqué plate to existing tank glacis to provide protection against projectiles comparable to the M111. The T-72B and later Uralvagon derivatives such as the T-90 will be passed over in this account, since they did not play a role in Operation *Desert Storm*.

In 1976, Ustinov decided to earmark the T-72 as the next export tank for Soviet clients in place of the T-62, notably for Warsaw Pact allies. In general, the Soviet practice was to allow export clients to build T-72 variants about a generation behind their Soviet counterparts in terms of armor protection and fire-control systems. The associated ammunition was also a few years behind the Soviet standard. In 1977 Ustinov visited India, and a tentative agreement was signed to sell the latter country 5,000 T-72 tanks and help it set up a T-72 plant. In the end, this deal was not completed on schedule due to political changes in India, but it did accelerate the process of preparing the T-72 for the export market. The first T-72 export tank manufactured at Uralvagon was internally designated as Obiekt 172M-E, (E for Eksportniy, or Export). By the time the Indian deal was under discussion, the Soviet government was also encouraging Poland and Czechoslovakia to begin license production and agreements were reached in 1978. Production of the T-72 Model 1975 export tank began at the Bumar-Labedy plant in Poland in July 1982 and at the Martin plant in Czechoslovakia in 1982. There were two versions of this tank built – the Obiekt 172M-E with the standard Soviet PRKhP and FTP-100M nuclear/biological/chemical (NBC) protective suite intended primarily for Warsaw Pact armies, and the Obiekt 172M-E1 with a modified protective system using hermetic sealing and a turboseparator intended primarily for export to Middle Eastern countries, including Libya, Algeria, Syria, and Iraq.

The second export version, the T-72M (Obiekt 172M-E2), began development in 1978, with production for export clients beginning at Nizhni-Tagil around 1980 and in Poland and Czechoslovakia by 1985. The T-72M was a hybrid of the Soviet T-72 and T-72A in terms of features. For example, it used the TPD-K1 laser rangefinder as found on the T-72A, but was still fitted with the monolithic steel turret. The initial production version, the Obiekt 172M-E2, had the original 2A46 125mm gun without the thermal shield and still carried the basic ammunition load of 39 rounds for the main gun. This version was followed by the Obiekt 172M-1-E3, which added a thermal sleeve to the 125mm gun, increased ammunition stowage from 39 to 44 rounds, introduced the improved TNP-1-49-23 nightsight in place of the earlier TNP-1-49, added the Tucha smoke grenade launchers to the front of the turret, and added the anti-HEAT sideskirts. In parallel, the Obiekt 172M-1-E4 was built for export outside of the Warsaw Pact and was essentially similar to the E3 except that it was fitted with the same NBC protective suite as the export T-72 (Obiekt 172M-E1).

The T-72M was finally cleared for the use of special armor in the turret in 1982; the resulting T-72M1 export tank was a close relation to the Soviet T-72A. This version had the improved turret front armor using ceramic rods and an upgraded glacis plate with 16mm steel appliqué. There were numerous other upgrades compared to the T-72M, including better shock absorbers and an improved driver's hatch. Production of the T-72M1 began in Poland and Czechoslovakia in 1986.

Two basic versions were manufactured – the Obiekt 172M-1-E5 for the Warsaw Pact, and the Obiekt 172M-1-E6 for export outside Europe with the alternative NBC protective suite. The main client for the Obiekt 172M-1-E6 was India, which built the model locally under license as the T-72M1 *Ajeya*.

These export variants are significant in the case of Iraq, since all Iraqi T-72s were export models – including the T-72 (Obiekt 172M-E1), T-72M (Obiekt 172M-1-E4) and T-72M1 (Obiekt 172M-1-E6). Iraq purchased its first batch of 100 T-72 Ural-1s (Obiekt 172M-E1) from the USSR in 1979–80. Following the outbreak of the war with Iran, the USSR restricted its sales to Iraq since it was also courting Iran; however, the USSR encouraged its Warsaw Pact allies to take its place. Thus, in 1982 Poland sold Iraq a batch of 250 T-72Ms (Obiekt 172M-1-E4), followed in later years by the improved T-72M1 (Obiekt 172M-1-E6). Iraq purchased a total of 1,038 T-72s of all types, mostly from Poland. In the late 1980s there were plans to begin T-72M1 production at Taji in Iraq in cooperation with Bumar-Labedy. The process was to begin in 1989 using knockdown kits from Poland, with the locally assembled tanks called *Asad Babil* ("Lion of Babylon"). There are conflicting accounts regarding how many, if any, were actually completed. Polish officials indicate that none were completed even though a T-72M displayed at an Iraqi arms show in 1988 was claimed to be a locally built tank. In the event, LtGen Amer Rashid pushed for complete manufacture of the T-72M1 in Iraq rather than simply assembly from knockdown kits. In 1991 Bumar-Labedy was upgrading the Taji facility, but during the course of the war Taji was destroyed by air attack.

As a result of the USSR's export policy, clients such as Iraq did not receive tanks comparable in quality to the best Soviet tanks. In 1990 the best Iraqi version of the T-72 was the T-72M1 – roughly equivalent to the Soviet T-72A, which was already a decade old and not as well armored as the newer T-72B or the preferred T-80B series. Just as importantly, the Soviet Union did not export its best tank ammunition: the Iraqi army relied primarily on second-rate ammunition for its T-72 tanks.

Old enemies, new friends. This is an interesting view showing the Abrams side-by-side with the T-72, though in this case nearly two decades after Operation *Desert Storm* and in very differennt circumstances. This photos was taken on October 31, 2008 at the Besmaya Gunnery Range outside Baghdad showing joint training of US and Iraqi forces. Around this time, the US government announced plans to provide the new Iraqi army with M1A1 Abrams tanks as part of their rebuilding effort. (US DoD)

TECHNICAL ASSESSMENT

The vagaries of Soviet tank design in the 1960s led to a host of standard tanks that were substantially smaller and lighter than their NATO counterparts. A combat-laden T-72M1 weighed 41.5 tonnes compared to 56.8 tonnes for the M1A1 – thus being one-third lighter. One of the most immediate results of this was the amount of internal space for the crew. The T-72M1 is extremely cramped, especially in the driver's compartment, with conditions being only marginally better in the turret. The M1A1, while not as spacious as the previous M60A3 tank, was positively luxurious compared to the T-72 with ample space for the loader and the rest of the crew. While this may seem irrelevant to tank design, it reflects the relative inattention of Soviet designers to crew ergonomics and the impact of these features on combat performance. The T-72M1 was not well suited to prolonged combat operations in desert climates because the extremely restricted space within the vehicle led to overheating, crew fatigue and excessive crew stress. Although Operation *Desert Storm* was fought during the winter months, temperatures even during February were sometimes warm enough to negatively affect crew performance. "Air conditioning" in the T-72 was provided by a small, unshielded plastic fan. This might be adequate in Russian or European climes, but was of dubious value in the desert.

Protection

Modern main battle tanks have their best armor towards the front, with the usual design requirement being for them to provide optimum protection in the forward 60-degree sector. This involves an inevitable design compromise, since it is impossible to provide equivalent protection in all directions while remaining within viable weight limits. As a result, in this text the focus is on frontal protection for these two tanks; the side and rear protection is inevitably significantly less. Most contemporary assessments of tank protection distinguish between protection against APFSDS projectiles versus shaped-charge HEAT warheads, since modern laminate armors offer different levels of defense against these two distinctly different threats.

The level of protection is usually expressed as equivalent to a certain thickness of rolled homogenous armor (RHA). It should be borne in mind that information on armor protection is still widely regarded as sensitive, so the data here cannot be regarded as definitive. The figures on T-72 protection are from official published Russian sources.

In general, the T-72 and T-72M were designed to be able to resist an strike equivalent to the Soviet 115mm tank gun firing a steel APFSDS projectile. This was considered roughly equivalent to the NATO 105mm gun of the time. The defense against HEAT was proof against a shaped charge roughly equivalent to the Soviet 9M14 *Malyutka* (AT-3 Sagger), which was viewed as equivalent to NATO types such as TOW; curiously enough, this was the same threat level for the original M1 Abrams tank. The T-72M1 was designed to be proof against the improved 105mm threats of the early 1980s, such as the Israeli 105mm M111 APFSDS with a tungsten-carbide penetrator, or its American equivalents such as the M735, M735A and M774. Data is also presented here for the T-72B1; this was not in Iraqi service but the data provides an idea of improved protective levels for newer generations of Soviet tanks, intended to counter the newer generation of NATO 120mm tank guns and improved antitank missiles such as TOW-2.

There is no unclassified data on M1A1 protective levels from US official sources. The data below for the M1A1 is based on Soviet estimates. No data has been released on the amount of additional protection offered by the M1A1 Heavy Armor upgrade, so the data here should be regarded as estimated.

As is evident from the table, the protective level of the best Iraqi T-72, the T-72M1, was inadequate to provide protection against the 120mm gun of the M1A1 at normal battle ranges. Conversely, the armor of both the M1A1 and M1A1HA could provide adequate frontal protection against the 125mm gun of the T-72M1 – especially when the gun employed the most commonly available tank ammunition, the

Comparative protective levels				
(mm RHA)	Hull vs APFSDS	Hull vs HEAT	Turret vs APFSDS	Turret vs HEAT
T-72	335	450	380	410
T-72M	335	450	380	410
T-72M1	400	490	380	490
T-72B1	530	900	520	950
M1A1	600	700	600	700
M1A1HA	600	700	800	1,300

3UBM7 round with BM15 penetrator. Both tanks could defeat each other in side or rear engagements.

The tanks differed significantly in internal layout, which affected survivability if penetrated. The T-72 had 22 of its 44 rounds of main gun ammunition in a two-tier carousel under the turret floor, which fed the autoloader; the rest was stowed in various locations around the fighting compartment. The location of so much ammunition in such a confined space was an invitation to catastrophe should the T-72 be penetrated. The T-72 had a greater tendency to "lose its cap" compared to earlier types such as the T-55, due to the increased volume of propellant carried inside the fighting compartment. A fully loaded T-72 carried double the propellant of the T-55 – 440kg compared to 220kg. The T-62 was inbetween at around 310kg.

The M1A1 had 34 of its 40 rounds of main gun ammunition in a protected bustle in the rear turret overhang and the remainder in protected ready racks inside the turret. The aim of this configuration was to minimize the risk of the ammunition being struck by hypersonic debris if the turret was penetrated, and if the ammunition racks were ignited, to vent the blast upwards through special blast

This overhead view of one of the M1A1 prototypes at Aberdeen Proving Ground in the United States shows the distinctive rectangular blast panels on the rear of the turret roof that are designed to vent away a fire or explosion should the tank's ammunition ignite. (US Army)

panels in the roof rather than forward into the fighting compartment. This was intended to prevent catastrophic destruction of the tank and to give the crew more time to escape. The combination of better armor and better ammunition protection gave the M1A1 a clear protection advantage over the T-72M1.

Firepower

The T-72

The T-72 was armed with the 125mm D-81TM (2A46) gun, an improved version of the D-81T (2A26) 125mm gun that went into service on the T-64A in 1968. This was a conventional smoothbore gun with a life expectancy of 600 rounds of HE/HEAT ammunition or 150 rounds of APFSDS, although export customers complained that the actual useful life was closer to 100 rounds of APFSDS. Barrel life was a significant issue for Iraqi tanks as a large proportion of the inventory had been employed during the Iran–Iraq War and the Iraqi army was not especially diligent about keeping its equipment in prime condition; accuracy suffered due to tube erosion.

The usual two types of antitank ammunition were available – APFSDS and HEAT. The 125mm ammunition was of the split type, with a projectile and a semi-consumable propellant case and a steel stub casing at the base. At least four types of APFSDS ammunition were available for export at this time, most of them already two decades old. Details of Iraqi ammunition stocks are not available; however, even though Iraq was manufacturing the 3VBM-7 ammunition in the late 1980s, the US Army regularly encountered the old 3VBM-3 ordnance during the 1991 fighting. By way of comparison, the best Soviet APFSDS around 1990 was the 3VBM-13 *Vant*, which had a 3BM-32 depleted-uranium penetrator with penetration capability of 560mm at 2km – about double the performance of the 3VBM-3 used by the Iraqis. One should note that Soviet ammunition designations

Soviet 125mm APFSDS ammunition						
Round	Projectile	Penetrator	Date of introduction	Initial velocity (m/s)	Weight (kg)	Penetration (mm RHA at 2,000m, 0 degrees)
3VBM-3	3BM-10	3BM-9	1962	1,800	3.6	290
3VBM-6	3BM-13	3BM-12	1968	1,800	3.6	315
3VBM-7	3BM-16	3BM-15	1972	1,780	3.9	340
3VBM-8	3BM-18	3BM-17	1972	1,780	3.9	330

are confusing since there were three GRAU (Main Missile and Artillery Directorate) designations: the overall ammunition round; the projectile, including the sabot petals and other housing; and the penetrator arrow itself. The table below lists all three. In general, the APFSDS performance of the Soviet 125mm gun was inferior to that of the US 120mm gun.

Two types of HEAT ammunition were available for export prior to Operation *Desert Storm*: 3VBK-7 and 3VBK-10. These employed conventional finned projectiles with copper liners for the shaped-charge warhead. Penetration capability for the 3BK-14M (3VBK-10) was about 500mm; neither type was capable of penetrating the M1A1 frontally.

The 125mm gun was fed by a mechanical autoloader from the rotating ammunition carousel under the turret basket. The carousel contained an assortment of 22 projectiles and 22 Zh40 propellant cases, stowed horizontally with the projectiles forming the bottom layer and the propellant cases the top layer. The additional rounds were stored in the hull around the turret: four projectiles and propellant cases in pockets in the right front fuel cells, two projectiles and Zh40 cases behind the commander's seat, two projectiles and one Zh40 case immediately behind the gunner, three projectiles on racks on the left rear hull side, six projectiles on the rear firewall, and eight Zh40 propellant cases in cavities in the rear fuel tank, on the floor behind the ammunition carousel. The only ammunition stowage above the turret line comprised five propellant charges near the gunner's and commander's stations.

The gunner sat on the left-hand side and the commander on the right-hand side of the gun. In the T-72M1 the gunner's sights comprised a TPN-1-49-23 active infrared nightsight on the left and the primary TPD-K1 daysight with integral laser rangefinder immediately in front of him. The TPD-K1 offered 8-power while the nightsight offered 5-power magnification. Turret traverse was controlled using a set of handgrips under the TPD-K1 sight, with manual backup provided in case the electric drive was turned off or disabled. To engage a target, on instruction from the tank commander the gunner would first select the proper ammunition type, which set the autoloader in motion. The gunner would meanwhile aim the main TPD-K1

The best Iraqi 125mm ammunition in 1991 was the 3VBM-7 APFSDS round, which used the BM-15 penetrator, seen here with an encapsulated tungsten-carbide slug. The associated sabot petals can be seen to the left. (Author's collection)

Iraqi 125mm ammunition

A-1-X-1

ЗБК 12M

БM9

БM10
125-ДB1
15 TP Ь/A Х/0
Ч
0-0-0

Н 40
125-ДB1
15 TP Ь/A Х/0
Ч Ь/A Х/0
BTX-20%0
0-0-0
0-0-0

СГ 0-0-0
14 г

The 3VBK-10 125mm HEAT round consisted of a 3BK12M projectile and a consumable propellant case.

The illustration here shows the two-piece ammunition as it would be stowed in the tank. After the 3BK12M projectile was fired, the fins at the rear of the projectile would pop out to help stabilize the round in flight. The long probe at the front of the projectile contains the fuze to detonate the shaped-charge. It is placed as far in front of the explosive as possible to detonate it in time and to establish an optimum stand-off range between the shaped-charge and the target. Shaped-charges are generally more effective when detonated at a distance away from the target since this stand-off distance permits the hypersonic stream created by the shaped-charge to form properly and maximize its penetrating power. The propellant case consisted of a metal stub casing at the bottom of the case plus a synthetic liner to contain the propellant charge; this liner would be consumed when the gun fired, leaning only the stub case.

The 3VBM-3 125mm APFSDS round was the oldest type of 125mm ammunition still in Iraqi service during the 1991 war. It consisted of a BM9 steel penetrator, a BM10 projectile, and a Zh40 consumable propellant case. The use of split, two-piece ammunition in the T-72 limited the potential length of the penetrator dart so it suffered from a shorter length/diameter ratio than the penetrator in US ammunition which degraded its performance. In addition, the penetrator dart was made of steel which had markedly poorer penetration than heavy metals such as tungsten carbide or depleted uranium. The Iraqi T-72 tanks also used the improved 3VBM-7 round which used a BM15 tungsten carbide penetrator. As can be seen in the illustration here, the BM10 projectile contained both the BM9 penetrator and an additional increment of propellant to increase the speed of the projectile.

Artwork by Jim Laurier, © Osprey Publishing

sight at the target and fire the laser rangefinder using a finger control. The range was displayed in the sight, and had to be manually entered into the tank's mechanical ballistic computer. The computer also required manual input of ballistic and meteorological corrections calculated from data available to the gunner before the engagement (degree of barrel wear, charge temperature, barometric pressure and ambient temperature). The only automatic data input was for vehicle movement, and the T-72M1 fire-control system did not incorporate corrections for crosswind data. Although the autoloader theoretically allowed a maximum rate of fire of eight rounds per minute, in practice the rate was likely to be more limited due to the time required to carry out the fire-control sequence. With limited training, Iraqi T-72 crews would often battle-sight the gun to a predetermined range, usually 1,800m, and leave these settings in place. The night-vision system for the gunner was active infrared using the Luna-2AGM turret searchlight and had an effective nighttime range of 800m; the tank commander's TKN-3 daysight/nightsight also had an infrared channel and the commander was provided with a small OU-3GK searchlight for independent illumination which provided coverage to about 400m.

The 125mm gun in the T-72M1 used a 2E28M electro-hydraulic stabilizer. This fire-control system performed similarly to those used in the early-1970s generation of Western tanks, such as the M60A1 RISE, Leopard 1A3, Chieftain Mk 5 or AMX-30. The system was poorly suited to firing on the move due to the complexities of manual data input and the inherent limitations of the gun stabilization system. Firing on the move in the T-72 was only accurate on level ground, at moderate speeds (up to 25km/h or 16mph) and against a target with small lead angles. The gunner's station was not well designed for firing on the move, with little thought given to providing large brow-pads or a chest rest to permit stability during high-mobility action. Because of these limitations and poor crew training, Iraqi T-72 tanks normally fired from a stationary position.

The M1A1

The M1A1 Abrams was armed with the M256 120mm gun, a license-built derivative of the German Rheinmetall gun used in the Leopard 2 tank. By the time of Operation *Desert Storm*, the preferred ammunition for tank fighting was the M829A1 APFSDS round, popularly called the "silver bullet" for its outstanding antiarmor penetration. In contrast to Iraqi tank ammunition, which relied on steel penetrators or steel with a tungsten-carbide insert, the M829A1 used a solid depleted-uranium rod. Depleted uranium (DU) was used in APFSDS penetrators due to its extreme density as well as its unique properties when impacting armor at high velocities. DU has a density of $18.6g/cm^3$ compared to only $7.8g/cm^3$ for steel. Heavy metal penetrators with comparable densities to DU, such as the traditional favorite, tungsten carbide, exhibit less armor penetration than DU due to differences in effect under the extreme pressure of impact. When a tungsten-carbide penetrator tip hits armor plate it deforms into a broad mushroom shape, much like other metals such as lead, making a wider crater and expending a relatively high amount of energy. In contrast, DU penetrators undergo adiabatic shear: during penetration small fragments flake off the tip, leaving a chisel tip which creates a narrow crater,

US 120mm ammunition

The M829A1 120mm APFSDS-T (armor-piercing, fin-stabilized, discarding-sabot, with tracer) was the premier US tank-fighting ammunition of Operation *Desert Storm*, variously nicknamed the "silver bullet" or "supersabot." In tanker's parlance, this type of ammunition is nicknamed "sabot," a contraction for the otherwise excessive full designation of the ammunition. Sabot, from the French word for a wooden shoe, refers to the light metal jacket around the penetrator dart that keeps it in place in the gun tube during the firing process and which peels away after the round leaves the gun tube. The M829A1 used a "long-rod" penetrator with a high length/diameter ratio, meaning that the dart was especially long compared to the diameter of the rod. The penetrator itself was machined out of depleted uranium, which offers both high mass and excellent penetrating qualities.

The M830 120mm HEAT-MP-T (high-explosive antitank multi-purpose with tracer) was the other combat round regularly used by US tanks in Operation *Desert Storm*.

By this time, the APFSDS was the preferred tank fighting round, but it was not ideal for use against light armored vehicles since it was so powerful it tended to pass completely through the enemy vehicle. HEAT ammunition was the preferred type when dealing with light armored vehicles since the shaped-charge, high explosive warhead could easily penetrate any armored vehicle, and the "behind armor" effect of the warhead was very substantial, causing a tremendous amount of internal damage to the enemy vehicle. The HEAT round was considered a "multi-purpose" round in the US Army since at the time, a dedicated high-explosive fragmentation (HE-Frag) round was not on hand for the 120mm gun; the T-72 had both a HEAT and an HE-Frag round. HE-Frag ammunition is traditionally used against "soft," that is non-armored targets such as trucks, emplacements and buildings. Lacking a dedicated HE-Frag round, the HEAT round was used in its place when engaging these targets.

Artwork by Jim Laurier, © Osprey Publishing

making better use of the energy. The second reason for preferring DU over tungsten carbide was its pyrophoric effects: the high-velocity impact of DU against steel creates small incandescent particles, creating a secondary incendiary effect after penetration which increases internal damage to the enemy tank. Although official figures are lacking, published estimates of M829A1 penetration capabilities are 670mm at point-blank range, 620mm at 1,000m, 570mm at 2,000m and 460mm at 4,000m. In other words, the M829A1 round was capable of penetrating the T-72M1 at normal battle ranges from any angle.

The much superior penetration capabilities of the M829A1 compared to Soviet 125mm ammunition were due to a variety of factors. The NATO 120mm gun offered higher chamber pressures than the Soviet 125mm gun: 5,650 bar versus 4,600 bar which provides some indication of the amount of energy exerted on the projectile. The Soviet use of split ammunition also limited the length of the penetrator dart. Although the Soviet 125mm gun had a higher muzzle velocity, the short penetrator length required wider fins that led to a more rapid loss of speed at longer ranges compared to the long-rod penetrator of the US projectile.

The performance of the M829 and M829A1 rounds during Operation *Desert Storm* surprised the Abrams crews. During peacetime firing, such rounds were not used; instead, training rounds with ballistic safety cones fitted to stop the rounds going too far were used; this in turn degraded the training rounds' ballistic performance and required a different ballistic solution in the tank's fire-control due to the high arch of their trajectory. Capt Mark Gerges commented about experience with combat loads during the fighting:

> At ranges out to 3,600, or even 4,000, there was no observable ballistic solution to the round – it was flat. The kick from the service ammo was also a surprise, and more violent than the not-so-gentle rock we were used to with training ammo. The tanks carried two types of sabot, a load of M829 and seven rounds of M829A1, which we called "supersabot." The plan was to use up the M829 on targets getting to the decisive showdown with the Republican Guards, and then shift to the supersabot because we thought the greater armor on the T-72M1s would need the better round to penetrate. Not quite. We fired only one or two supersabots in my entire company during the fighting.

The M1A1 used an integrated gun/turret stabilization system with line-of-sight stabilization in elevation and gun/turret stabilization in azimuth with hydraulic power for the gun and the turret. The gunner's station was designed from the outset to permit fire-on-the-move operations. For example, the gunner was provided with a large brow-pad to keep his face comfortably away from the sight aperture and other obstacles. The gunner was also provided with a chest rest so that during jarring tank motion he could wedge himself into a firm operating position between the seat-back and fire controls. The fire-control system was designed to minimize the need for numerous data inputs, which instead were handled automatically; the laser rangefinder was integrated into the gunner's primary sight. The fire-control system utilized a digital ballistic computer designed to be operated with minimal training, using automatic data inputs to improve overall gun accuracy with

A remarkable photograph of an APFSDS projectile in flight, with the aluminum sabot petals peeling away from the long-rod penetrator. The sabot holds the small-diameter penetrator centered in the gun tube during firing, and is the source of the US Army's nickname for this type of ammunition – "supersabot." (Alliant TechSystems)

minimum attention from the gunner. It would automatically input data from wind and cant sensors, as well as data on tracking rates for lead corrections based on the turret traverse. The gunner would manually enter other data, such as air temperature, ammunition temperature, barometric pressure and tube wear, but this could be done prior to the engagement to minimize the need for attention during combat. The gunner's primary sight was configured for both a 3-power wide field of view for surveillance and target acquisition, and a 10-power narrow field of view for aiming.

The most substantial difference between the fire-control systems for the M1A1 Abrams and the T-72M1 was the provision in the M1A1 of an integrated thermal imaging subsystem (TIS) two generations more advanced than the T-72M1's active infrared system. Active infrared systems required infrared searchlights for nighttime illumination, which made any tank using such a system glaringly evident to enemy tanks. Most major NATO armies shifted from active infrared to image-intensification night-vision systems in the late 1970s. Image-intensification sights were passive, without the need for dangerous searchlights; they relied on ambient moonlight or

other sources for illumination. These electro-optical sights collected the small amounts of light available even with partial moonlight, and amplified them sufficiently for the gunner to be able to acquire and engage targets. Their main disadvantage was that they needed some form of natural illumination, at least one-quarter moonlight, and this might not be available on totally moonless or cloudy nights. The next generation of sights, thermal imaging or FLIR (forward-looking infrared) sights, got around the limitations of the image-intensification sights by sensing minute differences in reflected or ambient infrared energy. Tanks moving at night have a very distinctive infrared signature since their engines give off thermal energy, as do their wheels and tracks. Even stationary tanks have a distinct signature since they collect solar heat during the day, which disperses at night. The thermal sights have a secondary function in daytime, since they have some capability to peer through atmospheric phenomena such as smoke, mist, and fog that would be opaque to normal human vision. Thermal sights were first used on the US Army's M60A3 (TTS) tanks. The TIS on the M1A1 was better integrated than the T-72M1 gunner's nightsight, which used a reticle separate from the gunner's normal fire controls.

The M1A1 had an auxiliary sight – a conventional telescopic sight – for use in the event of failure of the primary equipment; the T-72M1 lacked a spare sight.

In terms of firepower, the M1A1 outclassed the T-72M1 in all respects: it had better ammunition, better penetration, better performance at longer ranges, more sophisticated fire-control, better fire-on-the-move capability, and better crew ergonomics. But regardless of the technical details, the bottom line was that the 125mm gun and the ammunition available to the Iraqis could not frontally penetrate the M1A1 tank, while the M1A1's 120mm gun could penetrate the frontal armor of the T-72M1 at typical combat ranges.

Mobility

The M1A1 Abrams was powered by an AVCO-Lycoming AGT-1500 gas-turbine engine. This offered 1,500hp or about 23hp per ton. Turbines provide more power for a lighter weight than did comparable diesels of the time, and offered superior sustained high-speed travel; their main drawback was higher fuel consumption. During typical peacetime training exercises, US tankers found that the M1A1 Abrams could operate for about a day on a single load of fuel compared to about three days for the earlier M60A3 tank. The M1A1 had a notional road range of about 290 miles; ideal fuel consumption was 1.8 gallons per mile. The Abrams' actual range was quite variable, and usually lower, because turbine engines consume more fuel at idle than comparable diesel tank engines. Modern tanks do not shut off their engines when static since it is necessary to keep the batteries charged to operate various electrical systems, including the radio and fire-control system. The M1A1 had an hourly fuel consumption of 10.8 gallons at idle, 44.6 gallons on the road and 56.6 gallons cross-country. The main solution to the Abrams' fuel consumption problem was to provide adequate logistical support – an Abrams tank battalion had 16 HEMTT tanker trucks each carrying 2,500 gallons of fuel.

The T-72M1 was powered by a V-46-6 diesel engine producing 780hp. This gave the T-72M1 a power-to-weight ratio of about 19.8hp per ton and a maximum road speed of about 37mph – somewhat less than the M1A1. Internal fuel capacity was 1,000 liters (264gal) and a further 400 liters were typically carried in two external drums. The T-72 had an optimal fuel consumption of one gallon per mile, so even though it only carried about half the internal fuel of the M1A1, its average road range was about the same.

The M1A1 had better mobility than the T-72M1 in terms of actual power per ton as well as better ergonomic design of the crew stations; however, the T-72M1 offered better fuel economy.

THE MEN

The most significant difference between the crews of the M1A1 Abrams and the T-72M1 Ural was the lack of a loader in the T-72M1, leaving it with a crew of three versus four in the Abrams. Otherwise, crew functions were very similar. There has been long-standing controversy over the desirability of autoloaders versus human loaders. The US Army has generally favored human loaders for two reasons. Firstly, there is some advantage of a human loader over an autoloader in the first critical moments of a tank battle, since a well-trained crew can get off the first three rounds in around 15 seconds compared to two rounds or fewer from the T-72 autoloader. Secondly, US tankers feel that additional crewmen are vital in day-to-day combat conditions due to the enormous amount of work required for maintaining and resupplying the tank, as well as providing security when at rest. In the Soviet view, using an autoloader saved a considerable amount of internal volume in the design, permitting a smaller turret and a smaller, lighter tank. Also, an autoloader permits a faster sustained rate of fire – about eight rounds per minute in the T-72M1 compared to about four rounds per minute for the M1A1 Abrams.

M1A1 tank crew

The M1A1 had a crew of four: tank commander (TC), gunner, loader, and driver. All were stationed in the turret except for the driver, who was positioned in the center of the front hull. In the turret the loader was on the left and the gunner and TC were on the right.

The tank commander was positioned behind the gunner and was responsible for leading the tank in combat. In a four-tank platoon, the leader was a second lieutenant (O-1); the platoon sergeant was usually a sergeant first class (E-7) or staff sergeant (E-6); the two "wingman" tanks would also be commanded by sergeants. The TC was stationed below a rotating cupola and hatch that provided all-round direct vision, when "buttoned up," by means of periscopes. The TC was also provided with an optical adjunct from the gunner's primary sight and the commander could aim the

Inside the M1A1 Abrams

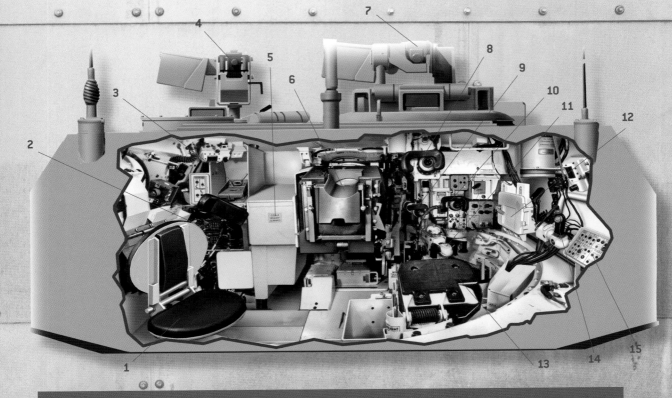

1. Loader's seat
2. Tank radio
3. Machine gun ammunition compartment
4. Loader's M240 machine gun
5. Coaxial machine gun ammunition stowage
6. M256 120mm gun breech
7. Commander's M2 heavy machine gun
8. Commander's sight
9. Gunner's auxiliary (telescopic) sight
10. Gunner's primary sight
11. Gunner's controls
12. Fire control computer panel
13. Gunner's seat (back rest folded down)
14. Commander's handles
15. Commander's control panel

Artwork by Jim Laurier, ©
Osprey Publishing

tank's weapon and fire it if necessary using these override controls. The TC's hatch had three positions: fully open, fully closed, and intermediate, in which the overhead hatch could be locked partially open to allow the TC to hear and see all around while offering some overhead cover. US Army training encouraged TCs to ride with their heads outside the tank, since this provided better situational awareness. The commander's station included a .50cal heavy machine gun on a remote-control mount; this could be operated from inside the tank when fully buttoned-up, and a periscopic sight was provided for this function. The commander also had controls for activating the smoke-grenade launchers on the front sides of the turret, which were used for defense.

Second in seniority in the tank crew was the gunner, a sergeant. The gunner's primary sight (GPS), located immediately in front of him, comprised an integrated day/night sighting system with laser rangefinder and a digital ballistic computer. The M1A1 fire controls were designed to be as automated as possible to permit the gunner to concentrate on his main task of acquiring the target identified by the commander, and accurately aiming the tank's weapons. The gunner's inputs included selecting whether to engage the target with the main gun or the coaxial machine gun and identifying the main gun ammunition type to ensure the ballistic computer set the proper offsets. The gunner's controls were operated using palm switches on the "Cadillac" grips which allowed him to turn the turret right or left, elevate or depress the main gun, and trigger the main gun or coaxial machine gun.

The loader was usually lowest in seniority. He armed the main gun on the instructions of the TC and had to be quite strong and agile as the rounds weighed more than 65lb each. The main ammunition stowage was in the turret bustle behind blast doors, with two 16-round racks on either side and one or two two-round ready racks at the extremities. There was an additional three-round ready rack in front of the loader in the left hull. Access to the main ammunition reserve in the left rear bustle was by means of a blast door actuated by the gunner using a knee switch which let him keep his hands free during the loading process. The loader's hatch was fitted with an M240 7.62mm machine gun for close-in defense of the tank. The tank radio was located in front of the loader's station.

The driver was isolated from the rest of the crew in the forward hull. The M1A1 driver's station represented a considerable departure from earlier US tank designs. Instead of sitting in a conventional seat, the driver lay on his back in a semi-prone position. However, the seat could be raised to let the driver sit up when operating with his head outside the hatch, or lowered to a more prone position when driving buttoned-up. The driver's main controls took the form of a steering yoke which operated much like motorcycle handlebars.

T-72M1 crew

The T-72M1 was conventionally laid out, with the driver located centrally in the hull and the commander and gunner on the right and left sides of the turret respectively. Due to the small turret volume and the enormous size of the gun breech the turret was extremely cramped, more reminiscent of World War II tanks than modern main battle tanks.

Inside the T-72

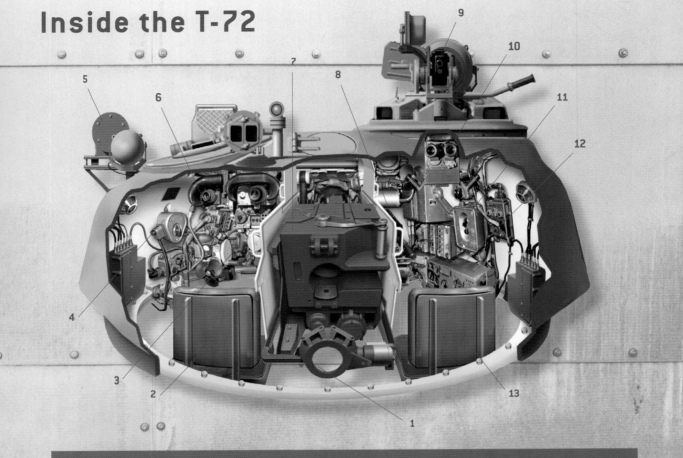

1. Autoloader rammer
2. Gunner's seat
3. Gunner's controls
4. Gunner's intercom switch
5. Electro-optical missile jammer
6. Gunner's TPN-1-49-23 infrared sight
7. D-81T 125mm gun breech

8. Coaxial machine gun
9. Commander's 12.7mm machine gun
10. Commander's cupola sight
11. Commander's intercom/radio switch
12. Tank radio
13. Commander's seat

The tank commander's main sight was the binocular TKN-3 sight, mounted in a fully traversable cupola; unlike the Abrams, the commander did not share the optical imagery with the gunner. The tank commander could override the gunner's controls to traverse the turret, and he could bring the turret to his line of sight with the control handle on the TKN-3. The commander also had several small optical periscopes; however, the view they provided was much more interrupted than that with the M1A1 Abrams. The commander's station included an R-173 tank radio, and the commander's cupola was fitted with an NSVT 12.7mm *Utes* ("Rock") heavy machine gun; however, this was aimed rearward when the commander's main sight was pointed forward and the cupola had to be rotated for the weapon to be used. This gun was designed to be manually operated by the commander from outside the vehicle, not by remote control from inside. One of the peculiarities of Soviet tank design was that the commander's hatch opened forward, blocking the commander's view and discouraging him from riding with his head outside the tank during combat. This represented a fundamentally different design philosophy to the US approach and offered further evidence of the relatively low priority afforded to ergonomics in Soviet tank design.

The gunner's station was even more cramped than the commander's, due to the bulky sighting system immediately in front of the gunner. The gunner's sights comprised a TPN-1-49-23 active infrared nightsight on the left and the primary TPD-K1 daysight with integral laser rangefinder immediately in front of him. Turret traverse was accomplished using a set of handgrips located under the TPD-K1 sight.

The driver sat centrally in the hull front, with a single large periscope mounted in the glacis plate, and two smaller periscopes mounted in the hatch over his head. The driver's controls were traditional braking levers rather than the steering yokes found in most contemporary Western tanks. These required more skill and strength to operate than the controls in the M1A1. This station was extremely cramped and the driver's controls were not well situated, being located to the side where they were harder to see during operations.

Crew training

Iraqi tank crew training

There is very little detailed information available about Iraqi tank crew training prior to Operation *Desert Storm*, although a certain amount can be inferred from the combat performance of Iraqi tank units. By the time of the invasion of Kuwait in 1990, the Iraqi army had grown from about six to about 60 divisions and was at the time the fourth largest army in the world. This massive expansion had come at a price, however, and the Iraqi army suffered from problems typical of developing countries – its troops were drawn from diverse cultural backgrounds, and often had poor education and limited technical training.

The army's tactical leadership was crippled by the paranoia of Saddam Hussein's Ba'athist regime. Loyalty was brutally enforced by secret police and by periodic officer purges; minor failures or missteps could prove fatal. Army control was heavily centralized and the pervasive fear instilled by the regime encouraged tactical commanders to follow orders strictly and discouraged personal initiative or flexibility. The Iraqi army, as in most developing nations, lacked an experienced and trusted cadre of NCOs, which has always formed the backbone of any technical combat arm such as tank forces. The authoritarian command-and-control tradition proved adequate against the slow-moving and equally inept Iranian army, but such rigidity was poorly suited to a fast-moving war of maneuver of the kind the Iraqi army would have to fight in 1991.

By the end of the war with Iran, the Iraqi army had a significant body of combat-experienced senior commanders, but further down the tactical ladder the quality of combat leadership tended to weaken. To compensate for the poor quality of most of the army's units, during the 1980s Iraqi commanders had learned to rely on carefully scripted combat operations, with units assigned a series of relatively simple and rehearsed tasks that did not depend on high levels of initiative or skill on the part of the lower tactical formations. Furthermore, the massive expansion of the army between 1980 and 1988 led to further dilution in quality of units, forcing the Iraqi army to rely more and more on a core of elite formations to carry out the most critical and demanding missions. Such units were primarily those of the Republican Guards Forces Command (RGFC) and the better regular army armored divisions.

The Republican Guards (Al-Haras al-Jamhaori) had originated as a praetorian guard to defend Saddam Hussein and his Ba'ath party leadership. Hussein favored fellow Sunnis – members of the same sect of Islam – for sensitive security posts, and especially those from his hometown of Tikrit. Loyalty to Saddam and the Ba'ath

Iraqi tactical doctrine favored entrenched emplacement of tanks during defensive operations. Lacking the time to prepare deep entrenchments, many Iraqi T-72M tank crews constructed small berms around their positions using the bow-mounted scraper, but this provided no protection against APFSDS rounds. (US DoD)

T-72M1: through the gunsights

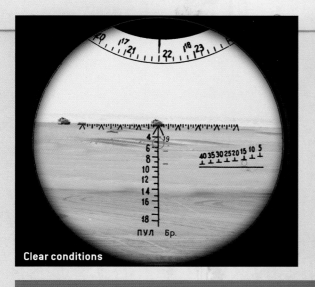

Clear conditions

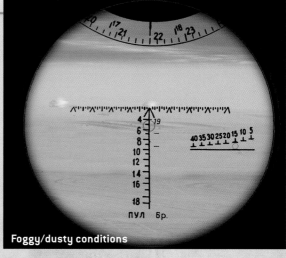

Foggy/dusty conditions

The T-72M1 gunner's reticle was considerably more cluttered than the comparable M1A1 gunner's sight, since it was a generation older in configuration and relied on more extensive manual inputs from the gunner. The T-72M1 had two reticles – the primary sight for the TPD-K1 daysight and laser-rangefinder as seen, and the TPN-1-49-23 active infrared nightsight. The gunner began by inputting the ammunition type which switched the sight reticle to the proper type – in this case, APFSDS (indicated by Cyrillic letters that transliterate as "Br" on the lower right sight of the vertical gradation; the Cyrillic letters that transliterate as "PUL" indicate "machine gun"). With this data incorporated, the gunner then placed the red laser aiming circle over the target, using the center one for the main gun or the one on the right of the range scale for the coaxial machine gun. After firing the laser rangefinder at the target, the gunner read the digital result off the reticle and entered it into the system; the reading appeared on the semicircular dial at the top of the reticle, with the top gradations for the coaxial machine gun and the primary gradations at the bottom of the circle for the main gun; "22" indicates a range to target of 2,200m. If firing on a moving target, the gunner had to place the red laser circle over the target for a few seconds while tracking the target, which entered data about the amount of lead required. Once the range was entered, the gunner then had to place the target above the main aiming mark, the inverted "V" at the center of the main set of gradations, as shown here.

This process was so complex, especially under the stress of combat, that Iraqi tankers were often instructed to "battle-sight" their guns, which meant entering a default set of range and ammunition data so that the gunner had only to place the aiming mark on target and fire. The default solution was usually APFSDS ammunition at a range of 1,800m. This may have been a major reason for the poor Iraqi shooting during Operation *Desert Storm*, since US tanks typically began engaging from ranges beyond 1,800m, and Soviet-made APFSDS ammunition was much more prone to dropping at extended ranges than American APFSDS due to the larger fins.

The main reason for the poor Iraqi gunnery during Operation *Desert Storm* is better illustrated by the second sight image, which depicts an engagement such as that at Medina Ridge. The overcast weather, rain, dust clouds and other conditions essentially made the US Army M1A1 tanks invisible to the Iraqi gunners through their sights. The only aiming points were occasional flashes from the Abrams' 120mm main guns. Even if the Iraqi gunner was well trained and attempted to use the laser rangefinder in the prescribed manner, the rangefinder was apt to provide false returns due to the rain and fog. This left the Iraqi gunners to try to aim at the flashes without proper range data, and if their guns were battle-sighted at the usual 1,800m the APFSDS round would fall considerably short.

Party were the primary criteria for serving in the Republican Guards. The poor performance of the Iraqi army in the first years of the Iran–Iraq War led to fundamental changes within the Republican Guards during 1986 – it expanded from the Ba'ath Party's elite guard force into a much larger formation of elite combat brigades and divisions. The RGFC armored units were given priority for the latest equipment, so the new T-72 tanks were found primarily in RGFC units. The enlisted men were mainly from the Sunni minority, and had better pay, uniforms and equipment. It is unclear whether training was markedly better than in the rest of the army, but the RGFC troops were certainly far better motivated than the rest of the army, as would become very evident in the 1991 Gulf War.

Although tanks were widely used by both the Iranian and Iraqi armies in the 1980–88 war, in the later years of the conflict tank-versus-tank fighting was very limited due to the small numbers of functional Iranian armor. Iraqi tank units were used primarily to provide fire support for the infantry, and this led to less emphasis on tank fighting skills. The Iraqi army fought a largely defensive war in the late 1980s, with tanks regularly fighting from fixed positions. This did not encourage the development of the kind of tactical skills associated with NATO or Warsaw Pact armies, which assumed that tanks would be used primarily in a mobile role. The widespread Iraqi use of tanks in an infantry support role also led to relatively high usage rates for the main guns. The lack of durability of Soviet gun tubes and the Iraqi propensity to cut corners in maintenance meant that by 1990 a significant proportion of tanks had worn-out gun tubes – limiting their accuracy, particularly if tank gunners were not trained to properly input barrel-wear data into the tank's ballistic computer.

These factors may partly account for the abysmal gunnery of Iraqi tanks in the 1991 war. Although US tankers repeatedly saw evidence of Iraqi tanks firing at them, reports of actual hits on US tanks were extremely few. Iraqi tankers were not as well trained in maintenance as US tankers, and repairs that in the US Army would routinely be undertaken within the company or battalion were delegated to specialized maintenance units or even to rear-area repair facilities. The level of training of Iraqi tankers was extremely poor by NATO standards; nevertheless, the Iraqi army was widely regarded as one of the more battle-hardened and combat-capable Arab armies of the time.

US tank crew training

The US Army had undergone a renaissance in the 1980s after the hollow years of the 1970s. During the Reagan period the Army had finally shaken off the legacy of the Vietnam War, and many young officers who had been platoon, company or battalion commanders in Vietnam had become senior leaders by the 1980s and were ardently intent on reform. The intellectual ferment within the officer corps culminated in the "Air-Land Battle" doctrine and greater emphasis on "train as you fight." At the same time, increased defense funding in the 1980s permitted both a rejuvenation of equipment such as the adoption of the M1 Abrams tank and M2 Bradley infantry fighting vehicle – as well as a substantial increase in operations and maintenance funding which permitted more and better-quality training. The shift from the Vietnam War's conscript army to a professional army was an important element in boosting the motivation and skills of the soldiers.

US tanker training has traditionally centered around Fort Knox, Kentucky, home of the Armor School since World War II. After basic training, US army tankers were sent to Fort Knox for specialist training. Young second lieutenants were sent to the Armor Officer Advance Course. The 1980s saw the beginning of a technical revolution in training. In the past, training on maintenance-intensive weapons such as tanks was invariably limited by budget, since training leads to considerable wear and tear on the equipment and the expenditure of costly training ammunition. The advent of the M1 Abrams was accompanied by the advent of computer-based training simulators. These could not substitute for hands-on training with real equipment, but acted as an invaluable supplement to traditional technical-skills training since they allowed new tankers to repeatedly rehearse basic combat skills more often and at a far more modest cost. The computer-based tank simulators at Fort Knox also allowed elementary small-unit training, since the individual "tanks" could be netted together by computer to conduct missions.

Once through their specialist training, tankers were dispatched to their units where training continued, as the US Army fostered a system of ongoing training within the unit. Fort Knox also served as the venue for continued career training, with the Advanced NCO Course and Armor Officer Advanced Course. The growing technical proficiency of US tankers became evident in tangible ways. The NATO armies in Europe had traditionally held a Canadian Army Trophy gunnery contest, and US Army teams had not won the event for nearly two decades until an M1 Abrams team won in 1986. Once crews were assigned to forward-deployed units in Germany, technical skills continued to be honed through training – for example, gunnery skills at the ranges at Grafenwohr and small-unit skills at the Combat Maneuver Training Center at Hohenfels.

Technological innovations helped add to the frequency and realism of small-unit tactical training – as with the introduction of laser simulation devices which made it possible to conduct more realistic tank-on-tank engagements during exercises. The culmination of this revolution in training was the refurbishment of the Army's Mojave Desert training center as the National Training Center (NTC). The NTC was computerized and fully instrumented to allow the recording of simulated battles, so post-mortems could be conducted and lessons learned. The NTC had its own highly trained "opposing force" (OPFOR) to ensure a constant and demanding test experience for visiting units. Rotation through the NTC encouraged units to practice and prepare in advance of their arrival on the desert battleground, which further polished small-unit tactical skills. Increased funding in the 1980s was instrumental in this process, since rotating a brigade through the NTC cost in the order of $10 million. By 1990 the US Army was arguably the best-trained military in the world.

The tank crew of Capt Mark Gerges, featured in the duel described later, provides a good example of the training of US Army tank crews. Capt Gerges's crew had been together for ten months as part of the 1st Armored Division in Germany. The company had been through a Hohenfels rotation in March–April 1990 and then undergone further tank gunnery training during the summer prior to being alerted for deployment. The crews had performed well at gunnery; Bravo Company was a high-scoring company in 2–70 Armor, gaining 842 out of a possible 1,000 points. The effect was increased confidence in the M1A1's fire-control system.

Capt Gerges was a distinguished military graduate of Norwich University (1984), and after being commissioned in armor he graduated from the Armor Officer Basic Course and the Nuclear, Biological and Chemical Officers' Defense Course. He had served in armor units in Germany and Texas prior to returning to Germany in the winter of 1989, then served on the staff of 2nd Brigade, 1st Armored Division for

M1A1: through the gunsights

Daylight channel

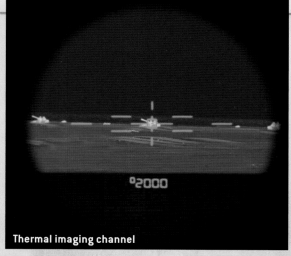

Thermal imaging channel

Artwork by Jim Laurier, © Osprey Publishing

The M1A1 gunner's primary sight (GPS) had both an optical daylight channel and a thermal-imaging channel which could be used day and night. Like the T-72M1 gunner, the Abrams gunner began the process by manually entering the ammunition type. The reticle in the center of the sight consisted of an aiming box one milliradian (mil) in size, equivalent to a target one yard wide at 1,000yd; the aiming mark totals 20mil across. The gunner squeezed the laser trigger, which provided a range in the green digital display below – in this case, 2,000m. Unlike the T-72M1, this data was automatically entered into the ballistic computer and the system made the appropriate gun elevation corrections. The small rectangle to the upper left of the laser range read-out is a "ready-to-fire" symbol. An "F" symbol appeared on the opposite side in the event of a system malfunction. The line above the laser readout indicated multiple laser returns,

which would be unlikely in this case and more commonly arose when attempting to determine range through trees or other obstructions.

One of the Abrams' main advantages during much of the *Desert Storm* fighting was the thermal imaging channel in the GPS, which sensed temperature differences between the objects being viewed. In this case the system is set at "white-hit," meaning that warmer objects appear as bright spots and cooler objects appear darker. Even in cases where light fog or rain might obscure the targets – as occurred at Medina Ridge – the thermal sight permitted the gunner to locate targets.

The system did have its limitations, particularly at ranges much beyond 2,000m, as the targets then appeared as little more than glowing blobs, making it very difficult for the gunner to differentiate between friend and foe, or between tanks and BMPs.

a year before taking command of Bravo Company, 2–70 Armor, in February 1990, a year before the Battle of Medina Ridge. He was 29 years old at the time of the fighting and was awarded the Bronze Star and Bronze Star with Valor device for his actions in Operation *Desert Storm*.

BATTLEGROUND: IRAQ 1991

On August 2, 1990, the Iraqi army overran Kuwait, spearheaded by T-72 tanks of the Republican Guards. President George H. Bush proclaimed: "This shall not stand," and the United States began mobilizing a coalition to liberate Kuwait. President Saddam Hussein had picked a particularly bad time to provoke the US and its allies as the climax of the Cold War had meant there was a substantial reserve of heavy combat forces in Germany that could quickly be deployed to the Arabian Gulf. The American strategic concern was not simply Kuwait; it was feared that Iraq would use Kuwait as a springboard for launching further troubling attacks in the region, potentially involving seizure of the nearby Saudi oilfields. Saudi Arabia perceived this threat as so serious that it quickly joined the anti-Iraq coalition and pressured other Arab states to do so as well, including Egypt and Syria.

Iraqi strategic plans

Hussein also seriously underestimated US resolve and so was obliged to reinforce his occupation of Kuwait, awaiting "the mother of all battles." This lull provided the US Army and Marine Corps with nearly six months to build up forces in Saudi Arabia. The two most obvious coalition options for liberating Kuwait were a thrust directly into the territory, or an envelopment of it through the trackless western Iraqi desert. Hussein and many Iraqi generals did not believe the coalition forces could conduct complex mechanized operations in the deep desert, so the focus of the Iraqi deployment was defense-in-depth of the Kuwaiti frontier. The Iraqi army's operational plans reflected the lessons of the Iran–Iraq War, and began with an initial line of resistance formed of second-rate regular army divisions and melodramatically dubbed "the Line of Death." A second line comprising the better regular armored divisions provided a tactical counterattack force, and a third line of RGFC divisions provided a reserve for reinforcement and counterattack.

Due to the limited capabilities of the regular Iraqi divisions, the Iraqi plan depended on static defense with an emphasis on the use of dug-in tanks and extensive obstacle barriers. This tactical pattern was simple enough for poorly trained troops to carry out, and it had proved very successful against Iranian infantry formations. Tanks were dug in to a hull-down position with only their turrets exposed, or were parked behind sand berms. Minefields, antitank ditches, and other obstructions were created along the initial line of resistance on the Kuwait frontier, and this sector was surveyed for preplanned artillery strikes.

A fatal flaw in the eventual RGFC deployment was that it stacked up three of the best heavy divisions in depth behind the Rumalyah oilfields – starting with the Tawakalna, then the Medina, and finally the Hammurabi. As a result, the US VII Corps was able to use overwhelming force to destroy the divisions piecemeal rather than confronting them simultaneously.

Although the Iraqi armed forces did anticipate a coalition air attack as part of the campaign, they had never experienced a major air assault during the Iran–Iraq War, and underestimated coalition airpower. While there were few expectations that the air defense network would shield the Iraqi army totally, Iraqi leaders did expect that it could inflict significant aircraft losses and that the Iraqi ground units could endure what survived.

The coalition plan

The coalition plan assumed that action would be taken against the Iraqi army along the Kuwaiti frontier, but that the primary thrust would be conducted into the western Iraqi desert to outflank, envelop and destroy the Iraqi army in Kuwait. The plan also included a significant deception effort aimed at convincing Hussein that the main thrust would be directed into Kuwait.

The right wing of the coalition assault into Kuwait consisted of two US Marine divisions with two Arab Joint Forces Commands (JFCs) providing formations on either side. The US Third Army controlled two corps on the left flank facing directly into the western Iraqi desert. The VII Corps was the primary heavy-maneuver force and included two US and one British armored divisions, two mechanized divisions, and an armored cavalry regiment. On the far left flank was the light-maneuver force, XVIII Airborne Corps, which included two US airborne/airmobile divisions, a mechanized division, an armored cavalry regiment, and a French mechanized division. The Third Army's two corps were deployed deep in Saudi Arabia through January 1991 and only began moving into strike position in the weeks prior to Operation *Desert Storm* in the hope of maintaining the ruse.

> **"** After 38 days of the air battle, I had 32 tanks. After 20 minutes against them [the 2nd Armored Cavalry Regiment], I had zero tanks. **"**
>
> A commander of the RGFC Tawakalna Division, on the effect of coalition aircraft and armor

A key element in the coalition plan was the incorporation of a significant pre-ground-attack air campaign to wear down the Iraq forces. This was conducted by coalition aircraft based in Saudi Arabia, from aircraft carriers in the Arabian Gulf, and from more distant bases such as the Indian Ocean island of Diego Garcia. Analysts at the time felt that a force ratio of three to one in favor of the attacker was needed to overcome a determined defense. In January 1991, Iraqi forces in the Kuwait theater enjoyed a marginal superiority in personnel, tanks, and artillery over coalition forces; the air attacks were intended to shift the balance in favor of the coalition.

T-72 tactical organization

The Iraqi army relied on British organizational practices, with tactical doctrine also influenced by later Soviet, Jordanian, and Indian advisers, and by the experiences of the war with Iran. The basic tactical formation was the brigade (*lawae*); brigades were generally formed into divisions with three brigades per division. The brigades in turn consisted of a number of *katiba*, which is often translated as "regiment" but which in the case of armor were closer in strength to a US battalion, nominally

The T-72 became the standard license-produced Soviet tank in the 1980s in Poland, Czechoslovakia, India, and Yugoslavia. Iraq was not the only army to use the T-72 in the 1991 war. The Kuwaiti 35th Fatah Brigade operated the Yugoslav-built M-84A version as part of the Joint Coalition Force Group. (US DoD)

Iraqi T-72 units in Kuwait Theater, 1991		
Brigade	**Division**	**Number of tank battalions**
12th Armored Brigade	3rd Saladin Armored Division	3
8th Mechanized Brigade	3rd Saladin Armored Division	1
8th RGFC Armored Brigade	RGFC Hammurabi Armored Division	3
17th RGFC Armored Brigade	RGFC Hammurabi Armored Division	3
15th RGFC Mechanized Brigade	RGFC Hammurabi Armored Division	1
2nd RGFC Armored Brigade	RGFC Medina Armored Division	3
10th RGFC Armored Brigade	RGFC Medina Armored Division	3
14th RGFC Mechanized Brigade	RGFC Medina Armored Division	1
9th RGFC Armored Brigade	RGFC Tawakalna Mechanized Division	3
18th RGFC Mechanized Brigade	RGFC Tawakalna Mechanized Division	1
29th RGFC Mechanized Brigade	RGFC Tawakalna Mechanized Division	1

having 55–60 tanks in three companies. The actual strength of Iraqi tank battalions is not known in detail. One battalion of the Tawakalna division had only about 40 tanks, according to its commander, and some regular army battalions only had around 35. In general, the RGFC divisions had the better equipment – usually T-72 tanks and BMP-1 infantry fighting vehicles – while the regular army divisions would have T-55, T-62 or Chinese Type 69 tanks along with Chinese armored personnel carriers or cheap Soviet MT-LB transporters. A few of the better regular army formations, such as the 3rd Saladin Armored Division, had at least one battalion of T-72 tanks, and conversely some RGFC brigades had T-62 tanks. A typical armor brigade would include two or three tank battalions and a mechanized infantry battalion; a mechanized brigade would reverse the balance of tank and mechanized infantry battalions. A fully equipped RGFC armored division might have about 220 T-72 tanks. Three of these RGFC heavy divisions saw combat in 1991; they were the Hammurabi RGFC and Medina–Manarawah armored divisions and the Tawakalna-al-Allah mechanized division. About 21 T-72 tank regiments saw service in the 1991 war, totaling close to a thousand T-72 tanks.

In a defensive engagement Iraqi tank regiments preferred to fight enemy tank units from static positions, due to the limitations of their small-unit training. Iraqi doctrine favored reverse-slope defense with the unit positioned down the opposite side of a hill or ridge. The aim of this tactic was to ambush an enemy tank formation as it crested the rise – the enemy's lead tanks could be picked off by the stationary tanks positioned below. At the same time, following waves of enemy tanks would be unable to locate and identify the Iraqi tanks until after they too had crested the rise, at which point they would still be vulnerable to Iraqi fire. This tactic minimized the tactical shortcomings of the Iraqi tankers, such as poor gunnery training, and placed minimal demands on the crew. The gunners of each Iraqi tank would be instructed in advance of the range to target, so the gun could be battle-sighted to engage at a predetermined range without the need for range input data, which would slow a poorly trained crew. To improve their survivability, Iraqi tanks were often dug in in advance by combat engineer units, which reduced the vulnerability of the hull to enemy fire and minimized the target presented to enemy gunners. The use of prepared defensive positions was especially common among the regular army armored divisions along the Kuwaiti border. As will be related below, the RGFC divisions in the Iraqi desert moved forward from prepared positions, but even in these circumstances the tank regiments attempted to create fixed defensive positions using available engineering assets as well as the scraper blade fitted to the front hull of the T-72.

Iraqi doctrine included a traditional combined-arms component with tank units often supported by intermixed infantry. This included dismounted infantry with large numbers of RPG-7 antitank rockets as well as their supporting BMP-1 infantry fighting vehicles. Likewise, Iraqi doctrine placed great faith in artillery support for forward tank positions. Despite substantial reserves of good-quality pieces, Iraqi artillery support was severely compromised by the poor quality of training and overreliance on tactics perfected in fighting Iran. The Iranian army was primarily an infantry force, so Iraqi artillery doctrine favored the use of preregistered kill-zones that could be prepared in advance of the enemy attack and which placed very limited demands on the Iraqi fire-direction network. However, such tactics were very poorly suited to engaging a fast-moving mechanized force, as would become blatantly apparent in 1991. Iraqi doctrine did not place significant emphasis on close air support as Iraq's air force had seldom shown the capability to use such tactics. While some Mil Mi-24 attack helicopters were available in the combat theater in 1991, they played little or no role in the ground campaign, and neither did fixed-wing strike aircraft.

M1A1 tactical organization

The first M1 Abrams units to arrive in Saudi Arabia were the battalions of the US 24th Infantry Division (Mechanized) which still had older M1 and IPM1 tanks. By November 1990 there were 580 M1/IPM1 tanks in Saudi Arabia, but only

The weather during the fighting in late February was mostly overcast, with frequent rain and sandstorms. This is a column of M1A1 tanks of VII Corps moving forward. (US DoD)

123 new M1A1 tanks. As the likelihood of a ground war increased the army reequipped as many units as possible with the M1A1, preferably the latest M1A1HA version. However, since there were not enough M1A1HAs available, a retrofit program was begun to upgrade M1A1 tanks with the Heavy Armor package. A total of 835 such upgrades were completed, also including fire-control upgrades, installation of an NBC-system heat exchanger, repainting with the CARC tan desert camouflage paint, and other improvements. This version had no specific designation but is sometimes referred to as M1A1 (mod) or M1A1HA; the table below lists them as M1A1 (mod) to identify the units that used them but elsewhere in this book they are simply called M1A1HA, since they were virtually identical in performance and features. At the start of the ground campaign only two battalions still had the M1 tank. By February 1991 the US Army had deployed 1,956 M1A1 tanks to Saudi Arabia (733 M1A1, 1,233 M1A1HA), plus 528 other tanks in war reserve stock not attached to combat units. Other upgrades were applied to the M1A1 fleet in the months prior to the fighting; this included the dispatch of the improved T-158 track.

US Army armored divisions were organized into six armor and four mechanized infantry battalions, while mechanized infantry divisions had the reverse mix of six mechanized infantry and four armor battalions. It should be noted that US heavy battalions relied on regimental lineage, so for example "2–67 Armor" refers to 2nd Battalion, 67th Armored Regiment. The armor battalions had a headquarters company with two M1A1 tanks, and four tank companies each with 14 M1A1 tanks, for a total of 55 tanks. The armored divisions were in turn each organized into three combined-arms brigades (comparable to the World War II combat command) typically consisting of two armor battalions, a mechanized infantry battalion, a self-propelled 155mm artillery battalion, and an air-defense battery along with supporting elements.

The 2nd Iron Brigade of the 1st Armored Division, featured later, provides a good example. It had three tank battalions (2–70 Armor; 4–70 Armor; 1–35 Armor) and one mechanized battalion (6–6 Infantry), supported by the 47 Support Battalion and 2–1 Field Artillery. The battalions in turn were mission-organized into combined-arms task forces. Thus, for example, Task Force 2–70 Armor (TF 2–70) comprised three Abrams tank companies – A, B, and D – and one Bradley mechanized company, C/6–6 Infantry, for a total of 44 tanks and 13 Bradleys.

A US Marine M1A1HA with mine plows passes a revetted Iraqi truck. The Marine 2nd Tank Battalion borrowed M1A1HA tanks from the Army until the M1A1 Common became available after the conflict. (USMC)

M1 Abrams tank battalions/squadrons, Operation *Desert Storm*						
	M1	M1A1	M1A1 (mod)	M1A1HA	M1A1 Common	Total
1st Armored Division		3	2	1		6
3rd Armored Division		3		3		6
1st Cavalry Division			4			4
1st Infantry Division	2		2	2		6
24th Infantry Division			4			4
Tiger Brigade (2nd Armored Division)			2			2
2nd Armored Cavalry Regiment				3*		3
3rd Armored Cavalry Regiment				3*		3
US Marine Corps				1	1**	2
Total	*2*	*6*	*14*	*13*	*1*	*36*

* Armored cavalry regiments were organized with three squadrons with 41 M1A1HAs each.
** Only two companies.

In the open desert, TF 2–70 moved in a modified diamond formation. Team Bandit (B Company, 2–70 Armor) led with Team Desperado (D Company, 2–70 Armor) on the right, Team Assassin (A Company, 2–70 Armor) on the left, and Team Bayonet (C Company, 6–6 Infantry) in the rear with battalion trains and headquarters in the center of the formation. Team Bandit, the focus of the duel described in the next chapter, comprised 14 M1A1 tanks, an engineer company, and an M88 recovery and medic vehicle with its remaining organic M88 and ambulance in the company trains.

The US Army also deployed two armored cavalry regiments to Saudi Arabia, the 2nd and 3rd ACR, one with each corps. Such regiments had three armored cavalry squadrons each with three armored cavalry troops with nine Abrams and 12 Bradleys. So a squadron had 41 Abrams and 32 Bradleys while the regimental strength totaled 116 M1A1 Abrams and 132 M3 Bradleys. The table below lists the squadrons as battalions for simplicity, although it should be noted that they had fewer Abrams than an armor battalion.

The US Marine Corps tank battalions in Operation *Desert Storm* were equipped primarily with the older M60A1 RISE/Passive tank, amounting to 277 of the 353 tanks deployed. The Marines were still awaiting delivery of the M1A1 Common – a modified version of the M1A1, intended to unify Army/Marine requirements by incorporating necessary Marine features such as deep-wading adapters for amphibious operations. The Marine 2nd Tank Battalion was equipped with M1A1HAs borrowed from the Army, while the two companies of the Marine Reserve 4th Tank Battalion had the new M1A1 Common tank. In total, the USMC deployed 76 M1A1 tanks in Operation *Desert Storm*, consisting of 60 M1A1HA and 16 M1A1 Common tanks.

US Army "Air-Land Battle" doctrine represented the culmination of more than a decade of intense debate over the ideal way to deal with a Warsaw Pact campaign in central Europe. Although primarily defensive in orientation, the doctrine did incorporate a strong emphasis on mobile counterattack and extremely aggressive tactics, and due to the high level of training at all levels this could easily be adapted for an offensive campaign. The US Army doctrine greatly stressed combined arms in the broadest sense of the term. The doctrine presumed a very heavy employment of airpower to wear down the enemy forces before contact with the ground element. In addition, the US Army had invested a tremendous amount of human and material capital in building up an organic aviation element within the heavy-maneuver divisions, most notably a battalion of AH-64 Apache attack helicopters. These provided the divisional commander with a powerful air cavalry force that could provide flexible flank security during mobile operations, as well as substantial antiarmor capability, which was of particular use in close-battle conditions where the US Air Force was less comfortable operating.

The advent of the M1 Abrams tank and M2/M3 Bradley infantry/cavalry fighting vehicle was accompanied by an evolution in doctrine that increased the tempo of small-unit tactics in direct combat, since both categories of combat vehicle could now fight on the move. This tactical innovation was stressed in training since the high speed of an assaulting force could help debilitate a slower-reacting opponent, and if properly exploited, speed could reduce the attackers' vulnerability to enemy weapons. This would become very apparent in combat with the Iraqi forces, which were unable to react quickly enough to deal with the US Army's offensive tactics. The forward-maneuver units' effectiveness was further enhanced by the substantial firepower of the divisional artillery, which had undergone a renaissance in the 1970s and 1980s in terms of equipment, munitions, and fire-direction. This broad modernization of technology and tactics acrosss the US armed forces amplified the Abrams tank battalions' advantage, since the Iraqi units had often already suffered from violent preparatory attacks from US fixed-wing aircraft, attack helicopters and artillery even before making contact with US tank units. In contrast, Abrams battalions could usually operate free from enemy air attack, and Iraqi artillery posed little threat both due to inherent tactical weaknesses and short life expectancy once engaged by US counterbattery fire.

THE ACTION

The air campaign began on January 17, 1991, and continued for 35 days. The US Air Force later claimed that 40 percent of the Iraqi tanks and 35 percent of the other armored fighting vehicles had been knocked out in the air attacks. However, this assessment was later judged to have been too optimistic. The US Marine Corps estimated that 10–15 percent of AFVs had been knocked out in Kuwait, while the US Army estimated about 15–25 percent in the western Iraqi desert. The lowest estimate comes from a Russian assessment that estimated 3,700 tanks in the combat zone at the outset of the air campaign and 3,400 at the end. Regardless of the precise number of tanks knocked out by aircraft, the air assault devastated the Iraqi army. The relentless bombing thoroughly demoralized the Iraqi troops and led to widespread desertion; a Russian assessment concluded that Iraqi strength in the combat zone dropped from 790,000 troops at the outset of the campaign to about 400,000 when the ground campaign began on February 24, 1991; some US estimates suggested that the Iraqi strength may have only been half this number. The air campaign also devastated the Iraqi logistics network, making it difficult to supply many units. The attacks had their greatest impact on the poorly trained and poorly motivated conscripts in the frontline divisions in Kuwait, but had far less effect on the better-motivated RGFC troops in the army reserve further back from the front lines.

G-Day, signifying the start of the ground campaign, began at dawn on February 24, 1991, with the assault by XVIII Airborne Corps, located on the western flank of the coalition. Meanwhile the Joint Forces Commands and US Marine Corps began breaching operations against the most substantial Iraqi defensive belts along the Kuwaiti frontier. Of the 36 Abrams battalions/squadrons in Operation *Desert Storm*, seven served with XVIII Airborne Corps on the left flank, 25 with VII Corps in the center, and four with the Marines on the right flank along the Kuwaiti border. Since the main concentration of Iraqi T-72 tanks faced VII Corps, this sector will be the focus here.

The primary mission of VII Corps was to rapidly breach the Iraqi frontier defenses, race through the Iraqi desert to the west of the Kuwaiti frontier, then envelop and destroy the Republican Guards divisions serving as the Iraqi army's main reserve.

The original plan envisioned VII Corps beginning its attack on G+1, but the Marines' unexpectedly rapid penetration of Iraqi defenses on the Kuwaiti frontier accelerated the plan and resulted in initial breaching maneuvers being undertaken on G-Day afternoon, with the 2nd Armored Cavalry Regiment in the lead followed by the corps' heavy-maneuver divisions. This massive force overran two brigades of the Iraqi 26th Infantry Division with few signs of coherent resistance or effective artillery.

Behind the thin crust of defenses along the border was the Jihad Corps, including the 10th and 12th Armored Divisions subordinate to Gen Ayad al-Rawi, commander of the RGFC. By late on February 24, Al-Rawi was well aware of the advance of XVIII Airborne Corps, but the late launch of VII Corps, the poor weather, and the annihilation of the 26th Infantry Division left him blind to the massive force heading towards his command. The threat posed by the coalition forces prompted him to dispatch two armored brigades of the 12th Armored Division and one from the 10th Armored Division to cover the Wadi-al-Batin along the western Kuwaiti border and to serve as a shield while he reoriented the RGFC heavy divisions towards the threat. The weather was "more like Germany than Arabia," in the words of one American tanker – cold, windy, rainy and overcast. The heaviest fighting on G+1 erupted along the corps' right flank as the US 1st Infantry Division continued the breach of the 26th Infantry Division defensive lines in preparation for exploitation by the British 1st Armoured Division. The Iraqi 7th Corps attempted to stem the advance by deploying its tactical reserve, the 52nd Armored Division, which became entangled and smashed in a one-sided night-fight with British Challenger tanks late on February 25. By midnight of February 25/26, most of the Iraqi 7th Corps had been routed.

Around noon on February 25, G+1, 2nd ACR began to encounter advance elements of the Iraqi 50th Brigade, 12th Armored Division, and it began a one-sided engagement against a battalion of T-55 tanks and MT-LB armored transporters. The Abrams and Bradleys fought for the remainder of the day against scattered armored and infantry elements of the Iraqi division, significantly weakening one of its brigades. A small number of T-72 tanks was encountered late in the day – most likely constituting advance elements of the RGFC Tawakalna Division. The US 1st Armored Division completed the destruction of the hapless Iraqi 26th Infantry Division, overrunning its surviving brigade. For most of G+1, the long columns of Abrams and Bradleys advanced at a rapid pace, screened by scout helicopters and AH-64 Apache attack helicopters.

During the evening of February 25, VII Corps commander Gen Fred Franks approved "Frag Plan 7," which started the "great wheel" of the 2nd ACR, as well as

The effect of APFSDS ammunition can be seen on this burnt-out Iraqi T-72 Model 1975; the impact point was circled with a chalk mark by a US evaluation team inspecting tank wrecks after the fighting. (US DoD)

the 1st and 3rd Armored Divisions and 1st Cavalry Division to the east along a phase-line to attack the RGFC corps. In the meantime, Gen Al-Rawi had ordered three RGFC heavy divisions to begin repositioning themselves to counter the rapidly approaching VII Corps. The Tawakalna Mechanized Division was placed in a defensive blocking position on the western Kuwaiti border, with surviving elements of the 12th Armored Division to its south, and the 10th Armored Division behind it to its east. The Medina and Hammurabi armored divisions were placed north on either side of the Rumaylah oilfields. This set the stage for the most intense tank fights of Operation *Desert Storm*.

Around 0600 on G+2, the 2nd ACR continued the advance, coming across isolated T-55 tanks and MT-LB transporters from the Iraqi 12th Armored Division's remaining brigades. The increasing numbers of better vehicle types encountered, including T-72 tanks, hinted at a growing RGFC presence. The intensity of the fighting increased to the point that the US regiment became convinced that it had finally entered the outer security zone of the RGFC Tawakalna Division. By mid-afternoon, the regiment as well as the neighboring 3rd Armored Division on their left encountered dug-in T-72 tanks and BMP-1 infantry fighting vehicles. Although much of the Iraqi army was now in full-scale retreat from Kuwait, the Tawakalna Division showed every sign of staunchly defending the line against the approaching VII Corps. Besides their own battalions, the Tawakalna Division had served as a collection point for battalions of the neighboring 12th Armored Division, which it incorporated into the defense.

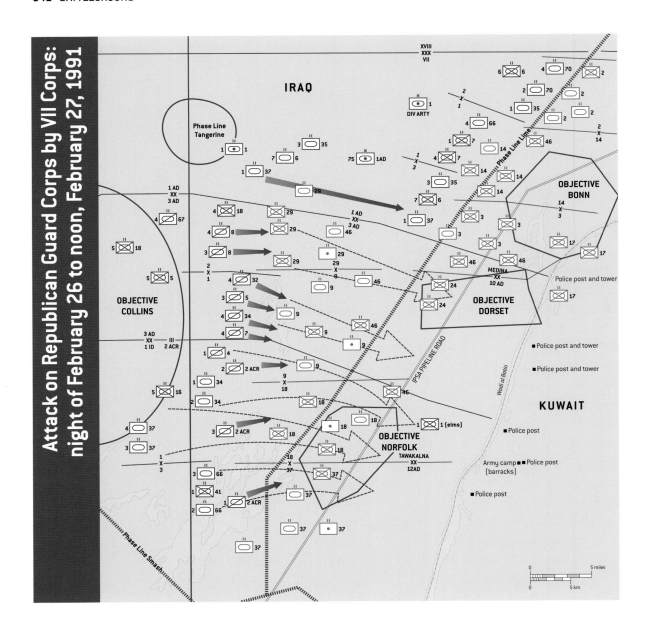

Attack on Republican Guard Corps by VII Corps: night of February 26 to noon, February 27, 1991

73 Easting

The fighting intensified in the late afternoon when 2nd ACR encountered elements of the Iraqi 9th Armored Battalion and 18th Mechanized Battalion on the left flank of the Tawakalna Division, in prepared positions to the west of the IPSA pipeline. E Troop and I Troop fought a series of skirmishes from around 1530hrs, pushing through the Iraqi position and reaching the 73 Easting gridline before being counterattacked by a company of T-72 tanks; however, these were destroyed by M1A1 tanks at 2,100m. The Iraqi defense position lacked an adequate security zone in front, so that when the American vehicles appeared out of the rain and mist they were completely unexpected. Some Iraqi crews were huddled down in trenches due to earlier air attacks in the area, and never managed to get back into their vehicles. Other tanks did try to fight back, but their crews could barely see the attacking American force and the tanks failed to properly adjust for range, with their sabot rounds hitting the ground well in front of the US Army vehicles. As the smoke cleared, it revealed that the 18 M1A1 tanks and 24 M3A1 Bradleys had destroyed more than 30 dug-in T-72 tanks and 12 BMP-1s with no loss to themselves. The mechanized infantry battalion commander captured by E Troop said he had started the fight with 900 soldiers, a few dozen BMP-1s and an attached battalion of 36 tanks; when he was captured all that survived were the 40 soldiers with him. A stunned Tawakalna tank battalion commander added: "When the air campaign started, I had 39 [T-72] tanks. After 38 days of the air battle, I had 32 tanks. After 20 minutes against them [the 2nd Armored Cavalry Regiment], I had zero tanks." After dark, 1–1st Aviation's Apache helicopters struck the second tactical echelon of these brigades, causing heavy losses to three emplaced battalions.

As contact with the Tawakalna Division developed, the US 1st Infantry Division passed through the overworked 2nd ACR in the dark to prepare for the following day's attack. In the process, two Bradleys conducting forward reconnaissance were silhouetted against the skyline by the burning wrecks of Iraqi vehicles and were hit by vehicles of the RGFC 18th Mechanized Brigade. The 3rd Brigade, 1st Infantry Division confronted an Iraqi regiment shortly before midnight along the IPSA pipeline and destroyed about 60 tanks and 35 infantry vehicles. The battlefield was littered with destroyed Iraqi equipment, burning wrecks, hidden Iraqi tanks in revetments, and roaming Iraqi RPG antitank rocket teams. One Abrams battalion remembered it as "fright night." During the fighting, M1A1 tanks on several occasions mistakenly engaged friendly forces, knocking out five other M1A1 tanks and two Bradleys; fratricide proved more costly than Iraqi actions. Friendly-fire incidents would continue to be a significant hazard because of the way US and Iraqi forces were intermingled, as well as due to the chaotic battlefield being obscured by darkness, rain and sandstorms. By dawn of G+3, the 2nd ACR and 1st Infantry Division had destroyed most of four Iraqi tank and mechanized brigades and had cracked open the left flank of the RGFC defenses.

In the center, the US 3rd Armored Division hit the right flank of the Tawakalna Division in the late afternoon of G+2, where about eight Iraqi tank and mechanized battalions, with 122 tanks and 78 BMPs, were pitted against ten US heavy battalions.

The fighting was not entirely one-sided. A troop of Bradleys from 4–7 Cavalry engaged a well-entrenched Iraqi position and nine of its 13 Bradleys were damaged before the unit withdrew; two more fell victim to friendly fire. Indeed, the Iraqi resistance was fierce enough that 1st Brigade, 3rd Armored Division temporarily halted the attack that night. The neighboring 2nd Brigade fought its way through much of the Iraqi 29th Mechanized Brigade defenses by the early hours of February 27.

The right flank of the Tawakalna Division – a tank battalion of the 29th Mechanized Brigade supported by a BMP company – was overwhelmed on the evening of February 26 by the 3rd Brigade, 1st Armored Division, with 24 T-72s and 14 BMP-1s knocked out. Four M1A1 tanks were mistakenly hit by Hellfire missiles from Apache helicopters but without crew injuries. The division's other two brigades continued to advance eastward that night, aiming at the RGFC Medina Division.

By midnight of G+2, after less than 30 hours of fighting, the Tawakalna Mechanized Division had been destroyed bit by bit by the overwhelming force of three US Army heavy divisions and the 2nd ACR. In contrast to press accounts which suggested that most Iraqi units "bugged out" and ran at the first opportunity, the Tawakalna fought tenaciously; nevertheless, its sacrifices were largely in vain due to its poor tactical skills.

Medina Ridge

On VII Corps' left flank, two brigades of the US 1st Armored Division continued to move forward on the night of February 26/27 in anticipation of encountering the RGFC Medina Armored Division on the outskirts of the Rumalyah oilfields. Gen Al-Rawi had dispatched a brigade of the Adnan Motorized Division to serve as a covering force, but this was identified during its movement forward and shattered by US artillery fire. By the morning of February 27, the 1st Armored Division had called a halt for refueling – M1A1 Abrams tanks typically refueled three times a day during the operation due to the distances covered. In the midst of this operation, 2nd Brigade was brought under intense artillery fire by the Medina Division's artillery regiment, but the Iraqis only struck preregistered boxes and did not adjust their fire, so 2nd Brigade emerged from the barrage unscathed. This was typical of Iraqi artillery which had excellent and plentiful weapons but poor fire-direction skills.

The Medina Armored Division's 2nd Armored Brigade had established a reverse-slope defense; however, the site had been poorly chosen, as the ridge that the brigade was using to ambush the advancing US force was too far away for its 125mm guns to reach, as the Iraqis had apparently not bothered to verify the distance. The weather was overcast and wet with visibility at only about 1,500m. The US 1st Armored

Division's 2nd Iron Brigade crested the rise shortly after noon on February 27. The Iraqis were unaware of their arrival, lacking a proper security zone and unable to see the Abrams due to the weather. The stage was set for the battle of Medina Ridge. The following account of the battle is in the words of Capt Mark Gerges, who led Team Bandit of TF 2–70 during the engagement.

Abrams vs T-72 at Medina Ridge

The Iraqis moved into position the day before to protect the withdrawal of Iraqi forces from Kuwait by covering the road along the Kuwaiti border. Oriented west in a generally north–south axis, the brigade was at 75 percent strength and consisted of T-72M1s and BMP-1s. The crews constructed hasty fighting positions by pushing sand up around their vehicles with attached scrapers so that only their turrets were visible, yet the entire vehicle extended above the desert floor. In reserve to the rear was a BMP-1 company; air defense and command-and-control vehicles were dotted along the position. Overestimating American capabilities in electronic warfare, the forward recon screen deployed with their radios off. Consequently, when TF 2–70 and 4–70 destroyed the screen at 0700, the presence of the Americans went unreported. The Iraqis had no idea that enemy forces were so close. At 1130, the Medina brigade cooked rice and chicken on small one-burner stoves near their vehicles.

American movement began at 1145, and leading the company was 1st Platoon under Lt Matt Howson in tank B11. As B11 crested a small wash less than 20 minutes

The Iraqi army introduced a number of local modifications, as seen here on the turret of a Medina 2nd Armored Brigade T-72M1 knocked out at the battle of Medina Ridge. A shelf has been added to the left of the gunner's hatch for an antimissile jammer, although the jammer itself has been knocked off by the explosion. Both infrared searchlights have had armored covers added over them to reduce their vulnerability to small-arms and artillery damage. (Mark Gerges) later, the driver suddenly slammed on his brakes lifting the rear of the tank into the air from the sudden halt. Almost immediately Lt Howson called "Contact, tanks, east" over the company net and backed into a hull-down position. Two T-72s and a BMP were oriented north, unaware of the American tanks. Howson's gunner, Sgt Manning, could see the crews on the back deck of the tanks. The other American

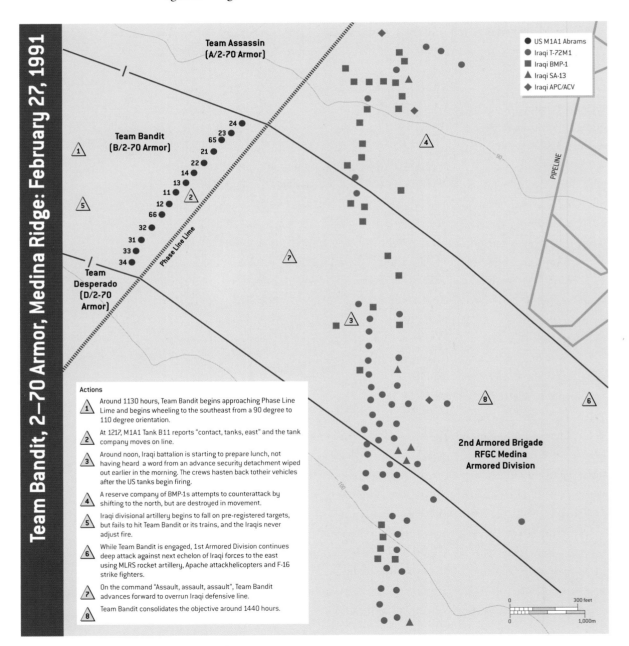

Team Bandit, 2–70 Armor, Medina Ridge: February 27, 1991

Team Assassin
(A/2-70 Armor)

Team Bandit
(B/2-70 Armor)

24
23
65
21
22
14
13
11
12
66
32
31
33
34

Phase Line Lime

Team
Desperado
(D/2-70
Armor)

PIPELINE

2nd Armored Brigade
RFGC Medina
Armored Division

- ● US M1A1 Abrams
- ● Iraqi T-72M1
- ■ Iraqi BMP-1
- ▲ Iraqi SA-13
- ◆ Iraqi APC/ACV

Actions

1. Around 1130 hours, Team Bandit begins approaching Phase Line Lime and begins wheeling to the southeast from a 90 degree to 110 degree orientation.

2. At 1217, M1A1 Tank B11 reports "contact, tanks, east" and the tank company moves on line.

3. Around noon, Iraqi battalion is starting to prepare lunch, not having heard a word from an advance security detachment wiped out earlier in the morning. The crews hasten back to their vehicles after the US tanks begin firing.

4. A reserve company of BMP-1s attempts to counterattack by shifting to the north, but are destroyed in movement.

5. Iraqi divisional artillery begins to fall on pre-registered targets, but fails to hit Team Bandit or its trains, and the Iraqis never adjust fire.

6. While Team Bandit is engaged, 1st Armored Division continues deep attack against next echelon of Iraqi forces to the east using MLRS rocket artillery, Apache attack helicopters and F-16 strike fighters.

7. On the command "Assault, assault, assault", Team Bandit advances forward to overrun Iraqi defensive line.

8. Team Bandit consolidates the objective around 1440 hours.

0   300 feet
0   1,000m

tanks in Team Bandit pulled into positions to the left and right of B11 and observed additional targets to the east. Simultaneously, Capt Mark Gerges's B66 sent a contact report to the task force commander requesting confirmation that there were no friendly vehicles to the front. Receiving immediate confirmation, the first tanks began firing at the Iraqi vehicles. Team Assassin to the north also reported tanks and BMPs to their front. The time was 1217.

The Abrams gunners saw hotspots through their sights at a range of nearly 3,000m. Invisible to the naked eye because of the weather, turrets showed up clearly above the sand berms surrounding each vehicle as did individual crew members as they moved about. Laser rangefinders reported ranges of 2,800–3,200m and the tanks alternated firing so that wingmen could observe the splash of a round and call out adjustments if needed. There was little need. The depleted-uranium sabot rounds flew practically flat in the two to three seconds it took them to reach the T-72s. There was no arch to the sabots' trajectory as there had been with training ammunition during gunnery practice in Germany. As a round struck a target, crews observed a flash through the thermal sight from the pyrophoric effect as the depleted-uranium penetrator struck the armor.

The experience of B66 under Capt Gerges in the center of the Bravo Company's line was typical. The tank gunner, Sgt Jerry Reynolds identified tanks on the ridge in front of the tank. The tank commander, Capt Gerges, issued the fire command "Gunner, sabot, tank" that began the crew's drill. B66 normally "battle-carried" a sabot round; this meant that a round was in the breech of the gun and the gunner preselected sabot as the ammunition type. All that was required was for the loader, PFC Bowie, to verify that the correct type of round was loaded, move his body from the path of the breech's recoil, and arm the gun, shouting "Up!" As this occurred, Sgt Reynolds selected a target through the thermal sight in 10-power, announcing "Identified," and ranged to the target with the laser rangefinder. After verifying the range, the tank commander, Capt Gerges, ordered "Fire." The gunner said "On the way" and pulled the trigger. The dust kicked up from the muzzle blast obscured the target for a second or two, but crews could normally see the tracer of the round flying to the target. After two to three seconds a flash showed that the round had struck the T-72. The American crews trained to fire center-of-mass as their sight-picture, so the sabot rounds often hit the sand berm directly in front of the tank and passed completely through the vehicle, causing a catastrophic kill. As the crews continued to engage the fire commands become more concise, with the tank commander and gunner discussing which target to fire at next. The driver, PFC Eugene Mendoza, attempted to assist in sensing the round and making no sudden vehicle movements as the gunner squeezed off the round.

After the first few rounds the crews began to notice a series of flashes from the Iraqi positions. Looking like the Hoffman charges used in tank maneuver training, the flashes appeared roughly simultaneously in groups of eight to ten. After observing this phenomenon two or three times and then splashes of sand a kilometer to their front, the crews realized what they were – Iraqi tank companies firing blindly in volley at the American muzzle flashes. The Iraqi crews had rushed to their vehicles and returned fire, but lacking thermal sights they could only fire at the muzzle flashes in the distance. This essentially blind fire often fell a kilometer too short of the American positions. Launches of AT-3 Sagger missiles from BMPs added to the Iraqi response. The missile left a telltale smoke trail, and American crews later remarked that the launches looked exactly like the Saggers in peacetime SIMNET training in Germany – a testimony to how well the simulator replicated the real missile. Trained to fire at the launch site, one or two M1s would immediately slew their turrets and fire the main gun at the BMP-1, killing the operator guiding the missile before it could cross the 3,000m to the American positions.

The thermal sights picked up heat rising from the turrets of the T-72s hit moments before. Shortly after, the first large explosions occurred – fire caused by sabot penetrations "cooked off" the T-72 ammunition located in the autoloader under the center of the turret. The spectacular and catastrophic explosions often lifted the turrets 30–40ft into the air and tore the vehicles apart. The American firing line was now

"Assault, assault, assault!" This remarkable photograph was taken by Capt Mark Gerges from the turret of his tank as Team Bandit overran the Iraqi 2nd Armored Brigade positions on Medina Ridge. The flaming debris appears to come from an SA-13 air-defense missile vehicle behind a berm and camouflage net, and the advancing line of M1A1 tanks can be seen beyond. (Mark Gerges)

Overleaf: Duel at Medina Ridge

"Contact, tanks, east!" This radio message around noon on February 27 started an engagement between Team Bandit of Task Force 2–70 Armor and elements of the 2nd Armored Brigade of the Medina Division. The Iraqi formation, a mixture of T-72M tanks, BMP-1 infantry fighting vehicles, and assorted light armored vehicles, were positioned near a slight rise in the flat desert which was subsequently dubbed "Medina Ridge." Team Bandit spotted the Iraqi armored vehicles from a range of about 3,000m (1.8 miles) and began engaging them almost immediately. At such a range, the US tanks were essentially invisible to the Iraqi tankers due to the weather conditions and the inadequate fire controls of the T-72 tank. About the only things the Iraqis could see were the violent flashes when the Abrams tanks fired their main guns as seen here in this illustration of the engagement. This huge flash was visible at long range, but it did not provide the Iraqis with enough range data to accurately aim their 125mm guns. (Artwork by Jim Laurier, © Osprey Publishing)

three battalions of 2nd Brigade on line, and in the distance, smoke plumes from burning T-72s marked the horizon of the area later known as Medina Ridge. Within 15 minutes of the start of the duel 37 plumes rose across the front.

The Iraqi crews fought back in vain as other elements of their brigade tried to stem the tide. Iraqi artillery, fired blind at preplanned targets, landed within a few hundred meters of the company trains located a kilometer behind the firing line. Nearly 400 rounds rained down during the engagement, but the undirected fire failed to shift to the American vehicles. In an effort to outflank the American line, the BMP-1 company in the Medina brigade reserve maneuvered to the north. They never made it. Zigzagging furiously, ten vehicles became nine, then eight as the M1A1s' fire took its remorseless toll. The final BMPs died on the northern extremity of the Medina's position.

Thirty-five minutes from the first contact, the momentum of the battle slowed. The 2nd Brigade commander, Col Montgomery Meigs, used the time to call in artillery, Apache helicopters, and A-10 Warthogs to attack a reported 40-plus tanks located a few kilometers from the engagement. Finally, not wanting to lose the initiative, he ordered the brigade to assault the Iraqi positions. The command of "Assault, assault, assault" has particular meaning to tank crews, with much the same resonances as "Fix bayonets" has for dismounted infantry. Advancing in line, all weapons on board the vehicles fired; the massive firepower generated by over 120 M1A1s had a shock effect on Iraqis already battered by the main-gun engagements.

As the TF 2–70 line moved forward, guiding on Bravo Company for orientation, loaders loaded one last sabot round and then stood on their seats to man their machine guns on the skate mount outside the turret. Tank commanders prepared the M2 .50cals, and gunners scanned the front looking for targets to engage with either main guns or co-ax machine guns. The assaulting line guided slightly southward to clear a pipeline complex to the north, 3km behind the Iraqi positions.

Moving forward, Iraqi vehicles hidden from sight by the ground suddenly came into view. Many were BMP-1s and SA-13s thought to be part of the brigade's command and headquarters; never stopping, M1A1s destroyed these vehicles by gunfire. Others were T-72s that had abandoned their positions in panic. These were destroyed as well. American tanks were soon within 600m of the main Iraqi defensive positions, and the crew's machine guns engaged individual infantry fighting positions. Burning tanks and BMPs littered the ground with tank turrets sometimes 40m away from the vehicles. As B66 approached the Iraqi line, the crew saw what looked like little white paper scraps waving in the breeze from one berm. As the tank approached, a group of 21 infantrymen suddenly stood up from the position, hands above their heads, to surrender. Tank B12 initially safeguarded the prisoners until the Bravo Company First Sergeant, Walter Wallace, and the maintenance team moved forward to secure them. The appearance of these prisoners stood in stark contrast to others captured during the past two days. While the regular army soldiers at Al-Bussayah wore dirty uniforms, were unkempt and unarmed, the Medina soldiers stood up with AK-47s in their hands, held over their heads. Load-bearing equipment was on and buckled, chinstraps on the helmets fastened, and their uniforms clean.

Within the Medina battle positions vehicles continued to burn, and American tank crews learned not to stop near a burning vehicle as the ammunition often unexpectedly cooked off. Next to some vehicles, small stoves boiled away full of rice and chicken – a testament to how quickly the end had come for the Iraqi soldiers.

The T-72 combat positions, spread about 75–100m apart, were strewn with the wreckage from the vehicles. The destruction was amazing but uneven. One turret might be in pristine condition, without a burn mark on it, except that it was 50m in front of its hull. Another turret might be slightly cocked off its turret ring, yet burnt out with only the major metal structure surviving. Some tanks had tried to run, backing out of position and turning to the rear before an American sabot round brought about their destruction. On one T-72 you could trace the flight of the sabot round through the sand berm to the front, through the front glacis plate, and out the back of the vehicle. The force of the explosion had blown the transmission out of the back of the vehicle, turning it upside down and throwing it 15ft from the tank.

To the north, the destruction of the reserve BMPs could be traced. From the rear of the Medina position a series of ten parallel APC tracks moved northwest. The BMPs advanced through a series of 45-degree turns intended to throw off American antitank guided missiles, but these maneuvers proved useless against tanks firing sabot rounds. The wreckage told the story of the failed counterattack. Suddenly one BMP fell, hit by a sabot round. A couple more zigs and zags and a second, third, and fourth BMP burned, until finally the survivors went to ground and were destroyed.

The fins of M829 sabots, entering the thin armor of the engine cover, did not even distort. Holes made by the fins were clearly visible in the BMPs' engine compartment armor. Ripping through the vehicle, rounds exited the rear crew doors, but the fire caused by the ignition of the ammunition and fuel ripped the rear doors open, and created a huge debris field extending 50ft or more behind the BMP. Iraqi losses to Bravo Company in this sector were 12 to 18 T-72s, 12 BMP-1s, 1 BTR, two to three BRDMs, and one AMX-10RC; TF 2–70 as a whole was credited with 59 T-72 tanks, 29 BMP-1s, six SA-13s, and four other armored vehicles.

After briefly consolidating on the position, 2nd Brigade moved further east five or six kilometers, halted to refuel and prepared to continue the attack.

The Medina and Hammurabi divisions

A similar situation prevailed in the US 1st Brigade sector facing the Medina's 14th Mechanized Brigade and elements of the 46th Mechanized Brigade of the 12th Armored Division, which were engaged at ranges of 4,000m using thermal sights while the Iraqis were in the process of rearming and refueling their vehicles. The Iraqi units were unprepared for the attack and generally oriented towards the south instead of facing west, from where the attack emanated. The US 1st Armored Division's 3rd Brigade was

The final tank combat of Operation *Desert Storm* occurred after the ceasefire on March 2, when the Hammurabi Division bumped into the US 24th Infantry Division while trying to escape, leading to the short but intense "Battle of Rumalyah." This is an M1A1 of Company C, 4–64 Armor, during the fighting. (US Army)

the last to crest the ridge around 1300hrs; it encountered the 2nd Mechanized Brigade and methodically destroyed it with long-range gunfire from the M1A1 tanks and TOW missile fire from the Bradleys. By the end of February 27 the 1st Armored Division had largely destroyed the Medina Division, knocking out 186 tanks and 127 armored infantry vehicles.

The third echelon of the RGFC was the Hammurabi Armored Division, which was further west behind the Rumalyah oilfields. This division did not engage US ground forces prior to the ceasefire. However, on the morning of March 2 a significant portion of the division attempted to escape north via an elevated causeway over the Hawr-al-Hammar waterway and through a sector controlled by the US 24th Infantry Division. The Hammurabi Division had apparently been ordered by Hussein to escape out of the Basra pocket, as it was needed to help suppress the revolts that were occurring in the Shi'ite regions of southern Iraq. The column was desperate enough to fire on the Bradleys of TF 2–7 Infantry and Abrams of TF 4–64 Armor, in violation of the ceasefire. The 24th Infantry Division responded by sealing off the causeway using artillery-fired mines, then proceeded to methodically destroy the column. The division's Apaches struck with 107 Hellfire missiles, scoring 102 hits; the column was then overrun by Abrams and Bradleys with the "Battle of Rumalyah" ending in the early afternoon after 187 Iraqi armored vehicles, 34 artillery pieces and 400 trucks had been destroyed. US losses consisted of a single Abrams, burnt out after being set on fire by a massive explosion from a nearby Iraqi vehicle. This constituted the last tank engagement of Operation *Desert Storm*.

The US Marine Corps experience with the M1A1 in *Desert Storm* largely mirrored that of the Army, though on a much smaller scale. Bravo Company of the Marine 2nd Tank Battalion had at least one violent confrontation with T-72 tanks of the 3rd Saladin Armored Division in the predawn hours of February 25. The company was coiled up in night defensive positions with a single crewman in each tank assigned to keep watch using the tank's thermal sight. An Iraqi T-72 battalion supported by BTR-63s (Chinese-built YW531) armored personnel carriers blindly approached the Marine defenses. An Iraqi lieutenant later recalled what ensued: "Our column was headed across the desert when all of a sudden, the tank in front of me, to the left of me, and behind me, all blew up." The lieutenant ordered his own crew to abandon their T-72, but before the men could do so their tank exploded. The lieutenant, standing in the open hatch, was blown free from the tank but the gunner and driver were killed instantly. In 90 seconds, 34 out of 35 T-72 tanks were knocked out, and then the Marine Abrams turned their guns on the poorly protected armored personnel carriers. One Marine crew was credited with hitting seven T-72 tanks with seven rounds in about a minute's time.

ANALYSIS

The tank fighting during Operation *Desert Storm* represented one of the most lopsided contests in 20th-century military history. The Iraqi army was outclassed in all respects and suffered appallingly high losses while inflicting minimal casualties on the coalition forces. In the case of the M1A1, more Abrams tanks were destroyed by friendly fire than Iraqi action. From later accounts it would appear that at least seven Abrams were hit by T-72 gunfire; one was temporarily disabled when a hit near the rear of the turret ignited crew stowage, and another may have been disabled by a shot through the thin armor of the engine compartment; however, no hits penetrated the frontal armor. Iraqi T-72 losses have never been tallied with any precision but were probably in the neighborhood of 750–800 tanks; total Iraqi tank losses to all causes were 3,200–3,900 plus 2,400–2,750 other types of armored vehicles lost. These T-72 losses were not exclusively to engagements against the M1A1 Abrams tank, but a significant portion were due to direct combat and not air attack.

The Iraqi T-72M1 tank performed poorly due to technical, tactical and training problems. On the firepower side, it was incapable of acquiring targets at worthwhile battle ranges, especially at night or in poor weather, and its gun/ammunition combination was incapable of penetrating the frontal armor of the Abrams. Better ammunition might have helped on the rare occasions when hits were scored, but the central problem was the lack of hits against the opposing M1A1 tanks. This was the result of both technical and training failures, as the T-72's fire controls were too complicated for rapid use by typical Iraqi crewmen. On the defensive side, the T-72's armor was vulnerable to the Abrams 120mm gun and its unshielded ammunition meant that penetrations usually led to catastrophic fires which incinerated the tank, often too quickly for the crew to escape. These spectacular explosions were profoundly demoralizing to the crews of neighboring tanks, who sometimes abandoned their own vehicles after witnessing such frightening conflagrations. On the training side, the Iraqi army was completely unable to operate effectively against a well-trained opponent operating at a much faster battle tempo; tactical success was not within its grasp since

A T-72M1 of the Hammurabi Division that "lost its cap" during the fighting with the 24th Infantry Division (M) along the causeway on March 2; two burnt-out BMP-1s are also evident. (US Army)

units were chronically unable to carry out ordinary tasks such as establishing security zones or conducting reverse-slope defenses even when they had the time and resources to do so. The popular perception that the Iraqi soldiers simply ran away from the fight was certainly not true of the troops of the RGFC heavy divisions, who fought bravely, though ineffectively, during the fierce clashes of February 25–27.

The success of the M1A1 Abrams in the 1991 Gulf War was as much about the qualities of the crews as the technology; the Marine Corps' old M60A1 tanks performed well and many US tankers argued that they would have triumphed against the Iraqis even if the equipment had been swapped. While the US Army might indeed have triumphed with older equipment, the superb protection of the M1A1 saved lives. Innovations in the M1A1 design had significant tactical effects, contributing to the fast tempo of operations and the ability to operate during the day or at night even in poor weather conditions. The 120mm gun and the associated fire-control system was stunningly lethal and this was the first war that saw tanks firing accurately on the move on a routine basis.

The Gulf War was also the first war to see the extensive use of thermal imaging sights; this technology alone was a major factor in the ability of US heavy-maneuver battalions to fight 24 hours a day and to stand off and destroy Iraqi units during poor daytime weather when targets were otherwise not visible. The turbine engine, for all the headaches caused by its prodigious fuel consumption, provided the Abrams battalions with the effortless speed to smash through Iraqi defensive positions before they could react. The primary lessons learned from tank battles in World War II had been that the side that found the enemy first, engaged first, and hit first was most often victorious. In the Gulf War this was still true.

AFTERWORD

The preceding chapters have provided a set of snapshots of tank-versus-tank skirmishes in the latter half of the 20th century. Such clashes remains a source of unending fascination to many tank buffs, wargamers, and military history enthusiasts, and they are certainly the most dramatic and exciting form of tank combat for most readers. Nevertheless, a history of tank fights should not be seen as a history of armored warfare. For the past century, tanks have been used in a far broader range of roles on the battlefield than simply fighting other tanks. In some conflicts since 1945, such as the desert wars in the Middle East, tanks have played a dominant role in land warfare with extensive tank-versus-tank fighting. In other conflicts, such as the 1965 Indo-Pakistan war, tanks played an important but not dominant role. In other Cold War-era conflicts in the developing world, the tank's role has varied enormously. In Vietnam, they were a minor support weapon in 1965–70, yet absolutely essential in the final North Vietnamese offensive that concluded the war.

The focus of this book by necessity avoids the issue of the broader mechanization of modern armies with other types of armored fighting vehicles such as armored infantry vehicles, armored scout vehicles, armored artillery vehicles and a host of other types. Indeed, tanks are substantially outnumbered by other types of AFVs on the contemporary battlefield.

Another issue that has not been detailed here is the technological interplay of tanks and antitank weapons. Since the rise of the tank in World War I, there has been a parallel rise in new types of weapons to defeat tanks. Starting with improvized antitank guns in World War I, an enormous variety of weapons has been used to fight against tanks, from individual antitank weapons such as bazookas and Panzerfausts to elaborate crew-served weapons such as specialized antitank artillery and modern antitank missiles, not to mention aircraft. Indeed, since World War I, antitank weapons have caused far more tank casualties than other tanks.

Tank-versus-tank combat is a fascinating area of warfare, and has been the most influential factor on tank design over the past century. But it is worth remembering that it has not been the only influence.

BIBLIOGRAPHY

Part I

Bessonov, Evgeni, Tank Rider: *Into the Reich with the Red Army*, Casemate, 2003

"Description of Sighting Equipment for 76 mm Tank Gun in Russian T-34 Tank," translated by School of Tank Technology, September 1943

Drabkin, Artem, and Oleg Sheremet, *T-34 in Action*, Pen & Sword, 2006.

Fey, Will, *Armor Battles of the Waffen SS, 1943-45*, Stackpole Books, 1990.

Gätzschmann, Kurt, *Panzerabteilung 51 Heeresgruppe II/Panzerregiment 33 1943–1945* (unpublished manuscript).

Glantz, David M., *Forgotten Battles of the German-Soviet War*, Vol. V The Summer–Fall Campaign, 1 July–31 December 1943, self-published, 2000.

Glantz, David M., and Jonathan M. House, *The Battle of Kursk*, University of Kansas Press, 1999.

Hughes, Dr. Matthew, and Dr. Chris Mann, *The T-34 Russian Battle Tank*, MBI Publishing Co., 1999.

Jentz, Thomas L., *Germany's Panther Tank: The Quest for Combat Supremacy*, Schiffer Military History, 1995.

Jentz, Thomas L., *Panzertruppen: 1943–1945*, Schiffer Military History, 1996.

Jung, Hans-Joachim, *The History of Panzer Regiment Grossdeutschland*, J. J. Fedorowicz Publishing, 2000.

Kolomyjec, Maksym, and Janusz Ledwoch, *Panthers and Tigers in the Kursk Bulge 1943*, Wydawnictwo Militaria, 2004.

Lehmann, Rudolf, *The Leibstandarte III*, J. J. Fedorowicz Publishing, 1990.

Lodieu, Didier, "Le Bataillon de Panther de la 9.Pz.Div." in Russie ou l'historique de la Pz.Abt. 51 (2e partie), *39/45 Magazine*, No. 187, February (2002).

Lodieu, Didier, "La Panther-Abteilung de la 9. Pz.-Div. ou la II./Panzer-Regiment 33 puis la Panzer Abteilung 51 Historique du Pz.-Rgt.33," *39/45 Magazine*, No. 169, July (2000).

Rahn, Walter, "Fighting Withdrawal of Kampfgruppe von Sivers as 'Floating Bubble' in the Vorskla Valley from Tomarovka via Borissovka-Grayvoron-Pirasevka-Kirovka as far as Achtyrka in August 1943," unpublished paper by former orderly officer of Panzer Battalion 52.

Schneider, Wolfgang, *Panzer Tactics: German Small-Unit Armor Tactics in World War II*, Stackpole Books, 2005.

Sewell, Stephen, "Why Three Tanks?" *ARMOR*, July–August 1998.

Sharp, Charles C., *German Panzer Tactics in World War II*, published by George F. Nafziger, 1998.

Sharp, Charles C., *Red Storm: Soviet Mechanized Corps and Guards Armored Units, 1942 to 1945,* George F. Nafziger, 1995.

Sharp, Charles C., *School of Battle: Soviet Tank Corps and Tank Brigades,* January 1942 to 1945, George F. Nafziger, 1995.

Sharp, Charles C., *Soviet Armor Tactics in World War II*, George F. Nafziger, 1999

Trojca, Waldemar, "Sd. Kfz. 171 Pz.Kpfw. V Panther," Model Hobby, 2003.

The German Tank Platoon in WWII: Its Training and Employment in Battle, George F. Nafziger, 2002.

Vuksic, Velimir, *SS Armor on the Eastern Front 1943–1945*, Fedorowicz Publishing Inc., 2005.

Zaloga, Stephen J., "Soviet Tank Operations in the Spanish Civil War," *Journal of Slavic Military Studies* Vol. 12 No. 3.

Zetterling, Niklas, *Kursk 1943, A Statistical Analysis*, Frank Cass, 2000.

Russia Battlefield website: www.battlefield.ru

Part II

Primary sources (unpublished)

Author's correspondence with Mr Joe Ekins, 2006

Imperial War Museum Sound Archive
Taped interviews with Trooper Ekins and Captain Boardman

The National Archives, Kew, London:
CAB 106/1047, British Army of the Rhine Battlefield Tour "Totalize'
WO171 (War Diaries)
/640, 33rd Armoured Brigade
/680, 154th Infantry Brigade
/859, 1st Northants Yeomanry
/878, 144th RAC
/1265, 1st Black Watch
WO179/3010, War Diary, Sherbrooke Fusiliers
The Tank Museum, Bovington
RH 88, War Diary and Associated Notes, 144th RAC
Taped interview with Trooper Ekins

Primary sources (published)

Meyer, Kurt, *Grenadiers* (Winnipeg: J.J. Fedorowicz, 1994)

Secondary sources (books)

Agte, Patrick, *Michael Wittmann and the Tiger Commanders of the Leibstandarte*, (J.J. Fedorowicz, 1996)

Chamberlain, Peter and Chris Ellis, *PzKpfW VI Tiger and Tiger I* (Profile AFV Series No. 48) (Profile, 1972)

Fletcher, David, *Tiger! The Tiger Tank: A British View* (London: HMSO, 1986)

Ford, Roger, *Tiger Panzer* (Karl Müller Verlag, 1998)

Fortin, Ludovic, *British Tanks in Normandy* (Histoire & Collections, 2005)

Gander, Terry J., *Tanks in Detail: Medium Tank M4 (76mm and 105mm) Sherman and Firefly* (Ian Allen, 2003)

Hart, Stephen A., "Teenaged Nazi Warriors: The Fanaticism of the 12th SS Panzer Division Hitlerjugend in Normandy," in M. Hughes and G. Johnson (eds.), *Fanaticism and Modern Conflict* (Frank Cass, 2005)

Jentz, Thomas, L., *Germany's Tiger Tanks – Tigers I and II: Combat Tactics* (Schiffer, 1997)

Jentz, Thomas, L., Doyle, Hilary and Sarson, Peter, *Tiger I Heavy Tank 1942–45* (Osprey, 1993)

Hayward, Mark, *Sherman Firefly* (Tiptree: Barbarossa Books, 2001)

Lupfer, Craig W.H., *Blood and Honor: The History of the 12th SS Panzer Division "Hitler Youth," 1943–45* (R. James Bender, 1987)

Meyer, Hubert, *Kriegsgeschichte der 12SS-Panzerdivision "Hitlerjugend"* (Osnabrück: Munin verlag, 1982); in translation as *History of the 12-SS Panzer Division "Hitlerjugend"* (J.J. Fedorowicz, 1994)

Neville, R.F., *The 1st and 2nd Northants Yeomanry 1939–46* (Joh. Heinr. Meyer, 1946)

Reid, Brian A., *No Holding Back: Operation "Totalize," Normandy, August 1944* (Robin Brass, 2005)

Schneider, Wolfgang, *Panzertaktik: German Small-Unit Armor Tactics* (J.J. Fedorowicz, 2000)

Spielberger, Walter J., *Tiger and King Tiger Tanks* (Haynes, 1991)

Secondary sources (articles)

Abbott, John "Bud," *"1st Northamptonshire Yeomanry, St. Aignan,"* Military Illustrated, No. 69 (February 1994), pp 12–18

Niemis, Renato, "Death of Wittmann," *Military Illustrated*, No. 132 (May 1999)

Taylor, Les, "Michael Wittmann's Last Battle," *After the Battle*, No. 48 (1985)

Part III

Government reports

Anon., *Technical Manual TM9-735, Medium Tanks M26 and M45*, Department of the Army (August 1948)

Anon., *Field Manual FM17-12, Tank Gunnery*, Department of the Army (November 1950)

Anon., *Technical Manual TM9-374, 90mm Guns M3 and M3A1 for Combat Vehicles*, Department of the Army (August 1950)

Anon., *Organization and Combat History of the North Korean 105th Armored Division*, Eighth Army G-2 (1950)

Anon., *Engineering Analysis of the Russian T34/85 Tank 1945 Production*, Chrysler Corporation Engineering Division (September 1951)

Anon., *Vseobecny popis tanku a jeho bojava a technicka charakteristika T-34-85*, Czechoslovak Defense Ministry (1956)

Coox, Alvin, *US Armor in the Anti-Tank Role: Korea 1950*, Operations Research Office (July 1952)

Thompson, Milton, et al., *Employment of Armor in Korea: The First Year*, Armor School, Ft. Knox (May 1952)

McDonald, H. W., et al., *The Employment of Armor in Korea*, Operations Research Office (April 1951)

McRae, Vincent and Alvin Coox, *Tank-vs.-Tank Combat in Korea*, Operations Research Office (September 1954)

Robertson, William, *Counterattack on the Naktong 1950* (Leavenworth Papers No. 13), US Army Combat Studies Institute (December 1985)

Articles

Conner, Arthur, "The Armor Debacle in Korea 1950: Implications for Today," *Parameters* (Summer 1992)

Kwang-Soo Kim, "The North Korean War Plan and the Opening Phase of the Korean War," *International Journal of Korean Studies* (Spring/Summer 2001)

Books

Daily, Edward, *Strike Swiftly: Korea 1950–53 – 70th Heavy Tank Battalion*, Turner (2000)

Estes, Kenneth, *Marines Under Armor: The Marine Corps and the Armored Fighting Vehicle 1916–2000*, Naval Institute (2000)

Gilbert, Oscar, *Marine Corps Tank Battles in Korea*, Casemate (2003)

Kolomiets, Maksim, *T-34: Pervaya polnaya entsiklopediya*, Eksmo (2009)

Ustyantsev, Sergey and Dmitriy Kolmakov, *Boevye mashiny Uralvagonzavoda Tank T-34*, Media-Print (2005)

Lototskiy, S. S. (ed.), *Voyna v Koree 1950–53*, Poligon (2003)

Vanin, Yu. V. et al., *Voyna v Koree 1950–53 gg.: Vzglyad cherez 50 let*, Pervoe Marta (2001)

Webb, Raymond, *The 72nd Tank Battalion in Korea 1950–1952*, Toppan (1953)

Zaloga, Steven, *M26/M46 Pershing Tank 1943–1953*, Osprey (2000)

Zaloga, Steven and Jim Kinnear, *T-34-85 Medium Tank 1944–1994*, Osprey (1996)

Zaloga, Steven and George Balin, *Tank Warfare in Korea 1950–53*, Concord (1994)

Part IV

Dunstan, Simon, *Centurion* (Ian Allan Ltd, 1980)

Dunstan, Simon, *Centurion Universal Tank 1943–2003* (Osprey, 2003)

Eshel, David and Dunstan, Simon, *Centurion Main Battle Tank* (Eshel Dramit Ltd, 1979)

Eshel, David, *Chariots of the Desert: The Story of the Israeli Armoured Corps* (Brassey's, 1989)

Fletcher, David, *Mechanised Force: British Tanks between the Wars* (HMSO, 1991)

Kahalani, Avigdor, *The Heights of Courage: A Tank Leader's War on the Golan* (Praeger, 1992)

Kahalani, Avigdor, *A Warrior's Way* (Israel, Steimatzky,1999)

Norman, Michael, *Soviet Mediums T-44, T-54, T-55 and T-62* (Profile Publications Ltd, 1978)

Rabinovich, Abraham, *The Yom Kippur War: The Epic Encounter that Transformed the Middle East* (Schocken Books, 2004)

Rabinovich, Abraham, *Stemming the Syrian Onslaught – Abraham Rabinovich* (The Quarterly Journal of Military History, Spring 2001)

Rabinovich, Abraham, "Shattered Heights" (*Jerusalem Post*), Israel, 25 September 1998 and 2 October 1998

Teveth, Shabtai, *The Tanks of Tammuz* (Weidenfeld and Nicholson, 1969)

Zaloga, Steven J., *Armour of the Middle East Wars 1948–78* (Osprey, 1981)

Zaloga, Steven J., *Modern Soviet Armour Combat Vehicles of the USSR and Warsaw Pact Today* (Arms and Armour Press, 1979)

Zaloga, Steven J., *Modern Soviet Combat Tanks* (Osprey, 1984)

Part V

Government studies and reports

Barto, Joseph, *Task Force 2–4 Cav: "First In, Last Out,"* US Army Combat Studies Institute (1993)

Bourque, Stephen, *Jayhawk! The VII Corps in the Persian Gulf War*, US Army Center of Military History (2001)

Hall, Margot, et al., *The 24th Infantry Division (M) Victory Book: A Desert Storm Chronology*, 24th Infantry Division (1991)

Scales, Robert, *Certain Victory: The United States Army in the Gulf War*, Office of the Chief of Staff (1993)

Schubert, Frank, and Theresa Kraus (eds), *The Whirlwind War*, US Army Center of Military History (1993)

Swain, Richard, *"Lucky War": Third Army in Desert Storm*, US Army Command and General Staff College (1994)

Anon, *Soviet T-72 Tank Performance*, CIA (1982)

Anon., *Armor/Antiarmor Operations in Southwest Asia*, Marine Corps Research Center (1991)

Anon., *The Iraqi Army: Organization and Tactics*, National Training Center (1991)

Anon., *Desert Shield and Desert Storm: Emerging Observations*, US Army Armor Center (1994)

Books

Cathcart, Tom, Iron Soldiers: *How America's 1st Armored Division Crushed Iraq's Elite Republican Guard*, Pocket Books (1994)

Clancy, Tom, Fred Franks and Tony Koltz, *Into the Storm: A Study in Command*, Penguin (1997)

Dinackus, Thomas, *Order of Battle: Allied Ground Force of Operation Desert Storm*, Hellgate (2000)

Hunnicutt, Richard, *Abrams: A History of the American Main Battle Tank*, Presidio (1990)

Pierson, David, *Tuskers: An Armor Battalion in the Gulf War*, Darlington (1997)

Pollack, Kenneth, *Arabs at War: Military Effectiveness 1948–1991*, Nebraska (2002)

Ustyantsev, Sergey and Dmitriy Kolmakov, *Boyeviy Mashiny Uralvagonzavoda Tank T-72*, Media-Print (2004)

Vernon, Al, et al., *The Eyes of Orion: Five Tank Lieutenants in the Persian Gulf War*, Kent State University (1999)

Woods, Kevin, *The Mother of All Battles: Saddam Hussein's Strategic Plan for the Persian Gulf War*, Naval Institute (2008)

Zaloga, Steven, *M1 Abrams Main Battle Tank 1982–92*, Osprey (1993)

Zaloga, Steven, *T-72 Main Battle Tank, 1974–1993*, Osprey (1993)

INDEX